CORNELL STUDIES IN CIVIL LIBERTY

Robert E. Cushman, *Advisory Editor*

The States and Subversion

THE STATES AND SUBVERSION

★ ★ ★

EDITED BY Walter Gellhorn

PROFESSOR OF LAW, COLUMBIA UNIVERSITY

Cornell University Press

ITHACA, NEW YORK, 1952

PREFACE

THIS volume is one of a series made possible by a grant from the Rockefeller Foundation to Cornell University. For three years a group of scholars working individually under my direction have studied the impact upon our civil liberties of current governmental programs designed to ensure internal security and to expose and control disloyal or subversive conduct. The research has covered the work of federal and state "un-American activities" committees and the operation of federal and local loyalty and security programs. The first report, published in 1950, was *Security, Loyalty, and Science,* by Professor Walter Gellhorn of the Columbia University School of Law. This dealt with the problems of government-imposed secrecy in scientific investigation and the loyalty and security clearance procedures applicable to government scientists. A volume on the House Committee on Un-American Activities, by Professor Robert K. Carr of Dartmouth College, will appear shortly; this will be followed by one on the President's loyalty program and the summary dismissal statutes, by Miss Eleanor Bontecou, formerly an attorney in the Department of Justice. A final report will summarize the findings of the entire study.

Besides these more general volumes the series includes detailed studies of the control of subversive activities in three states. *The Tenney Committee,* by Edward L. Barrett, Jr., Professor of Law at Berkeley, tells the story of the California committee on un-American activities. *Loyalty and Legislative Action,* by Dean Lawrence H. Chamberlain of Columbia College, recounts and analyzes thirty years of legislative control of subversive activity

v

in the state of New York. *Un-American Activities in the State of Washington*, by Vern Countryman of the Yale Law Faculty, reviews the work of the Canwell committee in that state.

The present volume, edited by Professor Gellhorn, presents a more general picture of state and local activity in this important field, although here also are selected samples of what our states and cities have been doing. For this purpose Professors Barrett, Chamberlain, and Countryman have provided condensations of their books, mentioned above; while Professors Harsha, Prendergast, and Mowitz prepared the chapters on the Broyles Commission in Illinois, the Ober Act in Maryland, and the Michigan loyalty program. In addition, Professor Gellhorn has contributed a wise analysis of the scope and significance of this "decentralization" of our efforts to protect our security and to root out disloyalty. An appendix compiles valuable documentary and factual material. It has been urged by thoughtful people that state and local security and loyalty programs are unnecessary and uniquely dangerous to civil liberty. This volume presents a body of evidence, and an analysis of that evidence, which may aid the citizen in forming a judgment upon this point.

The volumes in this series state the views, conclusions, and recommendations of the individual authors. There have, of course, been consultation, discussion, and exchange of criticism among the group engaged in the entire study, and valuable aid and suggestion have come from a number of distinguished persons outside this group. Each volume, however, as well as each chapter in this volume, remains the work, and states the opinions, of the person who wrote it.

ROBERT E. CUSHMAN

Cornell University
Ithaca, New York

vi

CONTENTS

The States and Subversion

I. CALIFORNIA

Regulation and Investigation of Subversive Activities

By EDWARD L. BARRETT, JR.   *November, 1950*

PRIOR to 1940 legislative regulation of subversive activities in California had been confined to a criminal syndicalism act, a Red Flag law, and general criminal statutes dealing with treason, rebellion, insurrections, and riots. During the decade of the 1940's, although a few statutes were added to the list, the emphasis shifted from legislative regulation to legislative investigation and exposure as a means of combating subversive activities. This chapter will deal principally with the activities of the legislative investigating committees during the decade and will consider the statutory developments only as they relate to the work of the investigating committees.

Three committees have carried the burden of legislative investigation of subversive activities in California. The Assembly Relief Investigating Committee under the chairmanship of Assemblyman Samuel W. Yorty (the Yorty committee) functioned only in 1940. The Fact-Finding Committee on Un-American Activities under the chairmanship of Senator Jack B. Tenney (the Tenney committee) operated continuously from 1941 to 1949. The Fact-Finding Committee on Un-American Activities under the chair-

[Mr. Barrett is Professor of Law in the University of California at Berkeley.]

1

manship of Senator Hugh M. Burns (the Burns committee) has been in existence since 1949. Minor investigations in the "subversive" field have been carried on by other committees, especially the Senate Investigating Committee on Education, but they will not be considered further in this study.

Because of its long period of operation and its voluminous output, the Tenney committee will receive the principal emphasis. A much fuller study of the Tenney committee, containing much of the evidence from which the conclusions in this brief treatment have been drawn, will be found in my book on the Tenney committee, previously published in this series, the Cornell Studies in, Civil Liberty.[1]

THE YORTY COMMITTEE

Legislative investigation of subversive activities was spawned in California by the chaotic local political situation of the late 1930's. The combined impact of the depression and the national Roosevelt administration had shifted party registration in California from 3 to 1 in favor of the Republicans in 1930 to almost 2 to 1 in favor of the Democrats in 1938. Upton Sinclair with his visionary End-Poverty-in-California program almost captured the governorship in 1934. Culbert L. Olson, running with the support of the Communists and other extreme left-wing groups as well as the old age pensioners, the New Dealers, and the regular Democratic machine, was elected governor in 1938.

During the opening months of his term—the first Democratic state administration since that of Governor Budd in 1895–1899—Governor Olson saw the unity which had led to his election destroyed. The drive for state jobs by patronage-starved Democrats was unprecedented. And Olson, who had promised many things to his supporters, soon learned that most state jobs were protected by civil service. Almost the only large agency free from these restrictions was the State Relief Administration. It became the chief hope of his diverse supporters. The Communists had already taken an active part in the organization of two unions, the Workers'

[1] Edward L. Barrett, Jr., *The Tenney Committee* (Ithaca, N.Y.: Cornell University Press, 1951).

2

Alliance, which enrolled recipients of relief, and the State, County and Municipal Workers of America, which enrolled administrative employees of the S.R.A. Through Olson they now sought to capture the S.R.A.'s top administrative positions as well. The local Democratic organizations claimed the right to appoint local S.R.A. supervisors and thus were in competition with the Communists. The trained social workers resisted these claims because they feared the relief organization might be destroyed by stuffing it with party hacks. Many businessmen opposed the whole notion of the relief program, asserting that it was far too expensive and that most of the recipients were *émigrés* from the dust-bowl areas rather than regular Californians.

In August, 1939, the Stalin-Hitler pact destroyed the loosely knit "United Front against Fascism" that had previously linked many people of diverse views. Many former Olson supporters then joined with the Republicans in a plea to "turn the Reds out of the S.R.A." Among those who became opponents of Olson at this time were two men who had been among his strongest supporters, Assemblymen Jack B. Tenney and Samuel W. Yorty. Tenney, a former piano player and song writer (author of "Mexicali Rose") turned lawyer, and Yorty were both elected to the assembly from Los Angeles County in 1936. In the 1937 and 1939 legislatures they were prominently identified with the "liberal" wing of the assembly. In 1937 they were among the authors of a bill to repeal the California criminal syndicalism act and of a resolution approving President Roosevelt's plan for reconstituting the Supreme Court. Tenney was chairman and Yorty a member of a committee set up to investigate the trial and conviction of several union men for an alleged dynamite plot in connection with a strike against a Standard Oil plant in Modesto. The majority report of the committee, signed by Tenney and Yorty, charged that the trial had resulted in a miscarriage of justice and stated that the district attorney who prosecuted the suit

> is a man who believes that Communists are lurking behind every pillar and post and that "Red" armies are apt to materialize out of thin air at any minute to destroy the government. He believes that every activity on the part of organized labor to better their [*sic*] working and living conditions of working

3

men is "subversive" and "un-American." He is burdened with the idea that every strike and every labor dispute is ordered and directed by Moscow. He thinks the present tendencies in government radical and very serious.[2]

In December, 1937, Tenney had been elected president of Local 47, American Federation of Musicians, a union which during his period in office supported such left-wing movements as Labor's Non-Partisan League and favored aid to the Spanish Republican government. Tenney and Yorty were among the eight members of the legislature who joined an American Newspaper Guild picket line before the *Hollywood Citizen-News* in June, 1938. In August, 1938, Tenney spoke at a rally of the Hollywood Anti-Nazi League in which the dissolution of the Dies committee was demanded. Tenney said:

> Fellow subversive elements, I have just heard that Mickey Mouse is conspiring with Shirley Temple to overthrow the government and that there is a witness who has seen the "Red" card of Donald Duck.
>
> When the Dies Committee stoops to calling President Roosevelt a Communist and says that Mrs. Roosevelt is a front for subversive elements, then I think the rest of us should be flattered to be put in that category.[3]

In November, 1938, both Tenney and Yorty were named in an affidavit before the Dies committee as having been active members of the Communist Party in 1936 and 1937.[4] Tenney was also listed in the Dies reports as a member of the National Committee, American League for Peace and Democracy [5] and a Los Angeles Sponsor of Friends of the Abraham Lincoln Brigade.[6]

[2] California Legislature, 52d sess., Assembly Journal (April 14, 1937), pp. 1918, 1922.

[3] *Hollywood Now* (a publication of the Hollywood Anti-Nazi League), August 26, 1938.

[4] Hearings before Special Committee on Un-American Activities, House of Representatives, 75th Cong., 3rd sess., vol. 3, p. 2084.

[5] Hearings before Special Committee on Un-American Activities, House of Representatives, 76th Cong., 1st sess., vol. 10, p. 6278.

[6] Hearings before Special Committee on Un-American Activities, House of Representatives, 76th Cong., 3rd sess., vol. 13, p. 7729.

4

During the 1939 legislative session Tenney was a coauthor of and both he and Yorty voted for a resolution requesting President Roosevelt to revoke the embargo on shipment of arms to the Spanish Republican government. Tenney was author of a bill which would have entitled a candidate for public office to damages if his opponents falsely called him a Communist and was quoted as saying that "such a law would end a lot of this vicious red baiting." He was also coauthor of a bill prohibiting inquiry by members of governing boards of school districts into the "political, religious or economic beliefs" of schoolteachers.

In August, 1939, Tenney lost a bitter intra-union fight in Local 47 of the A.F.M. over the adoption of a new constitution proposed by him. He blamed this defeat on "communistic" elements in the union and started a campaign to have them tried and expelled for subversive activities. Despite this campaign Tenney was overwhelmingly defeated for re-election as president in December, 1939.

During the fall of 1939 Yorty joined with those who were expressing concern about Communist influence in the state government and particularly in the relief administration. In December he was quoted in the press as charging, following an interview with Governor Olson, that "communistic elements" controlled the S.R.A. management in Los Angeles County and predicting that the legislature would not appropriate relief funds until rumors to this effect were confirmed or disproved. This prediction proved accurate, and a major contest developed between the governor and the legislature.

Throughout 1940 the war between the two branches of the state government continued. It was marked by five extraordinary sessions of the legislature.

When the first of these convened in January, 1940, anti-Olson Democrats joined with Republicans to upset the administration control of the assembly and select a new speaker. Several investigating committees were set up by the legislature to look into the relief situation. The one that became most important in the field of subversive activities was the Assembly Relief Investigating Committee under the chairmanship of Samuel W. Yorty and with Jack B. Tenney as a member. This committee, although empow-

5

ered to investigate "the entire problem of the relief of hardship
and destitution," confined itself to alleged subversive influences
in the relief picture and was known from the outset as the "little
Dies committee." On February 5 the committee held a hearing in
Los Angeles. On February 13, it filed a preliminary report charging that Communists had successfully infiltrated the Los Angeles
County Relief Administration and condemning the Olson administration for failing to take decisive steps to combat this menace. On the same day Yorty made a radio speech announcing that
he had broken with Governor Olson because he "is playing a dangerous game in failing to rid his administration of Communist
termites." Early in March Tenney took to the airways to denounce
the Workers' Alliance and Labor's Non-Partisan League. He
stated: "Smear campaigns have been started against individual
legislators who have had the courage of their Americanism,
the courage to speak out against subversive activities in the
S.R.A."

The committee was given additional funds and a wider authorization and held hearings throughout northern California. These
hearings were explosive in character. Witnesses refused to answer
questions. Their lawyers were ejected from the hearing room when
they protested too much. Eighteen persons were sentenced to jail
for actions in contempt of the committee. On May 24, the committee filed a long report which dealt in some detail with alleged
Communist infiltration of the S.R.A. and the alleged inefficiency
of the governor in dealing with the situation. Among the recommendations of the committee was one "that a thorough investigation of all subversive activities in California be undertaken as
soon as possible."

The culmination of the legislative anti-Communist activity in
1940 was the passage of a statute designed to ban the Communist
Party from the ballot. Assemblyman Tenney was the leading sponsor of the bill for this purpose; it was passed by overwhelming
majorities during the fourth extraordinary session of the legislature in September and was signed by the governor. Large parts
of this legislation were declared unconstitutional by the California
Supreme Court in 1942.[7]

[7] *Communist Party v. Peek,* 20 Cal. 2d 536 (1942).

THE TENNEY COMMITTEE

The Committee in General

Instead of returning to the legislature in 1941, Yorty ran unsuccessfully in the primaries for nomination as a United States senator. Tenney, however, was re-elected and immediately assumed the leadership of the anti-Communist investigations. In December, 1940, he announced that the returning members of the Yorty committee would request the legislature to set up a committee authorized to (1) investigate asserted communistic influences in state universities, (2) continue the study of the S.R.A., (3) investigate the German-American Bund and other Fascist groups, (4) study the activities of the Workers' Alliance and certain "mothers' patriotic groups," and (5) inquire into other state agencies. In January, 1941, he introduced a resolution to that effect, which later was consolidated with a resolution presented by other assemblymen calling for investigation of activities of Communist, Fascist, and Nazi groups in the schools.

As finally approved by the assembly and senate on January 25, 1941, the resolution set up a committee of three senators and four assemblymen and empowered it to "investigate, ascertain, collate and appraise all facts causing or constituting interference with the National Defense Program in California or rendering the people of the State, as part of the Nation, less fit physically, mentally, morally, economically or socially" and to "investigate the activities of groups and organizations whose membership include persons who are members of the Communist Party, the Fascist organizations, the German Nazi Bund, or any other organization known or suspected to be dominated or controlled by a foreign power, which activities affect the preparation of this State for National defense, the functioning of any State agency, unemployment relief and other forms of public assistance, educational institutions of this state supported in whole or in part by State funds, or any political program."

The committee thus created was continued from biennium to biennium as a joint committee (except for a brief period as an assembly committee in 1941 and 1942) until 1947. Since 1947 it has

7

been a senate committee, bearing the official name of Senate Fact-Finding Committee on Un-American Activities.

From 1941 to 1949 this committee was under the chairmanship of Jack B. Tenney, as an assemblyman in 1941 and 1942 and as a senator from 1943 to 1949. Senators Hugh M. Burns and Nelson S. Dilworth also served on the committee throughout this period. The other members changed from biennium to biennium.

During this period the committee was almost entirely the responsibility of Senator Tenney. Although the committee was constantly bipartisan in character, all the members appear to have been in accord with Tenney's general objectives, and they did little more than appear at hearings and sign the committee reports. The committee had able counsel in the person of R. E. Combs, a Visalia attorney, who did much of the detail work of preparing for hearings and conducted the bulk of the examination of witnesses. The operation of the committee, however, was in the main the responsibility of Tenney. He decided upon the hearings, sometimes without even consulting Combs in advance. He issued press releases and interjected his own lines of questioning into the hearings at many points. He personally wrote most of the reports of the committee and prepared committee legislation, both operations without consulting committee counsel. The committee files were maintained in his office, and he carried on extensive correspondence in the name of the committee.

During Tenney's term as chairman, the committee received total appropriations of $153,000 and expended approximately $146,000. It received $30,000 for each of the first two bienniums, $28,000 for the third, and $65,000 for the fourth. This money was expended principally in holding about 72 days of public hearings, which were reported in over 50 transcript volumes totaling over 11,000 pages, and in issuing five formal reports, totaling 2,241 pages.

Scope of the Committee Investigations

Pro-Axis Groups. During the period 1941 to 1945 the committee spent almost half of its time investigating individuals and groups thought to be sympathetic to the fortunes of Berlin, Rome, or Tokyo. In 1941 and 1942 the committee held nine days of public

8

hearings concerning such allegedly pro-German movements as the German-American Bund, National Copperheads of America, Friends of Progress, America First committees, and the Ku Klux Klan. California leaders of these organizations were called to the stand for questioning, and the resulting testimony was summarized in the 1943 report of the committee. In 1943 the committee delved into charges that one Hans Wilhelm Rohl, while a German alien, exercised improper influence to obtain contracts for the construction of secret installations at Pearl Harbor and other Pacific bases. Committee attachés later provided Fulton Lewis, Jr., with the material for a long series of broadcasts on the Rohl case. The committee's hearings were summarized in the 1945 report.

Between 1941 and 1945 the committee held about seven days of public hearings dealing with the activities of Arthur L. Bell and his two organizations, Mankind United and Christ's Church of the Golden Rule. The committee justified its investigation of these fabulous rackets by pointing to their opposition to the war effort, and, in fact, a number of the leaders of Mankind United were tried for sedition. Nearly forty-five pages in the 1943 and 1945 reports were devoted to summarizing the testimony at these hearings.

In early 1942 the committee held a short hearing on Japanese activities in California. In 1943 the committee convened to hear a Dr. John R. Lechner, the most vocal of the anti-Japanese in California. In the 1943 report the committee summarized the testimony of Lechner and repeated his call for permanent exclusion of the Japanese and for military rather than civilian control of the relocation centers. In 1943 and 1944 various committee members made trips to the relocation centers in California, but no further public hearings were held. The 1945 report, reflecting the changed tenor of public opinion, reported in a much more moderate manner upon the Japanese problem as it then existed.

In May, 1942, the committee held a sensational three-day hearing in San Francisco regarding alleged pro-Fascist activities in the San Francisco Italian colony. The testimony at this hearing was summarized in the 1943 report.

Communism and Labor. In its investigations of communism in California the committee gave a large portion of its attention to

9

alleged Communist infiltration and control of labor unions. In its very first hearing in July, 1941, the committee questioned a number of witnesses in an attempt to prove that a Communist fraction had organized the opposition to Tenney and his proposed new constitution in Local 47 of the A.F.M. A number of other witnesses were questioned about Communist activity in other unions in the Los Angeles area. Later in 1941 the committee held five days of public hearings on the politically explosive King, Conner, Ramsay case. These three men, union officers who with another had been convicted of the murder of the chief engineer of a ship, were released on parole late in 1941. California Attorney General Warren charged that they were free not because they were rehabilitated criminals "but because they are politically powerful radicals." The committee heard witnesses in San Francisco and at San Quentin and concluded that "King, Ramsay and Conner are free today merely because the Communist Party had obtained great influence in the political arena of the State of California." The 1943 report of the committee recounted at length the King, Conner, Ramsay hearings and contained about thirteen pages of discussion on Communist infiltration of labor unions in California.

In October, 1944, a report prepared by committee Counsel Combs on alleged Communist domination of the C.I.O. Political Action Committee was "read into the record" at a public hearing. This report, which was based in the main on a report made by the Dies committee in June, 1944, concluded with the charge that the C.I.O. Political Action Committee "constitutes a menacing subversive force in the Nation and in this State." The report was set out in full in the 1945 committee report.

At a hearing in Oakland in September, 1946, two expelled members of the Marine Cooks and Stewards Union appeared voluntarily before the committee to testify regarding what they charged to be Communist control of that union. In the 1947 report their testimony was set out at length along with an affidavit by a third expelled member of the same union.

In January, 1946, at a hearing in Los Angeles the committee brought forth the testimony of a handwriting expert to show that the signature on a Communist Party card was that of Herbert K. Sorrell, leader of a jurisdictional strike in the motion picture industry. In the 1947 report the committee summarized this testimony and presented other evidence thought by it to show that Sorrell was a Communist or fellow traveler.

In September, 1946, the committee held extensive hearings in Oakland on alleged Communist control of the International Federation of Architects, Engineers, Chemists and Technicians, C.I.O., and on charges that this organization was used in attempted espionage on atomic research at the University of California radiation laboratory. As a result of this investigation, Counsel Combs prepared a long report on the organization which was printed in full in the 1947 report.

At a hearing in Oakland in November, 1947, the committee delved again into charges of Communist control of the Marine Cooks and Stewards Union. Also Sidney Roger, a San Francisco radio commentator sponsored by a group of C.I.O. unions, was questioned regarding his associations and charged by Tenney with following the Communist Party line and being "a paid spokesman for a Communist dominated group of unions." At a hearing in Los Angeles in February, 1948, the committee heard testimony regarding other union activities, including charges that a news vendors' union was Communist-dominated. In its 1948 report the committee listed a large number of organizations as "Communist front organizations." At one point in this listing it charged nineteen C.I.O. unions "to be so thoroughly entrenched with Communist leadership as to be dominated by the Stalinites in America." Specific treatment was given to additional charges regarding the Federation of Architects, Engineers, Chemists and Technicians. A long section dealing with the Marine Cooks and Stewards Union included more affidavits from expelled members. Charges of Communist domination were also made against the News Vendors Union, Local 75, C.I.O., and the Screen Writers Guild.

In August, 1948, the committee held a hearing in Sacramento regarding the Food, Tobacco and Agricultural Workers Union, C.I.O. In its 1949 report under the general heading of "Important Communist Front Activity" the committee included a few pages on the "Labor Union Caucus" in which it detailed its charge that an "essential feature of the Communist revolutionary conspiracy

11

is the promotion of revolutionary industrial trade-unionism."

Communism and the Schools. During 1941 and 1942 the committee heard a few witnesses regarding alleged radical activities in the schools of the state. In its 1943 report the committee stated that most of its investigation had been made quietly. "As a result of this investigation, your committee is convinced that Communism is not being *taught* in the universities, or in any of our public schools throughout California. Your committee, however, is convinced, that . . . there are a considerable number of instructors and faculty members who are either active members of the Communist Party or whose positions relegate them to the role of 'fellow traveler.' "

In August, 1943, a Writers' Congress was announced to be held on the campus of the University of California at Los Angeles October 1–3, 1943, under the joint sponsorship of U.C.L.A. and the Hollywood Writers' Mobilization. In September Senator Tenney sent a fifteen-page report to President Sproul of the University of California charging that the congress was Communist-inspired, that the sponsors of the congress were the same as those who formed the first American Writers' Congress in 1935 under Communist Party auspices. Tenney's charges were denied by the university officials responsible for the congress. Tenney then publicly threatened to order an investigation by his committee if the congress was not canceled. The congress was held as scheduled. On October 9, 1943, the committee held a brief "hearing" which consisted of Counsel Combs's reading into the record eighty transcript pages of material relating to the League of American Writers. In October, 1944, the committee held a hearing, taking testimony regarding the League of American Writers, the Hollywood Writers' Mobilization, and the U.C.L.A. Writers' Congress. In the 1945 report the committee charged that the Writers' Congress was Communist-dominated. The bulk of this report was devoted to showing Communist control of the League of American Writers and detailing the alleged Communist affiliations of two or three individuals who had been connected with the league and who were among those on the committee for organizing the U.C.L.A. Writers' Congress.

In the 1945 report the committee gave three pages to telling

12

of the starting of a workers' education school—The Peoples Educational Center—in Los Angeles in 1943. This report detailed the associations of some of the people connected with the center and concluded that it was "inspired and controlled by the Communists." At Los Angeles in January, 1946, the committee held a hearing in connection with the Peoples Educational Center: in this hearing the committee questioned various members of the faculty of the University of California at Los Angeles and others regarding their participation in the work of the center by lectures or otherwise. In the 1947 report the committee discussed again the Peoples Educational Center and the people who were associated with it.

A considerable portion of the January, 1946, hearing was devoted not to the center but to the University of California at Los Angeles. Six members of the faculty were called for interrogation. Dr. Clarence A. Dykstra, U.C.L.A. provost, was questioned extensively regarding the *Hollywood Quarterly,* a magazine which then was published under the joint sponsorship of the university and the Hollywood Writers' Mobilization. He was also insistently asked his opinion of the propriety of lecturing by university faculty members at the Peoples Educational Center. These hearings were reported at some length in the committee's 1947 report under the heading, "University Professors and Communist Schools."

In hearings in Oakland in September, 1946, the committee took testimony regarding alleged Communist control of the California Labor School, a San Francisco institution, and regarding the professors from the University of California at Berkeley who were sponsors or otherwise associated with this school. A lengthy report of the testimony at these hearings and of the various individuals who had been connected in one way or another with the school was given in the 1947 report.

In October, 1946, the committee heard at Los Angeles charges by a few witnesses that two teachers at the Canoga Park High School had been slanting their teachings and discussions for the purposes of indoctrinating the students with Communist philosophy. As a result of this hearing the Los Angeles County board of education appointed a special committee which held extensive hearings. The report of this committee largely exonerated the

13

teachers, who were accordingly retained on the staff. In the 1947 report the Tenney committee summarized the testimony at its hearings, quoted substantial portions of the report of the board of education committee, and concluded that the latter committee had exercised "a serious lack of intelligence and realism in its attempt to cope with the skilled propagandists for Communist totalitarianism. It should be obvious that the task of investigation was one for professional investigators trained in piercing smoke-screens. The employment of members of the teaching profession in such an investigation is a waste of energy. The palpable 'white-wash' of the affair might easily have been anticipated."

In February, 1947, the committee held in the small town of Chico, California, a one-day hearing on charges that a Communist-inspired sex education program had been conducted at the local high school. This investigation chiefly focused upon whether or not certain textbooks which discussed physical sex relationships were proper for use by high-school students and whether they had been made available to the students. Very little attempt was made to relate the investigation to the subject of un-American activities, beyond the general proposition that the books in question tended to destroy the moral fiber of students, to break down respect for religion and the family, and to justify changes in the social order as a means of increasing sexual adjustment. The hearing was reported in the press under headlines such as "Tenney Fears Sex May Be Un-American." It was covered fully in the 1947 report, in which the committee concluded that the sex education program was part of "a carefully laid Communist plan for the corruption of America's coming generation." In a sequel to the Chico investigation, Senator Tenney in April, 1949, successfully opposed a bill proposing the establishment of family relations courses in teachers' colleges and high schools. "The only experience we have," he stated before the Senate Education Committee, "is the course at Chico." The books there were "obscene and Communistic," and the committee "definitely concluded it was a Communist plot to destroy the fibre of youth in Chico."

The 1947 report also contained a discussion by the committee concerning a booklet "Land of the Soviets" published under the auspices of the Institute of Pacific Relations and used in some of the schools. This report, which consisted of an examination of the booklet itself and of the record of associations of its author, concluded that the booklet was part of a program "for the softening of the coming generation by orienting youthful minds to the glories of Communism and directing disrespect and contempt for our traditions, our Flag and our Country."

In its 1948 report the committee stated that no "phase of education is immune from Communist infiltration, strategic and tactical attack. From teachers' unions to child care centers; from textbooks to the classroom, Communist infiltration proceeds steadily and persistently." Among the organizations listed by the committee in this report as "Communist front organizations" were several in the educational field.

In February, 1948, at a hearing in Los Angeles the committee interrogated additional witnesses concerning the Peoples Educational Center. And in September, 1949, after the P.E.C. had suspended operations and the California Labor School had opened up a Los Angeles branch, the committee held hearings in Los Angeles concerning the latter school. In its 1949 report the committee devoted several pages to a discussion of youth and education groups thought by it to be Communist-controlled, as well as reprinting its former discussions of the Peoples Educational Center and the California Labor School.

Communist Front Organizations. The committee devoted a considerable portion of its time to the problem of identifying and exposing organizations which it thought were mere fronts for the Communist Party. The committee held public hearings in which it either heard testimony or read into the record prepared reports concerning, among others, the following list of organizations outside the labor and educational fields: Actors' Laboratory Theatre, American Civil Liberties Union, American-Russian Institute, Committee for the First Amendment, Congress of American Women, Hollywood Community Radio Group, Hollywood Independent Citizens Committee of the Arts, Sciences and Professions, Joint Anti-Fascist Refugee Committee, Mobilization for Democracy, National Sharecroppers Fund, *People's Daily World,* Progressive Party, and Screen Writers Guild.

In 1948, instead of reporting on the hearings it had conducted during the preceding year, the committee issued a report which was designed, in the words of the committee, "to present a definitive explanation of the Communist front organization; an analysis which will provide, within one concise and factual compilation, the material that public officials, police agencies, journalists and leaders of all organized segments of the community must have readily available to them in authoritative form if they are to carry out their obligations to their organizations, their State and their Nation in meeting the problems raised by the Red Fascist conspiracy within the United States."

This report commenced with an analysis of Communist front organizations, classifying them according to the proportion of Communist influence and according to the Communist purpose and objective. The committee then found that "Stalinism is the most apt and appropriate descriptive label for the theories of violent revolution, and the concept of totalitarian government" and that any person "who supports the program of the Communist Party in any nation as part of the program of world revolution laid down by the Comintern in Moscow is a Stalinist. Any person who consistently works to serve the interests of the foreign policy of Soviet Russia, and who promotes discord, disunity, dissension and class strife, for the purpose of preparing the way for revolution, is a Stalinist." The great bulk of the report consisted of a listing and discussion of organizations found by the committee "to be controlled, to a lesser or greater degree, by the Communist Party of the United States." Several thousand individuals were also listed in this portion of the report and their affiliations discussed. The committee stated that so far as possible it had "deleted the names of officers and sponsors of Communist front organizations, who were, in fact, merely dupes and innocents of Communist manipulation" and that it was "concerned in this analysis with the bona fide, iron disciplined Communist revolutionary." The committee also stated that the "interested reader will carefully check the index of this report and the index of previous reports, and, by following the classifications listed herein and evaluating the degree of control and disguise of the front, easily arrive at indisputable conclusions susceptible to the most thorough documentation and proof."

The committee then listed and discussed some two hundred organizations. The discussion of each organization ranged from merely a few lines giving the policy of the organization or naming a few of its officers to ten or fifteen pages in which the alleged Communist front affiliations of the people connected with the organization were set out in detail. Most of the organizations and individuals named in this report had not been the subject of public hearings before the committee, and many of them had no connection with California. Included in the list were labor unions, relief organizations, and religious or racial societies as well as groups that devoted themselves directly to political or economic issues. The Tenney committee in 1948 characterized as "Communist fronts" approximately twice as many organizations as have been similarly labeled by the attorney general of the United States in connection with the federal loyalty program.

Miscellaneous Investigations. In 1942 and 1943 the committee investigated the "zoot suit" rioting which swept Los Angeles. When a citizens' committee sprang up to defend twenty-two Mexican-Americans who were put on trial for the murder of one Joseph Diaz in a brawl, the Tenney committee called members of the citizens' committee before it for interrogation and later issued a report charging that the citizens' committee was a mere front for Communist racial agitation. After a serious outbreak of rioting in June, 1943, between the Mexican-Americans and servicemen in the Los Angeles area, the committee held hearings and charged that the rioting resulted from Communist-inspired agitation in the left-wing press which fomented racial antagonisms. In tragic oversimplification the committee ignored the basic causes of the riots, such as poor housing and living conditions and widespread community discrimination against certain racial groups, and focused public opinion on a convenient scapegoat—the Communists caused it all.

In 1946 the committee came out against a Fair Employment Practices Initiative measure, charging that it had been inspired by the Communist Party and that it "was deliberately designed to create racial frictions and agitations, rather than to remedy such discriminations between ethnical groups as actually existed." In reporting on the incident in its 1947 report the committee ignored the widespread support of the measure by moderate groups in the community and condemned the measure because more than half of the members of a southern California committee for promotion of the measure "had been prominent in movements sponsored by the Communists and left-wingers in California."

In 1946 one of the members of the committee had been defeated in the Democratic primary for the state assembly. Five days before the general elections in November the committee held a hearing in Oakland, California, in which it attempted to show that the man who defeated the committee member had Communist sympathies. The defeated committee member himself conducted much of the questioning and gave some of the testimony. The political motivation of this was so obvious, however, that the man it attacked was elected and started on a career in the state legislature where he has been one of the strongest opponents of the committee.

In October, 1947, the committee permitted itself to become embroiled in a local political squabble. The small northern California city of Fairfax was engaged in a bitter local fight over planning, garbage, streets, and sewage. A member of the city council translated the whole affair into un-American activities terms simply by charging that a member of the planning commission appointed by the opposition group had engaged in "Communistic and un-American" activities. At the request of the majority of the city council the Tenney committee came to town and held a one-day hearing. Later Tenney issued a report concluding, on the sketchiest of evidence, that the "Communist Party was doing its level best to create a chaotic situation within that city." The report also congratulated the one group on the city council "on their vigilance in attacking the forces that are determined to destroy, not only Fairfax and California, but the United States of America as well." This report was used as campaign literature in the 1948 city election. Again the activity of the committee backfired. The candidates who relied on the Tenney report were roundly defeated.

Legislative Program

Over the years the committee sponsored a rather large number of bills in the state legislature. It succeeded, however, in having but a few of them enacted into law.

In 1941 Tenney and others who had been members of the Yorty committee introduced the bill which became the Subversive Organization Registration Act, an ineffective attempt to compel public registration of organizations seeking to overthrow the government or subject to control by foreign governments.[8] They also succeeded in procuring the enactment of legislation requiring state departments to discharge any employee who commits a contempt before a legislative committee and prohibiting the employment in any state department of any person who "carries on, advocates, teaches, justifies, aids, or abets a program of sabotage, force and violence, sedition or treason" against the government. They were unsuccessful in securing the enactment of a law requiring a loyalty oath for lawyers and making membership in a subversive organization ground for disbarment.

In 1943 the committee tried again unsuccessfully to procure legislation directed at lawyer members of subversive organizations. It was successful in securing the enactment of legislation regulating Japanese and German language schools.

In 1945 the committee sponsored legislation barring the use of public-school buildings by groups with subversive objectives. This legislation was declared unconstitutional by the California Supreme Court in 1946.[9] The committee was unsuccessful in securing the passage of legislation permitting labor organizations to expel members found to be subversives and authorizing employers

[8] In January, 1948, California Attorney General Howser announced that no organizations had registered under the act. There has been only one prosecution for failure to register; in that case a conviction of the officers of the Friends of Progress movement was reversed on appeal for lack of evidence to sustain the judgment. *People v. Noble,* 68 Cal. App. 2d 853, 158 P. 2d 225 (1945).

[9] *Danskin v. San Diego Unified School Dist.,* 28 Cal. 2d 536, 171 P. 2d 885 (1946).

to discharge employees upon "reasonable ground for belief" that they were subversive.

In 1947 the committee introduced a series of eight bills designed to prevent the teaching of controversial subjects in the elementary schools and to increase the legislative control over the selection of textbooks and educational policies. Of these eight only one became law, providing that basic instruction in geography, United States history, civics, the Declaration of Independence, the Constitution of the United States, and American institutions and ideals shall be prerequisite to advanced courses involving problems in sociology, political science, economics, foreign trade, and foreign affairs.[10]

In 1949 the committee introduced a comprehensive program of legislation designed, as it stated in its 1949 report, to "isolate, expose and remove from positions of power and influence persons who are a dangerous menace to our freedom and security." This program included bills broadly defining communism and Communist; making it a misdemeanor to teach any of the "isms" except Americanism upon school property with the intent to indoctrinate the pupils; requiring candidates for public office and all state employees to subscribe to special loyalty oaths; requiring subversive organizations to keep written public records of their meetings and declaring all places where such organizations hold meetings to be nuisances subject to abatement; prescribing a special loyalty oath for lawyers; permitting unions to expel and

[10] At this session of the legislature the Senate Investigating Committee on Education was established with Senator Nelson S. Dilworth (of the Tenney committee) as chairman. This committee has made six reports to the legislature, three of which have dealt with matters relating to subversive activities. The first report, filed in June, 1947, attacked the reinstatement by the state board of education of a high-school teacher who had previously been discharged for pro-Soviet sympathies. The third report, filed in March, 1948, contained an elaborate indictment of a series of supplementary textbooks for grade schools, the *Building America* series, as subversive in character. The sixth report, filed in June, 1949, dealt with alleged Communist charges of racial discrimination against an elementary school principal in Los Angeles. R. E. Combs, counsel for the Tenney committee, also acted as counsel for the education committee in connection with these three reports.

defense contractors to discharge subversive employees. A constitutional amendment was proposed to take from the Regents of the University of California and give to the legislature the power to ensure the loyalty of officers and employees of the university. It was to forestall the enactment of this measure that the regents of the university imposed their now famous loyalty oath. A constitutional amendment was also proposed to set up a special loyalty oath for members of the legislature and all public officers.

This legislative program was vigorously attacked and defended. Seven of the bills passed the senate by large majorities. They were defeated in the assembly only at the last moment as the climax of a bitter fight over the continuation of the Tenney committee which (as will be described later) led to the resignation of Tenney from the committee and a promise of improved methods for the future.

The Committee's Approach to Investigating Subversive Activities

The way in which the committee ran its hearings, wrote its reports and otherwise carried on its work can be understood only in the light of its assumptions as to the nature of the Communist movement, the objectives it sought to achieve by its investigations, and the standards of evidence it employed in seeking to identify Communists and Communist front organizations.

The committee's appraisal of the nature and extent of the Communist movement runs somewhat as follows:

A world-wide Communist conspiracy directed from Moscow has swept eastern Europe and is moving ahead in China and other Asiatic countries. The grand objective of this conspiracy is to capture America, and war between Russia and the United States is inevitable and imminent. The Communist Party in the United States is the local agent of this world-wide conspiracy, and its basic aim is the abolition of our present system of government and the establishment of a Soviet dictatorship in its place. "Thus, every Communist in the United States is a potential traitor, saboteur and espionage agent of Soviet Russia."

Because of its strategic location California is a principal target for the Communist conspiracy, and Communist agents are spreading their insidious propaganda from positions of influence and power throughout the state. Communists are devoted to this conspiracy with a fanatical single-mindedness. "While small in number they are great in influence because they fool many people into believing they are merely liberals and progressives who want to do something for the working class in general. Actually everything they do is done for the sinister purpose of destroying the governmental institutions in this country." They never waste any time or motion. They support only those causes that will benefit Moscow and associate only with those individuals who are useful to Moscow. Because of their single-mindedness and devotion, one of them can infect an entire organization. "When a trusted Communist functionary appears as the member of the Board of Directors of an organization, the Communist character and control of the group is firmly established." "It only takes two or three Communists on any Board, no matter how big it is, and eventually it will be taken over."

These assumptions colored all the work of the committee. It is impossible to understand the way in which Tenney operated the committee without realizing that he pictured himself as the heroic figure carrying on the battle against communism on the ramparts while the populace, ignoring its dangers, disported itself within the walls. He was battling the spies and traitors and saboteurs whose sole aim was to render our country defenseless in the coming inevitable war with Russia. All his activities were within this frame of reference. Each of his reports began with an elaborate discussion of world communism as the background against which accounts of local activities were set. In his conversation he referred constantly to the menace of international communism and complained of the criticism he received from those who should have known that their best interest would be served by joining his crusade. The same attitude carried over to his office staff and the others who surrounded him.

Objectives. Among the generally accepted objectives of legislative investigating committees are fact finding in aid of the legislative process and informing and molding public opinion. The first of these objectives was emphasized in the resolutions setting up

22

the committee; and the committee did in fact introduce legislation from time to time. The second, in the form of public exposure of subversive activities, was, however, the principal announced objective of the committee. As expressed in Senator Tenney's picturesque language, "the purpose of this Committee, in addition to the introduction of legislation from time to time on the subject, is to expose these Communists for what they are so that the people will not be taken in as a lot of suckers helping to cause their own destruction and financing that destruction as well."

In practice, the Tenney committee went far beyond either of these well-recognized objectives. Not content with mere exposure the committee sought to punish alleged subversives and their sympathizers, taking upon itself the functions of prosecutor, judge, and jury. Once it had established to its satisfaction that a particular individual was a Communist or fellow traveler it sought literally to banish him from all normal community life. The objective was to quarantine him as though he were infected with smallpox. Efforts were made to prevent association with him, to forbid lawyers defending him in his troubles with the law, to cause his employer to discharge him and his union to expel him. People were warned that they should not rent him a hall for a meeting, or join any organization of which he was a member, or read any book or attend any play or motion picture written by him, or even espouse any cause espoused by him.

In order to achieve these objectives the committee assumed a duty to compel the public at large to comply with its standards of conduct with reference to Communists. Increasingly the emphasis in the committee's activity shifted from the actual subversives to those who associated with them or supported any of their causes. Once it determined that a particular organization was a Communist front, the committee felt that its first duty was to drive all non-Communist individuals from the group. The more important and respected the individual the more dangerous was his association because he served as the window dressing necessary to lure innocents into supporting the Communist cause. Support of alleged Communists or Communist causes in any form was forbidden. Thus, the committee stated in its 1948 report, for a federal judge to make a single speech at a labor school found by the committee to be a Communist front was "a disgraceful reflection upon the federal bench. For anyone to fraternize with the enemies of the people of the United States, its Constitution and government, is bad enough in itself, but when a judge of the federal bench lends his position and name to dignify traitorous organizations, such as the Communist Peoples Educational Center, then no condemnation is strong enough to characterize such action."

Evidence. The committee operated on the theory (apparently common to investigative agencies in this field) that Communists and their sympathizers can be detected quite objectively by examining "documentary evidence" of their associations. In its 1948 report it said: "The symptoms of Stalinist activity are such that it is possible to interpret the Communist fever chart of an individual or organization, just as a physician who has studied the stigma and symptoms of disease, can chart the condition of a patient." In the same report it stated that by examining the material presented in its reports the reader can "easily arrive at indisputable conclusions susceptible to the most thorough documentation and proof."

Insofar as can be ascertained from studying the public record of the committee's activity this "thorough documentation and proof" which would lead to "indisputable conclusions" regarding an individual's sympathy for the Communist movement rested almost wholly upon that individual's associations. He belonged to certain organizations found to be Communist fronts. He signed a petition in favor of a known Communist. His name was mentioned favorably in a Communist newspaper. He spoke before a Communist front organization. He joined in a protest against the Dies committee or the Tenney committee. These were the "indisputable" facts which could be thoroughly "documented." From them the committee drew its "indisputable" conclusions.

The committee rarely made an effort to get a complete and well-rounded picture of a suspected individual's associations. The emphasis was always on associations with organizations thought to be Communist fronts. Other associations were treated as somehow irrelevant or mere camouflage. Only a Communist sympathizer or at least a Communist "dupe" of unusual stupidity would get himself mixed up in very many front organizations. Most of the people listed by the committee, in fact, were never given an opportunity to explain their associations. Only a small fraction of those named in the reports were ever called before the committee. Many of those called were, of course, evasive and unsatisfactory witnesses who made no attempt to provide the committee with information. But even those people who were willing to answer questions and anxious to explain their philosophies and associations were rarely permitted to do so. The committee had lists of their affiliations with organizations found to be Communist fronts, and the purpose of the hearings was to see if they would admit membership in them, not to discover other evidence regarding their beliefs and activities. In the few instances where the committee did permit a witness to testify at length regarding his own philsophy this testimony was disregarded, and the committee made findings on the basis of the associations revealed by its files.

The committee's conclusions regarding individuals were further affected by the standards it adopted for determining whether or not particular organizations were Communist front organizations. Here again the committee reached "indisputable conclusions" through "thorough documentation and proof."

This "thorough documentation and proof" in most instances consisted either in a determination that the announced objectives of the organization coincided with the Communist Party line or in a listing of its officers, members, and sponsors, or in a combination of the two. The greatest weight was given to the identity of the individuals connected with the organization. Here, particularly, the assumptions by the committee regarding the nature and extent of the Communist conspiracy colored its findings. Since Communists never waste time, they become members of organizations only to advance the interests of Moscow. And one or two of them can soon infect an organization and take it over. Therefore, it is rarely necessary to look further for evidence of the Communist character of an organization than to the names of its officers, directors, and members.

Most of the organizations listed by the committee as Communist fronts had not been the subject of testimony before the committee. As to such organizations the committee's findings appeared to be based on the letterheads and other documents in its own files and on the similar evidence presented in Dies commit-

25

tee publications. Even in the few instances where organizations were made the subject of committee hearings, little attempt was made to get a rounded picture of their activities, policies, and objectives. Instead, the hearings were largely confined to determining the names of individuals connected with the organization and setting forth their associations with other organizations found to be Communist fronts. In only a few instances did the committee present additional evidence regarding the policies and objectives and actual operations of the organizations.

As a result of such standards of evidence the committee's findings with respect to both individuals and organizations were inevitably unreliable. Individuals were found to be Communist sympathizers because they belonged to a number of organizations termed "Communist fronts." And the organizations were found to be Communist fronts because the individuals were connected with them. Such circular reasoning created an ever-increasing group of individuals who could be listed because of their membership in organizations and an ever-increasing group of organizations which could be listed because these individuals were connected with them. By 1949 the group of people involved was so large as to make patently ridiculous many of the committee's findings.

The Committee Hearings

In most instances the committee appeared to plan its hearings as a means of confirming and publicizing the results of previous investigation rather than as a means of finding facts. This technique resulted in giving to the public only a one-sided and fragmentary view of the matters at issue. The hearings were roughly comparable to a judicial trial in which only the prosecution was allowed to present evidence, bound by no rules and with its witnesses free from cross-examination, and in which the judge was absent and forced to reach his verdict on the basis of newspaper accounts of the trial.

Since the committee never had an active minority group, the planning and conduct of the hearings was left exclusively in the hands of Tenney and committee Counsel Combs. They chose both the subject matter of the hearings and the witnesses to be called. The typical pattern was for a decision to be made that a particular individual was a Communist Party member or a fellow traveler or that a particular organization was a Communist front. The individual or officers of the organization would be subpoenaed along with other witnesses selected by the committee who would give testimony adverse to the witness or organization. The latter were not given an opportunity to produce witnesses of their choosing to testify on their behalf. This preselection of witnesses invariably resulted in the committee's getting only a partial view, selected by themselves, of the situation.

As the hearing date approached, the committee frequently used publicity releases to stimulate interest. Statements would be made as to what the committee expected to prove about various named individuals and organizations. When process servers were unable to reach some of the people on the committee's list, another release would be given as to the Reds who were evading subpoenas.

The hearings themselves were conducted along a prepared line of inquiry. Counsel for the committee would have a hearing brief designed to elicit the information desired by the committee. The witness usually was given no general opportunity to explain himself. Nor was he permitted to produce witnesses on his own behalf or to cross-examine witnesses who gave testimony adverse to him.

In many instances, the committee would interrogate a series of witnesses regarding charges against individuals who were not before the committee. At one hearing held in Los Angeles in 1948, for example, several witnesses were called to testify regarding a member of the California assembly who, though presumably available, was not brought before the committee. These witnesses were questioned regarding his alleged prior police record and membership in the Communist Party. Documents were read to show his associations with other people charged to be Communist sympathizers. The assemblyman's only chance to present his side of the story was in statements to the press which, of course, did not receive the same publicity as the original charges.

The tone of many of the hearings, particularly in the later years, was that of prosecution rather than fact finding. Tenney frequently interrupted the questioning by Counsel Combs to pursue his own lines of inquiry in a manner which provoked immediate antagonism. Departing completely from the role of the fact finder, he would make statements such as the following to witnesses: "Let me tell you that you are not fooling everybody. Many Communists have lied about their connections. . . . That is perfectly all right with this committee and we're glad to have you speak, but it is very obvious that you are a Communist." In the course of questioning one witness, Tenney made the following statements: "Your activities indicate to me and this committee that you follow the Communist Party line, that you are a paid spokesman for a Communist dominated group of unions." "We are concerned with the enemies of this country, the potential quislings in what might come." "We feel that a person following a philosophy supporting a foreign power is an enemy to this country and therefore a dangerous person."

The tone of oppression which pervaded the hearings was amplified in other ways. Tenney would denounce attorneys for witnesses as "Communists" and eject them from the hearing room when they protested the tactics of the committee. Audience laughter or applause at the sally of a witness would bring forth an order from Tenney to the state police in attendance to eject the demonstrators along with a general denunciation of all the "Communists" in the audience.

The publicizing, as opposed to fact-finding, objective of committee hearings was made most evident by the large amount of material "read into the record" at such hearings. For example, long reports prepared by Counsel Combs charging that such organizations as the C.I.O. Political Action Committee, the Federation of Architects, Engineers, Chemists and Technicians, and the Congress of American Women were Communist-controlled, were read into the record at public hearings and later printed in the reports as findings of the committee. In one of the most extreme examples of this kind, Combs, at a hearing in 1948, read into the record, without prior notice to the organization, 300 pages of material prepared by Tenney concerning the American Civil Liberties Union and the alleged subversive affiliations of people connected with it. This was the committee's only public "hearing" regarding an organization which had protested vigorously a finding made in the committee's 1943 report that it was a Communist front and which had demanded a public hearing at which it could state its side of the case.

Another serious defect in the hearings as a basis for rational fact-finding was their inconclusive character. The committee would announce its intention to investigate a particular episode or organization and would then subpoena a group of people. Many of the witnesses would not be found. The testimony of those who did appear would suggest new lines of inquiry and would name people with intimate knowledge of the situation. In most instances, however, no attempt was made to follow up these matters and complete the investigations. The hearing was over. No matter how fragmentary the evidence presented, it became the basis for a committee report on the situation. Even in its role as an investigative agency the committee usually confined itself to discovering and reporting sensational charges against individuals and organizations without making a serious attempt to determine their truth or falsity.

The prosecution complex of the committee was also illustrated by the way in which it treated witnesses. Those who came before it to expose the Reds were treated with the greatest deference. Their testimony was in the main assumed to be true, and no attempt was made to probe their interest or to test the reliability of their statements. Adverse witnesses, on the other hand, were treated almost like convicted traitors; their testimony was challenged at every turn, and every unsavory episode in their private lives which could be discovered was exposed. In at least one instance, a witness who was treated as a gentleman and a patriot when he testified concerning Communist activities in a union, later found himself charged as a man without honor and with a long criminal record when he attacked the committee and opposed its legislative appropriations.

The Committee Reports

The Tenney committee filed five formal reports with the legislature. Thousands of copies of these reports (ranging from 10,000 of the 1943 report to 27,000 of the 1948 report) were printed and distributed.

The 1943 Report. This report of 445 pages was filed in April,

29

1943. The first 175 pages dealt with the subject of Communism. Much of this portion of the report was given to a textbookish discussion of the theory and strategy of the Communist movement, with headings such as "Communist Theory and Practice," "Trotskyism," "Six Periods of Communist Strategy in the United States." The testimony of witnesses on the subject of communism during the 1941–1943 period was summarized, and conclusions were drawn as to the Communist character of many individuals and organizations.

The remainder of the report consisted of summaries of the testimony of witnesses regarding the other organizations (primarily Nazi, Fascist, and Japanese) which had been the subject of committee hearings. Little attempt was made by the committee to evaluate the testimony thus recorded.

The report concluded with recommendations for the continuance of the committee and the enactment of legislation for the control of "subversive" groups.

The 1945 Report. This report of 236 pages was filed in April, 1945. The first sixty-five pages contained summaries of the testimony of witnesses regarding the activities of Hans Wilhelm Rohl and of the Mankind United organization and a report on Japanese activities which was written from newspaper accounts and visits made to the relocation centers by members of the committee.

The remainder of the report fell under the heading of "Communism." In this section the committee failed to differentiate between admitted Communists and Communist organizations and other organizations suspected only because of the records of a few of the individuals connected with them. The first four headings in the section were "Red-Baiting and Red-Baiters," "Communist Philosophy, Sources and Background," "Development of Communism in the United States," and "Communist Strategy in the Western Hemisphere." These sections dealt with the Communist Party itself, its members, and its literature.

The fifth heading was "Writers' Congress at U.C.L.A." The coverage of the report in this section has already been described.

The sixth heading was "Peoples Educational Center" under which a new labor school in Los Angeles was condemned as "a

Communist organization for the dissemination of Marxism." No hearing had been held, and the committee supported its conclusions by pointing to the associations of a few of the members of the provisional committee which organized the center.

The seventh heading was "West Coast Communist Press" and dealt principally with the *People's Daily World,* a West Coast newspaper.

The eighth heading was "The C.I.O. Political Action Committee" under which was reprinted a report on the organization prepared by R. E. Combs, counsel for the committee. The Political Action Committee had not been the subject of a committee hearing, but the report by Combs had been "read into the record" during a 1944 hearing.

The last heading was "Zoot-Suit Riots in Southern California," in which the committee reported its hearings on that subject and its conclusion that the riots had resulted in large part from "Communist technique in fomenting racial prejudices and antagonisms."

The 1947 Report. This report of 403 pages was filed in March, 1947. It contained an increased amount of "documentation" from various sources as opposed to actual summaries of testimony before the committee.

In this report, aside from the opening pages on Communist tactics and strategy, the emphasis was not upon the Communist Party itself but upon the various organizations thought by the committee to be Communist-controlled. The bulk of the report was devoted to charges of Communist influence in educational institutions. Two labor schools, the California Labor School in San Francisco and the Peoples Educational Center in Los Angeles, were discussed at length. Members of the faculty of the University of California were charged with participating in the activities of these labor schools and with assisting other allegedly Communist causes. Widespread Communist influence in the public schools was declared to exist, and detailed consideration was given to charges that two Communist sympathizers were on the faculty in one high school, that a text containing Soviet propaganda was used in some of the schools, and that a Communist-inspired sex education program had been started in another high school.

The report examined the activities of Mobilization for Democracy, a Los Angeles group organized in 1945 to protest the activities of Gerald L. K. Smith and the Ku Klux Klan, and concluded that it was a part of the over-all Communist network in California. The Hollywood Community Radio Group, a Los Angeles organization which was seeking a license to operate an FM station, was also discussed along with a related group which had protested the dropping of certain radio commentators from a local station.

Three episodes of alleged Communist influence in labor unions were reported. In one section the testimony of three expelled members of the Marine Cooks and Stewards Union charging Communist domination of that union was set forth in some detail. In another section alleged Communist leadership of the Hollywood motion picture strike was discussed. A third section contained a long report by R. E. Combs charging that the International Federation of Architects, Engineers, Chemists and Technicians had been used as a front for Communist espionage in connection with atomic research in the University of California radiation laboratory.

Also included in the report was a section containing short, selected excerpts from the testimony of most of the witnesses who had appeared before the committee and another devoted to an excellent discussion of the problem of anti-Semitism in America.

The 1948 Report. This report (of 448 pages) departed sharply from the pattern of earlier reports. Very little space was given to reporting on matters covered in committee hearings. In the introduction the committee gave a short account of a one-day hearing held at Fairfax, California, and merely listed the persons who had been called at the other hearings during the preceding year. The great bulk of the report consisted of a generalized analysis of Communist front organizations followed by a listing of approximately two hundred organizations with evidence alleged to demonstrate their character as Communist fronts. This aspect of the report was discussed in earlier pages of this chapter.

In this report the committee began the practice of assuming the Communist character of organizations. Thus in reporting on the associations of a particular individual the committee would proceed as follows:

In April of 1947 [he] became a sponsor of the *Communist* Committee for a Democratic Far Eastern Policy. He also became a director of the Northern California Chapter of the *Communist* front, Progressive Citizens of America. He chairmaned a meeting on the twenty-third of February, 1947 . . . under the auspices of the *Communist* Spanish Refugee Appeal Committee. He was the chairman of the fifth anniversary meeting of the *Communist* California Labor School. . . . [Italics added.]

Even more unfair use was made of this device in reporting the testimony of witnesses. Thus when one witness admitted having been a delegate to the Western Writers Congress, to having attended luncheons of the Inter-Professional Association and meetings of the John Reed Club, and to the fact that her name was listed as associate editor of *Black and White,* the committee reported her testimony as follows:

[She] testified that she had been a delegate to the *Communist* Western Writers Congress in San Francisco. She admitted having attended luncheons of the *Communist* Inter-Professional Association in 1937. . . . She attended meetings of the *Communist* John Reed Club in San Francisco. She admitted that her name was listed as associate editor of the *Communist* publication, *Black and White,* but stated that she had never been active in that capacity. [Italics added.]

The 1949 Report. This report was the longest to be filed by the committee, containing 709 pages of text (and no index!). Unlike the previous reports which had been almost wholly written by Senator Tenney himself, this one was written by Mr. Ed. Gibbons, editor of *Alert,* a Los Angeles publication that describes itself as "A Weekly Confidential Report on Communism and How to Combat It." It is published by Jacoby and Gibbons and Associates, who describe themselves as "Anti-subversive Public Relations Specialists." Gibbons was hired by Tenney and paid for his work out of committee funds.

The 1949 report failed even to mention the hearings held by the committee during the preceding year. Nor did it purport to expose and publicize additional Communist organizations and activities. Instead, it was devoted to an attempt to present a definitive statement of the whole problem of communism in the United States and of the desirable solutions to the problem.

The first part of the report contained the following section headings: "The World Situation," "The Domestic Situation," "The California Situation," "The Major Legislative and Legal Problem," "Official Citations of Communist Fronts and Publications," "Important Communist Front Activity," "Legislation and the Courts." Much of the material contained in this part was quoted directly from publications of House Committee on Un-American Activities or from former reports of the Tenney committee.

The second part of the report discussed the problem of what should be done about the menace of communism. The committee made four recommendations. The first was the enactment of additional legislation designed to "isolate, expose and remove from positions of power and influence persons who are a dangerous menace to our freedom and security." The second was to improve the quality of the work of investigation in the Communist field. The third was for more active court enforcement of laws already on the statute books. The fourth was for increasing community action by responsible organized groups interested in combating the menace of communism.

In one section of this part of the report, headed "Repudiations and Denials of Communism," the committee made explicit its position that its investigations and reports had been "factual" and "irrefutable" and that those who criticized it were either participating in or unwittingly aiding the Communist conspiracy. After calling attention to all the attacks made upon the committee and its members and charging that these attacks had been in general terms without specific challenge to the facts cited in the reports, the committee listed the names of several hundred persons as being among its "more notorious critics." It also stated that "these individuals all persistently, viciously and dishonestly have attacked and denounced this committee and its members without once directly challenging a single finding of the committee"; that they "are typical of the individuals within the various Stalinist orbits"; and that they "have conspicuously followed or appeased some of the Communist Party line program over a long period of time, and . . . they all have participated in . . . protests . . . and organizations specifically working for and publicly advocating the destruction of the Senate Committee on Un-American Activities and the smearing and discrediting of the committee's personnel and staff."

In the newspaper publicity given to the 1949 report this list of names was referred to as a "Red list," and attention was called to the listing of names of individuals prominent in stage, screen, and literary worlds. Many of these people issued irate denials which were also given prominent newspaper space. As a result of this the Tenney committee issued a thirteen-page 1949 "Final Report" in which it denied that the list of names was a "Red list." The committee then referred to the denials and attacks upon the committee and stated that the people who issued the denials should have an opportunity to refute the facts reported by the committee. The bulk of this report then consisted of "a tabulated list of specific citations of participation in Communist fronts, causes, activities, committees, organizations and campaigns by the individuals who publicly protested or denounced the mention of their names in the 1949 (Fifth Report)."

The Impact of the Reports. Brief mention should be made of the use to which the committee's reports have been put. They have had, of course, no wide circulation among the public generally. Press descriptions of them have necessarily been fragmentary and have given a generally distorted picture of the reports by emphasizing the sensational charges against prominent individuals.

The chief impact of the reports has come from their circulation to governmental investigating agencies and private organizations. They have been used, of course, as a source of information by such governmental organizations as the Federal Bureau of Investigation. Private anti-Communist publications, such as *Alert* and *Counterattack,* have made extensive use of the material in the reports as have veterans and other patriotic and service organizations.

A few examples will serve to illustrate the way in which the reports have been employed. In October, 1947, Bartley Crum was dropped from a list of Chico Community Forum speakers on a

35

protest by the Butte County chapter of the Veterans of Foreign Wars that the Tenney committee had named Crum as affiliated with two Communist fronts—the Progressive Citizens of America and the San Francisco Labor School. On February 24, 1949, the Riverside County school department canceled two speeches scheduled to be given to local teachers by author Carey McWilliams after protests by the American Legion that McWilliams had been named forty-seven times in the latest report of the Tenney committee. On May 22, 1950, Mrs. Hester R. McCullough testified in the libel suit brought against her by Larry Adler and Paul Draper that she relied in part on the 1948 report of the Tenney committee in protesting a concert by them in Greenwich, Connecticut. Findings of the committee that particular organizations are Communist fronts are repeated elsewhere without the supporting evidence which reveals the strength or weakness of the findings. Thus the House Committee on Un-American Activities in a publication entitled "Citations by Official Government Agencies" repeated the Tenney committee charges. In a publication distributed to members of the American Legion by the National Americanism Commission of the legion on "Communist Front Organizations . . . Their Nature and How to Spot Them," the Tenney committee citations were again repeated along with those of other governmental agencies. And when in August, 1947, the Los Angeles County board of supervisors established a loyalty check program as a part of which all employees were required to sign affidavits listing past or present membership or support of some 150 organizations, press reports indicated that the list of organizations came from the Tenney committee findings.

The 1949 Reorganization of the Committee

By 1949 opposition to the committee was building up in many responsible quarters. A number of church groups, such as the Presbyterian Synod of California and the Southern California-Arizona Conference of the Methodist Church, had publicly condemned the activities of the committee. The committee's 1949 legislative program brought other respectable and influential agencies into the opposition camp. The board of governors of the State Bar of California, for example, vigorously opposed the loyalty oath bill for lawyers. The League of Women Voters denounced the entire series of loyalty oath bills. The California national C.I.O. Political Action Committee, even while engaged in its own fight against alleged Communists in the ranks of the C.I.O., came out in opposition to the Tenney committee bills.

Several conservative and influential newspapers, notably the *San Francisco Chronicle,* the *San Francisco News,* and the *Los Angeles Daily News,* had been growing increasingly critical of the committee and its activities. Several episodes during 1949 increased this criticism. The *San Francisco News* printed in its January 19, 1949, issue an article by its political editor in which she quoted Tenney as admitting that some of the criticism of his committee was justified and promising major changes in the committee's procedure. Shortly after this article appeared Tenney wrote to the editor of the *News* that he had been deliberately misquoted and demanded front-page space for his letter. The editor rejected his accusations and refused to print the letter. At this point, the news letter *Alert* entered the controversy by printing the exchange of letters between Tenney and the *News* and referring to the "weird role" of that paper "as leadoff batter in an involved and sinister conspiracy to smear, discredit and destroy" Tenney and his committee. Ed Gibbons, *Alert*'s editor, then started a campaign in that publication against the critics of the committee. He commenced by attacking the *Los Angeles Daily News,* the *San Francisco Chronicle,* and the *San Francisco News,* stating that their attitude was "stupid and inexcusable."

These newspapers joined with others in opposition to much of the committee's 1949 legislative program. In its 1949 report the committee reacted to this criticism, stating that these three newspapers

> have continued to misrepresent, misreport and attack falsely in editorial comment the committee and its reports. The attitude of these newspapers has been characterized by an almost total unwillingness to cite a single specific criticism or refutation of any specific hearings or reports by this committee, while blithely publishing untruths, half-truths, and vague, generalized attacks upon the committee and upon public officials who have supported the committee in its work. These newspapers

also have bleakly refused to correct, retract or repair the damage done.

One result of this report was to add to the critics of the committee the influential McClatchy newspapers, the *Sacramento, Fresno,* and *Modesto Bees.*

The Democratic Party was brought officially into opposition to the committee as a result of an issue of *Alert* published by Gibbons while he was engaged in the preparation of the 1949 report for the committee. In the course of assailing the committee's critics, he stated: "Not all those involved in today's rat's nest of intrigue and duplicity are Communists. Some are opportunists; others politically ambitious and willing to go to almost any lengths to gain their ends; others are cheap crooks and racketeers; and others are befuddled dupes and dopes." He then listed more than a hundred individuals, stating, "The names are in alphabetical order and this list does not indicate their immediate importance or Stalinist fever-chart reading at this time." The list included on the one hand several open officials of the Communist Party, such as William Schneiderman, state secretary, and on the other six members of the state assembly, all Democrats; two members of the state senate, both Democrats; Democratic Congressman Frank R. Havenner; San Francisco District Attorney Edmund Brown, a leading Democrat; Oliver J. Carter, then state chairman of the Democratic Party and now a federal district judge; Mrs. Edward Heller of San Francisco, Democratic national committeewoman; James Roosevelt, who became the 1950 Democratic candidate for governor of California; John F. Shelley, then state president of the A.F.L., now a member of Congress and a Democrat; and others.

Senator Tenney distributed copies of that issue of *Alert* to members of the legislature. In the resulting furore on the floor of the senate, Tenney subscribed to everything that Gibbons had said in his publication. He argued that the people listed by Gibbons were at least "dupes" and that many of the senators were not fully aware of the danger of communism and did not take time to read the reports of the committee. "The fact is this legislature has spent $100,000 to bring the grim story to us," he said. "The Red armies are poised behind the Iron Curtain and there are more than 20,000,000 labor slaves of the Soviet Union." Other members of the senate denounced Tenney for employing Gibbons, and an investigation was held of the conditions of his employment.

The mounting opposition to the committee was reflected immediately in the votes on committee bills as they came up for passage in the assembly. Sam Yorty, who had been chairman of the 1940 committee on which Tenney served, issued a statement in the assembly in opposition to the bills. In this statement he said: "Senator Tenney has headed this committee for almost ten years. He has worked very hard and faithfully, at this tiresome, nerve-wracking, and thankless job. It is obvious to me that he is completely exhausted, and that his constant scrutiny of Communist activities has resulted in distortion of his perspective, causing him to have an exaggerated opinion of the immediate threat of Communist success in the United States."

By June 20, sufficiently strong pressures had been placed on the legislature from various forces to compel the retirement of Tenney from the committee and the defeat of his legislative program. Labor organizations and Democratic Party officials were in open opposition. It was widely rumored that famed liquor lobbyist Arthur H. Samish had swung his influence against Tenney and his bills. The politically potent forces for old age pensions, led by George H. McClain of Los Angeles, irate at Tenney for opposing their program and activities, joined the anti-Tenney movement.

It became known that the Senate Rules Committee, which controls committee appointments for that body, would not approve the continuance of the committee with Tenney as a member. Strong pressure was placed on the senate for the complete abolition of the committee. A compromise solution was worked out under which Tenney would withdraw and Senator Hugh M. Burns would be appointed chairman. Tenney publicly announced his withdrawal, stating:

> The Communist Party in particular uses the committee chairman as the target of obscure factual and shocking findings. . . . I feel that a new committee under new leadership will confuse them to some extent because they will have to re-aim their smear artillery.

Regardless of where I am and what position I hold I will

39

continue to fight these organizations and individuals as vigorously in the future as in the past until this menace is completely eliminated or the United States is subjugated by continued and ruthless assault.[11]

Following this announcement all of the Tenney committee bills were defeated in a theatrical session in which the speaker of the assembly, Sam L. Collins, joined with former committee chairman, Sam Yorty, in support of a motion to re-refer them all to committee.

THE BURNS COMMITTEE

On July 2, 1950, the Senate Fact-Finding Committee on Un-American Activities was continued by a unanimous vote of the senate with an appropriation of $50,000. On August 2, the Senate Rules Committee formally appointed Senator Hugh M. Burns as chairman of the new committee. Senators Clyde Watson and Nelson Dilworth were also retained from the old committee. New members appointed were Senators Nathan Coombs, a Republican, and Earl Desmond, a Democrat. R. E. Combs was continued as counsel for the committee. In the fall of 1949 the committee records and files were removed from Senator Tenney's office in Los Angeles to a new committee office set up in Fresno, where Senator Burns resides.

This new committee was created by the senate with the understanding that its methods would be improved. Senator Burns does not appear to have the fanaticism or personal ambition of Tenney. Committee Counsel Combs, a man of integrity, ability, and moderation, was given greater control of the planning and conduct of the committee hearings. It is (in November, 1950) still too early for an adequate appraisal of the work of the committee under Senator Burns, since it has held only five or six days of public hearings and has as yet filed no reports.[12] However, some evidence

---

[11] *Sacramento Bee,* June 21, 1949.

[12] Since this chapter was written the Burns Committee has filed its first report and held one or two additional hearings. See California Legislature, Senate, *Sixth Report [on Un-American Activities in California],* 1951 ([Sacramento, 1951]), 427 pp.

of the approach and methods of the committee can be gained from an examination of the one major hearing held by the committee, that in Oakland, California, May 8 to 10, 1950.

The hearing received considerable advance publicity. The press, citing the committee's counsel as its news source, reported that the hearing would be a continuation of a 1946 hearing where it was charged that employees of the University of California radiation laboratory were organized by the Communists while engaged in research on the atomic bomb; that more than forty subpoenas had been issued for scientists and others in the Bay area; that the session would be devoted to alleged Communist activity at the University of California's Berkeley campus in general and at the radiation laboratory in particular. Counsel Combs also was reported as naming certain individuals upon whom subpoenas had been served and as referring to two of these individuals as "friendly witnesses" who were not suspected of subversive activities. All of this made sensational news, provoking headlines such as "New UC Spy Quiz Due Monday."

The hearing opened on the morning of May 8 before a small crowd which rarely ran to more than fifty or sixty people. A large contingent of press representatives was present throughout the hearings.

In certain respects there was a dramatic improvement in the procedure of conducting the hearing over the procedure under the chairmanship of Senator Tenney. Substantially all the questioning was conducted by committee Counsel Combs. Interruptions by members of the committee were infrequent, and their questions were usually routed through Combs or asked after seeking his permission. Witnesses were treated with courtesy and consideration, whether friendly or antagonistic. The whole tone of the hearing was relaxed, without the denunciations of witnesses and spectators which had marked many of the hearings under Tenney. Witnesses were given ample opportunity to explain their statements and clarify their positions. Counsel were permitted to argue objections to the committee, the rulings on the objections were made courteously without denunciations of counsel, and counsel were permitted to consult freely with their clients.

In many other respects of more substance, however, the hearing was open to serious criticism. These criticisms can be suggested only by first giving a list of the witnesses heard by the committee and something of the matters testified to by them.

On the first day only two witnesses were heard. Vern Smith, an expelled Communist who had been convicted of contempt for refusing to testify before the committee in 1947, was called again. In his forty-five minutes on the stand he refused to answer questions put to him and denounced the committee roundly. Steps were again taken to cite him for contempt. The second witness was Paul Crouch, a former member of the Communist Party who had been party organizer in Alameda County, California, in 1941. Crouch, who had previously testified for the federal government in the trial of Harry Bridges and on other occasions, described at some length his experience in the party in California and elsewhere. He also gave some rather unusual testimony regarding a group of persons whom the committee had not been able to serve with subpoenas. As to each of these witnesses, in response to questions by Combs, he told the committee what the person *could have* testified to of his own knowledge *if* he had been served and had appeared and had testified. Throughout the rest of the hearing Crouch sat at Combs's elbow and consulted with him frequently as other witnesses testified.

The first two witnesses on the second day of the hearing were former members of the Communist Party who refused to answer questions put to them about party organization and procedure. The third witness was a former official of the C.I.O. who refused to answer questions regarding his alleged connections with the Communist Party. The fourth witness was Erle Loran, professor of art at the University of California. He was asked if he was acquainted with the famous atomic physicist, Dr. J. Robert Oppenheimer. He replied that he was and that he had rented his house at 10 Kenilworth Court to Oppenheimer for eight months in 1941. He described the house and its location.

The committee then called Mrs. Paul Crouch. She testified at length concerning her long career in the Communist Party. Then she was asked about a particular meeting in July of 1941. She said that the meeting was a closed meeting of a special section of the Communist Party held for the purpose of hearing her husband explain the changes in party line occasioned by the German invasion of Russia. She stated that she and her husband were driven to the meeting by Kenneth May, whom she described as educational director for the party at that time. She described the location of the house where the meeting was held and its exterior appearance. Her description matched that given earlier by Professor Loran of his house at 10 Kenilworth Court. Then, just before the noon recess, in ample time to catch the afternoon editions of the newspapers, she testified that while she did not at the time recognize any of the people at the meeting she had since identified two of them from photographs. One was Dr. J. Robert Oppenheimer; the other Dr. Joseph Weinberg, the famous "Scientist X" of the House Un-American Activities Committee hearings. She also stated that she had subsequently seen both of these individuals at social affairs arranged by the Communist Party.

During the afternoon session Mrs. Crouch testified further concerning this particular meeting. She positively identified the house in which it was held as that at 10 Kenilworth Court. She said that a few days prior to the hearing she had been taken for a ride through the hills by committee investigators and had then identified the house. The latter part of her testimony was given to describing her activities as a "courier" for the Communist Party in connection with a state C.I.O. convention held in Oakland in 1941. She charged that the party prepared resolutions which were adopted by the convention and that the C.I.O. official who had been on the stand earlier had handled the resolutions for the party. She also told of the circumstances which led up to her leaving the party.

The last witness called was William Schneiderman, state chairman of the Communist Party. When Schneiderman's lawyer presented a legal defense to the first question asked of Schneiderman, the committee adjourned for the day.

That night Dr. J. Robert Oppenheimer, who as director of the Institute for Advanced Studies resided in Princeton, New Jersey, issued the following statement from Washington, D.C.:

> I learned this evening of testimony concerning me given by Mrs. Paul Crouch, said to be a former Communist and wife of a former Communist party official, in an appearance before the

Un-American Activities Committee of the California Senate.

I have not yet seen the details of the testimony, but I understand the general import is to the effect that a group of people assembled with Mr. and Mrs. Crouch at my house in Berkeley in mid-July 1941, for a closed Communist meeting. The implications of this testimony are obvious, and I should like to comment at once.

I have never been a member of the Communist party. I never assembled any such group of people for any such purpose in my home or anywhere else. I am unable to recall any gathering in my house that could reasonably have been mistaken for such a meeting. Neither the name Crouch nor the accounts of Mr. and Mrs. Crouch recall to me anyone I have ever known.

I should like to make a further comment. I have made no secret of the fact that I once knew many people in left-wing circles and belonged to several left-wing organizations. The Government has known in detail of these matters since I first started work on the atomic bomb project.

These matters also came up in a story about me in Time Magazine some 18 months ago, in which an interview with me was reported in part as follows: "Until 1936 Oppenheimer had never even voted; he was certainly one of the most unpolitical people in the world. But in the depression he watched young finely-trained physicists cracking up because they were unemployed. He also heard about relatives forced to leave Nazi Germany. Says Oppenheimer: 'I woke up to recognition that politics was a part of life. I became a real left-winger, joined the Teachers' Union, had lots of Communist friends. It was what most people do in college or late high school. . . . Most of what I believed then now seems complete nonsense.' "

Senator Nathan Coombs opened the third and last day of the hearing with the remark that he had read Dr. Oppenheimer's statement and could not find anything in it to refute the testimony of Mrs. Crouch. "Dr. Oppenheimer," he said, "says that he cannot recall the meeting at his house; he does not say that there haven't been such meetings. Then, speaking of the follies of youth, he says he became aware of the importance of politics and had many left-wing friends. It seems to me a rather weak, left-handed denial." Chairman Burns announced that the committee was ready to listen to testimony under oath from anybody whose name comes up in the proceedings and offered to let Dr. Oppenheimer appear before the committee to make a statement, "under oath, of course." Senator Nelson Dilworth then arose and stated: "It seems to me that Dr. Oppenheimer should be fully aware of the proper way to reply to matters of this kind. The proper course is not by a roundabout denial in the public press. The charge has been made before this committee under oath by a former functionary of the Communist Party—with members of which Party Dr. Oppenheimer admits association. Something more than a hasty denial, not in the press, is in order."

The first witness on this day was a hotel manager who brought records purporting to show that the Crouches, registered under the name of Wilson, had been at his hotel during the 1941 C.I.O. convention regarding which Mrs. Crouch had testified. The next witness was William Schneiderman who presented a blanket objection to all questions on constitutional grounds. After he left the stand, the committee directed its attorney to take action on a contempt citation. A former Communist was then called to the stand and testified that he had been at a housewarming with other Communists in 1941 and had seen present Dr. Oppenheimer and Dr. Weinberg. He said that Dr. Oppenheimer was pointed out to him by a Japanese girl named Alice, with whom he was dancing. He said that he had identified Dr. Weinberg later from pictures. He was then shown a picture and identified it as Weinberg. Later in the hearing, Combs took a second look at the picture and recalled the witness who reiterated his identification. It then turned out that the picture had been that of another scientist, not Weinberg. The witness said perhaps he was mistaken as to Weinberg but could not be as to Oppenheimer.

The next witness testified that she had been engaged in man-power work at the University of California during the war and that in connection with that work she met Marcelle Scherer, an officer in the International Federation of Architects, Engineers, Chemists and Technicians (the organization which had been the subject of the committee's 1946 hearings). She stated that Scherer had attempted to get members of his union trained in synthetic rubber manufacture but that the request was not granted.

The remainder of the hearing was given over to further testimony by Mr. Crouch. He explained that the special section of the Communist Party was made up of people whose identity had to be protected; that Kenneth May supervised this section locally; that it had branches composed of public officeholders, professionals, professors, radiation laboratory employees, and persons working at the Shell Development Company. He told of a Communist underground school which had been conducted in the area. He confirmed his wife's identification of Dr. Oppenheimer as being present at the meeting, adding that the meeting was definitely "a secret, closed meeting of top ranking Party members." He told of his searches for the house in which the meeting had been held, searches only recently successful. He also related aspects of the tale of alleged transmission of atomic secrets from the University of California radiation laboratory to the Soviet consul through Scientist X and Steve Nelson, Communist functionary.

The hearing then adjourned with the following statement by Senator Burns: "Simply for the reason that the name of Dr. J. Robert Oppenheimer has been brought into this hearing we do not presume to judge whether or not he is a member of the Communist Party, but we want to repeat that he is welcome to testify under oath."

Many objections of substance suggest themselves immediately regarding the method of handling this hearing. Perhaps they can best be developed by asking at the outset what was the committee's purpose in holding the hearing. While many collateral matters were gone into (such as the 1941 C.I.O. convention), the principal focus of the hearing was upon charges that one of the nation's foremost atomic scientists, J. Robert Oppenheimer, had been a member of a special section of the Communist Party in 1941. Despite the inference of Senator Burns's closing statement that Dr. Oppenheimer's name had merely been "brought into this hearing," it is apparent that the committee planned to have the testimony regarding Oppenheimer given and buttressed at the hearing. Why the committee wanted to air such charges against Oppenheimer, what purpose the publicity was to serve, has yet to be made clear.

Assuming then that the principal objective of the hearing was to put into the record and publicize the charges against Oppenheimer, one can see immediately the unfairness and inadequacies of the hearing. Dr. Oppenheimer, so far as appears, was given no advance notice of the proceedings. He was not even requested to appear and explain his position. Preliminary correspondence with him might have given even the committee some doubts as to the reliability of the witnesses it proposed to use, but no apparent attempt was made by committee investigators to get Oppenheimer's side of the story. So the only witnesses present were those selected by the committee. Having no prior notice that the hearing was to deal with him, the "defendant" was not only deprived of any real chance to appear in person, but also of any opportunity to present evidence on his own behalf. To tar a prominent American with the brush of communism under such circumstances is inexcusable. And the suggestion that Dr. Oppenheimer was guilty of an improper action in issuing a denial to the press (instead of meekly requesting some future opportunity to appear before the committee and make his denial under oath) was an excellent example of the arrogant and self-righteous attitude frequently taken by members of such unreviewable agencies as legislative investigating committees.

This hearing also served to high-light the difficulties with evidence which is not subject to cross-examination. Mrs. Crouch's story that placed Dr. Oppenheimer at the alleged Communist meeting cried aloud for testing. She described the house but admitted she had seen it a few days previously in the company of committee investigators. What were the circumstances under which she picked it out? Was the possibility excluded that someone looked in an old directory to find where Dr. Oppenheimer lived in 1941? How was it that she recognized none of the people at the meeting even though they were supposed to be prominent individuals? How was it that she later recognized only two? Under what circumstances did she make the original identification? Was her identification more reliable than that of the other witness before the committee who named the wrong scientist from pictures?

This hearing also illustrates again the inconclusive character of the committee investigation. Subpoenas were requested for forty people, but only ten appeared. No subsequent attempt to subpoena the missing witnesses and hear their testimony has been reported. Furthermore, it was apparent throughout the hearing that certain individuals could testify much more directly and fully concerning the facts being brought out. Kenneth May, for example, who was stated to be the supervisor of the special section of the Communist Party and who took the Crouches to the meeting, would be a key witness in any rational inquiry. Yet, so far as revealed, no attempt was made to get him before the committee. Only a fragmentary picture was presented, and the committee has given no indication of an intention to round it out. Although the committee cannot compel the attendance of witnesses from outside the state, it can at least invite their voluntary appearance.

The *San Francisco Chronicle* in an editorial on May 12, 1950, reached the following conclusion concerning the hearing:

> We would challenge the propriety of the committee's tactics in any event, but in this case much more is involved than propriety. Here the committee is lending itself to a purpose dear to the hearts of the Communist themselves—the careless spreading of confusion and distrust through the undermining of confidence in those in whom we have placed the utmost trust, and for the soundest reason.

THE SEPTEMBER, 1950, SESSION OF THE CALIFORNIA LEGISLATURE

As a result of the emergency created by the Korean war, Governor Warren issued a proclamation on September 14, 1950, calling the legislature into an extraordinary session on September 20, 1950. One of the purposes for which he called the session was to "consider and act upon legislation relating to civil defense, disaster relief and subversive activities, and civil and military services in connection therewith." The changed tenor of public opinion resulting from the situation in Korea and from the nationwide attacks upon alleged Communists in government was reflected in a quite different approach by the legislature to the problem of regulating subversive activities than it had taken in 1949.

48

A number of bills and proposed constitutional amendments calling for loyalty oaths and investigations and providing for the compulsory registration of members of subversive groups were immediately introduced. One of the bills was passed by both houses and signed by the governor; and a constitutional amendment was proposed to be voted on by the people in the fall of 1952.

The bill adds Sections 3100–3109 to the California Government Code under the heading "Oath or Affirmation of Allegiance for Civil Defense Workers and Public Employees." For the purposes of the act the term "civil defense worker" is defined to include "all public employees and all volunteers in any civilian defense organization accredited by the State Disaster Council." It then provides that subject to the provision of the California Constitution providing an exclusive oath for public officers, all civil defense workers shall take the following oath or affirmation:

I, _____, do solemnly swear (or affirm) that I will support and defend the Constitution of the United States and the Constitution of the State of California against all enemies, foreign and domestic; that I will bear true faith and allegiance to the Constitution of the United States and the Constitution of the State of California; that I take this obligation freely, without any mental reservation or purpose of evasion; and that I will well and faithfully discharge the duties upon which I am about to enter.

And I do further swear (or affirm) that I do not advocate, nor am I a member of any party or organization, political or otherwise, that now advocates the overthrow of the Government of the United States or of the State of California by force or violence or other unlawful means; that within the five years immediately preceding the taking of this oath (or affirmation) I have not been a member of any party or organization, political or otherwise, that advocated the overthrow of the Government of the United States or of the State of California by force or violence or other unlawful means except as follows: _____

(If no affiliations, write in the words "No Exceptions") and that during such time as I am a member or employee of the _____ I will not advocate nor be-
(name of public agency)

come a member of any party or organization, political or otherwise, that advocates the overthrow of the Government of the
United States or of the State of California by force or violence
or other unlawful means.

The act then provides that no "compensation nor reimburse-
ment for expenses incurred shall be paid to any civil defense
worker by any public agency unless such civil defense worker has
taken and subscribed to the oath or affirmation"; that every person
"who, while taking and subscribing to the oath or affirmation
required by this chapter, states as true any material matter which
he knows to be false, is guilty of perjury, and is punishable by
imprisonment in the state prison not less than one nor more than
14 years"; and that every person having taken the oath or affirmation who, while in the employ of any state agency or civilian
defense organization "advocates or becomes a member of any
party or organization, political or otherwise, that advocates the
overthrow of the Government of the United States by force or
violence or other unlawful means, is guilty of a felony" punishable
by imprisonment from one to fourteen years.

By interpretation of the attorney general of California the act
has been held applicable to all persons who in any way work for
any governmental organization in the state, including volunteer
unpaid workers, precinct employees at election time, and faculty
and employees of the University of California and all other state-
supported schools and colleges. Many people are troubled by the
dilemma presented in the act: What organizations "advocated the
overthrow of the Government of the United States . . . by force
or violence or other unlawful means"? No list of organizations
has been promulgated, and each person taking the oath is required
to make his own determination with, presumably, a risk of a
perjury prosecution for either listing too few or too many organizations. A very small number of people have refused to sign
the oath and have been discharged from their positions. A number
of legal tests of the constitutional validity of the law are now
under way.

The proposed constitutional amendment, if adopted by the
people, will add the following section to the California constitution:

Notwithstanding any other provision of this Constitution, no person or organization which advocates the overthrow of the Government of the United States or the States by force or violence or other unlawful means or who advocates the support of a foreign government against the United States in the event of hostilities shall:

(a) Hold any office or employment under this State, including but not limited to the University of California, or with any county, city or county, city, district, political subdivision, authority, board, bureau, commission or other public agency of this State: or

(b) Receive any exemption from any tax imposed by this State or any county, city or county, city, district, political subdivision, authority, board, bureau, commission or other public agency of this State.

The Legislature shall enact such laws as may be necessary to enforce the provisions of this section.

The legislative proposals for compulsory registration of members of subversive groups were dropped when Congress passed the Internal Security Act of 1950. Instead of acting on them, the senate authorized the Burns committee to decide if there were any necessity for state legislation on the control of subversive activities as a result of the Congressional action and to report back to the 1951 session. The assembly directed the Subcommittee to Control Communism, Subversive Activities and Sabotage of the Interim Committee on Judicial System and Judicial Process to make a similar study.

The change in attitude of the legislature and other members of the state government was shown in other ways. The civil defense loyalty oath bill was proposed to the legislature by Governor Warren who, as a member of the board of regents, had consistently voted against the imposition of a loyalty oath on members of the faculty of the University of California. The bill was passed by votes of 69 to 5 in the assembly and 28 to 0 in the senate. The proposed constitutional amendment on loyalty oaths passed both houses without a dissenting vote. Senator Tenney, who had been so discredited at the 1949 session, joined with Senator Burns and other members of the Burns committee in originating a number of bills relating to subversive activities and was the successful

51

sponsor in the senate of the loyalty oath constitutional amendment. Speaker Sam L. Collins, who had taken the lead in securing the defeat of the Tenney bills in 1949, proposed a constitutional amendment to give the legislature power to impose any oath, declaration, or test as a qualification for any office or public trust. He withdrew the proposed amendment only after it had been criticized on the floor of the assembly as "rather dangerous," "a blank check," and "an attempt to give the Legislature power to exclude minority members." And the assembly, which had not engaged in legislative investigation of subversive activities since the Tenney committee became an exclusively senate committee in 1947, set up a Subcommittee to Control Communism, Subversive Activities and Sabotage of its Interim Committee on Judicial System and Judicial Process.

One resolution adopted by the assembly suggests that the legislative attitude toward the investigation and regulation of subversive activities may have come full circle in the decade since the Yorty committee was established in 1940. This resolution directed the chief clerk of the assembly to have printed for distribution to and by the members of the assembly 1,000 copies of the report of the Assembly Relief Investigating Committee (the Yorty committee) made to the assembly at its 1940 session.[13]

[13] A great many bills dealing with subversive activities were introduced into the 1951 session of the California legislature, and a few were passed. No person "who advocates the overthrow of the Government of the United States or of this State by force, violence, or other unconstitutional means" shall be certified for a license to practice law, and such advocacy is also made a specific ground for disbarment or suspension. (Bus. & Prof. C. §§ 6064.1, 6106.1, added by Cal. Stats. 1951, c. 179.) Every candidate in the primary elections is required to swear in his declaration of candidacy and in his declaration of acceptance of nomination, "I am not engaged in one way or another in any attempt to overthrow the government by force or violence, and . . . I am not knowingly a member of any organization engaged in such an attempt." (Cal. Elections Code, §§ 2601, 2619, as amended by Cal. Stats. 1951, c. 876.) Teachers in the public-school system are specifically forbidden to "advocate or teach communism with the intent to indoctrinate any pupil with, or inculcate a preference in the mind of any pupil for communism." (Educ. C. § 8275, added by Cal. Stats. 1951, c. 538.) A constitutional amendment to require

the civil defense workers' oath, discussed above, of all public officers and employees was proposed to go on the ballot in 1952. (Cal. Resolutions, 1951, c. 69.) A bill providing for the dismissal of teachers in state colleges for "membership in, or active support of, a 'communist front' or 'communist action' organization, as those terms are now defined in the federal 'Internal Security Act of 1950'" or for "persistent active participation in public meetings conducted or sponsored" by such organizations was passed by both houses of the legislature but vetoed by Governor Warren. (S.B. 1836.)

II. ILLINOIS

The Broyles Commission

By E. HOUSTON HARSHA   *July, 1949*

DURING the last decade and a half the Illinois legislature has launched two investigations of alleged subversive activities. In the first, attention was focused solely upon the University of Chicago. The second investigation, although authorized to engage in a wider scope of inquiry, also concentrated upon the University of Chicago, with ancillary attention paid to the recently formed Roosevelt College. Aside from this surface similarity the contrast between the two investigations is marked. The so-called "Walgreen" investigation in 1935 was touched off by widely published charges of Charles Walgreen, owner of one of Chicago's leading retail drug chains, that his niece had been indoctrinated with communistic ideologies by certain members of the University of Chicago faculty. Lengthy public hearings conducted by a committee of five state senators resulted in four of the five senators' concluding that there were no Communists on the faculty of the University of Chicago, that the faculty made no effort to indoctrinate students with communism, and that existing sedition laws of Illinois were adequate to restrain advocacy of violent overthrow

[Mr. Harsha was a Research Associate (Assistant Professor) at the University of Chicago Law School when this was written. Currently, he is a Trial Attorney with the Antitrust Division, United States Department of Justice.]

54

of the government.[1] In contrast, the Seditious Activities Investigation Commission, popularly known as the Broyles commission, devoted two years to secret investigation of subversive activities throughout the state, then publicly investigated alleged subversion at the University of Chicago and Roosevelt College, and, while formulating no conclusions as to whether Communists were on the faculty of either school or students were indoctrinated with communism, issued a statement in June, 1949, condemning conditions at the two schools and recommending that tax exemptions be withdrawn from them both. Reporting widespread subversion within the state, the commission also proposed sweeping legislation to combat subversive activities not only among teachers in public and private schools, but also among all state and municipal employees and the legislators themselves. It also proposed outlawry of the Communist Party and "Communist front" organizations.

CREATION OF THE BROYLES COMMISSION

According to the statement of its chairman, Senator Paul Broyles (Republican; Mount Vernon), the Broyles commission, officially designated the Seditious Activities Investigation Commission, "was caused to be created by a resolution of the Legislative Commission of the American Legion, Department of Illinois, in the State Convention in 1946. By reason of this resolution, Senate Bill 313 was passed." [2] Organized in August, 1947, the commission was composed of five members of the Illinois senate, five members of the house of representatives, and five public members appointed by the governor. As public members former Governor Dwight H. Green appointed two past state de-

[1] For an excellent review of the Walgreen investigation see the *University of Chicago Magazine* (1935), pp. 345–352.
The reconciliation of Charles Walgreen and the University was perhaps the most surprising long-range result of the investigation. About two years after the investigation, Mr. Walgreen made a gift of $550,000 to the University. *University of Chicago Magazine,* June, 1938, p. 23.

[2] *Report, Seditious Activities Investigation Commission, submitted pursuant to the provisions of an Act of the 65th General Assembly* (1949), p. 95. (Hereafter cited as *Report.*)

partment commanders of the American Legion, a member of the Illinois State Chamber of Commerce, the assistant counsellor of the University of Illinois, and a Chicago attorney.[3] Of the fifteen-man commission, two members appointed from the house of representatives took no part in the commission's work, and two other legislators, Senator Norman C. Barry (Democrat; Chicago) and Charles J. Jenkins (Republican; Chicago), refused to sign the report submitted by the commission and issued separate dissents when Chairman Senator Broyles in June, 1949, published a special statement regarding the investigation of the University of Chicago and Roosevelt College.

The enabling legislation, Senate Bill 313, empowered the commission "to investigate any activities of any person or persons, co-partnership, association, organization, group or society, . . . which are suspected of being directed toward the overthrow of the Government of the United States or the State of Illinois." By amendment, the commission was also empowered "to investigate as to whether the Ku Klux Klan has organized again in Illinois, to investigate its activities if it is organized, and to investigate any other association . . . that foments or attempts to foment racial and religious hatreds." [4] The commission made no findings or recommendations regarding the Ku Klux Klan.

EXISTING LAWS AGAINST SUBVERSION

At the outset it should be observed that Illinois is not devoid of laws designed to curb subversion. It is unlawful in Illinois to advocate the reformation or overthrow, by violence or other unlawful means, of the representative form of government secured by the constitution of the United States or the constitution of Illinois.[5] It is unlawful for any person to publish or knowingly sell or distribute any printed matter which advocates the violent overthrow of the constitutional form of government.[6] In addition, it is unlawful for any person to organize or join any society the

[3] *Ibid.*   [4] *Report,* pp. 5–7.

[5] Ill. Rev. Stat. c. 38, sec. 558 (1947); constitutionality sustained in *People v. Lloyd,* 304 Ill. 23, 136 N.E. 505 (1922).

[6] *Ibid.,* sec. 559.

object of which is to advocate the reformation or overthrow of the existing form of government by violence or other unlawful means.[7] Illinois is one of a number of states to adopt a Red Flag law.[8] However, an enactment of the legislature denying a place on the ballot to any political organization which is associated "directly or indirectly, with Communist, Fascist, Nazi, or other un-American principles and engages in activities or propaganda designed to teach subservience to the political principles and ideals of foreign nations" [9] was considered unconstitutional by one federal district court.[10]

A member in a Communist, Nazi, or Fascist organization or one who participates in any activity of such organization is ineligible for appointment to any position in the classified state Civil Service.[11] The legislature has forbidden use of state moneys to pay any employee of the state who "directly or indirectly" advocates the overthrow of the government of the United States or of Illinois by force or by "allegiance and subservience to the political principles of any foreign government, or who knowingly joins . . . any organization which advocates the overthrow of the Government. . . ." [12]

Finally, the legislature has singled out the University of Illinois and forbidden use of any of the university's facilities by any subversive, seditious, and un-American organization.[13]

---

[7] *Ibid.*, sec. 560.   [8] *Ibid.*, sec. 563.

[9] Ill. Rev. Stat. c. 46, sec. 7–2, 8–2, 10–2 (1947).

[10] *Feinglass v. Reinecke,* 48 F. Supp. 438 (D.C.N.D. Ill. 1942). The court regarded such terms as "un-American" and "the political principles of foreign nations" as being so vague and indefinite as to make the act invalid. The court also stated that "a party may not be excluded from a place on the ballot because it advocates economic ideas which may happen to be unpopular at the time" (at p. 441).

[11] Ill. Rev. Stat. c. 24½, sec. 8 (1947). This provision does not appear to have been tested in the courts.

[12] Ill. Rev. Stat. c. 127, sec. 166a (1947).

[13] Ill. Rev. Stat. c. 144, sec. 48.8 (1947).

LEGISLATION PROPOSED BY THE BROYLES COMMISSION

Yet, as a result of its investigation, the Broyles commission concluded that existing statutes were insufficient to cope with present dangers to the state. Apart from the not unusual request that additional funds ($75,000) be appropriated [14] to carry on its work, the Broyles commission recommended adoption of a resolution which, after a somewhat flamboyant preamble condemning foreign "isms," [15] calls upon each member of the legislature to file *voluntarily* an affidavit that

> he is not and has never been a member of, or affiliated with, the Communist Party, or the secret, underground, illegal branch of that party, and that he does not believe in, is not a member of, and does not support any organization or subversive group, which advocates, advises or practices the political theories of Marx, Lenin, and Stalin, or that presently existing form of government of the United States or this state should be changed by force, violence or other unconstitutional means. . . .[16]

Undoubtedly, the fact that the constitution of Illinois specifies the qualifications for membership in the Illinois legislature [17] led the commission to refrain from adding any sanction to the proposed resolution, unlike the other bills proposed by it.

[14] *Report,* p. 443.

[15] "Whereas, The integrity, welfare, and peace of freedom-loving peoples and nations, if not of the world itself, are threatened by the persistent dissemination, by sly, covert, and subtle methods, of foreign 'isms' and infiltration into private and public groups of artful advocates of totalitarian theories and adherents of subversive movements; and

"Whereas, To ignore the presence of this insidious poison is to violate the cardinal principle that eternal vigilance is the price of liberty; to condone the activities of these sly purveyors of political and economic venom is to invite the growth of political cancer; the failure of groups, public or quasi-public, to identify the loyalty of their individual members is to subject the innocent to suspicion; now, therefore, be it Resolved. . . ." (*Report,* p. 444.)

[16] *Report,* p. 444.   [17] Ill. Const. Art. IV, sec. 3.

58

Senate Bill No. 152, sponsored by the Broyles commission, would require every membership corporation, and every unincorporated association having a membership of twenty or more persons, which requires an oath as a condition of membership (with the exception of labor unions, college fraternities and sororities, and benevolent, educational, or religious societies not sponsoring candidates for public office), to file with the secretary of state a copy of its constitution, bylaws, rules, records, regulations, oath of membership, and roster of members and officers.[18] Section 2 of the proposed act would require every such corporation or association to file with the secretary of state every resolution or the minutes of any action of such corporation or association providing for concerted action of its members to promote or defeat legislation, federal, state, or municipal, or to support or defeat any candidate for political office. Section 3 would make it unlawful for such corporation or association to mail to anyone not a member any anonymous printed matter or letter and would require that all such letters or other written or printed matter "intended for a member" of such corporation or association bear the name of the corporation or association together with the names of the officers and their addresses. Violation by any corporation or association would be a misdemeanor punishable by a fine of not less than $1,000 nor more than $10,000. Any officer who violated or permitted or acquiesced in a violation by his corporation or association would be subject to a fine of not more than $1,000 or imprisonment for not more than one year or both. Any person joining such corporation or association with knowledge that such organization had failed to comply with the provisions of the act would also be subject to the same penalty.

Senate Bill No. 153 would amend the "School Code" to permit the dismissal of any public schoolteacher "advocating in his teaching any doctrine to undermine the form of government of this State or of the United States by force and violence. . . ." [19]

Senate Bill No. 154 would deny eligibility for election or appointment to any public office or prohibit employment as a teacher

[18] *Report,* pp. 445–446.   [19] *Report,* p. 447.

in any "public school, college or university in this State" [20] to any person "who directly or indirectly" is affiliated with "any Communist organization or any Communist front organization" or any "foreign political agency which advocates the overthrow of constitutional government" by force or other means not permitted under the United States or Illinois constitution or "who directly or indirectly teaches or advocates the overthrow by force or other unlawful means" of the government of the United States or Illinois.[21]

Section 2 of No. 154 would require all persons appointed or elected to public office (save those whose qualifications are fixed by the constitution) and all teachers "in any public tax-supported school, college, or university" to file an oath of allegiance to support the constitution of the United States and of the State of Illinois. Section 2 provides for the removal from office of any of the above designated classes of public servants who engages in the activities interdicted in Section 1 of the act save that in this section advocacy of the overthrow of government "by foul or other means not permitted by the Constitution" appears at one point in place of the phrase "by force or any unlawful means."

Senate Bill No. 156 is aimed at the definition and outlawry of communism. Section 1 defines communism as "the doctrine which advocates crime, physical violence, destruction of property, corruption of governmental agencies, or other acts of force or violence or insidious or treacherous acts for the purpose of accomplishing the destruction of the free systems of representative government." [22]

A Communist front organization is defined as any organization which "has been in fact primarily organized to accomplish the purpose of promoting the interests of Communism." A Communist is defined as one who "espouses, directly or indirectly, or openly or secretly, furthers the cause of Communism." Finally, the bill declares that any person who is a Communist or "who attends meetings of Communist organizations or Communist front organizations to further the cause of Communism, or who pays

[20] It is not clear whether this phrase applies to teachers in private schools.

[21] *Report,* pp. 448–449.   [22] *Report,* p. 450.

60

dues to or carries a membership card in any such organization, or who is in any way active in behalf of Communism . . . or a Communist front organization" is guilty of a felony, punishable by imprisonment for not less than one year nor more than five years.

This, then, was the legislative program recommended by the Broyles commission. None of it was enacted by the Illinois legislature, nor was a further appropriation made for continuation of the commission. Accordingly, the constitutional problems and the merits or demerits of the bills as sound public policy might appear to have lost much of their urgency. But such repressive measures are seldom permanently defeated; in the next or subsequent sessions of the legislature they may be reintroduced, thereby revitalizing the issues. It seems important, therefore, to examine the case presented on behalf of the bills by the Broyles commission. Almost equally important is an inquiry into the operations of the commission itself. Both may have future significance.

REPORT OF THE BROYLES COMMISSION

A flavor of mystery usually surrounds the activities of an investigative body. It is often reticent about its sources of information. It seldom reveals the private forces influencing its work and almost never does it disclose discussions *in camera* of whom it will investigate and how it will conduct its inquiry. But the Broyles commission is the startling exception. Perhaps unique among all antisubversive investigative committees, the Broyles commission in its official report has published the apparently verbatim transcript of its secret, "executive" sessions covering a period of almost two years. It has published the transcript of its private conferences with other governmental agencies investigating subversive activities. It has revealed the reports submitted by the investigator hired by the commission. In the writer's opinion the *Report of the Broyles Commission* is not a self-serving document. A record is afforded of the biases and predilections of members of the commission, of the unguarded statements of witnesses who do not realize they are speaking for publication, and of the private groups and individuals that have influenced the commission's action. In this sense the report of the commission is an extraordinarily valuable public document. One can be grateful that the Broyles commission has seen fit to release this information, but as to its reasons one can only conjecture.

The report contains reference to thirty-four executive sessions of either the full commission or its subcommittee held in the period, August, 1947 to February, 1949. An early section of the report summarizes the evidence received by the commission in these secret sessions. Interspersed in the summary are some of the commission's conclusions with respect to the evidence. This important segment of the report, quite apart from the thought content, is a grammarian's nightmare. It suffers from hasty composition, an evident lack of the proofreader's touch, and a startlingly flamboyant "high" style.[23] Entitled "Facts and Data Revealed at Hearings," it begins:

> In the initial study of the subject matter, the testimony presented by informed persons, both former card-holding members of the Communist organizations and citizens who had made the investigation of Communism their chief aim, it was stated that an active Communist will never admit his membership and will use every artifice humanly possible to disuade any person seeking information that he as an individual is not in any way connected with any such organization or is interested in subversive methods or programs.[24]

If this be true it casts some doubt on the efficacy of the commission's proposal to require oaths of all public servants.

In the section devoted to education the commission's résumé reads:

> The clever methods used in the schools was fully described by witnesses who stated that certain texts used did not contain enough valuable information on subjects they were written to teach—schools provide the most fertile field for Communistic and subversive activities and are the spot that is most dangerous. . . . Testimony was received relative to the presence of organizations upon the campuses that, although seemingly

[23] No alterations in spelling or grammar have been made in quoting portions of this section.

[24] *Report,* p. 16.

social, in their activities, in reality are the hotbeds of promoting, inculcating and stimulating Communist ideologies. It was also stated that certain members of the teaching personnel in specific courses that have to deal with the economics of governments and civics, stress too strongly in their comparison with our governmental machinery, the Communist form of government.

It was brought to the attention of the Commission that the School situation was a very difficult problem in that the philosophy of governments in the schools of higher learning are discussed as to their comparative differences in the theory of government. The elementary schools are in no way effected by subversive propaganda except as to the teaching personnel who are adherents of subversive study and activities. The secondary grade schools present as important a problem as the universities in that the high school teachers, for example in certain high schools in the city of Chicago, are ardent followers of subversive movements and in teaching such courses that are related to the history of government and its functions, are prone to praise certain foreign isms and philosophies of government, together with the economic phases of their operation, as against our form of government. It is unnecessary to say that the students are much effected by the statements in open class-room discussions that result in the belittling of our form of government by comparison.[25]

However ungrammatical, these are serious charges indeed.

After reference to a conference between the commission and the presidents of the normal colleges of Illinois, the report states:

It was unanimously asserted by the leading educators of Illinois who testified before our Commission that the subject of Americanism and American History should be given emphasis in the curriculum, of the grades, high schools, and the colleges, both private and public, with a thorough treatment of the establishment and subsequent development of our Nation and its heroes in the *histrionic* sense.[26] [Emphasis supplied.]

There is doubt that the "leading educators of Illinois" actually said this!

[25] *Report,* pp. 16–17.   [26] *Report,* p. 17.

The commission also makes this trenchant observation about our educational system: "A fallacy of our educational system is that the Universities set the pattern and the teaching methods used there are supposed to be the best. High schools follow that, grade schools follow high school, then we go back to the axium that the best teaching is done in the elementary schools." [27] This is a little confusing.

Other "facts" revealed at the commission's hearings:

> The various publications that are sent to the students in schools are subversive in that they give one side of the theory of government strange to our own. It was said that the un-American attitudes are not solely of the teachers, but everyone is hampered by the books that they use, and it said that *a Liberal in current American society is a political thinker or actor whose feelings, thought, and actions are in favor of the Kremlin, not without friendly criticism.*[28]

Obscure though the interrelation of statements regarding subversive school publications and liberalism may be, it is shockingly clear that, to the Broyles commission, liberalism is, indeed, a suspicious political philosophy.

The commission also heard testimony regarding the infiltration of communism into other segments of our society.

> Also testimony relative to the presence of many Communists in our Housing Projects who are actively engaged in the promotion of Communist propaganda and active in support of Communist organizations, was given to the Commission. It was thought that a survey of these Housing Projects should be made with a view of their rejectment. Other facts concerning the Housing Projects were brought out to include the placing of persons in new housing projects and the payment to many other persons to remain there in order to incite riot. It was also stated that in the Public Library are complete reference books on the subject of Communism, dealing with this subject at great length and stressing the advantages of the Communist system of government in preference to our type of government.[29]

[27] *Report,* p. 21.   [28] *Report,* p. 20.   [29] *Report,* p. 19.

In fact, on the subject of communism, the authors of the report become agitated to the point of incoherence. One characteristic of communism revealed by the report is described as follows: "The Communistic movement seizes upon all types of welfare programs or sudden catastrophies and thereby ingratiate themselves with the unfortunate victims of situations that result from the general misfortunes of persons either through natural destruction by the Hand of God or *dissilitory* reactions of the unthinking citizens." [30]
And of communism in our larger cities the report states:

There are many persons who follow the communist doctrine who seize upon their opportunities in the major cosmopolitan areas to speak to those who are not very mentally alert, *orating upon our capitalistic system and appealing, not to the intellectual type, but makeshift individuals who are rather disgruntled over their own financial condition.* These speakers, who are propagandists, deal with their subject matter competently, thus creating a sounding board for the itinerant speakers.[31] [Emphasis supplied.]

Revealing it received information that there are 6,500 Communists in Illinois "and for each card carrying member there are ten persons who stand ready and willing to do the bidding of the communists," [32] the commission states:

All the factual data tends to prove that the main purposes of the followers of Communism are:
(1) The overthrow of capitalist government, by which is meant, of course, the United States Government.
(2) The establishment of a dictatorship of the proletariat, which means, a government like the one now in power in Soviet Russia.
(3) Acceptance and submission to discipline of the Communist Party and the Communist Internationale.
(4) Unconditional defense of the Soviet Union in any war between it and capitalistic countries.[33]

In the light of such data and by way of summation the commission declares:

[30] *Report,* p. 19.   [31] *Report,* p. 21.   [32] *Report,* p. 21.
[33] *Report,* p. 22.

Communist criminals are least entitled to refuge under our laws, than any other criminal who holds all moral, spiritualistic and patriotic concepts in contempt.

May we further state that *this Commission fearlessly and without any pretence of dealing with the subject matter of its investigation; without docility, are anxious to advocate legislation to absolutely curb their operations because of their violation of the basic principles of the very constitution which they seek to destroy, and so this Commission, strongly advocates the passing of nihilitory legislation so needed to treat them as the mongrel class of citizenry.*[34] [Emphasis supplied.]

This impassioned appeal for legislation (whether to be directed against the commission or against Communists is not quite clear, grammatically) is somewhat undercut by the commission's admission: "Many experts have endeavored to qualify these terms [communism and subversion] in a legal sense. None have, at least in a legislative sense, realized this goal." [35]

Insofar as the foregoing quotations are intelligible, it seems clear that the majority of the Broyles commission believed that there was widespread subversion, particularly in the schools of Illinois, and that the need was great for drastic countermeasures. Since the commission obligingly published the transcript of its executive sessions, an independent assessment of the evidence relied upon by the commission is possible.

Selection of education as a field for investigation is partially attributable to certain preconceptions of the commission's chairman, Senator Broyles. At the second meeting of the commission, designated by the chairman as a "policy-making" session, Senator Broyles said:

Should we spread ourselves all over, or go after a specific group? It is my opinion that we should concentrate our efforts on a specific group. I think the greatest danger is in the over-liberal educators who have a tendency to glamorize the various isms, especially communism, to our young people who are sent to our various colleges and universities in the State.[36]

[34] *Report*, p. 22. [35] *Report*, p. 20.
[36] *Report*, pp. 121–122.

At this meeting, held October 3, 1947, it was decided to create a subcommittee to formulate a program for the commission. To help the subcommittee in its task Worth Schumaker, Americanism Committee, National Department of the American Legion, was invited to give his advice. In reply to the question, "What is the most dangerous condition now that is presented on Communistic or subversive activities?" Mr. Schumaker replied: "I think your schools would be the spot that is most dangerous." [37]

The advice of Ellidore Libonati, another spokesman for the American Legion,[38] and brother of a member of the commission, was not so generalized. In response to a question asking the names of persons the commission should investigate the witness said: "I would subpoena some of these persons who are around town here —Professor Pooche of the University of Chicago—he is an avowed communist."

> *Broyles:* Do you have sufficient information that we could give the Committee—I mean proof of that?
> *Ellidore Libonati:* Yes, I could show you a paper he marked of a "GI." Notations on the paper definitely show him to be a communist. He was discharged from a New Jersey school for his avowment of Communism.[39] I would subpoena Bloggert, University of Illinois, who has written a book on social science—in other words, I would go after the college professors.

Warming to this advice, Senator Broyles asked another witness at this meeting: "In your opinion, if we would subpoena a known red professor in the University of Chicago, what could we accomplish? What could we benefit generally in doing that?"

The witness, Frank Hughes, identified as an editorial writer for the *Chicago Daily Tribune,* replied with feeling: "You would

[37] *Report,* p. 127.
[38] Identified in the records as chairman of the Americanism Committee, Department of Illinois, American Legion (*Report,* p. 134).
[39] Professor Pooche, a promising candidate for the *New Yorker*'s Department of Improbable Names, is not listed in the University of Chicago catalogue. Despite the fact that he is an "avowed communist," his name does not appear in the public hearings involving the University of Chicago.

accomplish damn little. He would probably just rant at the charges of 'witch-hunting.' " [40]

A little later, Senator Broyles returned to this subject, asking: "Is there any way that we can get these 'red' professors out of our colleges? What would be the approach?" Hughes replied:

There was a publication printed privately in 1935 entitled "How Red is the University of Chicago." This was taken from the files of the Daily Maroon. It is a thorough job for those years. To do a completely up-to-date thorough job would be a monumental task. It is true that you could get a few of the "red" professors out, but you would leave a mess of them absolutely untouched. New York University is the only college that has two faculty members convicted and sentenced for perjury and contempt of Congress. The professors who follow that line go to Chicago to get their Doctors! How to get at it, Senator, I just don't know. It is a necessity to have no one but a staff of highly trained investigators, who can delve and read and subpoena whenever necessary.[41]

Seeking further advice on subversive activities, the Broyles commission sent a delegation in August, 1948, to Washington, D.C. to confer with various federal investigative agencies. William Rogers, identified in the transcript as the chief investigator, "Senate Investigations Committee" (Ferguson committee), reviewed the workings of the federal loyalty program with members of the Broyles commission and then stated: "One thing that is valuable —if you get to the stage where you hold hearings, get some of these people who have been Communists and changed. It is very helpful because I think there is going to be a tendency along those lines. You give a good idea as to how they work. I think one of the places you ought to be more conscious of Communism, is in the schools; a high percentage of the professors are in the Wallace movement."

Johnson [Kermit E. Johnson, member of Broyles commission]: What kind of legislation could we pass to get rid of that?" *Rogers:* "It is tough." [42]

[40] *Report*, p. 149.   [41] *Report*, p. 150.   [42] *Report*, p. 215.

The minutes of the conference then read: "Broyles told of the existence of groups on the campus at the University of Chicago which call themselves the young Communist League, AYD, etc. and asked, 'What can be done about a situation like that.'"

Rogers: "Do you give them any State money?"
Broyles: "No, but they are tax exempt."
Rogers: "I assume you don't have any trouble in the State universities, do you?"
Broyles: "We don't think we have, but it seems though the real hot spot of the universities is the University of Chicago."
Rogers: "If there is anything you can do financially to them, that is what hurts."[43]

In a conference with Representative J. Parnell Thomas, chairman of the House Un-American Activities Committee, August 27, 1948, Congressman Thomas is quoted as stating:

If you are going into the education phase, thoroughly, the University of Chicago would be the one of the places we would start. We have more literature on infiltration of Communism in educational institutions—but over a period of time, different matters have come in to us and just off hand I happen to think of the University of Chicago. We run into it as much as any other university in the States.[44]

To which Representative Richard B. Vail of Illinois added:

In attacking the educational institutions, I would do it under a general heading, without approaching the Univeristy of Chicago directly. In Chicago you have a close tie between Roosevelt College and Chicago University. You will draw a measure of criticism by selecting the University of Chicago as your main objective. If you include Roosevelt College, you have two elements there that are very vital in the development of the Communist thinking. It is a subject that should receive attention.[45] [Emphasis supplied.]

It would be misleading, however, to conclude that education in general and the University of Chicago and Roosevelt College in particular were the sole areas the commission was advised to ex-

[43] *Ibid.*   [44] *Report,* p. 225.   [45] *Report,* p. 225.

plore. At its first executive session, the commission received testimony from United States Congressman Fred E. Busby that there were 6,500 Communists in the State of Illinois.[46] During the round of conferences with federal investigative agencies in 1948, the Broyles commission was admonished by Robert B. Young, a member of the staff of the Senate Committee on the Judiciary, that Illinois ranked fourth in the number of Communists.[47] Officer Frank Heimoski of the Industrial Squad of the Chicago Police Department informed the commission: "Since 1929 that organization has gathered and maintained files on Communistic, Bund and other un-American individuals and organizations. We have a file containing over eighty thousand names throughout the entire United States—thirty thousand names in Chicago. That takes in everything." [48]

These three statements constitute all the evidence to be gleaned from the minutes or transcripts of the executive sessions of the Broyles commission bearing upon the number of persons engaged in alleged subversive activities in Illinois. Although specifically authorized to investigate the activities of such persons, the commission does not appear to have made any recorded effort to verify the accuracy of such data and, even more surprisingly, in view of the commission's strictures against the Communist Party, it failed to investigate the operations of the party in Illinois. A clue to the reason why the Broyles commission decided to ignore the Communist Party and its adherents appears in a series of exchanges between the chairman and several of the witnesses active in American Legion affairs. Senator Broyles outlined to the witnesses a procedure for summoning officers of the Communist Party before the commission to "air them good before the people of Illinois." [49] But when Senator Broyles asked the first of such witnesses whether this proposal would assist the commission "in educating the people to the danger" he received the following reply from Ellidore Libonati: "I don't think so. If you read the Committee proceedings of the un-American Activities Investigation Committee . . .

---

[46] This appears to be the sole basis for the commission's statement that there are 6,500 Communists in Illinois (*Report*, p. 123).

[47] *Report*, p. 233.   [48] *Report*, p. 130.   [49] *Report*, p. 135.

you'll find that the communists turned that meeting upside down and you can't get an answer from them." [50]

Despite Mr. Libonati's counsel that Communists not be subpoenaed to appear before sessions of the Broyles commission, the members of the commission returned to a lively discussion of tactics to be employed against the Communists.

> *McMackin* [Omar J. McMackin, public member of the Commission]: Getting back to the thing that Paul [Broyles] asked a while ago. Some time back we discussed the possibility of subpoening the records. Then they would refuse and there could be publicity that they refused to do that, and they would be held in contempt and could be prosecuted because of that.
>
> *Thomas* [Senator John T. Thomas, Belleville, member of the commission]: Let's say, put the head of the communist party on the stand and he refused to answer on the grounds that it would be incriminating or degrading. That would give you a long speech that will give a message to the State of Illinois.

. . . . .

> *Ryan* [Lowell D. Ryan, Chicago public member of the commission]: Assuming they decline to produce these records and you have to cite them for contempt, then you will have a law suit on your hands. Assuming the court rules that they must do it and you get the list—then publish it.
>
> *Broyles:* Win or lose, we are developing something here for the public to see.[51]

The transcript of the meeting indicates that Mr. Ryan was delegated the task of preparing suitable questions.

But still another witness with American Legion affiliations, Edward Clamage, chairman of the Anti-Subversive Committee, Department of Illinois, American Legion, discouraged calling Communists before the Broyles commission. Said Mr. Clamage: "I, therefore, question the advisability of inviting these communists to your meetings. They would probably do the same thing that they did in the Congressional Investigating Committee on un-American Activities. If they are not allowed to read these statements it gives them an opportunity to release these items." [52]

---

[50] *Report*, p. 135. [51] *Report*, pp. 136–137. [52] *Report*, p. 185.

It would appear the advice of the American Legion witnesses prevailed, for the commission tabled Senator Broyles's suggestion. The minutes for the meeting of February 13, 1948 state:

It was agreed that the purposes of the Commission could best be accomplished by a minimum of publicity until the laws to be recommended to the General Assembly were ready for publication. It was brought out that even now the subversive and Communistic groups are beginning to wonder and ask what the Commission is doing. It was decided to keep them in the dark until the Commission is ready to release the proposed legislation.[53]

It was the consensus that when the laws to be suggested were prepared, the subversive groups would ask for an audience to oppose legislation. The Commission would then confront them with the information that has been compiled against them.[54]

The commission thereafter continued to invite before it only witnesses who were sympathetic to the objectives of the commission. For an appreciation of the distorted picture of subversive activities in Illinois which the commission obtained by relying solely on such witnesses, one must turn to verbatim extracts of the testimony.

Ellidore Libonati testified:

Then you would come to another subject—the Chicago Housing Authority. I think definitely one or two of their people are communists. I know two of them. One of them is a member of eleven front organizations, another one, prior to 1945 was a member of twenty-two front organizations. That Miss Wood [Elizabeth Wood, Executive Secretary, Chicago Housing Authority] is definitely a sympathizer and on these Airport riots that you have on Airport Projects—the Legion has made an investigation, but unfortunately we figured we would be subjected to too much debate. For example, they pass it out that 10% of the project should be given to the colored families. As a result, you have the colored families going in there. They did not want those folks there. There was a riot. They threw

53 *Report*, p. 152.   54 *Report*, p. 154.

72

over the furniture of the colored families and we understand that somebody got them new furniture and was paying them to live there.

In the Public Libraries you have a situation. The Marx books are too numerous. I believe you should know something about communism—just the highlights of it. But the way they do now, they develop the subject at length and by so doing put in the young mind a yearning for that.[55]

. . . . .

We should have an investigation of the Railroad Retirement Board. The Legion has a special committee in Cook County that has to do mostly with that because of the discrimination against veterans.[56]

The next witness spoke on some matters which seem of dubious relevance to an inquiry into subversion in Illinois. The transcript reads:

Arthur L. Conrad, Associate Administrator of the National Physicians Committee for the Extension of Medical Service was introduced and spoke to the group on the implications and background of Communist influence in the field of medicine and education. He briefly summarized the attempts that have been made to socialize medicine in the United States. He emphasized that a concerted and planned drive has been on since 1939.

There ensued a lecture by Mr. Conrad denouncing the Wagner-Murray-Dingell Bill for compulsory health insurance. Although the transcript at one point attributes to Mr. Conrad the statement that "the socialization of medicine was in reality an international plot or program which definitely fitted into the world domination program of the Soviet Union," [57] nothing in Mr. Conrad's testimony on this subject points to subversive activity, even by his definition, in Illinois. In the field of education, Mr. Conrad testified regarding a textbook on civics, which in his opinion was dangerous, written by Mary Elting, allegedly a teacher in the

[55] *Report,* p. 138. This appears to be the sole basis for the commission's statement that there are "many communists in our Housing Projects."
[56] *Report,* p. 139.   [57] *Report,* p. 142.

73

Jefferson School of Social Science [58] in New York. According to Mr. Conrad the textbook had been withdrawn from use in the public schools of Cook County and Chicago.[59] It is not indicated when this occurred.

Frank Hughes, who identified himself as an editorial writer for the *Chicago Tribune,* was invited to speak next. His concept of subversion was unimpeded by customary definitions of the term. Said Mr. Hughes: "What are you going to call subversive—anybody who presents controversial theories in public school rooms to the extinction of the other side of the issues is guilty of using subversive propaganda." [60]

Rhetorically, Mr. Hughes asked: "The Phi Beta Capa [Kappa?] fraternity pledges to the United Nations. . . . One government of all people by all people, etc. . . . Is it subversive to use such a statement in public schools without giving the other side of the argument?" [61]

Mr. Hughes viewed the progressive education theories of John Dewey and George S. Counts as subversive, as well as the American Education Fellowship for its purported advocacy of national and international planning of production, public control of basic resources, and world citizenship. He found socialism subversive and considered suspicious if not subversive U.N.E.S.C.O.'s [62] alleged proposal to rewrite history textbooks "so that the student can get a fair picture of one world—one history." [63]

Although comment is probably superfluous, it seems clear that subversion encompasses political, economic, or educational activity with which the witnesses disagree. Evidently lacking sufficient perception to detect this basic error, it is small wonder the commission was dismayed by the presence of the hydra-headed monster subversion in so many aspects of contemporary society.

But despite the discursive testimony of Messrs. Libonati, Hughes, and Conrad, the commission held fast to its decision to concentrate on the field of education. Although continuing its procedure of hearing only "friendly" witnesses in executive ses-

[58] Listed as subversive in the attorney general's letter of Nov. 24, 1947.
[59] *Report,* p. 144.   [60] *Report,* p. 147.   [61] *Ibid.*
[62] United Nations Educational, Scientific and Cultural Organization.
[63] *Report,* p. 147.

sions, the commission proposed to obtain evidence of subversion by two other methods. At a meeting of the subcommittee Dwight Anderson, chairman of the Legislative Commission of the American Legion, Department of Illinois, stated: "You are going to do your own investigating, and don't you have an enormous force right at your finger tips—communicate with every post of the V.F.W. and American Legion and ask those post commanders to appoint committees in different localities to report back by mail whatever activities they have in their schools and towns." [64] This suggestion was received favorably, apparently, for the minutes of that meeting contain this further notation: "In keeping with the pertinent suggestion of Dwight Anderson, Mr. McMackin asked Senator Broyles to send the letter requesting assistance from the various posts of the four veteran organizations." [65]

The Broyles commission also hired an investigator. His function was described in the minutes as follows: "It was agreed that the primary purpose of the investigator would be to investigate and find proof and basis for the need of the legislation to be recommended. The investigator would substantiate the legislation by his findings." [66] In a startling departure from precedent, the findings of the investigator are set forth in full in the report of the commission. Analysis of the contents of the investigator's report raises some question as to whether he fulfilled the function contemplated by the commission.

After interviewing members of the commission, Lieutenant Heimoski, Chicago Police Department, Ellidore Libonati, and Edward Clamage of the American Legion, and a number of other persons who might be expected to have information regarding subversive activities in Illinois, the investigator, Charles E. Kruger, made the refreshingly frank observation:

None [was] of any particular assistance in the investigation. All of them had one item in common, and that was to subscribe to as many as possible of the papers, pamphlets, and booklets containing communist teachings and start documenting individuals and organizations. They also agreed that they believe there was a considerable amount of communistic activity in the

[64] *Report,* p. 131.   [65] *Report,* p. 133.   [66] *Report,* p. 153.

State. *But none of them could cite any specific instances of what is occurring.*[67] [Emphasis supplied.]

Having found his contacts devoid of firsthand information concerning subversive activities, the investigator launched his inquiry.

These are the high lights of his report:

Northwestern University: I interviewed Mr. Jay Gerber, a former F.B.I. man and Secretary of Public Relations. He is of the opinion that the student body and faculty and the administration is very conservative and doubts if there is any activity in this school worthy of attention of this Commission. . . . Dean Seulberger [Dean of Students] recognizes the fact that there are several members of the faculty that he describes as liberal, but at the same time he believes them to be good American citizens.[68]

University of Chicago: The student body on the campus is probably more politically minded than on other campuses because they are somewhat older, more serious, and have specialties. A large percentage of them are strictly intellectual students. Procedure for forming a club or organization at the University of Chicago is practically identical with that of Northwestern; however, the difference lies in the administration. At Northwestern Paul Robeson was denied permission to speak on the campus, but the officials at the University of Chicago permitted Ge[r]hardt Eisler to address a meeting. Dean Strozier admitted that giving his sanction to Ge[r]hardt Eisler was one of the hardest problems he had to face, but it was his opinion that if he had to remain consistent to the university policy of freedom for the students so long as they do nothing contrary to the university policy, and it was not illegal, he was forced to concede to their request for Eisler as a speaker. . . . It is Dean Strozier's opinion that professors in the faculty do not impose their personal views on the students. . . . It was his belief that all legal groups should be permitted to operate in the open as the various types of clubs serve to counteract the influence that may be exerted by any one. He believes that the Communist Club which is recognized on the campus at the University has its functions and is more than offset by such clubs known as

[67] *Report,* p. 417.   [68] *Report,* pp. 418–419.

the Conservative Club, and Calvert Club which is a Catholic Youth organization. . . . It was also his opinion that the number of people engaged in programs conducted by the AYD and Communist Club and others that might be front organizations is so small compared to their 8,500 students enrolled that they could be discounted almost entirely. . . . I have reviewed their files of the known members of the [Communist] Club and have reached the opinion that *the present members probably were inculcated with the Communist philosophy prior to the time they entered the University.*[69] [Emphasis supplied.]

Roosevelt College: Dean Emery Balduf was cooperative and furnished a list of organizations and their officers at the College. He explained that the College prides itself on being very democratic and enumerated these things of which President Sparling boasts: (1) academic freedom, (2) democratic administration, (3) equality of opportunity.

Dean Balduf and John B. Schestman, Assistant to the President, were interviewed jointly. They agreed that the administration would tolerate anything within legality and decency. The administration may not approve of an organization and its purpose, but will give it official recognition. This was done when American Youth for Democracy petitioned for recognition. The student body organization wanted to refuse recognition and, so voted, but the administration officials requested the student body organization to reconsider what they did, and the AYD was recognized. Dean Balduf casually mentioned that some of the administration officials are now sorry they permitted the AYD to organize because their members are never satisfied and make "too much noise." Some students wanted to form a vigilantes committee and break up the AYD meetings, but the administration issued a memo to prevent it. . . .

President Sparling was very aggressive to me and antagonistic to this Commission. His attitude was entirely different than was met at any other institution. This may be because he was the only president interviewed. . . . Several times during the interview, in which I participated very little, President Sparling made the remark: "And you can go back and tell that to Governor Green." . . . Sparling indicated that if he had a communist professor on the faculty, he would do nothing about it, if the

[69] *Report,* pp. 419–421.

77

man was qualified to teach the subject. It is also Sparling's opinion that there is very little subversive activities in our educational institutions.

A review of subjects taught and of the instructors at this College—there is only one conclusion to be derived—Roosevelt College is very liberal. This is not meant to be any discredit to the College as no thorough study has been made. Without any intention of jeopardizing the reputation of this institution, it is believed the activities at this institution should remain under scrutiny.[70]

Illinois Institute of Technology: The school does not recognize any organization on the campus that is political in nature. The administration never lets this type of group get started in the campus, and at the present time they are free from trouble of this nature. . . .

The school is primarily an engineering school and has close relationship with Industry, which may account for its effort to maintain a conservative student body.[71]

University of Illinois: Dean Turner and Security Officer, Joe Evers, have their own sources of information as to what is going on at the University. Since recent legislation banned AYD, the Dean believes his sources of information are not too good. In a sense the door has been closed because his "sources" no longer know what is happening. Formerly he knew the number of members of the organization, together with their speakers, where they met, background of the group and members, as well as the general movement. Now he has no control if a group meets off campus. Sometimes pamphlets are found near the University that have no identifying names, this could be the work of students or towns people.

It is believed by Dean Turner that the student body is rather conservative. . . .

The PCA placed a petition for recognition, but the administration stalled for several weeks and soon the faculty advisor withdrew his name, and the petition was dead. There were only seven or eight signers to the petition.

Dean Turner . . . does not believe there are any Pink or Red organizations on the campus now, but he does feel they are trying to get in.[72]

[70] *Report,* pp. 430–431.   [71] *Report,* p. 431.
[72] *Report,* pp. 432–433.

Abraham Lincoln School: This school is alleged to have been operated by the Communist Party for a number of years. It is now believed, however, that the school is gradually becoming defunct and has no finances to carry on.[73]

Mr. Kruger's investigation of these institutions can scarcely be described as exhaustive. On the other hand his investigation does not lend credence to Senator Broyles's assumption that "Red" teachers, particularly at the University of Chicago, were indoctrinating students with subversive ideas. It is perhaps significant that when the Broyles commission publicly investigated the University of Chicago and Roosevelt College, Mr. Kruger was not asked to testify.

The Chicago public high schools and junior colleges were also investigated by Mr. Kruger, with largely negative results. Visiting three junior colleges and six high schools, he was informed that the number of "Red" students was either nonexistent or infinitesimal. He found no evidence that Chicago public schoolteachers indoctrinated their students with communism. Shunning publicity, Mr. Kruger did not visit the one high school, Senn High, where students had recently charged one of the teachers with publicly stating her Communist affiliation. Although Senator Broyles, at one of the executive sessions, referred to the story as illustrative of the Red menace he wished to curb,[74] the transcript of the same meeting deflates these charges: "It was brought out that the students who signed the statements against the teacher had changed their statements and it was strongly probable that they were simply students who were not making good marks and were trying to 'get even' with the teacher for conscientiously grading them low." [75]

In light of these findings by its own investigator, it is strange that the report of the commission should repeat charges that "the high school teachers, for example in certain high schools in the city of Chicago, are ardent followers of subversive movements. . . ." [76]

Pushing ahead its investigation of education, the Broyles com-

[73] *Report,* p. 434.   [74] *Report,* p. 164.   [75] *Report,* p. 168.
[76] *Report,* p. 16.

mission invited Vernon L. Nickell, state superintendent of public instruction, to attend an executive session. Mr. Nickell proved an enthusiastic witness. He advocated formation of a textbook committee to censor all texts used in Illinois public educational institutions. Superintendent Nickell recommended two prerequisites for membership on this board of censors: "What I had in mind was a committee of veterans. I would want them to have some connection with the schools." [77] Another suggestion of Superintendent Nickell was to invite the presidents of the Illinois teachers' colleges to appear before the Broyles commission to report any subversive activities they might have detected. Both recommendations met with the approval of the Broyles commission.

The presidents of five Illinois state teachers colleges, the state director of the Department of Registration and Education, Frank G. Thompson, and Superintendent Nickell, appeared before the Broyles commission in May, 1948. The meeting was unproductive of evidence of subversive teaching in these schools, although some of the educators cited additional dreary instances of accusations leveled at teachers for "Red teaching," which upon investigation proved baseless. For example, President Karl L. Adams, Northern Illinois State Teachers' College, stated:

> We had a letter circulated on the floor of the Senate about one of the members of our faculty at DeKalb. The letter was supposed to be from a parent of a student from Sycamore. The letter stated that we had a man in our school of Russian birth who was teaching things he shouldn't. A complete investigation revealed that the address and name of the student as well as those of the parent were ficticious and the accusations totally unfounded.

But some of the educators, in their choice of episodes illustrative of the administration of their respective campuses, created the impression that the nonconformist, student or teacher, receives short shrift in these institutions. President F. A. Beu, Western Illinois State College, is reported as stating: "In our institution of 1500 we have only two liberalists. . . . We had a faculty member named Walch that was reported, and he became very angry

[77] *Report,* p. 166.

80

and resigned and went to New Mexico. We had another man this year. We are not employing this man next year." [78]

With respect to the deviatory student, President R. W. Fairchild of Illinois State Normal University stated:

> I think of all the things we should not overlook, either as faculty members or students, is that frustrated individual who has not found his particular place and must compensate for it by doing something to get notice. As a matter of knowledge of government, we give the students an opportunity to set up certain types of political clubs on the campus—republican and democratic—and lo and behold appears a third party group, called together by a young man who was a veteran and one who is a frustrated individual seeking a place in the limelight. Six people came, he made the seventh, out of somewhat over 3,000 students. *That group has passed out of existence. You won't hear of it any more.* This same young man was the one who took up the question of Negro students. We have no discrimination, but there was one eating place that they thought was discriminating against the Negro students, and when they started to picket the place we questioned them and this fellow was a leader of that type. He is just a frustrated individual who tries every way possible to let people know he is on campus. [Emphasis supplied.]
>
> *McMackin* [member of commission]: "Would a man of that type make a good teacher?"
>
> *Fairchild:* "Not unless he gets out of that way of thinking." [79]

Resort to indoctrination of college students was justifiable according to some of the educators, so long as directed to a desirable end. President Chester F. Lay, Southern Illinois University, stated:

> Personally I think we are in a state of civilization in which some of us professors and administrators may have to admit that now it is time for indoctrination in the American way of life. Most of them might say we ought not indoctrinate our students. Personally, I think the advantages of our way of life ought to be set forth so persuasively that only the keenest minded students would be thinking over and above what they were taught about government. [80]

[78] *Report*, p. 174.　　[79] *Report*, p. 175.

[80] *Report*, p. 177. The transcript of the meeting ascribes the following

Senator Broyles added his educational views somewhat plaintively:

> If the truth could be taught and end up by this: This is why we are the greatest nation in the world. You could end up with something like that and you wouldn't have any of the youngsters wanting any of the other isms. There should be some book in American history and our way of living, making favorable comparisons. There should be some way out of the situation.[81]

Before creating a textbook censorship committee, as recommended by Superintendent Nickell, the Broyles commission sought the advice of Edward Clamage, chairman of the Anti-Subversive Committee of the American Legion, Department of Illinois. Informed by Mr. Clamage that it was a "splendid idea," [82] the commission shortly thereafter selected a fourteen-man committee based largely upon the recommendations of Superintendent Nickell, State Director of Education Frank G. Thompson, and Ellidore Libonati, American Legion.[83] The *Report of the Broyles Commission* makes reference to only one meeting of the Text-Book Committee. At this meeting Senator Broyles suggested the procedure to be followed: the committee would examine the schoolbooks for objectionable material and report its findings to the Broyles commission which, in turn, would communicate with the offending schools and suggest "in a quiet way" [84] the elimination of the objectionable texts. The only meeting reported was devoted largely to a discussion of standards and procedures. The first member of the Text-Book Committee called upon, Hal J. Connor, made a number of sensible and pertinent observations:

---

to Frank G. Thompson, director of registration and education: "Director Thompson agrees with President Lay that the time has come to realize that we must teach and indoctrinate Americanism" (*Report,* p. 181). This view was not held unanimously, however. President Karl L. Adams of Northern Illinois State Teachers' College said: "You cannot teach people what to think. You have to teach them how to think" (*Report,* p. 166).

[81] *Report,* p. 182.   [82] *Report,* p. 186.   [83] *Report,* p. 193.
[84] *Report,* p. 369.

I have not seen any books or pamphlets that I would consider subversive in whole, or in part. I hear things about such text-books, but I have never seen them. One of the things that was in my mind, namely, what is the method of procedure if you find something subversive? Would it be in the nature of legal action, or would it be to get in touch with the publisher, or the author, or the school? . . . Would it be enough just to get the certain school or all the public schools in the State from using them? Then, of course, there is the question of how to go about finding the material we are looking for. . . . There have been hundreds of text-books written, and how would they be made available and what method would we have of perusing even a large proportion of the text-books that are in use. It seems to me that a fundamental point would be for the Committee to sit down and try to define what constitutes subversive or seditious material in a text-book. I think we should start there. We should set up a definition, or a set of standards that might be applied.[85]

Unfortunately, the answers were not of the caliber of the questions. Thus one member is reported as stating he would recommend use of those textbooks "that come out strictly for Americanism rather than those that tend to take that somewhat false scholarly attitude that you must give full recognition for all concerned." [86]

In the course of the meeting discussion wandered to the greater importance of censoring teaching personnel rather than text-books. As one member put it: "Even with the finest text-books their teachers can do the dirty work." [87]

The same member had a novel standard for determining subversive teaching, suggesting that: "there could be subversive activities even in mathematics. For an example, when the boys entered the Army it was found that most of them had a deplorable lack of training in mathematics. . . . Inadequate and improper

[85] *Report*, p. 369.

[86] *Report*, p. 371. Since the Text-Book Committee was composed largely of educators, it seems strange this statement was not challenged as overly chauvinistic. But such was not the case.

[87] *Report*, p. 372.

teaching of any subject could be considered as subversive." [88]

The minutes reflect the breadth of view of still another member who "explained about academic freedom using the example of a teacher who wanted Russian in the curriculum."

This member is then quoted as stating: "They are perfectly innocent, but I think that is flirting with danger. I think some definite law would tend to do away with this confusion." [89]

Fortunately, there is no indication that the standards suggested were adopted. Indeed, the record is silent as to whether the Text-Book Committee thereafter functioned.[90]

The attention of the Broyles commission was again directed to the University of Chicago by James Simpson, secretary of the Legislative Commission, American Legion, Department of Illinois, at a meeting of the subcommittee held July 16, 1948. The minutes of that meeting state:

> Mr. Simpson told the Commission of a friend of his who is a student at the University of Chicago who would come in and tell a closed meeting about his difficulties in having to answer the questions the way the instructors wanted them answered— in a sympathetic manner towards subversive and communistic tendencies, in order to please the instructor and remain in the upper rank and be admitted to Annapolis. It was stressed that the name of the student must be kept secret or else he would fail in his classes.[91]

The following month the unidentified University of Chicago student appeared before the subcommittee. The student first ad-

[88] *Ibid.* There is no indication in the record of objection to this statement. One might suppose that any group of teachers would shudder at the thought of applying such a standard.

[89] *Report,* p. 376. It should be observed that Chairman Broyles had informed these gentlemen at the beginning of the meeting that "there would be no publicity concerning what they had to say" (*Report,* p. 369).

[90] Much as one might condemn use of improperly "slanted" texts (assuming there are such), especially in primary schools, the Text-Book Committee seems hardly qualified to undertake such a task in view of the caliber of opinions expressed. There is some indication that such an undertaking would be duplicative, since some local boards of education have already prepared lists of recommended textbooks (*Report,* p. 370).

[91] *Report,* p. 92.

dressed himself to the Communist Club and the A.Y.D., stating that there were eleven members of the Communist Club at the University of Chicago and approximately seventy-five members of the A.Y.D. He stated that several members of the Communist Club were acknowledged Communists.[92]

When questioned about subversive teaching, the student's testimony became more lively, though perhaps less factual.

> *Knox* [member of the commission]: In your opinion, the student body out there, what would you say would be about the approximate number of these people?
>
> *Student:* I would hate to make a guess because I haven't come in contact with too many of the students. I am still in the college, and in my Social Science clubs that I go to, discussions always are swinging to the left, either by the professors or by the students.
>
> *Knox:* In your opinion, if you can give me this, do you think this is on the up-grade now and becoming more prominent or is it a stand-still?
>
> *Student:* Do you mean this communistic tendency? I would say it is definitely on the up-swing. On their English essays and comprehensive tests they write on leftist subjects because they know they will get a better grade. When I was living at the Boys' Dorm I was talking to a lad there who told me when he wrote his English placement, he wrote on the University of Chicago, upholding the way they operate.

> .   .   .   .   .

> *Hodges:* Do you think your Social Science teachers were advocating leftist views or was it open discussion? In other words are they salesmen for it?
>
> *Student:* I would say they are salesmen for it. I had a professor, Kitness,[93] Soc. I, who damned Ford up and down the day he died, saying that he was not liberal enough with the working men.
>
> *Jim Simpson* [guest of the commission]: It is more serious than we realize that 60% of the voters have known no other president but Roosevelt.

[92] *Report,* p. 204.

[93] The university directory lists an Ira A. Kipnis, instructor in social science.

McMackin: Do you hear very much discussion of the Wallace candidacy?

Student: There is a very strong "Wallace for President" group out there.

Simpson: Is it based on his economic principles or delay of war?

Student: I don't know.

Hodges: Are there any organizations of students out there who make it their business to combat this Communist business?

Student: No, there is no organized group.[94]

The transcript of the meeting then records the following:

"It was agreed to present the evidence to the Board of Trustees who appoint the professors and ask them to clean up, and then contact the Alumni." [95]

The minutes of the meeting of the Broyles commission during the latter months of 1948 and the first quarter of 1949 refer principally to decisions relative to the legislative program to be presented by the commission. Two ancillary activities are noted in the record of this period. The commission sent a four-man delegation to the Area Conference on Subversive Activities, National Department of the American Legion, at Indianapolis, Indiana, February 12 and 13, 1949. Senator Broyles addressed the legion, giving a résumé of the work of the commission. The commission also sent a delegate to the Interstate Legislative Conference on Un-American Activities, a meeting in Los Angeles, California, September 20 and 21, 1948, sponsored by the Legislative Committees on Un-American Activities of California and Washington. The meeting was called to formulate (in the words of Senator Broyles) "a program to be followed by each state *which would keep any one state from receiving all of the criticism* and would tend to make any recommendations for legislation uniform in all the states." [96] (Emphasis supplied.)

Senator Broyles's characterization of the conference, however, may have been inexact, for more praiseworthy objectives were presented to the delegates. The need for intensified efforts to educate the young in the meaning and processes of a democratic soci-

[94] *Report,* p. 205.   [95] *Report,* p. 206.   [96] *Report,* p. 183.

86

ety was stressed. Delegates were advised not to advocate legislation barring the Communist Party from a place on the ballot. In the realm of legislative investigations of subversive activities, they were warned against "the reckless smearing of a single sincere Liberal by calling him a Communist or fellow-traveler or a Communist sympathizer . . ." [97]

The major portion of the conference was devoted to lectures and discussions regarding the approved techniques for conducting a state antisubversive investigation and the need for uniform antisubversive legislation. The dangers posed by communism, the devices utilized by Communists to avoid detection, and the most appropriate countermeasures also received attention. The delegates heard a rather complete exposure of Communist tactics with considerable emphasis upon the readiness of Communists to lie and dissemble. Yet the delegates were not attentive, apparently, for at the close of the conference, one of them remarked guilelessly: "I have never taken an oath . . . in connection with my work, and I don't have any way of knowing whether or not anybody here is, and they don't know whether I am engaged in subversive activities, and it might be an excellent suggestion that we here start the practice of declaring our allegiance." [98]

This suggestion was warmly greeted, all delegates thereupon taking an oath in which they denied past or present membership in the Communist Party. [99]

To illustrate the advantages which would accrue from establishment of an antisubversive activities committee in each state and closer co-operation among them, R. E. Combs, chief counsel of the California Senate Fact-Finding Committee on Un-American Activities, stated:

> If a college professor, a known Communist or professional agitator, or some joiner of Communist Front[s], is kicked out of one university, for example, why should he find haven in a university in Georgia, Alabama, Illinois or Washington? Here is

[97] *Report,* p. 307. Unfortunately, the evil foreseen was solely the resulting injury to the committee's work. Ignored was the damage to reputation of the innocent (*ibid.*).

[98] *Report,* p. 364.   [99] *Report,* p. 365.

87

a concrete example. A fellow was on his way from Washington where he was kicked out of the university. He was to get a berth at one of our universities, but as a result of our trip to Seattle we were ready to get him at the border, as it were, and he is not on the payroll, nor will he ever be. That is why liaison between committees is a tremendously important thing.

. . . . .

I can see no reason against, and I can see every reason for, the establishment of a committee on un-American activities in every state of the Union. Then we won't have such people as Dr. Frank P. Graham,[100] horsing about in Alabama and Georgia as head of an organization which he called the Conference for Southern Welfare, which has been established by the United States Department of Justice and by the records of the Congressional Investigating Committee as a Communist-dominated organization [101] enthusiastically supported by known members of the Communist Party.[102]

The delegates to the Interstate Conference concluded their deliberations with adoption of a resolution urging establishment of an un-American activities committee in each state. The delegates also voted to establish a permanent Interstate Conference which would facilitate interchange of information and prepare uniform antisubversive legislation.

THE GREAT INVESTIGATION [103]

By the end of February, 1949, the Broyles commission, without benefit of public hearings, had completed its legislative proposals

[100] At the time United States senator from North Carolina and formerly president of the University of North Carolina.

[101] This is apparently a reference to the Southern Conference for Human Welfare, which is not listed as subversive in the attorney general's letters of November 24, 1947, and May 27, 1948. The House Committee on Un-American Activities filed a report describing the Southern Conference for Human Welfare as a "communist front." For discussion of this report see Gellhorn, "Report on a Report of the House Committee on Un-American Activities," 60 Harv. L. Rev. 1193 (1949).

[102] *Report,* pp. 316–317.

[103] With apologies to a student publication of the same name which reproduced portions of the public hearings.

and introduced them in the Illinois senate. Referred to the senate judiciary committee, the five so-called Broyles bills were recommended for passage following a boisterous one-day public hearing. Newspapers reported that about five hundred people crowded the chambers to protest against the bills. Included in the group were approximately 150 students from the University of Chicago and Roosevelt College.[104] The students' criticism was reported as vehement—the reaction of the legislators equally so. The house of representatives unanimously adopted a resolution the next day directing the Broyles commission to investigate "any and all subversive activities . . . at the University of Chicago and Roosevelt College." [105] The resolution was quickly adopted in the senate the following week by a 38 to 1 vote.[106]

Thereupon, Senator Broyles introduced a measure calling for an emergency appropriation of $2,500 for the investigation of the University of Chicago and Roosevelt College. By the end of March this measure had passed both houses by overwhelming majorities and had been sent to Governor Adlai Stevenson for signature. Permitting the bill to become law without his signature, Governor Stevenson issued an accompanying message, stating in part:

> I doubt the necessity for this investigation. The resolution says that a large number of students from these universities appeared in opposition to pending legislation to control subversive activities. It goes on to say that "it appears that these students are being indoctrinated with Communistic and other subversive theories." Because some one hundred students from institutions numbering 15,000 exercise their right as citizens to oppose anti-subversive legislation it hardly follows that they are being indoctrinated with Communism as this resolution seems to imply.
>
> Nevertheless, I am reluctant to interfere with the legislature's power of investigation. Also, in view of the serious charges, I

[104] *New York Times*, March 3, 1949, p. 30, col. 5.

[105] Ill. H.J.R. No. 21, 66th Gen. Assembly. Reprinted in *Seditious Activities Investigation Commission, Report of Proceedings, Investigation of University of Chicago and Roosevelt College* (1949), p. 4. (Hereafter cited as *Proceedings*.)

[106] *Chicago Herald and American*, March 9, 1949, p. 1.

think the University of Chicago, one of the great centers of learning in the world, and Roosevelt College, a new institution dedicated to education of those of limited means, should be given an opportunity to be heard.[107]

While the Broyles commission was preparing for the forthcoming investigation, Benjamin Gitlow, head of the Communist Party in America until 1929, was introduced by Senator Broyles to a joint session of the general assembly. Mr. Gitlow spoke of his experiences as a Communist and the reasons for his break with the Communist Party.[108]

The following day Senator Broyles announced that the commission had employed Mr. Gitlow to investigate the University of Chicago and Roosevelt College.[109] Senator Broyles was also reported to have stated that the commission might employ students at the two schools as "undercover agents." [110] About the same time the Broyles commission retained Dr. J. B. Matthews to conduct the interrogation of witnesses at the forthcoming public hearings.[111]

Dr. Matthews, like Mr. Gitlow, enjoys a record of drastically revised political affiliations. The *Report of the Broyles Commission* attributes to Representative J. Parnell Thomas the statement that "Dr. J. B. Matthews was the number two man to Earl Browder." [112] However, Dr. Matthews was reported as denying membership in the Communist Party but admitting he held at one time "a strategic non-membership in the party." [113] Upon reformation, Matthews had become director of research for the House Committee on Un-American Activities.[114] More recently Matthews had been active at the state level, appearing as a witness before the Massachusetts Legislative Committee on Constitutional

---

[107] *Chicago Daily Tribune,* April 11, 1949, Part 2, p. 4; *Chicago Daily News,* April 11, 1949, p. 16, col. 7.

[108] *Report,* p. 451. Gitlow's conviction for violation of the New York criminal anarchy statute was affirmed by the Supreme Court of the United States in *Gitlow v. New York,* 268 U.S. 652 (1925).

[109] *Chicago Sun-Times,* March 30, 1949, p. 4, col. 5.

[110] *Ibid.*   [111] *Proceedings,* p. 6.   [112] *Report,* p. 226.

[113] Milburn P. Akers, *Chicago Sun-Times,* April 5, 1949, editorial page.

[114] *Chicago Daily Tribune,* April 7, 1949, p. 6, col. 1.

Law to advocate adoption of antisubversive legislation.[115] And in an address before the American Legion in February, 1949, Dr. Matthews had asserted:

> I had a hand in the recent case in Seattle at the University of Washington. Last July I testified two days before the legislative committee which initiated the investigation of professors at the University of Washington. I recited the records of the Communist affiliations of the professors that were dismissed.[116]

In the several weeks intervening before the public hearings began on April 21, 1949, the Broyles commission and its legislative program became a focal point of public attention. Contrary to the commission's earlier opinion that only subversive groups would oppose its legislation, three of the four major newspapers in Chicago came out against the bills.[117] The Broyles commission and its activities also became a high priority target for a number of newspaper columnists for the Chicago newspapers.[118] The general tone of these articles, it can be said safely, was caustic.[119]

[115] *Ibid.*

[116] *Report,* pp. 393–394.

[117] See editorials of *Chicago Daily Tribune,* March 5, 1949, and March 26, 1949; *Chicago Daily News,* March 25, 1949; *Chicago Sun-Times,* March 7, 1949. The *Chicago Herald American* was the only Chicago newspaper favoring the Broyles bills (Editorial, April 11, 1949).

[118] Edwin A. Lahey, *Chicago Daily News,* April 20, 1949, April 21, 1949; Herb Graffis, *Chicago Sun-Times,* March 7, 1949; Milburn P. Akers, *Chicago Sun-Times,* March 15, 16, 18, 21, 22, 23, 24, 25, 28, April 1, 3, 5, 6, 10, 14, 18, 19, 20, 1949.

[119] Typical is Milburn P. Akers' column in the *Chicago Sun-Times* of April 5:

"Senator Broyles, whose penchant for ex-commies is somewhat akin to that of a backwood revivalist for sinners who hit the sawdust trail, has hired another investigator, consultant, researcher or something for his ever increasing Gestapo, Ogpu, or posse commitas. Anyway, the good Senator, who appears convinced revolution is brewing in the University of Chicago's Great Books Course, or at Roosevelt College's Class in Freshman Composition, has gathered unto himself another recanting brother.

"This time, the brother didn't have quite so much to recant. For, so says J. B. Matthews, the latest addition to Broyles' squad of campus snoopers, he was never a member of the Communist Party. But he insists, does J. B. Matthews, that he was almost as big a sinner as was Ben Gitlow, another Broyles agent for the investigation of co-eds and their boy friends.

"Gitlow had a card. But Matthews, one-time Methodist preacher, didn't. Instead, Matthews held what he once described as 'a strategic non-membership in the party.'

" 'I hope it will not appear immodest,' he said on the same occasion, 'but for a period of years I was probably more closely associated with the Communist Party's united front movements than any other individual in this country.'

"So now Broyles is all set for his drive against the campuses: Gitlow, it appears, will spearhead the frontal attack while Matthews conducts a flanking operation. And woe unto any co-ed, college man or faculty member who chances to believe General Dwight Eisenhower was expressing good Americanism at Columbia University Oct. 12, 1948 when he said:

" 'There will be no administrative suppression or distortion of any subject that merits a place in this university's curricula. The facts of Communism, for instance, shall be taught here—its ideological developments, its political methods, its economic effects, its probable course in the future. The truth about Communism is, today, an indispensable requirement if the true values of our democratic system are to be properly assessed. Ignorance of Communism, Fascism, or any other police state philosophy is far more dangerous than ignorance of the most virulent disease.'

"Both schools—Chicago and Roosevelt—should scan their libraries before either Gitlow or Matthews stop on the campus.

"Any books by Milton should be burned, at once. For didn't he write in his Aeropagitica:

" 'And though all the winds of doctrine were let loose to play upon the earth, so Truth be in the field, we do injuriously by licensing and prohibiting to misdoubt her strength. Let her and Falsehood grapple; whoever knew truth put to the worse, in a free and open encounter.'

"And rid yourselves, Chicago and Roosevelt, of any books by Jefferson, who said, in his first inaugural:

" 'If there be any among us who wish to dissolve this union or to change its republican form, let them stand undisturbed, as monuments of the safety with which error of opinion may be tolerated where reason is left free to combat it.'

92

Chicago newspapers during March and April recorded mounting criticism directed principally at the Broyles bills, and, in some instances, at the pending investigation of the two schools. This opposition stemmed from civic, religious, labor, veteran, professional, and academic groups.[120]

One of the calmest, most dispassionate voices raised against the controversial Broyles bills emanated from the Chicago Bar Association. Its committee on civil rights reported:

> An examination of these bills reveals that none of them sets forth the acts or associations sought to be proscribed with sufficient definiteness. It is impossible to do more than guess from their texts what acts, associations or even beliefs are made ground for the imposition of civil disqualifications or criminal penalties.

"Broyles, flanked by Gitlow and Matthews, rides again. Hi, ho, Silver, away. The co-eds and their boyfriends must be saved from Eisenhower, Milton and Jefferson."

[120] Among the groups mentioned in the press as protesting either the Broyles bills or the pending investigation were the following: a campus committee representing all student organizations at the University of Chicago (*Chicago Herald-American,* March 10, 1949); a group of fifty professors and instructors at the University of Illinois (*Chicago Daily News,* April 2, 1949, p. 6, col. 4); American Civil Liberties Union, Chicago Division (*Chicago Daily News,* April 5, 1949); the Chicago Methodist Ministers Association (*Chicago Sun-Times,* April 7, 1949); five clergymen serving the campus of the University of Chicago (*Chicago Daily News,* April 7, 1949); the Chicago Federation of Labor (*Chicago Sun-Times,* April 12, 1949); the Illinois Congress of Parents and Teachers (*Chicago Sun-Times,* April 13, 1949); the Chicago Metropolitan Area Building Service Employees Council, the Illinois Conference of the American Association of University Professors (*Chicago Sun-Times,* April 14, 1949); the South Side Committee to Protest the Broyles Bills (*Chicago Sun-Times,* April 15, 1949); the Citizens Schools Committee (*Chicago Sun-Times,* April 16, 1949). Of those approving both the Broyles bills and the investigation, the American Legion and the *Chicago Herald-American,* a Hearst newspaper, appear to have been leading proponents (*Chicago Herald-American* editorial, April 11, 1949; for American Legion approval see *Chicago Tribune,* April 4, 1949, Part 4, p. 6, col. 6.

Referring to the lack of specific definition or accepted common-law meaning for such words or phrases appearing in the bills as "doctrine to undermine," "insidious," "espouses indirectly," or "in any way active in behalf of," the committee concluded:

> While this Committee concurs with the legislature in its opposition to the methods and objectives of the Communist Party, it is our opinion that these bills should not be enacted. Their indefiniteness would make them administratively unworkable and subject to valid constitutional objections. Moreover, to the extent they propose to prohibit the advocacy of the overthrow of government by force or other unlawful means, they add nothing to existing law. . . . In addition, these bills infringe upon guaranteed civil rights, and would become a source of suppression and intimidation which would inhibit education and discussion effective in counteracting subversive doctrines.[121]

An episode indicating that publicly expressed criticism of the Broyles commission was not being totally ignored by the commission involved the request of Laird Bell, chairman of the board of trustees of the University of Chicago, for certain procedural safeguards. Mr. Bell, in a letter made available to the press, asked Senator Broyles to assure the two schools the right to reasonable notice, to have counsel present, and to cross-examine. He also requested opportunity to present rebuttal witnesses, to have open hearings, and to obtain a full transcript of the hearings.[122] Senator Broyles was reported in the press as disposed to agree to the suggestions save one. He was reported unwilling to grant the right of cross-examination of witnesses. Several Chicago newspapers editorially criticized Senator Broyles's stand on this issue, asserting such denial would seriously jeopardize a fair hearing.[123] The press subsequently reported dissension among the members of the commission over the rules of procedure to govern the hearings and finally, on the night preceding the first public hearing, the com-

[121] *Report on Sedition Bills,* Committee on Civil Rights, Chicago Bar Association, April 20, 1949. Approved by Board of Managers, April 21, 1949.

[122] *Chicago Sun-Times,* April 9, 1949.

[123] See editorials of the *Chicago Sun-Times* and *Chicago Daily News,* April 18, 1949.

mission reversed itself, agreeing to permit the schools to cross-examine witnesses.[124]

At the opening of the public hearings [125] Senator Broyles announced the rules of procedure which would govern the sessions. The right to counsel and to make a statement at the close of his testimony was to be accorded to every witness. Any person named in the hearings was to have the right to file a rebuttal statement which would be incorporated into the records. If testimony should reflect adversely upon any person, that person would have the right to cross-examine, through counsel, the witness making the charges.[126]

Save for the failure to afford reasonable notice to those being investigated of the nature of the charges to be presented against them,[127] the Broyles commission had adopted impressive procedural safeguards.

Robert M. Hutchins, chancellor of the University of Chicago, was the first witness. He began his testimony with a statement vigorously defending the university.[128] Speaking first of the subpoena served upon him calling for his testimony concerning "subversive activities at the University of Chicago," Hutchins said: "This is a leading question: the answer is assumed in the

[124] *Chicago Sun-Times,* April 21, 1949.

[125] The investigation of the University of Chicago and Roosevelt College was held in the chamber of the house of representatives in the State Capitol Building in Springfield. The hearings lasted three days in April (21–23) and closed with a one-day session on May 19, 1949.

[126] *Proceedings,* p. 11.

[127] The matter of surprise witnesses was later to cause difficulty; see footnote 145.

[128] Hutchins was permitted to make an opening statement after a procedural skirmish between members of the Broyles commission. Hutchins had hardly taken the witness chair when Senator Barry moved to suspend the rules so that Hutchins might make an opening statement. After sharp debate the vote was tied, 6 to 6. Senator Broyles, one of those voting against the motion, thereupon announced he was changing his vote to assure a fair hearing. The chairman then ruled the motion was carried by a 7 to 5 vote. Senator Barry and Representative Jenkins grinned broadly but said nothing. Their amusement was explained later by their assertion that under rules of parliamentary procedure, a motion to sus-

question. I cannot testify concerning subversive activities at the University of Chicago, because there are none." [129]

Following his flat denial with a more detailed statement, Hutchins said of the university's faculty:

The faculty of the University is, as everybody knows, one of the most distinguished in the world. The faculty number 1,000. None of its members is engaged in subversive activities. The principal reason why the University has such a distinguished faculty is that the University guarantees its professors absolute and complete academic freedom. Nobody has ever ventured to say that any member of the faculty of the University of Chicago is a Communist. It has sometimes been said that some members of the faculty belong to some so-called "Communist front" organizations. The University of Chicago does not believe in the un-American doctrine of guilt by association.

The fact that some Communists belong to, believe in, or even dominate some of the organizations to which some of our professors belong does not show that those professors are engaged in subversive activities. All that such facts would show would be that these professors believed in some of the objects of the organizations. It is entirely possible to belong to organizations combating Fascism and racial discrimination, for example, without desiring to subvert the government of the United States, even though some other members of these organizations may desire to subvert the government of the United States.[130]

Completing the dichotomy of his denial of subversive activities at the university, Hutchins said of the student body:

---

pend the rules requires a two-thirds vote rather than a simple majority. The opposition had neglected the point.

[129] Transcript of hearings prepared by private reporter for the University of Chicago, p. 22. The writer, who attended the hearings, has found that the official transcript issued by the Broyles commission contains many inaccuracies, and in some instances the sense of the statements of the witnesses has been materially changed. Citations to the transcript prepared for the University will be hereafter designated as "U. of C. transcript." The writer has checked the U. of C. transcript, and, while it, too, contains inaccuracies, it is on the whole more reliable than the official transcript.

[130] U. of C. transcript, pp. 25–27.

The University has many thousands of students. None of them, so far as I know, is engaged in subversive activities. One or two students are alleged to have said publicly that they are Communists. I am not aware that they have advocated the overthrow of the government by violence. If they have, they have broken the law of this state, and the proper officials should have instituted proceedings against them.

As is well known there is a Communist club among the students of the University. Eleven students belong to it. The club is not thought to subvert the government of this state. Its members claim that they are interested in studying Communism, and some of them, perhaps all of them, may be sympathetic toward Communism. But the study of Communism is not a subversive activity. I am not sympathetic toward Communism; but I do not see how the sympathetic feelings of ten or a dozen students at the University of Chicago can be a danger to the state.

The policy of the University is to admit law-abiding students who have the qualifications to do the University's work. It would not be in the public interest to exclude students of Communistic leanings. If we did, how would they ever learn better? [131]

Chancellor Hutchins then reminded the commission that fourteen years ago a legislative committee had attempted to find evidence of subversive activities at the university but had found none. He stated that since that time there had been no changes which would justify the present investigation. Rather he pointed to the fact that the university had been entrusted by the federal government with the "most momentous military secret in history" —the creation of the first atomic chain reaction. He also stated that the university presently manages for the government its principal laboratory of atomic research and is engaged in many other secret research projects on behalf of the government. Said Hutchins:

The government maintains a security officer on the Campus. Because of the secret projects I have referred to, Federal agents constantly visit the Campus. It is unlikely that if there were subversive activities there they would not have reported them.

[131] U. of C. transcript, pp. 27–28.

An investigator for this Commission spent days on the Campus a year ago. Neither the legislature nor the University has been informed that he discovered any subversive activities at the University. I can only conclude that he found none.[132]

Speaking of the motivations underlying the investigation, Chancellor Hutchins said:

> The resolution calling for this investigation originated in the House of which the Chairman of this Commission is not a member. The reason given was that some hundreds of young people, about 20% of whom were students at the University of Chicago, demonstrated in an impolite manner against certain bills pending in the Legislature.
>
> The penalty does not seem to fit the crime. Rudeness and redness are not the same. I recognize that it is provoking to the Legislature to be impolitely treated when it is conscientiously performing its duties. But even if I admitted that students of the University of Chicago were as impolite as they are alleged to have been, I could not admit that impoliteness was even presumptive evidence of subversive activity or that the fact that students were impolite showed that they had been taught to be impolite or subversive by the faculty of the University of Chicago.
>
> The bills against which these students demonstrated were not so obviously perfect as to suggest that anybody who demonstrated against them was subversive or engaged in subversive activities. . . .
>
> These students exercised their right as American citizens to protest against pending legislation of which they disapproved. They were entirely right to disapprove this pending legislation. The Broyles bills are unnecessary, since any dangers against which they are designed to protect us are already covered by laws now on the statute books. They are, in my opinion as a former professor of law, unconstitutional. And, worst of all, they are un-American, since they aim at thought-control. They aim at the suppression of ideas.

[132] U. of C. transcript, p. 29. Chancellor Hutchins' reference to Investigator Kruger's report was a particularly well-aimed shot in the dark since at this time Kruger's report had not been made public.

It is now fashionable to call anybody with whom you disagree a communist or a fellow-traveler. So Branch Rickey darkly hinted the other day that the attempt to eliminate the reserve clause in baseball contracts was the work of communists.

One who criticizes the foreign policy of the United States, or the draft, or the Atlantic Pact, or who believes that our military establishment is too expensive, can be called a fellow traveler, for the Russians are of the same opinion. One who thinks that there are too many slums and too much lynching in America can be called a fellow-traveler, for the Russians say the same. One who opposes racial discrimination or the Ku Klux Klan can be called a fellow traveler, for the Russians claim that they ought to be opposed. Anybody who wants any change of any kind in this country can be called a fellow traveler, because the Russians want change in this country, too.

The constitution of the United States guarantees freedom of speech and the right of the people peaceably to assemble. The American way has been to encourage thought and discussion. We have never been afraid of thought and discussion. The whole educational system, and not merely the University of Chicago, is a reflection of the American faith in thought and discussion as a path to peaceful change and improvement.

The danger to our institutions is not from the tiny minority who do not believe in them. It is from those who would mistakenly repress the free spirit upon which those institutions are built. The miasma of thought-control that is now spreading over the country is the greatest menace to the United States since Hitler.

There are two ways of fighting subversive ideas. One is the policy of repression. This policy is contrary to the letter and the spirit of the Constitution of the country. It cannot be justly enforced, because it is impossible to tell precisely what people are thinking; they have to be judged by their acts. It has been generally thought that the widest possible attitude could be given to freedom of speech and publication, on the ground that the expression of differing points of view, some of which are bound to be unpopular, is the way to progress in the state. Hyde Park corner in London, where anybody may say anything, has long been a symbol of the confidence of the Anglo-Saxon world in the ability of democratic institutions to withstand criticism, and even to nourish itself upon it. There are numerous laws already on the books which provide for the punishment of subversive acts.

The policy of repression of ideas cannot work and never has worked. The alternative to it is the long, difficult road of education. To this the American people have been committed. It requires patience and tolerance, even in the face of intense provocation. It requires faith in the principles and practices of democracy, faith that when the citizen understands all forms of government he will prefer democracy and that he will be a better citizen if he is convinced than he would be if he were coerced.

The Legislature and the University of Chicago are both opposed to communism. The task of the Legislature is not merely to protect the people by passing laws that prevent the minority from overthrowing the state. It is to eliminate those social and economic evils and those political injustices which are the sources of discontent and disaffection. The members of the faculty of the University have many times assisted the Legislature in its effort to discover and remedy these evils and injustices, and they are ready at all times to assist it.

The task of the University is to enlighten the community, to provide citizens who know the reasons for their faith and who will be a bulwark to our democracy because they have achieved conviction through study and thought. The University does not claim that it is perfect or that it always succeeds. It asserts, however, that the policy of education is better than the policy of repression and that it is earnestly dedicated to making the policy of education produce the results that the American people have believed it can produce. All the University asks of the Legislature, and all that it has ever asked of it, is a sympathetic understanding of this task.[133]

In the interrogation of Chancellor Hutchins that followed, it is significant that Dr. Matthews did not attempt to challenge Hutchins' statement that there were no Communists on the faculty of the university, nor was any serious attempt made to prove students were being indoctrinated with communism by any member of the faculty. Indeed, much of the questioning pertained to matters rather irrelevant to the administration of the university—the

---

[133] U. of C. transcript, pp. 29–35.

views of Hutchins with respect to the dismissal of certain professors by the board of regents of the University of Washington; with respect to whether the Communist Party was a conspiratorial fifth column; whether the attorney general of the United States was justified in indicting and trying the leaders of the Communist Party; whether Russia and the American Communist Party were a "clear and present danger" to the United States; whether advocacy of world federation was subversive. Hutchins' responses to these and to other questions more nearly pertinent to the issue of subversion at the university were a cross-examiner's nightmare. To matters pertaining to university policy Hutchins conducted a calm, thoughtful, and consistent defense; to questions which struck him as frivolous or irrelevant he gave an extraordinary demonstration of the lightning-quick riposte.

Matthews first attempted unsuccessfully to elicit from Hutchins an admission that the membership of the Communist Club on the campus was far greater than that registered with the dean of students.[134] Failing in that Matthews then turned to the two students who had publicly admitted being Communists and asked: "Would you not assume that their purposes must be subversive by definition?"

> *Hutchins:* I would assume that if a man joined the Communist Club saying that he was a communist, his interest was in studying it, discussing and perhaps promoting Communism. It has not yet been established that it is subversive to be a communist.
>
> I might add perhaps the only student I have ever known well, with marked communistic leanings, was a student of my own, whom I met at Marquette University the first week in March when I lectured there and then he was a Dominican father. I do not say that if he had not been a student of mine that he would not have become a Dominican father, but I do say that it does not follow that because students join communist clubs when they are in universities that they will be communists when they get out." [135]

Central to the theme of Matthews' questions was the thought that the university should take action against some members of

[134] U. of C. transcript, p. 37.   [135] U. of C. transcript, p. 40.

the faculty for their off-campus affiliations. But Hutchins remained adamant. Matthews said: "The records which I shall present through other witnesses, Chancellor, show in summary that some sixty-odd persons listed in the latest available directory of the University of Chicago as professors or professors emeritus have been affiliated with 135 Communist Front organizations in 464 separate affiliations. Now I should like to know if that is not something for which the University might well be alarmed?"

> *Chancellor Hutchins:* I don't see why.
>
> *Mr. Matthews:* You don't think that that is indicative of the fact that the University of Chicago is allowing its prestige to be used in the Communist Front movement?
>
> *Chancellor Hutchins:* I don't think so, especially when you consider the alternative.
>
> *Mr. Matthews:* You are indifferent to it? . . .
>
> *Chancellor Hutchins:* I didn't say I was indifferent to it. I said, "Consider the alternative." Suppose now that you have a Nobel prize winner undoubtedly competent in his field, and he joins an organization of which the Attorney General at the moment happens to disapprove. Is it suggested that I am to interfere with his freedom of association, freedom of speech and freedom of thought? I hope not.[136]

But the question continued to arise. At one point Hutchins said: "The question is not what our professors belong to but what they are doing."

> *Mr. Matthews:* Suppose they belong to the Ku Klux Klan or the German-American Bund, would the University be indifferent to such associations?
>
> *Chancellor Hutchins:* The University does not like many of the associations of its faculty members but the University does not feel that an individual is bound by all the tenets of all the groups with which they belong.
>
> *Mr. Matthews:* You are acquainted, I take it, to a considerable degree with the recent action of the Board of Regents of the University of Washington at Seattle, are you not?
>
> *Chancellor Hutchins:* Yes.

· · · · ·

[136] U. of C. transcript, pp. 74–75.

Mr. Matthews: You are aware of the fact that one of the three dismissed professors did not affirm or deny his membership in the Communist Party, namely Professor Ralph Gundlach? You are acquainted with that fact, are you not?

Chancellor Hutchins: I have heard that.

Mr. Matthews: And the evidence against Gundlach, so far as there is anything tangible, was that he was affiliated with, roughly, a score of communist front organizations . . . and that he was dismissed on that basis. Would you be willing to have administrators of the University of Chicago use the University of Washington action as a precedent?

Chancellor Hutchins: You mean that if a man joined a group of organizations that were so-called communist fronts and he was entirely competent as a professor and there was no other objection to him than that and there is no evidence that he was engaged in subversive activities other than that; there was no evidence that he ever advocated the overthrow of the government by violence?

Mr. Matthews: That is the decision in the case of the University of Washington.

Chancellor Hutchins: The answer is "no." [137]

But Matthews continued to press the matter of alleged Communist front affiliations of members of the faculty. Said Mr. Matthews: "I notice on the American Sponoring Committee [for the World Congress of Peace, Paris, April 20–23, 1949] the name of a Dr. Maude Slye. Is Dr. Maude Slye on the faculty of the University of Chicago? Is she listed in the current directory?"

Chancellor Hutchins: You recall, I think, that she is listed as "Emeritus."

Mr. Matthews: That is correct.

Chancellor Hutchins: Dr. Slye retired many years ago after confining her attention for a considerable number of years exclusively to mice. [Laughter.]

Mr. Matthews: Dr. Maude Slye was an Associate Professor Emeritus—this is the latest obtainable directory.

Chancellor Hutchins: "Emeritus" means retired.

Mr. Matthews: She is retired on pension?

Chancellor Hutchins: Oh, yes.

[137] U. of C. transcript, pp. 56–58.

Mr. Matthews: And has at least the prestige of the University of Chicago to some degree associated with her name, inasmuch as she is carried in the directory of the University?

Chancellor Hutchins: I don't see how we can deny the fact that she has been all her life a member of the faculty of the University. She was one of the most distinguished specialists in cancer we have seen in our time.

. . . . .

Mr. Matthews: Is it the policy of the University to ignore such affiliations on the part of the members of the faculty? . . .

. . . . .

Chancellor Hutchins: As I indicated, Dr. Slye's associations were confined on our campus to mice. She could not, I think, have done any particular harm to any of our students even if she had been so minded. To answer your direct question, however, I am not aware that Dr. Slye has ever joined any club that advocated the overthrow of the government by violence.

Mr. Matthews: May I ask if in your educational theory there is not such a thing as indoctrination by example?

Chancellor Hutchins: Of mice? [Laughter.] [138]

The status of a professor emeritus proved a baffling one to Mr. Matthews. Said Mr. Matthews: "Suppose we enter into some more such situations and assume one of your professors Emeritus were convicted as a dope peddler. Would you carry him?"

Chancellor Hutchins: How could we deny him if he were a member?

Mr. Matthews: Would you carry him in your directory if he were convicted as a dope peddler?

Chancellor Hutchins: He is still a professor emeritus. I don't want to lie and say I would take his name out of the book and thus tell a falsehood. What "emeritus" means is that this man has been a professor at the University of Chicago. Period. It is impossible, no matter what his future acts may be, to say that that isn't so if he has ever been a professor.

If I am asked then whether a man who committed a felony has been a professor at the University of Chicago and he has, I have to say that he has.

[138] U. of C. transcript, pp. 52–54.

Mr. Matthews: I am getting at the facts.

Chancellor Hutchins: You have some notion that having been a professor that you can stop being a professor Emeritus. You cannot. There isn't any way you can.

Mr. Matthews: I want to establish one way or another this simple fact: does the University lend its prestige to these individuals, regardless of their conduct?

Chancellor Hutchins: If you have worked at the University of Chicago until you were sixty-five, there is no way in which the University can deprive you of the prestige of having been there.

Mr. Matthews: Are all professors emeritus listed in the directory?

Chancellor Hutchins: All professors emeritus are listed until they die.

Mr. Matthews: But are they all recipients of the pension?

Chancellor Hutchins: There are two pension plans at the University. Would you care to have me explain them?

Mr. Matthews: No.

Chancellor Hutchins: Every member of the staff who works sufficiently long and contributes to the retirement plans or who by contract is entitled to be on a pension plan gets the benefits of his contributions, and there is no way in which the University can deprive him of those benefits which he has legally earned.

.   .   .   .   .

Mr. Matthews: So that regardless of how many of these professors emeritus become members of the Communist Party, assuming some do, there is nothing the University could do about it, is that right?

Chancellor Hutchins: It would be like saying if an Ex-President of the United States became a member of the Communist Party you could prevent him from having been an Ex-President of the United States.[139]

Nor were Mr. Matthews' sallies into constitutional law and the foreign policy of the United States particularly rewarding from his standpoint. Said Mr. Matthews: "You are somewhat of a student, I would take it, of world affairs. You speak frequently on the matter."

[139] U. of C. transcript, pp. 65–68.

Chancellor Hutchins: I am a student of those subjects on which I speak.

Mr. Matthews: You must have some definite opinions on the nature of the Communist Party and its potential menace in the United States and throughout the world?

Chancellor Hutchins: Oh, I have some general views, such as I suppose every citizen would have.

Mr. Matthews: They are not flattering to the Communist Party, I take it. I assume that is the case?

Chancellor Hutchins: No.

Mr. Matthews: Do you consider that the Communist Party in the United States comes within the scope of Justice Holmes' "clear and present danger" decision?

Chancellor Hutchins: I wouldn't think so. . . .

. . . . .

Mr. Matthews: I was going to ask if it is not clear that the expenditure of 15 billion dollars on our military establishment reflects the government's belief, supported by the overwhelming majority of the American people that Soviet Russia is a clear and present danger to this country?

Chancellor Hutchins: Well, I do not believe that Mr. Justice Holmes was speaking of foreign countries, but of citizens of the United States. It is a very important constitutional doctrine.

. . . . .

Mr. Matthews: Now, in 1949 as in 1948, 1947 and 1946, the government of the United States and the people of the United States in supporting their government believed that Communism in the world at large is a clear and present danger for which there is the need to sacrifice fifteen billions of dollars.

Chancellor Hutchins: If you wouldn't mind omitting "clear and present danger"—it seems to me you are taking Mr. Justice Holmes' words, having one context, and putting them in another—I think I can answer the questions more readily.

Mr. Matthews: I shall be glad to delete it.

Chancellor Hutchins: If you mean do I think that the government of the United States and a good many people of the United States believe that Russia is a danger, the answer is "yes."

Mr. Matthews: An abnormal danger, isn't that also clear?

Chancellor Hutchins: $15,000,000,000 is an abnormal amount of money.[140]

Undaunted, Mr. Matthews insisted on returning to this line of questioning. Though of doubtful relevancy, Matthews wished to know whether Hutchins believed the Communist Party was a conspiratorial fifth column or a political party. When Hutchins confessed that Matthews probably had better information than he, Matthews continued, "Thorez, in France, and Togliatti in Italy, as you recall, made it quite clear that in the event of an invasion of their countries by the Red Army they would call upon the peoples of France and Italy to support the Red Army."

Chancellor Hutchins: Yes.

Mr. Matthews: A few days later the two leaders of the Communist Party in the United States, Eugene Dennis and William Z. Foster . . . issued a statement which seemed to have the same purport. You are acquainted with that statement?

Chancellor Hutchins: I have heard that.

Mr. Matthews: Do you recall the manner in which President Truman characterized Communist Party members when he asked about it?

Chancellor Hutchins: I do.

Mr. Matthews: His statement was that they are all traitors.

Chancellor Hutchins: I recall his statement.

Mr. Matthews: Do you concur with the President?

Chancellor Hutchins: Am I required to?

Mr. Matthews: No, not at all, but I think it would be a matter of great interest to the people of the United States to know your views on that subject.

Chancellor Hutchins: Doubtless, Mr. Truman's information is superior to mine. Doubtless your information is superior to mine. If it is true that all members of the Communist Party are traitors, I should suppose that they should be proceeded against as such, and that we should not go through miscellaneous media and make charges that have not been established by due process.

Mr. Matthews: Do you favor the enactment of legislation to make the Communist Party illegal?

Chancellor Hutchins: No.

[140] U. of C. transcript, pp. 76–79; Transcript, pp. 38–39.

Mr. Matthews: Then you wouldn't proceed against them either now or ever?

Chancellor Hutchins: Oh, I beg your pardon. You completely have misunderstood me. If an individual is a traitor, there are laws that go back—you will remember the case of Aaron Burr —in common law to take care of these individuals.

I share the views of the late, or I beg your pardon, recent candidate of the Republican Party for the Presidency in regard to legislation directed against the Communist Party as a party. Governor Dewey, as I recall, took violent issue in the State of Oregon with the proposition to enact such legislation.

The newspapers in Chicago have never been called subversive in the sense of being Communistic, but they have also opposed such legislation. Therefore, it doesn't seem to me to say one is opposed to legislation to outlaw the Communist Party suggests either that we are without a remedy against Communists or that one is sympathetic toward the Party.

Mr. Matthews: There is certainly no inference in my question that you were in the slightest.

Chancellor Hutchins: I understand.

. . . . . .

Mr. Matthews: I think we probably will agree that the President of the United States was using the word "traitor" not in a technical or legal sense but in a moral sense.

. . . . . .

Chancellor Hutchins: You will forgive me for saying that there is some question whether we should mold our vocabulary on the President's. [Laughter.] [141]

It was not a particularly fruitful day for Mr. Matthews.[142]

[141] U. of C. transcript, pp. 100–103. Chancellor Hutchins' remark was made shortly after President Truman's widely publicized statement that a certain Washington columnist was a S.O.B.

[142] As the *Chicago Daily News* observed editorially April 25, 1949: "Chancellor Robert M. Hutchins of the University of Chicago has achieved in reality one of the pleasantest day-dreams by which lesser men entertain themselves: he made a monkey of the cross-examiner. . . . Dr. Hutchins' deft disposal of J. B. Matthews, the Committee investigator and no slouch himself at dialectics, will, we predict, come to rank high in the literature of squelching."

The interrogation of witnesses following Chancellor Hutchins was anti-climactic. The student chairman of the Communist Club at the university was called to the stand, and, after answering questions concerning the membership of the Communist Club he was asked whether he was a member of the Communist Party, whether he would fight for the United States in the event of a war with Russia, and whether the Communist Party was an illegal organization. To all of Dr. Matthews' questions the student refused to answer on the ground that his answers might tend to incriminate him or were an inquiry into his political beliefs, protected by the constitution. Breaking with the precedents of other un-American activities committees, Senator Libonati moved that the student be instructed that he need not answer the question. The motion carried, and the student was excused.[143]

Dr. Edward J. Sparling, president of Roosevelt College, the next witness called, traced the phenomenal growth of Roosevelt College from an enrollment of 1,200 in the fall of 1945 to its present enrollment of over 6,000 students. Dr. Sparling testified that there were no Communists on the faculty to his knowledge and that the Communists had opposed the development of Roosevelt College since its inception. He numbered the membership of the Communist Club at Roosevelt College at about ten students and stated that the American Youth for Democracy had dissolved at that school.

Mr. Matthews' questions of Dr. Sparling paralleled the earlier examination of Chancellor Hutchins. Matthews interrogated Dr. Sparling about the affiliations of a few of the Roosevelt College faculty with alleged Communist-front organizations. Matthews laid particular emphasis upon the alleged affiliations of Dr. Thomas Mann and Dr. Albert Einstein, members of the advisory board of Roosevelt College. In response to Matthews' suggestion that Einstein and Mann should be disqualified from membership on the board, Dr. Sparling stated that Roosevelt College was proud to have them as members of the board, and that he, too, disapproved of the doctrine of guilt by association.

Dr. John B. Thompson, dean of the Rockefeller Memorial Chapel and associate professor of Christianity of the Divinity

[143] U. of C. transcript, pp. 126–135.

School in the University of Chicago, was next called. Dr. Thompson had made a number of public speeches denouncing the Broyles bills and the activities of the commission. Mr. Matthews' interrogation of Dean Thompson was devoted almost entirely to matters which would seem irrelevant to a determination of whether subversive activities existed at the university. Mr. Matthews developed that Dean Thompson had been active, prior to his appointment to the faculty of the university, in the Southern Conference for Human Welfare and in the American Peace Mobilization. Matthews never indicated why these matters were germane to the inquiry, save for the inference that Dean Thompson's past conduct was tainted. Dean Thompson had had no connection with either organization after joining the university's faculty.

Dean Thompson closed his testimony with a note of censure. He said:

> To some of us whose social action stems primarily from our religious conviction, and from our belief in democracy, it is extremely discouraging and alarming to see committees or legislators, or newspapers, glibly lump into one category all the members of a group or an organization which is standing for some important social cause simply because it is known or suspected that some Communists are members of the same organization or cause.
>
> I have never been a Communist, nor have I ever had any inclination to be one, but I should hate very much as a Churchman to have any less concern for justice than any Communist. I should hate to think that my energies or my convictions are any less than that of a Communist . . . and the other word is simply this: that those of us who cherish the great convictions of Jefferson and Lincoln, the tradition of democracy that has grown up in this country, that is due primarily to the hunger of people for freedom so that they can express human dignity, it seems we should have enough faith in democracy, to use democratic methods in attacking these problems. The problem of civil liberties does not exist except in relation to minorities with whom we disagree. . . .
>
> You don't believe in liberty unless you believe in it for the person you disagree with. The thing that alarms me is our present debate over matters of grave policy popularly known as the

Broyles Bills, namely that when we resort to this kind of legislation we betray the fact that we don't really trust ourselves.

A great many of us are not particularly alarmed about investigations like this this afternoon. I mean this isn't a personal thing. It has happened before and it will happen again . . . but we are alarmed about the spirit that is spreading over America, a spirit of intolerance for social change, a spirit that intimidates people who want to use the ordinary democratic processes of social change and who themselves want to work for a greater measure of justice, a greater extension of democratic rights than even this country with its great heritage has ever known.[144]

Having heard the accused, the commission, in an inverted procedure, then heard the accusers. As a surprise witness,[145] Mr. Matthews called to the stand Representative G. William Horsley (Republican–Springfield), sponsor in the house of the resolution authorizing the investigation. Representative Horsley introduced a large number of documents which he said were furnished by an unidentified employee of the University. These documents consisted of a list of student organizations from which Horsley selected for mention the Communist Club, the Socialist Club, the American Veterans Committee, and the Young Progressives of America; notices from bulletin boards of the University advertising meetings of a selected group of student organizations such as the Communist Club, the Socialist Club, the AVC, Young Progressives of America, the Student Forum, and the campus Committee against Conscription.[146]

Representative Horsley also introduced copies of magazines and

[144] U. of C. transcript, pp. 265–267.

[145] The university's understanding that it would be given reasonable notice, not less than a week, of all witnesses to be called, was repudiated by Chairman Broyles, who asserted he had not made such a commitment. See discussion, U. of C. transcript, pp. 272–279.

[146] The irrelevancy of one item appealed even to Representative Horsley's sense of humor. Said Representative Horsley: "The next exhibit is that of the bulletin posted on the board under date of March 3, 1949, with the approval of the University, advertising a 'Beer Party,' to be held March 5th, by the student captains." Mr. Tenney, attorney for the university, asked, "Do you think that is subversive?" "It depends on how much beer they have," Horsley replied (U. of C. transcript, p. 291).

pamphlets sold by the Communist Club and the Politics Club at their respective meetings.

When Representative Horsley had completed his documentary case, Representative Jenkins asked the following pertinent question: "Representative Horsley, did you find anything in these documents that advocated the overthrow of the government by force? . . ." Mr. Horsley replied, "No, I didn't find anything directly in that regard. . . ." [147]

The next surprise witness was Howard Rushmore, who identified himself as a reporter for the *New York Journal-American* and a writer of magazine articles dealing with communism. Giving his qualifications as an expert on communism, Mr. Rushmore stated that he had testified for the government in the Harry Bridges deportation case, had testified before the House Committee on Un-American Activities, in connection with the Hollywood writers' hearings, had testified before the Washington State legislative committee on the subject of Communist infiltration of education, had been the first to expose the Canadian atomic bomb spy ring and the alleged Hiss-Chambers espionage ring, and had been officially listed, decorated, or commended by the Knights of Columbus, the American Jewish League against Communism, the American Legion, the Exchange Club, and the Catholic War Veterans. Other qualifications omitted by Mr. Rushmore until brought out upon later examination were membership in the Communist Party for three years prior to 1939 and membership on the staff of the *Daily Worker* during the same period.[148] In what appeared a well-rehearsed interrogation, Dr. Matthews requested Rushmore to produce the "Communist Front records" of the University of Chicago faculty. Rushmore mentioned the alleged "front" affiliations of approximately twenty of the faculty but singled out eight for particular attention.[149] Some of the affiliations charged occurred as early as 1934; Rushmore made no attempt to

[147] U. of C. transcript, p. 308.   [148] U. of C. transcript, p. 532.

[149] They were Wayne McMillen, professor of social service administration; Harold C. Urey, professor of chemistry; Robert J. Havighurst, professor of education; Ernest W. Burgess, professor of sociology; Malcolm P. Sharp, professor of law; Rexford G. Tugwell, professor of politi-

distinguish past from current affiliations, a matter which was later to cause controversy. He followed the well-established procedure for establishing Communist front affiliations, relying on old letterheads of organizations and newspaper accounts of "front" meetings. Rushmore failed, however, to give the commission any evidence bearing on the possibly relevant consideration of whether the particular professors had evidenced in their writings, speeches, or teaching a sympathy for communism. Interlarded with his testimony of Communist front affiliations, Rushmore gave the commission the benefit of his knowledge of the Alger Hiss case, the Judith Coplon case, the Elizabeth Bentley episode, and the Canadian atomic spy ring.

Mr. Rushmore also expressed his views concerning restrictions needed for the teaching profession. In his opinion teachers who failed to discern the Communist front nature of organizations to which they might belong should be prohibited by law from teaching.[150] Applying his generalization to a specific case, Rushmore stated that Professor Harold C. Urey, who, even Mr. Rushmore admitted, was one of the five scientists that had contributed most to the development of the atomic bomb, should be barred from working on atomic energy at the University of Chicago, "in view of his long and continuous support of the Communist front organizations. . . ."[151]

With the close of Mr. Rushmore's testimony, the hearings ended with the right reserved to the University of Chicago to offer rebuttal evidence.

Reaction from the University of Chicago administration was not long in forthcoming. Lynn Williams, a vice-president of the university, was quoted as saying that the testimony against Professor Urey was a "deliberate smear" and that the university would reply to the charges.[152]

---

cal science; Maude Slye, associate professor emeritus of pathology; and James Luther Adams, professor of religious ethics.

[150] U. of C. transcript, p. 344; *Proceedings*, pp. 143–144.

[151] U. of C. transcript, p. 367; *Proceedings*, p. 151.

[152] *New York Journal American*, April 25.

Five days after the hearings closed Laird Bell, chairman of the board of trustees of the university, transmitted to the Broyles commission affidavits of the seven [153] active professors whom Mr. Rushmore had singled out in his testimony. In an accompanying letter Mr. Bell directed a stinging attack upon Rushmore's testimony, stating:

> Despite a mass of hearsay and innuendo, when we come down to cases only one instance out of the 50 involves current membership in an organization listed by the Attorney General.

> . . . . .

> We understand that witness Rushmore insisted that his identity and the nature of his testimony be kept secret until his last minute appearance. The conclusion is inescapable that Rushmore was willing to make irresponsible charges but not to confront those whom he accused.[154]

In a statistical breakdown of Rushmore's testimony it was pointed out that of the thirty-eight organizations termed Communist fronts by Rushmore, only eleven of these were listed by the attorney general as Communist, or "suspected" in the language of the letter. Of the fifty memberships or affiliations attributed by Rushmore to the seven faculty members in Communist fronts the letter pointed out that only one was current (January 1, to April, 1949) in an organization listed by the attorney general; seventeen were terminated either before the war, during the war, or at the war's end; for twenty-one of the alleged affiliations the professors had no present recollection of ever belonging or had never heard of the organization; and the remainder—eleven affiliations—were with organizations not listed by the attorney general.[155]

Mr. Bell's letter and the affidavits of the seven professors having been made public,[156] the Broyles commission concluded that matters could not be left in this posture. On May 9 the commission

---

[153] No affidavit was secured from Professor Slye, who had been retired for five years.

[154] U. of C. transcript, p. 384.

[155] U. of C. transcript, pp. 385–386.

[156] *Chicago Sun-Times,* April 28, 1949; *Chicago Daily News,* April 29, 1949.

114

voted to reopen the investigation and to subpoena the professors to testify concerning discrepancies between their affidavits and the Rushmore testimony.[157]

When public hearings were resumed May 19, 1949, it soon became apparent that vindication of Mr. Rushmore was the central issue. Dr. Matthews was quick to develop a number of flaws in the analysis prepared by the university of Rushmore's testimony. Whereas the university had submitted affidavits from seven of the eight professors "specifically named in the testimony of Howard Rushmore," it was, of course, true that Rushmore had mentioned the names of about twelve others in connection with descriptions of particular organizations which Rushmore had termed subversive.[158] Rushmore had not, however, attempted to give the full list of affiliations with alleged Communist front organizations for these other twelve in contrast with the eight he had singled out for intensive treatment. Matthews seized on this discrepancy.[159] In the haste of preparing an early reply to Rushmore's accusations, the university committed another rather technical error. One of the professors, James Luther Adams, who at the time was in the East, had been reached by telephone and the proposed affidavit read to him. He had indicated its accuracy and requested that it be sent to him for execution. In the meantime the affidavit, unsigned, was released to the press together with the executed affidavits of the other professors. When the unsigned affidavit reached Professor Adams for execution, he discovered he had misunderstood one of the statements made to him over the telephone and had to change his answer. He also changed one other statement for the sake of greater accuracy. These discrepancies also furnished Dr. Matthews with openings for adverse criticism.

[157] *Chicago Sun-Times,* May 10, 1949; *Chicago Daily News,* May 10, 1949; *Chicago Daily Tribune,* May 10, 1949, p. 4.

[158] Thus, Rushmore had mentioned a circular letter announcing a meeting in 1937 of the American League for Peace and Democracy, which eleven members of the faculty had signed; he had charged that eight of the faculty had acted as sponsors of the meeting at the Waldorf-Astoria in March, 1949, of the National Council of the Arts, Sciences and Professions.

[159] U. of C. transcript, pp. 387–388; *Proceedings,* p. 176.

In the interrogation of the professors who had executed affi-davits, Dr. Matthews was able in a few instances to refresh the recollections of some of the professors concerning old affiliations which in their affidavits they had either denied or indicated no recollection of the organization. On the other hand several pro-fessors were able to establish instances in which organizations had listed their names wholly without authorization.[160]

Howard Rushmore was called in rebuttal to demonstrate that he had relied on documentation for his charges—clippings from the *Daily Worker,* old letterheads of organizations, petitions, and advertisements of meetings. As has been indicated, in some in-stances these documents were inaccurate. One source of confusion arising from Rushmore's previous testimony was his failure in a number of instances to specify whether the accused professor had been a member of the organization or had attended or perhaps addressed a particular meeting. If a professor, believing himself charged with membership, flatly denied it he might be faced with a document indicating he had addressed or endorsed a particular meeting.[161]

Although it did not appear to this observer that Dr. Matthews and Mr. Rushmore proved anything approaching bad faith on the part of the administration or professors of the university, the re-duction to sworn affidavits of professors' recollections covering a period of fifteen years appeared somewhat rash.

However muddied were the conclusions derivable from the comparison of Rushmore's testimony and the affidavits of the seven professors, no such opacity attended the oral testimony of the five professors who took the stand.

Professor Havighurst, employing an aggressive tactic followed by others of the group, turned the tables on the commission by asking at the outset of his testimony: "I should like to know what the general nature of the charges are against me, Mr. Chairman. . . . May I ask if anybody has raised any suspicion of there being any subversive tendency as to my teaching at the University of Chicago?"

[160] U. of C. transcript, pp. 460–461, 551–552.
[161] U. of C. transcript, pp. 539–542.

116

To which the chairman, Senator Broyles, replied: "That question has not been raised." [162]

Professor Sharp phrased the issue a bit more acutely at the outset of his testimony by asking: "Am I charged with subversive teachings in these proceedings?"

The chairman replied, "No, you are not, Professor Sharp."

> *Professor Sharp:* Is it felt that my testimony will throw some light on subversive organizations in Chicago, *or is it the question of Mr. Rushmore's veracity only?*
>
> *The Chairman:* I think you might be of some help to the Commission and also to the University, Mr. Sharp. Your testimony might be worth while.[163] [Emphasis supplied.]

Having firmly established that there were no charges of subversive teaching on their part, the professors fired a few direct shots at the innuendoes of Rushmore's testimony. Said Professor Sharp: "I should like to say that in my judgment the testimony of the sort given by Mr. Rushmore is systematically misleading. I have broadcasted, I think I counted, sixteen times since the summer of 1945, on the University of Chicago Round Table. Those broadcasts can be obtained for 10 cents apiece. I stated publicly my position on most of the issues involved here. I think if Mr. Rushmore had been a careful man—I think indeed if he had been an honest man, he would have paid some attention to those public statements. He might even have read some of my articles before insinuatingly charging, as he has in other hearings, by innuendo that I hold a position which I don't hold at all."

> *Mr. Matthews:* Is that the end of your statement?
>
> *Mr. Sharp:* I should like to find stronger words to express my distaste for Mr. Rushmore's type of testimony. One says a lawyer has gone to prison, then it turns out he has gone to prison to consult a client. It is a very different story. The half truth is a very well known way of misleading.[164]

---

[162] U. of C. transcript, p. 493; Transcript, p. 230.

[163] U. of C. transcript, p. 535; *Proceedings*, p. 249. Similarly, Senator Broyles informed Dr. Urey, in response to the latter's direct question, that there was no charge of subversion against him (*Proceedings*, p. 267).

[164] *Proceedings*, p. 258; U. of C. transcript, pp. 554–555.

Dr. Matthews' questioning of the renowned atomic scientist, Dr. Urey, brought this comment on Rushmore's testimony:

Mr. Matthews: I would like to ask you if you seriously, or in any respect, challenge the accuracy of the testimony of Mr. Rushmore in your affidavit of April 28th, 1949?

Mr. Urey: You see, the events recorded here happened about ten years ago, and in the last ten years, I have had one five-year job that was the hardest job I have ever had in my life. My gray hair is largely due to it. There are many things since 1940 that I no longer recall clearly. I kept no records of political activities before the war. I do not impugn the testimony of Mr. Rushmore, except in one detail. It is a partial story, and the partiality makes it wholly false.

Mr. Matthews: But on explicit details, with respect to your affiliations with these organizations, you do not challenge the accuracy of the testimony?

Mr. Urey: As stated in my statement, there are many times when my memory does not recall to mind any of these organizations, but it would also be impossible for me to deny that I had some connection. I was in favor of the loyalists in Spain. I am wholly unreconstructed on the point. I think Franco is a "stinker" and I am wholly against him.

.   .   .   .   .

This record is incomplete. I was also a member of other organizations. I was a member of the Committee to Defend America by Aiding the Allies. You will recall that it met before Russia was attacked by Germany. This was not the Communist Party line. I cannot help it if the communists fellow traveled with me on the Spanish situation. I didn't fellow-travel with them. It was the reverse. Since then, they have seen fit not to fellow-travel with me.[165]

Nor did the professors leave the commission in doubt as to their personal views on communism. The first of the professors to testify, Professor Ernest W. Burgess, chairman of the Department of Sociology, informed the commission in unmistakable terms:

I have never been and I am not now a communist. I have never been and am not now in sympathy with Communism. In all the thirty-three years that I have taught at the University of

[165] *Proceedings,* pp. 267–268; U. of C. transcript, pp. 575–578.

Chicago, I have never heard of a single member of the faculty who was accused or even suspected of being a communist.

Communism as exemplified at present in the Soviet Union, combines three principles. I am opposed to all three. First, Communism advocates state socialism. Although socialism has been tried for thirty years in the Soviet Union its results are far inferior both as to productivity and especially in quality of goods to those of our American economic system. Second, Communism in the Soviet Union has maintained a political dictatorship with one party government and final power in the hands of the Politbureau. Third, the Communist Party has abolished freedom of speech and freedom of teaching in every country where it has taken over power.

．　．　．　．　．

As a sociologist I am interested in studying two questions about communists. The first is, under what conditions a person becomes a communist. The second is, under what conditions a communist becomes an anti-communist. I suspect that a college education does not make communists but instead turns those already communists into anti-communists. Actually, in my opinion, the best way to convert a person from Communism is to have him make a trip to the Soviet Union and let him actually see for himself how Communism works.

In conclusion, I would like also to state that other sociologists and I are on the blacklist in the Soviet Union.[166]

Professor Urey was even more vitriolic in his denunciation of communism. He stated:

I think the Communist Party is a conspiratorial party. I believe that it reports directly to Moscow, and I believe its objective is to bring revolution the world over in favor of Communism, by fair means or foul—by foul mostly. I thoroughly abhor the organization, and I think it has no part in American life. However, I believe in law as it is administered in the United States. The trial being conducted in New York should give us all information instead of prejudices and beliefs. Perhaps that statement is strong enough on the communist situation so that no questions on my attitude are necessary. I hope so.[167]

[166] *Proceedings,* pp. 227–228; U. of C. transcript, pp. 486–488.
[167] *Proceedings,* p. 268.

Those professors who were questioned with respect to the highly controversial issue whether Communists should be allowed to teach in educational institutions displayed in their replies a wide divergence of views for men who purportedly followed too closely the Communist Party line. Professor Burgess stated his position as follows: "I would not be opposed to a university discharging a member of the Communist Party from its faculty because as a member of the Party he does not have freedom of speech but, I wouldn't necessarily say that a university should do it. I say it has the right—the Board of Trustees and the President, have a right to do it, . . . I would trust the President and the University trustees of the University of Chicago in exercising good judgment on this question. I have the greatest confidence in their integrity and in their support of the principle of freedom of speech and teaching."

Mr. Matthews: Have you made any special note of the case of the three professors who were discharged from the faculty of the University of Washington in Seattle?

. . . . .

Mr. Burgess: Well, I would state that the President and the Board of Trustees, if they found they were Party members, and I think they did, were justified in doing it. That is my personal conviction.[168]

Professor Havighurst, who followed Professor Burgess to the stand, was asked a similar question by Dr. Matthews.

Mr. Matthews: You are not willing to state categorically, as Professor Burgess did, that members of the Communist Party are subject to thought control and, therefore, unfit to be instructors or professors in our educational institutions?

Mr. Havighurst: I think that is the question: How much are they subject to thought control?—I don't believe in thought control, and I don't believe a clear case was made that these men at the University of Washington were subject to thought control. One of them was professor of English, as I remember it, and the other was a professor of philosophy, the other psychology. None of them were teaching economics, none of them teaching

[168] *Proceedings,* p. 227.

government—I have considerable doubt as to whether or not there was sufficient thought control to make these teachers subversive.

Representative Jenkins: Professor Havighurst, from the account in the newspapers, it appears to have come out in the New York trial that in some of these communists' schools they taught the doctrine of overthrowing the government by force. I believe I am correct in saying that the Thomas Jefferson School in New York is one of them and the Abraham Lincoln School in Chicago. My question is: Do you think that those schools have a right to teach that doctrine in our country—to overthrow the government by force?

Mr. Havighurst: If I were satisfied that these schools were teaching the doctrine of overthrow of the government by force, I would be opposed to them. I would say they do not have the right.

. . . . . .

Representative Jenkins: Do you think they have the right to organize these communist schools over the country for the express purpose of indoctrinating Americans with Communism or with the philosophy of Communism?

Mr. Havighurst: Senator, it seems to me that if we deny one group the right to teach people who come freely to it, its own views, I don't know where we are going to draw the line. I feel that if we really believe in freedom to learn, in freedom to speak we have to allow a lot of unpopular things to be thought and to be said.

Representative Jenkins: Isn't it true that the professor, no matter what the subject he is teaching—is an ideal of the student if he admires him? If he hates him, of course, it is the opposite. If he happens to admire that teacher and he has an engaging personality then—even in the teaching of Philosophy—and Philosophy particularly, wouldn't he have the opportunity to indoctrinate the students in that class with his philosophy of Communism?

Mr. Havighurst: If it were proven that a teacher was indoctrinating his students with Communism in a public university, I suspect that he should not be allowed to continue to do it.

Representative Jenkins: Well, if not in the classroom, when he meets him casually or socially on the campus he should inevitably seek to indoctrinate him with Communism, do you think that would be a cause for dismissal?

Mr. Havighurst: If you think I have arrived at my position without a lot of difficulty I assure you it is not true. It cost me a lot to take this position in favor of freedom of speech. I know something about the way education is conducted in Germany. I have studied it. I have been over there twice in the last eighteen months looking at the picture and I know that after Hitler took over the first thing that happened or one of the first things was that communist teaching was eliminated, very shortly after that democratic teachers were eliminated and very shortly after that a number of church leaders, both Lutheran and Catholic, were intimidated and prevented from speaking freely and shortly after that religious teaching became subject to a great deal of control by the State.

I feel if you start limiting freedom at one point it is hard to stop and so I argue that in our society, which can afford to take a lot of chances, I think we have got to allow people to do some awfully unpopular things in order to protect this policy of freedom. But it is an awfully difficult thing to think through and I wouldn't blame anybody else for disagreeing with me on this point.

Representative Jenkins: Would you adopt the principle that you have to wait until you reach the line where they are teaching absolutely the overthrow of the government before preventing or prohibiting it?

Mr. Havighurst: I think the place to draw the line depends on a great many different things. At the present time, I think the overthrow of the government would be a good place to draw the line, as far as teaching in a university is concerned. I make a distinction here between teaching in high school and universities. I think we should be much more free to teach controversial subjects at the university level where our students are much more mature and much more able to be critical of the professors, etc.[169]

The mild-mannered Professor Burgess, whose views on communism and the treatment to be accorded Communist teachers had not ruffled the feathers of the Broyles commission, proved a tartar on the issue of freedom of association and the inferences to

[169] *Proceedings*, pp. 240–242; U. of C. transcript, pp. 514–519.

be drawn therefrom. Taxed with sponsorship of the National Council of American-Soviet Friendship [170] by Dr. Matthews, Professor Burgess admitted the charge and referred to the endorsement of the organization by President Franklin D. Roosevelt in November, 1944, and by General Dwight D. Eisenhower in November, 1945. Referring to the postwar activity of the organization, Professor Burgess stated:

Now when the war ended, it seemed to me that the encouragement of American-Soviet Friendship was an important objective, perhaps an even more important objective for the success of the United Nations and for achieving peace in the world, than it was before. The Council did not change its activities. It continued the same activities which President Roosevelt and General Eisenhower so eloquently and whole-heartedly approved, and I further believe that the Attorney General made a mistake when he listed this organization as subversive, and I hold also, as an American citizen, I have a free right to judge what evidence there is. The Attorney General gave the National Council no hearing before it listed its name—gave no hearing after it listed its name. I don't think the American people, who, following the American way of life, establish free associations, should be governed by what a governmental official may say in regard to the organization to which they are related. Now, I was a sponsor of this National Council and of the Chicago Council, which meant that I agreed with the objectives, but didn't mean that I agreed with all the activities of the National Council of American-Soviet Friendship.

When Dr. Matthews, despite Professor Burgess' admission of sponsorship, offered documentary proof, he evoked a rather pat defense to the doctrine of guilt by association. Said Professor Burgess: "I see my name is here with many prominent persons throughout the country. Three United States Senators—who apparently do not agree with the Attorney General that this organization is subversive."

[170] This was the only current membership in an organization listed by the attorney general as subversive which any of the seven professors acknowledged.

Mr. Matthews: Are you implying that you are going to establish innocence by association?

Mr. Burgess: Well, it seems to me that if you imply guilt by association you should also be able to prove innocence by association.

Mr. Matthews: You then accept guilt by association?

Mr. Burgess: I am not saying that. I don't subscribe to either one but if one is brought forward, then the other should also be brought forward.[171]

In a similar vein, Professor Urey protested the uncritical use of the attorney general's blacklist of organizations when Dr. Matthews pointed out that the American Committee for Protecting the Foreign-Born to which Professor Urey had belonged in 1940 had been designated a Communist front organization by the attorney general. Professor Urey replied: "Of course, I think the designation of organizations by the Attorney General as subversive is one of the most dangerous things in our present American life. I do not accept his word as final and as a citizen I reserve the right to hold my own opinion. I think it is extremely dangerous when the Executive Department of the United States can think for us and make an ultimate, final decision as to what is good and what is bad. I still believe that the citizens of the United States are really the boss of this country and that the president and his whole office is only our servant and he takes orders from us, not the other way around."

Mr. Matthews: The question that I wish to ask you is whether or not you know that the Attorney General's listings are based upon exhaustive investigation by the Federal Bureau of Investigation?

Mr. Urey: Oh, I suppose they are.

Mr. Matthews: Do you think it is not a matter of great public concern that communists, whom you have castigated, should not be employed in the federal government?

Mr. Urey: I don't want them employed in any responsible position anywhere.

Mr. Matthews: Do you have any better program for weeding

[171] *Proceedings,* pp. 219–220.

124

them out of the federal government than the President's loyalty program?

Mr. Urey: Oh, I haven't criticized trying to weed them out. I object to organizations being specified as subversive by the Attorney General and then that statement being accepted as though it were the Bible by everybody in deciding whether it is right or wrong to belong to the organization. I don't object to the government weeding out Communists.[172]

Professor Urey, the last university witness, in closing his testimony, did not bother to defend himself, but, rather, aimed a barb directly at the commission, stating:

I am a newcomer to the University of Chicago. I came there after the war, in 1945. The fame of that institution and what it stands for has been contributed to only in a very slight degree by my efforts. It is one of the great universities of the whole world. It is so regarded the world over. In my years there I have intimately associated with the members of the staff of that organization and it is strictly loyal and American. It is a great university and *deserves better from the people of Illinois than this investigation.* Thank you.[173] [Emphasis supplied.]

The following day, May 20, 1949, the Broyles commission, meeting in executive session, agreed that the report to the general assembly covering the investigation of the University of Chicago and Roosevelt College should consist merely of the transcript of the testimony and that "no comment would be necessary, inasmuch as the testimony speaks for itself." [174]

But the matter was not to end so quietly and ambiguously. Representative Jenkins, who had been an outspoken critic of Dr. Matthews' methods of interrogation, stated to the press that the failure of the commission to submit specific recommendations "gives the two schools a clean bill of health." [175] Shortly thereafter, a resolution exonerating the University of Chicago and Roosevelt

[172] *Proceedings,* pp. 269–270; U. of C. transcript, pp. 579–581.
[173] U. of C. transcript, pp. 581–582; *Proceedings,* p. 270.
[174] *Proceedings,* pp. 272–273.
[175] *Chicago Sun-Times,* May 21, 1949; *New York Herald Tribune,* May 22, 1949.

College of implications of Communist influence was introduced in the house by Representative Charles M. Skyles (Democrat–Chicago). The proposed resolution stated in part that the Broyles commission had "discovered no subversive influences" and that "each of these institutions is exonerated of any stigma arising from the investigation." [176] The measure was referred to the house Executive Committee. Meanwhile, two Chicago newspapers protested the failure of the Broyles commission to issue specific findings. Both newspapers took the position that if the Broyles commission had found no subversive activities on the campuses of the two schools it should so state; that if it failed to do so then the legislature should adopt the Skyles resolution.[177]

Evidencing sensitiveness to such criticism Senator Broyles shortly thereafter issued a "statement," [178] concurred in by two other members of the Broyles commission, setting forth his findings and recommendations. The "statement" opens on a note of commendation for the "splendid work of the Commission," coupled with injured surprise at the opposition to the commission stemming from certain quarters:

> In a sense, the storm of opposition to the activities of the Commission is a tribute to its achievement in the field of investiga-

[176] *Chicago Sun-Times,* May 27, 1949.

[177] *Chicago Sun-Times,* May 30, 1949; *Chicago Daily News,* May 31, 1949; and see Milburn P. Akers, *Chicago Sun-Times,* May 22, May 27, 1949.

[178] In a preliminary paragraph of the statement it is asserted, "We have been urged by the press and many persons to give a brief statement in an analysis of the findings of The Seditious Activities Investigation Commission in its inquiry into whether there are seditious and subversive activities at the University of Chicago and Roosevelt College in Chicago. It was the opinion of the Commission that we should let the record of the testimony speak for itself, but since another member has given out a statement, I feel that I, as chairman, and joined by other members of the Commission, should issue a brief statement" (Press release, "Statement of the Chairman and members of the Seditious Activities Investigating Committee reporting briefly, their findings at the University of Chicago and Roosevelt College and recommendations in accordance with House Joint Resolution No. 21, June 14, 1949").

126

tion of those who threaten our state and national security. It is to the credit of the great majority of the people of the State of Illinois that they have not been blinded by the cheap attempts of some to belittle the work of the Commission through petty ridicule. The left wing press, which includes among others, the Daily Worker, the official organ and mouthpiece of the Communist Party, led the way in a smear campaign against the Commission—a Commission composed of 13 veterans, including two Past-State Department Commanders of the American Legion, one Congressional Medal of Honor winner of World War II, a representative of the Illinois State Chamber of Commerce, and former investigator for the Federal Bureau of Investigation, and a Chicago Attorney, and Grand Knight of the Knights of Columbus.

In the main, such opposition came from the following sources [the statement continued]:

1) The Communists and their close fellow travelers who fear exposure.
2) Those who have been duped or compromised by the Communists and who seek to cover up their own gullibility.
3) Those who are too naive to believe that there is a serious Communist menace to our way of life.

We have been told by competent observers, that never in the recent history of our State has there been encountered by a Committee or Commission, such an extensive and highly coordinated effort to challenge its authority and stop its activities by organizations and individuals, some of subversive character, seeking to shelter their activities behind legal safeguards—which reassures and further confirms the exacting and splendid work of the Commission and is highly complimentary.

The "findings" of the majority statement are less than clear cut. Senator Broyles stated:

The Commission's investigation did reveal activity that could be classified as undesirable in an institution of learning: The many evasive answers of some witnesses—the admission of the official recognition of the Communist Club by faculty witnesses—the student president of the Communist Club, who under oath refused to answer the question "Are you a member of the Communist Party?," who refused to answer the question, "Would you defend the United States at war with Russia?"—this student succeeded Hans Freistadt as leader of the Communist Club movement at the University of Chicago. Freistadt is an avowed Communist and has just recently been exposed in connection with his receiving a scholarship to the Atomic Energy Commission.

The testimony of the witnesses, including the faculty members and administrators of the institutions, did reveal such extensive connections, over the last several years, of these men with communist dominated organizations, that I am sure the public was startled, and decidedly, did not approve.

The Commission, at no time, indicated a desire, either by action or recommended legislation, to "control thought," "curb academic freedom," or prove "guilt by association." These are all "catch" phrases, employed by the communists, to defend their activities and to cover the real facts behind the scenes and discredit anyone who exposes them. These phrases are all too often used by well-meaning, but duped people. Regardless of how these phrases are used, most loyal American citizens would not feel friendly toward the idea of their Minister of the Gospel, their banker, or the teacher of their children, being associated constantly with people of ill-repute and doubtful reputations.

While the professors apparently could see no real harm in such activities, we cannot but feel that they were on very unsound ground, and did, despite their protestations to the contrary, suffer in some degree from "guilt by association." [179] It was disturbing, and in fact appalling, to find that some of the faculty members refused to accept the right of the Justice Department and other governmental agencies, to list certain organizations as "subversive," "communist" or "communist-front organizations." They held to their point of view even though they were advised, and agreed, that these listings were not made until a thorough investigation had been made by the Federal Bureau of Investigation and all other investigative agencies of the federal government.

If this investigation produces a salutory effect on such activities of the professors, as we believe it will, it will have been very much worthwhile.

In conclusion, we feel that any person who has membership in a communist or communist-front organization or a subversive organization as listed by the Justice Department of the

[179] Cf. this statement with the first sentence in the paragraph preceding.

United States, is an undesirable person to teach our American school children of any age.[180]

The résumé of evidence completed, the majority then made the recommendations which, they apparently believed, logically flowed from the "findings."

We recommend that any student attending a tax-exempt or tax-supported educational institution, who refuses to answer the question whether or not he is a communist, and whether or not he will fight for the United States in the event of war with Russia, and any student, who, under oath, states that he is a communist, and that he will not fight for the United States in the event of war with Russia, be immediately expelled by the authorities of such school, college or university, in order to prevent the contamination of other students in the student body.

With respect to teachers, the majority of the Broyles commission recommended that "any teacher or professor who refuses to resign from known communist or communist-front organizations and groups as listed by the Justice Department of the United States, be dismissed from the faculty of any tax-exempt, or tax-supported institution of learning."

The majority of the commission also recommended that all schools in Illinois

take immediate steps to stop the sale of Communist propaganda in the form of books, magazines, newspapers, pamphlets, leaflets, and other materials, and that steps should be taken to deny the use of the bulletin boards and campus publications for the purpose of advertising communistic gatherings, and that campus facilities should be denied for the purpose of holding communistic meetings and the hearing of those individuals who advocate the principles of communism.

It is further recommended that a survey should be made of text books, as well as required reading material, such survey to be made by responsible authorities of such educational institutions, for the purpose of eliminating material which advocates

[180] This is a complete, unabridged statement of the "findings" made by Senator Broyles.

the theories and doctrines of communism and any other subversive doctrine.

The majority of the commission also recommended that all schools within the state "make a personal investigation of the conditions relative to the students' activities, also the affiliation of their faculty members, and that they take immediate steps to discontinue the Communist Clubs and other like organizations listed by the Justice Department of the United States or any other governmental agency" and that "all educational institutions should investigate any newly-named organization that has in its membership, persons who have been members of questionable organizations listed by governmental agencies—such as the American Youth for Democracy, now defunct, since it was spot-lighted as a communist-front organization—which shall include at the present time, so-called communist study groups as well as the Young Progressives of Illinois, which is fast becoming infiltrated with known communists who have joined after their known communist organizations have been spot-lighted by investigation."

As a preliminary to its final recommendation, the majority of the commission reached this possibly irrelevant yet startling conclusion:

After nearly two years of contact with top officials of our State and Nation, which included many conferences with people in all walks of life, we have come to the conclusion that: The truth being taught by our educators, the truth being preached by our clergymen, *and sufficient laws to control those who will not be educated and have no faith in their God* will be the most successful way to combat this organized conspiracy and "red menace" in our midst.[181] [Emphasis supplied.]

Finally, the commission recommended:

that any school or university that continues to employ professors or teachers who have been or continue to be affiliated with subversive, communist or communist-front organizations; or any school or university that recognizes as a student organization those organizations listed by the Justice Department as subversive, communist, or communist-front organizations, shall be

[181] Is the Broyles Commission recommending that belief in atheism and agnosticism be made illegal in Illinois?

denied tax exemption. Regarding tax-supported schools and universities, it shall be the duty of the Board of Trustees, and governing officials, and the employing bodies to comply with these recommendations. If the Board of Trustees, the governing officials, or the employing body, refuse to comply, it is recommended that such board of trustees, governing officials or employing body, be by law, removed from office. If the present statutes do not cover this situation, it is recommended that the necessary laws be enacted.

A short dissent by Senator Norman C. Barry (Democrat–Chicago), one of the two active members of the commission who refused to sign the majority statement, took issue with the conclusions the majority had drawn from the testimony. Said Senator Barry:

This Commission was directed to investigate subversive activities. It found none. No faculty member was even charged with teaching or saying anything subversive. When at least three professors asked whether they were charged with being subversive, Chairman Broyles stated in open hearing that they were not so charged. The professors who testified stated their opposition to communism.

The statement of Chairman Broyles and others rests in part upon the discredited notion that membership in an organization makes a man guilty of all the thoughts and acts of other members. But at no time did any witness or any Commission member dare assert that any faculty member had engaged in subversive activities or even harbored principles other than those wholly American. As to the student communist club, there is honest and sincere difference of opinion about permitting students of any political belief to exercise our freedom to assemble peaceably. No law forbids it now. It has yet to be proven that suppression will really help in the battle against communism. The whip is not always the best teacher. To combat communism among young people requires all the skill our educators can command. Any university will stand or fall on how well it meets that problem.

After paying tribute to the achievements of the university, Senator Barry concluded his dissent, stating: "The Trustees of the University have intelligences, ability and responsibility. They know the University and its work. They know its problems. They know all these things, better than the members of the Commission. I want no part in dictating to these men how to do their job. To do so is both unwise and un-American."

Another member of the Broyles commission, Representative Charles J. Jenkins (Republican–Chicago), issued a separate dissent a few days later.[182] Although disagreeing vehemently with the "findings" of the majority, Representative Jenkins' position on recommended policy was approximately midway between that of the majority and Senator Barry. Representative Jenkins believed that the Communist clubs at the two schools should be disbanded and not again reformed under any other name, that professors should resign from organizations listed by the attorney general as subversive and should exert "the utmost care" in joining organizations or permitting use of their names. But, with respect to the "findings" of the majority, Representative Jenkins held they were "not in accord with the known facts and . . . not supported by evidence." Said Representative Jenkins:

> It is impossible to cite any word, written or voiced, by any professor or any officer of either institution which indicates that any one of them ever made a statement which could be regarded in any way as subversive. In fact, there was not one word of testimony as to what any professor ever said to any student in class or elsewhere except only the letter introduced by Professor Sharp of the University of Chicago urging the Communist Club to invite anti-Communist speakers to present their points of view.
>
> J. B. Matthews, designated by the Commission to be chief interrogator of witnesses, introduced throughout his examination a number of accusations against the two institutions and members of the faculties. He was not under oath, and sought by clever insinuation and innuendo to accomplish by indirection what he failed to prove. In our opinion he did not prove his case. It is unfair to the institutions and personalities involved, therefore, for the Commission to place reliance on such testimony.

. . . . .

[182] House Journal, Illinois Assembly, June 24, 1949, pp. 30–32.

If communistic indoctrination exists on either campus, it would reveal itself frequently in documented form and the investigators would have something more to show than a few paragraphs written by a Columbia professor and used as optional reading. Among the many students, past and present, there are certainly thousands of loyal Americans who, if they had detected any subversive teachings, would eagerly have taken the opportunity to testify.

.   .   .   .   .

Even in the press statement of the majority, they do not condemn the schools or the professors except by innuendo, which we may call guilt by assumption. They should have said the two institutions and the professors were not proven guilty by the evidence and therefore, exonerated.

Articulating a protest against use of the "smear" technique, Representative Jenkins said:

It seems to us that the way to expose Communism is to expose Communists. The widespread smears of persons who are not Communists or even Communist sympathizers simply divert attention from the real dangers. We can even be lulled into the mistaken idea that attacks on loyal Americans are of some help in preserving democracy. Moscow must cheer when we brand as Communists those who work for peace, repeal of poll taxes, elimination of racial conflict, and slum clearance. Those who fall into this practice perform a service to Stalinists which Communists can get in no other way.

.   .   .   .   .

Our hearings and observation of similar investigations by other governmental agencies lead us to suggest that a new and real Communistic danger is arising in the country—the failure to keep the meaning of Communism clear. Communism in our opinion is fallacious in theory and vicious in practice. We should always so regard it. But the practice of tagging the Communist label on everyone with whom we do not agree is so prevalent that we are in danger of obscuring the true meaning and danger of Communism.

But this did not conclude the advice rendered to the Illinois legislature, Representative G. William Horsley (Republican–

Springfield), although participating solely as a witness in the investigation, issued a pamphlet giving his own analysis of the testimony adduced in the hearings, together with what he described as "comments and additional materials" purportedly describing conditions at the two schools. Not a member of the Broyles commission, Representative Horsley issued the booklet, according to his statement, "in order that a complete picture will be given of the issues involved prior to the time the members of the General Assembly will be called upon to vote upon a resolution concerning these issues." [183]

Representative Horsley's "analysis" of the testimony is merely prelude, being limited to approximately three and a half pages of the twenty-three page pamphlet. The thrust of Representative Horsley's "comments and additional materials," which comprise the bulk of the pamphlet, is that Chancellor Hutchins has introduced "radical" theories of higher education at the university, the principal vice of which had been the admission of students to the college at the ages of fifteen or sixteen. Toward them, according to Horsley, the university has disclaimed any responsibility for the moral conditions existing on the campus. Low moral standards are asserted to prevail on the campus, fostered by communistic indoctrination of the students. Representative Horsley cites twenty-nine cases of crime purportedly involving students or staff of the university.[184] These are listed as "ample proof of the fact that communism, lawlessness, disrespect for religion and family life go hand in hand." One can only speculate as to the motivation

[183] *Analysis of Testimony Given before the Seditious Activities Investigation Commission with Regard to the Investigation of the University of Chicago and Roosevelt College, Together with Comment and Additional Materials Collected by Representative G. William Horsley,* Foreword (1949).

[184] Without attempting an exhaustive analysis to determine the extent to which the students of the university were involved, the writer found some of the cases cited by Representative Horsley would have little relevance to his charges since they involved crimes committed *upon* students or staff of the university by unknown criminals. Such examples are relevant, of course, if Representative Horsley's intention is to discourage parents from sending their children to the university.

of Representative Horsley in making these charges. They were not made when he was subject to cross-examination as a witness before the Broyles commission.[185]

With the issuance of the Horsley pamphlet, the array of "reports," "statements," and "comments" was completed. Attention shifted to the Illinois house of representatives where the remnants of the Broyles antisubversive activities bills were awaiting action. The Illinois senate had previously defeated Bill No. 152 requiring registration of organizations using an oath as a condition of membership.[186] The senate had also given the coup de grâce to the Broyles commission by rejecting a bill to extend the life of the commission for two years and give it an appropriation of $75,000. The remainder of the Broyles proposed legislation had been passed by the senate and was then pending action by the house. All of these remaining bills were allowed to die when the house adjourned on June 30, 1949, without voting upon the measures.[187] Neither the Skyles resolution exonerating the two schools nor a resolution condemning the schools which Representative Horsley wished to introduce was put to a vote.

CONCLUSION

It appears that the Broyles commission failed on two counts to perform the function delegated to it by the legislature—to investigate activities "suspected of being directed toward the overthrow of the government." On the one hand, the commission failed to investigate that area of political activity ordinarily suspected of subversion, and on the other, the commission departed from its own frame of reference by conducting inquiries into the opinions and associations of persons whom even the commission did not accuse of subversion.

[185] Horsley's "analysis" was denounced by Chancellor Hutchins and President Sparling. Chancellor Hutchins was quoted as characterizing the Horsley accusations as "vicious and untrue." Hutchins stated, "It is a lie to say, as Horsley does, that immorality is tolerated or encouraged or that the University is not vigilant concerning the morals of its students" (*Chicago Sun-Times,* June 24, 1949).

[186] *Chicago Sun-Times,* July 5, 1949.

[187] *Chicago Sun-Times,* July 5, 1949.

While the commission was rabid in its denunciation of communism and advocated "nihilitory" legislation to deal with Communists, it is extraordinary how little reliable information concerning the Communists' activities in Illinois emerges from the record of the two-year investigation. Informed there were 6,500 Communists in Illinois, the Broyles commission made no recorded effort to determine the accuracy of this figure and failed to uncover any hitherto unknown activity of Illinois Communists. Rather the operations of the Communist Party in Illinois were almost completely skirted by the commission. It is significant that the commission's witnesses largely related twice-told tales of the operations of Communists not in Illinois but in the federal government, in other states, and in other lands. On the state of evidence which the Broyles commission has presented it is entirely possible to conclude that Communists in Illinois constitute but a tiny, ineffectual minority. If the facts are otherwise the Broyles commission failed to adduce them. For this reason it is a tenable conclusion that the public and the legislature are no better informed as to what Communists are doing to imperil the state than before the investigation. Rather than contributing to an informed public opinion, the commission has tended to compound confusion by largely ignoring Communists and by scrutinizing activities which the commission conceded were not subversive.

In the field of education the Broyles commission made more intensive inquiries. Despite vague references to education as the "danger spot" for communist infiltration and unsubstantiated allegations of "redness" in schools, the startling fact emerges that the commission could not discover a single teacher in Illinois who was a Communist or advocated communism in his teaching. As for student Communists, the commission found two at the University of Chicago who had previously asserted publicly their adherence to communism, and Chancellor Hutchins estimated there might be twenty-five in all at the university. These, together with the ten members of the Communist Club at Roosevelt College (assuming *arguendo* that membership in the club is coordinate with being a Communist), hardly constitute a frightening figure. Here again, if the facts are otherwise, the commission failed to establish them.

Perhaps the most glaring reflection of the commission's failure to uncover evidence of actual subversion within the state was the manner in which it conducted the public investigation of Roosevelt College and the University of Chicago. Faced with the fact that its own investigator had failed to find evidence of subversive activities at the two institutions, the commission was forced to fall back on testimony regarding the off-campus affiliations of some of the professors. Though ultimately disclaiming adherence to the doctrine of guilt by association, the commission, lacking evidence of subversion in the speeches, lectures, or writings of these professors, was clearly placing its entire reliance on this doctrine to make its case. The inherent shortcomings of guilt by association were never more clearly exposed than when the professors whose associations had been impugned were permitted to articulate their pronounced anti-Communist views. Moreover the patent irrelevancy of inquiry into off-campus affiliations of the several professors was implicitly recognized by the chairman when he informed the professors that no charge of subversion had been made against them. That, one might have concluded, should have ended the matter. The rest was merely a gratuitous inquiry into opinions and associations. The integrity of the majority of the Broyles commission suffered when it failed to clear explicitly the two schools and the several professors of subversive activities. The commission should have admitted the difference between "undesirable" activities and subversive activities.

In the area of proposed legislation, the record of the Broyles commission fares no better. A strong inference is derivable from the record that the legislative proposals had no necessary connection with the evidence collected by the commission. Certainly if the commission had found subversive activity at the University of Chicago and Roosevelt College it is doubtful that measures more punitive could have been suggested. The commission was recommending withdrawal of tax exemption from the two schools regardless of the presence or absence of subversive activities in those schools. In essence the commission concluded that schools should be punished for employing professors who, though not engaged in subversive activities in performing their academic duties, were associated with disapproved organizations. This is guilt by associa-

137

tion with a vengeance. It is almost analogous to decreeing that a corporation shall lose its right to do business within the state if one of the employees of the corporation has after-hours affiliations with undesirable groups.

Apart from the recommendations of the Broyles commission addressed specifically to the two schools, the commission's other legislative recommendations appear unsupported by cogent evidence of subversion in Illinois. It might, of course, be argued on a priori grounds that, even without demonstrated need, additional legislation to restrain subversive activities can do no harm. Although it is a somewhat inverted rationale—to justify legislation for which a need had not been shown—this tenuous basis crumbles under the weight of a constitutional objection. The widespread opinion among members of the legal profession that the Broyles bills were unconstitutional, though obviously not ultimately determinative, might have caused a commission more sensitively attuned to constitutional guarantees to refine and perhaps reject such patently unconstitutional measures.

This study has not attempted to assess the damage to reputation of individuals and institutions impugned by the Broyles commission. (On the other hand, it might be pointed out the activities of the Broyles commission as reported in the press and in the commission's own documents probably did not enhance the reputations of many of its members.) Nor has much space been devoted to an analysis of the repercussions which the Broyles commission's investigation may have had upon the willingness of citizens to think independently even though unpopularly. Chancellor Hutchins made the point eloquently soon after the close of the Broyles investigation when he said:

> We hear on every side that the American Way of Life is in danger. I think it is. I also think that many of those who talk the loudest about the dangers to the American Way of Life have no idea what it is and consequently no idea what the dangers are that it is in.
>
> You would suppose, to listen to these people, that the American Way of Life consisted in unanimous tribal self-adoration. Down with criticism; down with protests; down with unpopular opinions; down with independent thought. Yet the history

138

and tradition of our country make it perfectly plain that the essence of the American Way of Life is its hospitality to criticism, protest, unpopular opinions, and independent thought. . . .

Asserting the dignity of man, and of every man, America has proclaimed and protected the freedom to differ. Each man is supposed to think for himself. The sum of the thoughts of all is the wisdom of the community. Difference, disagreement, discussion, decided by democratic processes, are required to bring out the best in the citizens. . . .

The heart of Americanism is independent thought. The cloak-and-stiletto work that is now going on will not merely mean that many persons will suffer for acts that they did not commit, or for acts that were legal when committed, or for no acts at all. Far worse is the end result, which will be that critics, even of the mildest sort, will be frightened into silence. Stupidity and injustice will go unchallenged because no one will dare to speak against them.

But quite apart from the broad consideration of inroads on basic civil liberties, the Broyles commission stands condemned by its own record as an antisubversive investigative agency which failed to find subversion yet lacked the good grace to say so. The oblivion to which the legislature consigned the Broyles commission should cause no regret.

III. MARYLAND

The Ober Anti-Communist Law

By WILLIAM B. PRENDERGAST   *June, 1951*

FRANK B. OBER played the leading role in the drama of Maryland politics in 1949. Though he holds no political office, though he is not connected with any political machine, Ober stole top billing from the legislature, which was in session for the first three months of the year, and from the prospective candidates for the governorship in 1950, who began to move downstage as the year approached its end. That Ober played his part effectively seems to be generally conceded, but the critics were not at all unanimous as to whether he was hero or villain in the historical drama. They were not even agreed that what they witnessed was drama, some regarding it as a low form of burlesque.

The split of opinion among the critics as to the leading player can be readily illustrated. A state senator delivered this encomium, "As long as our flag flies, as long as Francis Scott Key is remembered, we shall remember Frank Ober." The state council of the Veterans of Foreign Wars considered the performance deserving of a special award, a certificate of meritorious service in the fight against communism. On the other hand, Representative Vito Marcantonio pronounced Ober a "two-bit Fascist" and a "small-town imitation of J. Parnell Thomas." Henry Wallace accused him of making a "brutal attack upon the constitutional guaran-

[Mr. Prendergast is Assistant Professor of Government in the United States Naval Academy.]

140

tees that are the life blood of our American system." And the Communist Party of Maryland and the District of Columbia called Ober "openly Fascist," a "notorious red-baiter," and (crowning insult!) a "corporation lawyer."

Ober's prominence on the political stage resulted from his service as chairman of a commission brought into existence by resolution of the state legislature in 1948 to prepare a program of anti-Communist legislation. A lawyer's lawyer, Ober had been a partner of Maryland's late governor, Albert C. Ritchie. He brought to his job indefatigable zeal, thorough knowledge of the legal problems involved, and an unshakable conviction that communism is an imminent menace to the United States. By virtue of these qualities he exercised a dominant influence over his commission. Although the draft law proposed by the commission was the product of joint effort, the members of the commission usually deferred to the judgment of their chairman. Appropriately, then, the law which the legislature adopted, adhering closely to the commission's recommendations, became known as the Ober Act, and the credit or the blame for the law fell largely upon Ober's head.

The selection of Ober as chairman of the commission was prompted by an address which he delivered before the State Bar Association shortly before the members of the commission were designated. That speech, a plea for sterner laws against subversion, reviewed past attempts to control communism by legislation and argued that constitutional authority is not lacking to outlaw the Communist Party completely or to impose any lesser controls upon it.[1] Ober was critical of decisions of the supreme court of the preceding decade which made the clear-and-present danger doctrine the touchstone by which the constitutionality of laws restricting speech is determined. Condemning "free speech fanatics" and "self-canonized liberals who are unwilling to sacrifice an ounce of free speech dogmatism for a pound of democratic survival," Ober invoked the following principle to justify legislative prohibition or restriction of the Communist Party: "Every one is

[1] This address was published as "Communism versus the Constitution," *American Bar Association Journal*, 34 (August, 1948), 645.

at liberty to advocate change in our government by the orderly methods prescribed by the Constitution. The moment he urges the substitution of the bullet for the ballot he becomes an enemy of society and should be treated as such. Freedom of speech should stop short of subversive activities." [2] Rejecting the doctrine that the freedoms of the First Amendment should enjoy a preferred status, Ober observed, "The survival of the Government is entitled to the preferred status."

What is probably the key to Ober's approach to the problem of controlling Communists was buried in a footnote to his address. The struggle in progress between the United States and Russia, he argued, justifies stringent measures against those who clearly belong in the enemy's camp. Cold war is war, and judicial notice should be taken of this state of affairs. "If it be recognized that fifth columns are but the advance skirmishers under the technique of warfare as practised by totalitarian powers, it would . . . clarify the judicial treatment of sedition by requiring that legislation be tested more from the standpoint of the war power and national security than by whether or not a formal state of war exists." [3]

The central thesis of the address was presented to the gathering as a resolution at the close of the speech. Though lawyers who were later to challenge the constitutionality of the Ober Act were present, not one voice was raised in dissent when the Maryland Bar Association voted that "it is within the constitutional power of Congress and of the State legislatures to pass laws outlawing the so-called Communist Party entirely or any other subversive organization seeking the overthrow of our Government by violence, if they wish to do so, and hence pass any properly drawn laws seeking to control the activities of such parties." [4]

Ober's concern about Communist influence in educational institutions was given pointed expression the following year when he refused to contribute to the Law School fund of Harvard Uni-

[2] *Ibid.*, p. 745.   [3] *Ibid.*, p. 746, n. 77.

[4] *Ibid.*, p. 733. In 1949 Ober was elected president of the State Bar Association. At the association's 1950 convention, a resolution was adopted endorsing the Ober Act. Although a few votes were cast against the resolution, no one took the floor to oppose it.

versity, of which he is an alumnus. His act of protest, Ober wrote to President James Conant, was prompted by the fact that two members of the Harvard faculty had participated in meetings sponsored by organizations commonly accused of following the Communist Party line. One of the offending professors, John Ciardi, had addressed a meeting called by the Progressive Party of Maryland to oppose the Ober Act. The other, Harlow Shapley, was a prominent figure in the Cultural and Scientific Conference for World Peace held in New York City in late March of 1949. "I do not believe," Ober wrote to President Conant, "a great university can properly permit the prestige which its name gives its professors to be used in a manner hostile to our country." He went on to suggest the dismissal of the two offenders. Noting that colleges are "not alive to the nature or dangers arising from Communism" in spite of the "prevalence" of communism on the campus, Ober urged college authorities to keep "closer watch on what its professors are doing." [5]

The Ober commission, which drafted the anti-Communist law, was composed of six members of the state legislature and five prominent citizens who held no public office. In addition to its chairman, the commission included the following members:

John W. Avirett, II, a Baltimore lawyer and naval reserve officer, who served during World War II as special assistant and aide to the assistant secretary of the Navy.

Henry H. Balch, a lawyer and state senator representing rural Talbot County, former state's attorney for the county and a veteran of both world wars.

Charles M. Bandiere, a prominent Baltimore realtor and member of the house of delegates since 1943.

T. Raymond Burch, a realtor and insurance agent; president of Prince George's County Real Estate Board; postmaster of Berwyn, Maryland (population 8,000), 1934–1946; member of the house of delegates from Prince George's County, which includes

[5] This correspondence received wide publicity. It can be found under the title, "Freedom at Harvard," in the American Association of University Professors *Bulletin,* 35 (Summer, 1949), 313–334, together with a reply from Grenville Clark on behalf of the university, firmly rejecting Ober's suggestions as a peril to academic freedom.

some suburbs of Washington but is controlled politically by tobacco-producing rural areas.

Wilmer C. Carter, a realtor and insurance agent, former president of the Baltimore Kiwanis Club, active member of other businessmen's organizations; state senator since 1939 and sponsor of the resolution for the appointment of the Ober commission, a man who has "dedicated his life to fighting communism."

Howard W. Jackson, a Baltimore insurance agent, mayor of Baltimore, 1923–1927 and 1931–1943; a municipal officeholder for 32 years, an anti-New Deal Democrat who supported Dewey in 1944.

David K. McLaughlin, a Hagerstown lawyer, a state senator representing predominantly rural Washington County, a veteran of the Naval Air Force in World War II.

William C. Purnell, a Baltimore lawyer, former assistant U.S. attorney for Maryland, general counsel for the Western Maryland Railroad, brigadier general in the Maryland National Guard, a veteran of World War II, a dark horse candidate for the Republican gubernatorial nomination in 1950.

Morton E. Rome, a Baltimore lawyer, former assistant state's attorney for Baltimore, Naval Reserve officer, World War II veteran, a member of the staff of Justice Robert H. Jackson at the Nuremberg trials for the prosecution of Axis Criminality in 1946, member of Americans for Democratic Action.

Leona M. Rush, a housewife, a member of the House of Delegates representing Montgomery County, which embraces many of the suburban areas around Washington.

Six members of the commission were lawyers, four of them graduates of the Harvard Law School. Business interests were amply represented both by realtors and insurance agents and by attorneys whose practice identified them with the business community. Five members of the body were veterans. Only three members were free from rather strong political ties. The commission was bipartisan, but no disagreement along party lines developed within it. On the whole it was a serious, able, and conscientious group. Its devotion to its job was manifested in long hours spent at its work over a period of five months. Certainly better balance would have been achieved among the personnel of the commission had it included representatives of such groups as labor, teachers, and organizations devoted to the cause of civil rights. But, in comparison with the general run of politically appointed investigative bodies, the Ober commission would rank high.

The proceedings of the group were shrouded in secrecy. No public hearings were held; no record of its deliberations was made public. The aura of mystery that surrounded its meetings provided both friends and foes of the commission's proposals with arguments to support their stand in subsequent public controversy. Opponents of the recommendations saw in the secrecy evidence of predetermined conclusions, of one-sidedness, if not of some sinister plot that had to be veiled from public scrutiny. They alleged that the concoction which the commission represented to be of its own making had been brewed by the Federal Bureau of Investigation and the Committee on Un-American Activities of the national House of Representatives.[6]

The secrecy of the deliberations was turned to good account by supporters of the Ober Act, and the impression that the F.B.I. had aided materially in the formulation of the act was cultivated by them. Proponents of the proposed law dropped hints that they knew much more than they could tell of Communist plots. They used the "it is later than you think" tactic, expressing regret that they could not reveal the correct time to other Marylanders since it had been made known to them in deepest confidence. By this method the question of the need for the legislation was in great part evaded. Such statements as "the Commission has been informed that there is substantial infiltration in some Maryland [educational] institutions" acquired a stamp of authenticity when attributed to an unnamed but unimpeachable source.[7]

In one particular the commission began its work with a predetermined conclusion, one that the legislature had embedded in the resolution establishing the body. The "whereas" clauses of that

[6] E. T. Baker, "Maryland Betrays Its Past," *New Republic,* 120 (April 25, 1949), 15–17.

[7] *Report of Commission on Subversive Activities to Governor Lane and the Maryland General Assembly* (January, 1949), p. 47 (hereafter cited as *Report*).

resolution, copied from the Mundt-Nixon Bill,[8] contained a finding that "the recent successes of communist methods in other
countries and the nature and control of the world communist
movement itself present a clear and present danger to the security
of the United States and the State of Maryland." The need for
legislation thus established, the commission had to draft something "to expose and expurgate subversive . . . activities."

The deliberations of the commission were confined largely to a
study of documents which are matters of public record. The Bolton report, various publications of the House Committee on
Un-American Activities, the Coudert report in New York State,
publications of the United States Chamber of Commerce, the
reports of the "Little Dies Committees" in Washington and California, relevant legislation in other states, the report of the Royal
Canadian Commission on the Rose-May espionage, and the record
of the hearings on the Mundt-Nixon Bill constitute the chief
sources cited by the Ober Commission in a bibliography appended
to its report.[9] In this bibliography no works of men who have in-

[8] H.R. 5852, 80th Cong., 1st sess.

[9] Bolton Report, *The Strategy and Tactics of World Communism,*
Report of Subcommittee 5, Committee on Foreign Affairs, U.S. House of
Representatives, 1948 (80th Cong., 2d sess., House Document No. 619).

Committee on Un-American Activities, U.S. House of Representatives,
*The Communist Party of the United States as an Agent of a Foreign
Power,* 1947 (80th Cong., 1st sess., Report 209); *Report on the Communist
Party of the United States as an Advocate of the Overthrow of Govern-
ment by Force and Violence,* 1948 (80th Cong., 2d sess., Report 1920);
One Hundred Things You Should Know about Communism, 1949.

Coudert Report, Report of the Subcommittee Relative to Subversive
Activity . . . , Joint Legislative Committee on the State Education System, New York State Legislature (Legislative Document No. 49, 1942).

U.S. Chamber of Commerce, *A Program for Community Anti-
Communist Action* (Washington, 1948).

Legislature of State of Washington, Joint Fact-Finding Committee on
Un-American Activities, *Reports,* 1948.

Legislature of State of California, Joint Fact-Finding Committee on
Un-American Activities in California, *Reports* (annual, 1943–1948).

Royal Canadian Commission to Investigate Disclosures of Secret and

vestigated the impact of antisubversion laws on civil liberties—men such as Zechariah Chafee, Jr., Robert E. Cushman, O. K. Fraenkel —are to be found. In addition to studying the documents listed in its bibliography, the commission received testimony from a representative of the Federal Bureau of Investigation and from officers of the intelligence services of the Armed Forces at one of its meetings. It refused to hear spokesmen for the Communist Party and the Progressive Party but offered to consider any information submitted by them in written form.

The Ober commission devoted great care to what it conceived to be its task—the drafting of legislation which would effectively suppress an evil, the existence and the nature of which had been established by the legislative directive creating the commission. Probably because of the background of its members, it seems to have been preoccupied with the legal problems it encountered. The professional work of drafting the law was performed with great skill. Scrupulously attentive to judicial opinions on earlier legislation of this character, the Ober commission strove to avoid the constitutional shoals on which its law might founder.

This preoccupation with the technical questions of legality did not blind the commission to problems of policy. The commission's avowed aim was to "destroy Communism without destroying Americanism." To that end it embodied in the law it proposed certain provisions designed to guard against the use of investigative power for character assassination. Because of "the criticism that has so often been made against some legislative committees," the Ober commission refrained from recommending the establishment of an un-American activities committee in the state. Investigations, it decided, should be conducted by grand juries and by a special assistant attorney general, who was charged with the duty of enforcing the act.

By the terms of the Ober Act grand juries may not charge any

Confidential Information to Unauthorized Persons, *Report* (Ottawa, 1946).

Committee on the Judiciary, U.S. Senate, *Hearings on H.R.5852*, 1948 (80th Cong., 2d sess.).

resident of Maryland with disloyalty unless the person so charged has been indicted; the special assistant attorney general may divulge information reflecting on the loyalty of a resident of the state only to effectuate the purposes of the law. These provisions are a thin shield for one under investigation, impressive more for the spirit which they manifest than for their practical effectiveness. Aside from the fact that they do not protect nonresidents of the state, they can be so easily circumvented in any case that they will become nugatory if the enforcement of the law is entrusted to a conscienceless official. The special assistant attorney general is under no real restraint when he is forbidden to publicize information except to effectuate the purposes of the law, for the purposes of the law (nowhere defined) are almost as broad as he cares to make them. The point here, however, is not the strength of these provisions but their presence in the Ober Act. From the fact that they are there it appears that the commission was not insensitive to the dangers that antisubversion legislation can entail. Considerations of policy, though taking second place to problems of legality in the commission's mind, were not ignored.

That the Ober commission did its work *in camera* rather than by the method of open sessions and public hearings was in itself of little consequence. It had power to do no more than offer recommendations. Publicity at this stage of the legislative process is the exception, not the rule, in American politics. As long as the lawmaking body grants interested parties a full hearing, considers the legislation carefully, debates and votes on it calmly and soberly before the public eye, it matters little that the law was not drafted on the front steps of the State Capitol at high noon.

THE PROVISIONS OF THE OBER ACT

The Ober commission submitted to the governor on December 30, 1948, a draft of a proposed statute to be known as the Subversive Activities Act of 1949 and a report justifying the proposal. In large part the statute was a synthesis of the Smith Act,[10] portions of the Mundt-Nixon Bill,[11] and the loyalty program established

[10] 54 Stat. 67 (1940), 18 U.S.C.A. 2385.
[11] H.R. 5852, 80th Cong., 1st sess.

148

for employees of the national government by executive order in 1947.[12] It was described by the American Civil Liberties Union as "the most sweeping measure" of its type enacted in 1949, and it drew from Senator Mundt the admiring comment that it was "as full of teeth as an alligator's jaw." A carbon copy of a large part of the Ober Act was placed on the statute books of Mississippi one year later with the enactment of that state's Subversive Activities Act of 1950.[13]

In its criminal sections the Ober Act attacks the Communist movement by describing its characteristics rather than by naming it. The terms of the law single out two objectives commonly attributed to American Communists—the overthrow of government by violence and the establishment of a puppet government in the United States. To prevent the forcible overthrow of government, the Ober Act declares felonious (1) acts intended to have such a result, (2) words advocating such acts if uttered "under such circumstances as to constitute a clear and present danger to the security of the United States or of the State of Maryland," and (3) participation in any organization advocating the forcible overthrow of government.

To forestall the erection in Annapolis or in Washington of a government subservient to a foreign power, the act makes criminal participation in a foreign-controlled organization seeking to establish in place of the existing national and state governments "any form of government the direction and control of which is to be vested in, or exercised by or under, the domination or control of any foreign government, organization, or individual. . . ." [14]

---

[12] Executive Order 9835, 12 F.R. 1935.

[13] General Laws of the State of Mississippi 1950, c. 451. In 1951 New Hampshire likewise adopted a statute copied from the Ober Act. Laws of the State of New Hampshire 1951, c. 193.

[14] The pertinent passages of the act run as follows: "Sec. 1, Par. 2. It shall be a felony for any person knowingly and wilfully to (a) commit, attempt to commit, or aid in the commission of any act intended to overthrow, destroy, or alter, or to assist in the overthrow, destruction or alteration of, the constitutional form of the Government of the United States, or of . . . Maryland, or any political subdivision of either . . . by revolution, force, or violence; or (b) advocate, abet, advise or teach

Subversive organizations and foreign subversive organizations are banned by the Ober Act. The former are defined as organizations "a purpose of which is to engage in or advocate, abet, advise or teach activities intended . . . to assist in the overthrow, destruction, or alteration of, the constitutional form of the government of the United States, or of . . . Maryland, or of any political subdivision of either of them, by revolution, force, violence or other unlawful means." The latter are organizations "directed, dominated, or controlled directly or indirectly by a foreign government" which seek by any means (violent or not) to supplant existing state and national governments with a form of government under the control of any foreign government, organization, or individual.[15] One familiar with the Mundt-Nixon Bill need not

---

by any means any person to commit, attempt to commit, or assist in the commission of any such act under such circumstances as to constitute a clear and present danger to the security of the United States, or of . . . Maryland or any political subdivision of either . . . or (c) conspire . . . to commit such act; or (d) assist in the formation or participate in the management or to contribute to the support of any subversive organization or foreign subversive organization knowing said organization to be a subversive organization or a foreign subversive organization; or (e) destroy any books, records or files, or secrete any funds in this State of a subversive organization or a foreign subversive organization, knowing said organization to be such."

Sec. 1, Par. 3, discussed in the text, p. 151, makes membership in subversive or foreign subversive organizations a crime. The statutory definitions of "subversive" and "foreign subversive" are given in the text above and in note 15.

[15] According to the complete statutory definition, a foreign subversive organization is "any organization directed, dominated, or controlled directly or indirectly by a foreign government . . . a purpose of which is to engage in or to advocate, abet, advise, or teach, activities intended to overthrow, destroy or alter, or to assist in the overthrow, destruction or alteration of the constitutional form of the government of the United States, or . . . of Maryland, or of any political subdivision of either of them, and to establish in place thereof any form of government the direction and control of which is to be vested in, or exercised by or under, the domination or control of any foreign government, organization, or individual . . ." Organizations "to promote world peace by alliances or

be told that the characteristics of a foreign subversive organization here described were taken in part from Section 4 of that bill.

An organization of either type, the law provides, is to be dissolved after being found illegal by a court; its property is to be forfeited to the state; and its records are to be turned over to the attorney general of the state—presumably for the initiation of legal action against individual members.

Any person found guilty of a violation of any criminal provision of the Ober Act automatically becomes ineligible to vote and to run for, or to hold, public office in the state. In addition to this mandatory penalty, the statute authorizes a maximum fine of $20,000 and/or a maximum prison sentence of twenty years for any offense other than mere membership in an organization made illegal by the act. A person convicted only of rank-and-file membership in a forbidden organization can be fined no more than $5,000 or given a maximum sentence of five years or both. Mere membership, of course, entails the loss of the political privileges specified above.

The act's provisions touching ordinary members of prohibited organizations were strenuously criticized by opponents of the legislation and were accepted with some misgivings by its skeptical supporters. In anticipation of such reactions, the Ober Act contains two provisions designed as safeguards for the innocent and unwary. In no case is membership criminal unless the member knows the organization to be a subversive or a foreign subversive organization. Again, although joining a condemned group was to constitute a felony as soon as the act became effective (on June 1, 1949, under normal circumstances), those whose membership had been established before that date were given until September 1, 1949, to sever their connection with the organization.

As insurance against innocuous desuetude, the fate that overtook most of the antisubversion laws passed immediately after World War I, Maryland's law provides for its continuous enforcement. It sets up a special functionary under the attorney general known

---

unions with other governments or world federations, unions, or governments to be effected through constitutional means" are expressly declared not to be foreign subversive organizations.

by the equivocal title of special assistant attorney general in charge
of subversive activities. This official is to devote his time to the
conduct of investigations and the collection of evidence on subversive activity within the state. Information gathered by him is
to be turned over to grand juries as a basis for criminal proceedings. Besides this method of enforcement, the Ober Act directs
grand juries to make special efforts independently to ferret out
violators of the law.

The foregoing criminal provisions constitute one of the two
major divisions of the Ober Act. The other is a loyalty section
aimed at excluding subversive persons from the public payroll as
well as from the payroll of any private educational institution
receiving financial support from the state. Declaring subversives
ineligible for appointment to, or employment in, any governmental office within the state, the act provides for a somewhat flexible
loyalty program. Every public job holder at the time the law became effective was required to submit a written statement that he
was not subversive, i.e., an advocate of the violent overthrow of
government or a member of a subversive or a foreign subversive
organization.[16] Candidates for public office are required to submit

[16] The declaration required of all to whom the loyalty provisions of
the law apply reads, ". . . I am not a person who commits, attempts
to commit, or aids in the commission, or advocates, abets, advises or
teaches by any means any person to commit, attempt to commit, or aid
in the commission of any act intended to overthrow, destroy or alter, or
to assist in the overthrow, destruction or alteration of, the constitutional
form of the Government of the United States, or of the State of Maryland, or of any political subdivision of either of them, by revolution,
force, or violence.

"I am not a member of a subversive organization . . . [then follows the
statutory definition of a subversive organization].

"I am not a member of a foreign subversive organization . . . [then
follows the statutory definition of a foreign subversive organization].

". . . this statement is made with the knowledge that it is subject to
the penalties of perjury . . . Under the penalties of perjury, I hereby
certify, affirm, and declare that all statements hereinabove contained are
true and correct, and that I have made no material misstatement or concealment of fact and no material omission of fact." Since the *Gerende*
decision (see page 165), the attorney general's office has prepared an

an affidavit to the same effect. Exemption is granted to candidates for president and vice-president of the United States; their loyalty must be vouched for, however, by "those persons who file the certificate of nomination for such candidates" in the state. Appointees to office after the act has become effective are to be screened for loyalty. Each appointing authority is directed to establish its own procedure for this purpose, no specifications being laid down in the law to guide state agencies. Appointments can be made only after it is established by such procedure that "no reasonable grounds" exist to believe that a prospective appointee is subversive.

One holding an appointive position in the service of the state is to be discharged if "reasonable grounds on all the evidence" exist for the belief that the job holder is subversive. The words quoted were borrowed from Executive Order 9835 of 1947, the presidential directive establishing the loyalty program of the national government. The Maryland law provides that notice of charges and opportunity to be heard be granted to a public servant before discharge "in accordance with the procedures prescribed by law for discharges for other reasons."

Finally, the act fixes its sights on subversive teachers by requiring all private institutions of learning receiving any state funds to report the procedures adopted by them for the detection of subversives in their employ and the steps taken to terminate such employment. The penalty for noncompliance is denial of state aid to the unco-operative institution. It was no secret that Johns Hopkins University was the target of this provision.

THE LEGISLATURE AND THE OBER ACT

The members of the lower house of the legislature were introduced to the proposed law at a seminar conducted behind closed doors by the members of the Ober commission. Most of the meet-

---

alternative oath which can be taken by one who objects to the terms of the foregoing declaration. The alternate form consists of a statement that the affiant "is not one who is engaged in one way or another in attempts to overthrow the government by force or violence and is not knowingly a member of an organization" engaged in such attempts.

ings of the legislative committees which reported the bill were likewise shut to the public and the press. Consequently little is known of this stage of the legislative history of the act. Two open hearings were held, however. The first took place before a joint committee of the two houses. The principal organizations interested in the legislation were heard at this session before galleries packed with supporters of the measure. The most prominent witness to appear was Arthur O. Lovejoy, eminent philosopher and professor emeritus at Johns Hopkins University, who spoke in opposition to the bill. The second open hearing was held for the purpose of receiving amendments proposed by individuals and groups outside the legislature. Only those who were generally sympathetic toward the bill appeared at this meeting.

From the outset it was clear that the bill would be passed by the legislature, but it was not certain that major amendments would not be made before final passage. Several members of the legislature expressed dissatisfaction with particular provisions of the law, and a more extensive revision of it might have occurred before it reached the governor had it not been for two factors. The truculence of the spokesman for the Communist Party at the committee hearing on the bill irked some lawmakers. Believing that they had been dared to pass the bill without change, they were disposed to accept the challenge. The second factor was of more consequence. The issue presented by the Ober Act crystallized in the public mind as communism versus anticommunism. One witness speaking for the bill at the committee hearing asserted, "The question is simply one of being for or against communism. I'm against it." The *Baltimore News Post,* the Hearst daily paper, presented the issue in the same terms. While the measure was under consideration by the legislature, it published in bold type daily a statement captioned "Show Your Americanism," urging its readers to write the legislators asking passage of the law without amendment. The general public, to some degree, accepted this appealingly simple analysis of the issue.[17] Few law-

[17] The writer has examined the correspondence received by Governor William Preston Lane relating to the Ober Act. Overwhelmingly, letters favoring the act said only that communism is a great evil, and therefore this bill should become law.

makers were willing to incur the political risks involved in taking a stand that might be interpreted as a manifestation of sympathy toward communism. In the climate of opinion in the spring of 1949, legislators found it discreet to refrain from pressing any amendments that would weaken the Ober Act.

The major amendment proposed was not designed to weaken the bill. It called for the establishment of a Maryland Bureau of Investigation as the enforcement agency for the law rather than the creation of a new assistant to the attorney general for that purpose. Offered by the attorney general, this revision of the measure was urged on the ground that the legal office of the state government was not an appropriate agency for police work. There is reason for the suspicion that the attorney general wanted no part in the execution of this particular law. This amendment was vigorously opposed by the Ober commission and by spokesmen for teachers. Abuse of the authority conferred by the act would be likely to occur, it was argued, if a special police force were set up to uncover violators. The attorney general found himself alone in supporting this alteration of the bill.

Two other amendments gained only a handful of votes when offered on the floor of the house of delegates. One especially desired by teachers would have deleted the word "teach" wherever it appeared in the act. The other would have eliminated the provisions punishing ordinary members of a prohibited organization.

During its consideration by the legislature the act was modified by two amendments, both of which were accorded approval by the members of the Ober commission. A guarantee of the right of appeal to the courts for any state employee threatened with discharge under the law was inserted. And the phrase "or by other unlawful means" was stricken from the bill. The commission's draft of the law had declared criminal acts or words intended to overthrow or alter the constitutional form of government "by revolution, force, violence or other unlawful means." The last four words, though commonly used in criminal syndicalism laws, were deemed dangerously vague by many legislators. This amendment was intended to limit the crime of subversion to acts or words involving or threatening violence.

The Ober Act was passed unanimously by the state senate. Only three senators took the floor to speak on the measure. All of them qualified their support of the legislation by voicing some misgivings and warning that later revision might be necessary to counteract abuse. In the house of delegates the spectacle was repeated. Delegate De Witt Hyde of Montgomery County took the floor to declare that he would vote for the bill as "a calculated risk." Confessing that he viewed the measure with "conflicting emotions," he asserted that he had resolved the "conflict between my duty to protect my country from its enemies and my duty to protect our constitutional freedoms" in favor of the former duty. Delegate Francis X. Dippel of Baltimore remarked that the bill posed a "dilemma." Announcing his intention to vote for it, he urged that a continuous scrutiny of its operation be maintained by the legislative council and by the bar associations in the state to determine "its effectiveness in combatting subversive activities and its effect upon the traditional liberties of the citizens." The Ober Act was passed by the lower house of the state legislature by a vote of 115 to 1; the lone negative vote was cast unexpectedly by a former country schoolteacher.

Governor William Preston Lane affixed his signature to the bill with only a perfunctory comment. From the time of the submission of the Ober commission's report he maintained complete silence on the measure. Sponsors of the law sought without avail to secure a benediction from the administration for the bill.[18] The governor's aloofness was certainly not due to any attachment to the theory of separation of powers. On other occasions in behalf of other measures Governor Lane has shown himself very ready to intervene in the lawmaking process to persuade, even to dragoon, the legislature to act favorably on administration bills.

Before the Ober Act had been signed, a movement to delay its enforcement was under way. Opponents of the law had begun the circulation of a petition for a referendum on the act. Under the state constitution the filing of such a petition bearing 10,000 signatures would postpone enforcement until the election of 1950 at

[18] *Baltimore News-Post,* Jan. 21, 1949, p. 1. A prominent state legislator summarized the governor's attitude toward the law in these words, "The Ober Act put Lane on the spot. Like some of the rest of us, he wished it had never been born."

which the voters would pass upon the law. By a three-fifths vote in each house, however, the legislature may pass "emergency laws" which remain in effect pending a referendum.

The course taken by the proponents of the Ober Act to frustrate the effect of the referendum petition was to make the act an emergency law. A bill declaring the act repealed and re-enacted with amendments making it an emergency measure "necessary for the immediate preservation of the public health and safety" was introduced in the legislature on April 1, the day following the signing of the law. The rules in both houses were suspended to permit the second reading on the day of introduction. On April 2 the emergency law passed both houses without opposition, and on April 22 it was signed by the governor.[19]

PRESSURES AND PRESSURE GROUPS

There is little room for doubt that the Ober Act would have been approved by the voters of the state at any time. The voters' sentiments on anti-Communist legislation were registered in 1948 when an amendment to the state constitution barring members of organizations advocating the forcible overthrow of government from public office was ratified by a vote of 202,910 to 84,132. Leaders of some organizations which are hostile to the act privately confess the futility of attempting to repeal the law by popular vote. It is significant that the Congress of Industrial Organizations and Americans for Democratic Action, both of which opposed the enactment of the law, refused to associate themselves with the movement to secure a referendum.[20]

Newspapers throughout Maryland supported the law almost unanimously. No journal of general circulation fought the law editorially, although the *Sunpapers* of Baltimore were critical of it. The *Sunpapers* were alone in advocating major amendments to

[19] Laws of the State of Maryland, 1949, c. 86; Md. Ann. Code Art. 85A.
[20] The Baltimore Industrial Union Council (C.I.O.), in explaining its attitude toward the petition for a referendum, declared "the majority of citizens are either indifferent or unopposed to the law" (*Sun* [Baltimore], May 22, 1949, p. 30). Both the C.I.O. and the A.D.A. actively participated in the campaign to defeat the law at the polls in 1950, however.

the Ober Act and suggesting that it contained serious dangers of abuse.

Besides the newspapers, the chief organized support for the Ober Act came from veterans' organizations—the American Legion, the Veterans of Foreign Wars, Catholic War Veterans, Jewish War Veterans, the 29th Division Association; from groups representative of business interests—chambers of commerce, Kiwanis, Rotary and Lions clubs, the Optimist Club, the Real Estate Board of Baltimore; and from such Catholic organizations as the Catholic Daughters of America, the International Federation of Catholic Alumnae, and the Ancient Order of Hibernians. Forty-five groups, including those named here, constituted a common front known as the Maryland Committee against Un-American Activities for the purpose of supporting the legislation.

The opposition to the act split sharply into two factions. Communists and those who did not object to association with Communists constituted one, and a somewhat heterogeneous anti-Communist group formed the other. Two distinct campaigns were conducted against the act, since the second faction eschewed any form of joint action with the first. Along with the Communists were found the Progressive Party of Maryland, the National Lawyers Guild, the Maryland Council of the Arts, Sciences and Professions, the United Electrical Workers, and the National Union of Marine Cooks and Stewards. The anti-Communist opposition was a fusion of Americans for Democratic Action, the Maryland Civil Liberties Union, the Congress of Industrial Organizations, various teachers' organizations, and an *ad hoc* committee of fifty prominent citizens of the state—college professors, clergymen, lawyers, and doctors.

The proponents of the act conducted a desultory campaign in its behalf, knowing that demonstrations of organized support were unneeded to secure its passage. Those in the camp of the Communist Party showed greater energy, organizing picket lines in front of Ober's office, staging protest meetings, circulating petitions, and sponsoring letter-writing campaigns. This wing of the opposition specialized in distortion of the provisions of the law and in wild invective against its authors in urging their cause. "Fascist," "Gestapo," "thought control," "witch hunt," "Red-baiting" were the principal clichés mouthed by Communist spokesmen in what was, all in all, a rather wearisome display of intellectual sterility.

The case of the anti-Communist opposition was presented in general as an appeal to reason.[21] Theirs was a difficult task. To engage in the same fight with Communists without closing ranks with them required some tactical skill. And to convince the public that the issue was not "simply a matter of whether you are for or against Communism" was a challenge to anybody's powers of persuasion.[22] So widely accepted was this version of the issue that some organizations which looked on the act with disfavor refused to take any strong public stand on the law. The Railroad Brotherhoods excused themselves with the comment that no issue of concern to labor was presented by the act. The State Federation of Labor hung back until the law had been declared unconstitutional by a lower state court before voicing vigorous opposition to it. The federation soft-pedaled its stand until that time because of fear of unfavorable reaction from union members within its ranks as well as fear of adverse reaction from the general public.

While Communists and their friends simply condemned the Ober Act from preamble to final paragraph, the anti-Communist opposition concentrated its efforts toward amending the measure. This line of attack was dictated by realization of the impossibility of defeating the bill outright. But efforts to amend extensively proved unavailing. Unless an amendment secured the acquiescence of the members of the Ober commission, it was doomed.

[21] A surprising and regrettable exception is the statement authorized by the executive committee of the Maryland State Teachers' Association, "Do You Want the Gestapo in Maryland?" (*The Maryland Teacher*, 6 [Feb., 1949], p. 4). "How would you like to turn from the blackboard some day to find the state or local police sitting in the rear of your room?" the statement asked. The power of the police to audit any teacher's class was not increased one whit by the law. Equally farfetched was the statement of an officer of the association that "logically the police would suppress" the writings of Marx, Plato, Bellamy, and Thomas More under the Ober Act (*Evening Sun* [Baltimore], Feb. 24, 1949, p. 32).

[22] A state legislator, who should have known better, remarked to the writer that the A.D.A. was a "Communist front." It is not surprising, then, that the politically naïve considered opposition to the Ober Act as evidence of Communist leanings.

Both the governor and the members of the legislature received a considerable quantity of mail dealing with the act. Although the correspondence directed to the governor was rather evenly divided pro and con, the enemies of the measure outdid its friends in writing to the legislators. This mail had no observable effect on votes. For one thing, letters registering opposition came almost entirely from urban areas—Baltimore, the satellite communities around Washington, and, in significant numbers, from cities in other states. Rural areas control the Maryland legislature, and the majority of the legislators are as unimpressed by letters from Baltimore as they are by letters from Boston. Further, there were too many form letters; too many were stereotyped; too many were obviously not the product of the signatories. As one legislator remarked to the writer, referring to communications that had come to him, "People in South Baltimore just don't use words like those."

To understand why the Maryland legislature enacted the Ober Act almost unanimously, one need only read the headlines of any newspaper during the last months of 1948 and the first few months of 1949. Daily they trumpeted news of Communist successes, Communist recalcitrance, Communist persecution of religious leaders, stories of Whittaker Chambers, Judith Coplon, and Alger Hiss. The pressure groups most influential in securing the passage of this law were located far from Annapolis—in Moscow, Peiping, Budapest, in courtrooms in New York and Washington. They were manning barricades in Berlin and casting vetoes at Lake Success.

When the voters of Maryland passed judgment on the law in November, 1950, hot war had bubbled up in Korea. The fact that American troops were locked in combat with Communist armies intensified anti-Communist sentiment in the United States. Voting for the Ober Act was one way of demonstrating that sentiment. For the campaign to win popular support for the act, an enlarged Maryland Committee against Un-American Activities adopted a slogan keyed to the desire to strike a blow that would aid our fighting men—"A Vote for the Ober Act Is a Vote against Communism." Some voters registered their disapproval of communism by voting against Millard E. Tydings, defeated in his bid for re-election to the position in the United States Senate he had held for twenty-four years, because of widespread suspicion that he had shut his eyes to the presence of subversive elements in the Department of State. Another casualty in the election was Delegate John R. Newcomer, the state legislator who voted against the Ober Act. Significantly, Newcomer was the only member of his county's delegation to either house of the state legislature seeking re-election who was rejected at the polls.

The vote on the Ober Act was 259,250 to 79,120. Rural areas supported the law with far more impressive majorities than did urban regions. In some of the less populous counties voters endorsed the law by margins as high as nine to one, whereas in the city of Baltimore the majority approximated two-and-a-half to one. Any question about the attitude of the people of the state toward antisubversive legislation was thus conclusively settled.

THE COURTS AND THE OBER ACT

Shortly after the passage of the Ober Act two suits were instituted against the attorney general to prevent its enforcement.[23] One was brought by the Communist Party. The other was initiated by six college professors, two doctors, a sculptor, and a salesman as taxpayers. Judge Joseph Sherbow of the court that originally heard both suits pronounced the Ober Act unconstitutional in its entirety.

The emergency law, Judge Sherbow declared, was defective in form and retroactive in application. Coming to grips with the Ober Act itself, the justice found it in conflict with national and state constitutions as an abridgment of "the basic freedoms guaranteed by the First and Fourteenth Amendments" (speech, press, assembly), as a bill of attainder, and as a violation of the due process clause because of vagueness.

"The law deals with overt acts, not thoughts. It may punish for acting, but not for thinking." This principle was not respected by the Ober Act, Judge Sherbow declared without specifying exactly which provisions were defective in this respect. Since the

---

[23] *Frankfeld v. Hammond, Lancaster v. Hammond,* Baltimore Circuit Court No. 2, Sherbow, J. (*Daily Record* [Baltimore], Aug. 16, 1949).

Ober Act's preamble speaks of communism and inferentially its provisions do the same, the act was found to be a bill of attainder, a legislative act imposing punishment without a trial.

Several provisions of the law were regarded by the court as too vague and indefinite to satisfy the constitutional requirements of clarity in the definition of the offenses it prohibits. The word "revolution" used in the statute, the court understood to mean any sort of sudden and drastic change, even though accomplished by peaceful means and orderly legal processes. Its ambiguity made it defective. Paraphrasing the provisions of the act somewhat inaccurately, the court asserted that they prohibited advocating or teaching "the commission of any act" which constitutes "a clear and present danger to the security" of the nation or the state. Here again is fatal ambiguity. The soundness of these conclusions is open to serious question. To reach them, the court had to ignore the words, "force or violence," used in the statute to qualify the expressions cited as vague. Further, the history of the act suggests that the word "revolution" was intended to mean a violent uprising. When used in parallel construction with "force or violence," it was tautological, but this would not be the first time that lawyers used two words where one would have been enough.

Several other examples of vagueness were cited by the court. It is not enough to declare membership in certain organizations criminal, Judge Sherbow declared, without providing in the statute a definition of membership. When the act introduces the element of *scienter*, punishing members of prohibited organizations who *know* their organizations to be subversive, it slips into indefiniteness again. Knowledge may be actual or constructive, and the law fails to indicate which type of knowledge is required for conviction on the ground of membership in a forbidden group. "Reasonable grounds on all the evidence" for the belief that a state employee is subversive constitute the standard to be used in determining whether to discharge such employee. But, the justice objected, "What may seem reasonable to one may seem extremely arbitrary and unreasonable to another." Finally, in defining a foreign subversive organization, the law used the expression "indirectly controlled by a foreign power." "Indirectly," the court said, suffers from the vice of vagueness. So much indefiniteness,

Judge Sherbow said, constitutes a violation of the due process clause of the federal constitution.

The loyalty affidavits required of candidates for public office were found by the lower court to be prohibited by the state constitution, which bars the legislature from demanding any oath from officeholders other than that specified in the constitution itself.[24] An affidavit of loyalty from candidates was regarded as an attempt to accomplish by indirection what could not be done directly.

The opinion of the lower court was noteworthy for what it failed to say as well as for what it said. It ignored the question of the severability of the provisions of the law, though it found no fault with many parts of the act. The whole law was declared bad because certain parts of it were bad. And it failed to take any notice of an imposing number of precedents in which higher courts, state and national, had upheld laws similar in many respects to the Ober Act.[25]

Maryland's highest tribunal, the Court of Appeals, reversed the decision of the lower court in February, 1950.[26] Unanimously it held valid the emergency act, which put the Ober Act into effect immediately and kept the petition for a referendum from suspending its operation. Unanimously it decided that those who had challenged the Ober Act presented no justiciable case to the courts. The law had not been applied against them. They did not allege that they had violated it or intended to violate it. They did not allege unwillingness to comply with any of its provisions. Using the words of Justice Cardozo, the court said, "The complainants have been crying before they are really hurt." Four members of the court stopped here, expressing no opinion as to the validity of the provisions of the act.

A minority of two justices, however, went on to indicate that they considered the major provisions of the Ober Act constitutional. The main features of the loyalty program set down in the statute—the loyalty affidavits required of public employees and

[24] Maryland Constitution, Declaration of Rights, Art. 37.

[25] Notes 35 and 36, pp. 170 and 172.

[26] *Hammond v. Lancaster,* 71 A. 2d 474 (1950); *Hammond v. Frankfeld,* 71 A. 2d 483 (1950).

candidates for office—were upheld. "No one has a right to be a government employee," the minority declared. They asserted that the act was not a bill of attainder.

The two justices indicated clearly their sympathy for the act. Calling the body which drafted the law "intelligent and able," they asserted that the law "is not a carelessly thought out enactment." "We should not create any doubt," they added, "that the people can adopt such a policy [as that embodied in the Ober Act] even if we do not now pass upon all the provisions of the act."

Elections in 1950 and 1951 afforded rulings on the merits of the loyalty provisions applicable to candidates for public office. In 1950 certain candidates offered by the Progressive Party refused to submit the loyalty affidavits required by the law. Upon being denied a place on the ballot, they instituted proceedings to secure a writ of mandamus directing the secretary of state to place their names before the voters. An unfavorable decision from a lower state court was appealed by Louis Shub, the Progressive candidate for governor, and Thelma Gerende, candidate for the House of Representatives from the Second Maryland District.

The Court of Appeals unanimously reversed the lower court's ruling insofar as it applied to Miss Gerende, holding that the Maryland legislature had no power to prescribe qualifications for a member of the United States Congress. By a 3–2 decision, however, it upheld the denial of relief to Shub.[27]

The majority of the court looked upon the loyalty declaration as a means of giving effect to the amendment to the state constitution adopted in 1948 barring advocates of the violent overthrow of government from public office. In demanding the declaration of candidates for state office, the judges asserted, "the Legislature has

[27] *Shub v. Simpson,* 75 A. 2d 842 (1950), 76 A. 2d 332 (1950). Because of of the imminence of the election, the court rendered its decision upon hearing argument without delaying for the preparation of opinions. Shub unsuccessfully sought an immediate review of the *per curiam* decision from the United States Supreme Court. By a 6–3 vote, the national tribunal refused to intervene until the Maryland justices issued opinions indicating the reasoning by which they had arrived at their decisions, precluding review before the election in which the appellant desired to run. 340 U.S. 861 (1950).

performed a duty, owing to the voters of the State, in requiring from those who seek their suffrages proof in advance . . . that if they are elected, they will be able to hold the office they seek."

The dissenting minority pointed to the provision of the state constitution which bars the legislature from imposing any oath of office other than that contained in the constitution itself and declared "one constitutional provision may not be violated in order to 'implement' another." Further, the dissenters observed, the loyalty declaration goes far beyond the scope of the constitutional amendment which it is supposed to implement, requiring a disavowal of membership in foreign subversive organizations which may not advocate violence at all. To this latter objection the majority had no convincing rejoinder to offer.

The majority opinion quickly disposed of the contention that the Ober Act violates constitutional guarantees of freedom of speech, an issue on which the minority was completely silent. Noting the findings of the legislature as to the extent and gravity of the Communist menace and expressing respect for the legislature's judgment, the opinion simply asserted, "The purpose of Chapter 86 . . . is not to restrict freedom of speech or thought, nor does it do so."

With this decision began the process of whittling down the Ober Act by judicial interpretation which was to be consummated by the United States Supreme Court. The majority of the Maryland Court of Appeals asserted that the "purpose" of the law "is to prevent infiltration in our state, county, or municipal governments of persons who are engaged in one way or another in the attempt to overthrow the government by force or violence."

When the law was next challenged, the Maryland tribunals simply pointed to the decision in the case of *Shub v. Simpson*. This time suit was brought by Miss Gerende, who sought to run for a seat in the Baltimore City Council in 1951 without filing a loyalty affidavit. Appeal was taken from the adverse decision of the state courts to the United States Supreme Court, which unanimously upheld the provisions of the law under attack.

What the Supreme Court upheld, however, was something much narrower than the loyalty declaration intended by the authors of the Act. Seizing upon the pronouncement of the Maryland court as to the law's purpose, the national tribunal declared, "We read this decision [*Shub v. Simpson*] to hold that to obtain a place on a Maryland ballot a candidate need only make oath that he is not a person who is engaged 'in one way or another in the attempt to overthrow the government by force or violence' and that he is not knowingly a member of an organization engaged in such an attempt. . . ." [28]

The Supreme Court was guided to this conclusion by Attorney General Hall Hammond, who, in the course of oral argument, assured the court that this restricted interpretation of the loyalty oath had been proclaimed by Maryland's highest court. Whatever the intention of the state court may have been in *Shub v. Simpson* (and its language was somewhat cryptic), the interpretation of the law can now be regarded as settled.

In effect, the construction placed on the law by the judges discards as verbiage the elaborate provisions relating to foreign subversive organizations. Phrases fashioned by skilled draftsmen with meticulous care have been declared meaningless. Judicial interpretation of the Ober Act was tantamount to judicial emasculation.

FIRST STEPS TOWARD ENFORCEMENT

The application of the Ober Act began with the process of executing loyalty affidavits. Four public employees, all in the service of the city of Baltimore, refused to sign the required statements and were consequently dismissed from their positions. Of these, two were teachers; one was a librarian; and the fourth was a physician in charge of the tuberculosis division of the city's Department of Health. Three of the four are Quakers who objected that their religious convictions prevented them from participating in any way in the enforcement of a law which they considered unjust. The other recusant asserted that her loyalty to democracy would not permit her to sign a statement which she deemed undemocratic. There is no reason to suspect that any of the four was involved in an undertaking that could by any stretch of the meaning of words be branded subversive. Certainly the Quakers are as far

[28] *Gerende v. Board of Supervisors of Elections,* 341 U.S. 56 (1951).

166

removed from the class of dangerous revolutionaries as anyone could be.[29]

The attorney general of Maryland, Hall Hammond, has displayed a marked reluctance to proceed in carrying out the provisions of the law. In a public declaration of policy he announced that he anticipated few prosecutions under the law and that the creation of a special agency for enforcing the act was intended chiefly for its "psychological effect." [30]

In interpreting the provisions of the law, Hammond proved to be a strict constructionist even before he urged upon the Supreme Court the restricted construction of the loyalty provisions given judicial sanction in the *Gerende* case. From the beginning he declined to exercise surveillance over the appointing authorities in the state's administrative system to determine whether loyalty affidavits are actually secured from all present and prospective public employees. The responsibility for securing such affidavits, he asserted, rests wholly with the appointing authorities. Again, when an election in the city of Cumberland gave rise to the inquiry whether the act required the execution of loyalty declarations by candidates for local office, Hammond ruled that it did not except in Baltimore.[31]

[29] Tribute was paid, by their supervisors and associates, to two of the dismissed employees for faithful and efficient service. When the Baltimore board of education considered the case of Vera Shank, elementary school teacher, the city's superintendent of schools expressed the "hope that a way can be found to make it unnecessary to terminate the services of capable, efficient public servants like Miss Shank" (*Sun* [Baltimore], March 31, 1950, p. 34). The Maryland Library Association lauded Elizabeth Haas, the dismissed librarian, for her personal and professional qualifications (*Sun,* May 21, 1950, p. 32).

[30] *Sun* (Baltimore), April 27, 1950, p. 25.

[31] The letter of the law seems to support this interpretation. But the assumption made by most who were familiar with the law (and the interpretation given by the city solicitor of Cumberland) was that loyalty affidavits were required of candidates for public office on any political level within the state. The Ober commission's Report contains no indication that this requirement would have less than universal applicability (*Report,* p. 45).

The special assistant attorney general in charge of subversive activities is O. Bowie Duckett, whose experience has been in general law practice. Duckett attended the United States Naval Academy and served in the judge advocate general's Department of the Army in World War II. For information on Communist activity he reads such publications as the *Daily Worker, Plain Talk,* and *Counterattack* and consults with the staff of the Un-American Activities Committee of the House of Representatives and the Federal Bureau of Investigation (which he finds uncommunicative).

Duckett is gradually developing a small investigative staff. Two state policemen and two members of the Baltimore city police department, specially selected for their jobs on the basis of a competitive examination, have been assigned to work under his direction. Military Intelligence is contributing to their training by schooling them in counterintelligence techniques.

Dossiers have been compiled on more than eighty residents of the state by the office of the assistant attorney general in charge of subversive activities. The information contained in them and the identity of the individuals concerned are jealously guarded secrets. Duckett will reveal only that the subjects are suspected of engaging in Communist activities in the recent past. As of the summer of 1951, seven or eight public employees are under investigation as a result of allegations that they are, or have been, in the service of the Communist Party.

Duckett receives a small number of complaints from private individuals who believe that they have detected some violation of the law. Complaints from such sources are likely to be trivial and irrelevant. Several people have asserted that the public libraries give undue prominence to their display of works dealing with Russia and communism while they bury books concerning the United States in remote and inaccessible stacks. Such allegations Duckett dismisses on the ground that the facts at best constitute no violation of the law he is enforcing.

A complaint that received considerable public notice was the charge that subversive influences were at work in the school system of Montgomery County. The complainant, a Washington attorney, Franklin T. Miles, specifically alleged that three series of textbooks used in the county schools were subversive [32] and that Russian-born Mrs. Shura Lewis delivered a subversive talk before the students of a high school in Silver Spring in 1947. He hinted, however, that investigation into the county school system would unearth evidence of further subversive activity.[33]

To this complaint Duckett replied that "the statement of charges does not set forth a cause of action against the State or County school officials under the Subversive Activities Act of 1949." His examination of such books cited in the complaint as were still in use in the school system led him to conclude that there was nothing subversive in them. This reply to his charges, Miles denounced as a "Millard Tydings type of whitewash attempt."

One public employee has been dismissed from his position since the Ober Act became effective on the basis of strong suspicion that he was a Communist. William W. Hinckley, a teacher of English in a Montgomery County high school, accused by Elizabeth Bentley of being a party member, refused to tell the House Committee on Un-American Activities in June, 1950, whether or not he was a Communist on the ground that his answer might be self-incriminatory. In 1939 he had denied before the same committee that he was a Communist. Hinckley did not contest his dismissal from the public school system.

Prosecution of Hinckley for perjury was not undertaken, although he had executed the loyalty affidavit required by the Ober Act. After an investigation Assistant Attorney General Duckett concluded that no evidence could be produced to show that Hinckley was a Communist at the time at which he made his declaration of loyalty.[34]

[32] Bruner-Smith Social Studies, *Building America* Series, and "certain books" by Harold O. Rugg.

[33] Miles is an old hand at spotting subversion in the schools. The charges here indicated were made by him to the county commissioners of Montgomery County, to the county board of education, to Governor Lane and to the state superintendent of schools at various times in 1948. His inability to impress any of these officers with the seriousness of his charges led him to ask the governor to investigate the state superintendent of schools.

[34] Two other high-school teachers were dismissed during the summer

Nor has any other prosecution taken place under the criminal provisions of the Ober Act. No applicant for public employment has refused to execute the loyalty declaration. No sort of investigation has been conducted to determine whether present or prospective public employees measure up to the statutory standards of loyalty. As far as the writer can determine, there is no loyalty check in operation at any governmental level within the state; nothing is done by appointing authorities beyond the practice of requiring public workers to sign the prescribed affidavits.[35]

The candidates of the major parties in the 1950 state election and in Baltimore's 1951 municipal election declared themselves loyal without a murmur of protest. Some—but not all—candidates of the Progressive Party refused to execute the required affidavits, thereby contributing to the judicial history of the act.

The private educational institutions in the state which receive public funds have filed statements certifying that their employees are not subversive. The presidents of the smaller institutions vouch for their faculties and administrative staffs on the basis of their personal knowledge of the employees concerned. Johns Hopkins University appointed a faculty committee to determine whether the procedures used in selecting faculty and administrative employees included adequate safeguards against infiltration by subversive individuals. The committee's investigation and affirmative answer to the question were accepted at compliance with the

---

of 1951 after being identified as Communist Party members within the past five years. The identification was made by Mary Stalcup Markward before the Committee on Un-American Activities.

[35] A canvass of all appointing officers within the state would be an impossible task. Extensive inquiry by the writer into the practices followed by state, county, and municipal appointing authorities, however, failed to reveal any use of investigative processes. Since the passage in the text above was written, one subdivision of the state, Montgomery County, has begun to inquire about the loyalty of prospective county employees. An applicant for a position in the county government is required to furnish the names of five character references. Both the applicant and the five individuals whom he has designated are asked whether he is a member of a Communist or Fascist organization or an advocate of violent revolution.

requirements of the Ober Act. Washington College in Chestertown, Maryland, has adopted a procedure of its own. Before the appointment of new faculty members, it secures statements that the prospective appointee "is a loyal citizen of the United States and has not engaged and is not now engaging in subversive activities." These assurances are sought from persons named as references by the applicant for a faculty position.

Compliance by educators with the law's provisions has been willing, though in many cases unenthusiastic. Dr. Richard D. Weigle, President of St. John's College in Annapolis, incorporated in his certification of the loyalty of his staff and faculty a statement summarizing the attitude most commonly expressed by educators toward this aspect of the law.

> The mere imposition of an oath completely fails to accomplish the desirable ends which the General Assembly had in view in passing this legislation. Experience has already shown that most individuals penalized by the terms of this Act have been persons of the Quaker persuasion who every one would agree constituted excellent security risks. The truly subversive person cannot be detected by the administration of an oath as he has no scruples as to the means to be followed in achieving his sinister ends.

Declaring that St. John's College would not harbor any individual who "engages in acts subversive of the State or the National Government," Weigle added that his college "stands firmly upon the principle of academic freedom" and will continue to encourage its students "to read fully and carefully works of varying political, economic, and social doctrine." He concluded by expressing distaste for combatting subversion by repressing ideas.

ESTIMATE OF THE OBER ACT

In dealing with what it defines as subversion the Ober Act adheres closely to the pattern of criminal syndicalism laws found in other states, a pattern to which the federal Smith Act conforms as well. The national government and thirty-nine other states now have on their statute books laws prohibiting the advocacy of violence to effect political change. In order to avoid a constitutional obstacle, the Ober Act incorporates the clear-and-present-danger rule in one of its provisions relating to mere talk. Thus not every utterance of an individual urging the violent overthrow of government is made criminal; to constitute a crime under the law, the utterance must be made in circumstances in which it amounts to a clear and present danger to the security of the national or the state government. This limitation is found only in a provision relating to the advocacy of violence by an individual.[36] An organization advocating the violent overthrow of government is illegal, and any member of it is subject to punishment, whether there is any clear and present danger that the organization's talk will erupt into violent acts or not.

Precedent suggests that the constitutionality of the foregoing provisions is unassailable. The Supreme Court of the United States upheld criminal syndicalism laws in three cases in the 1920's [37] and the highest courts of at least seventeen states have taken the same stand.[38]

---

[36] The force of this limitation may not be all that it seems. In the preamble of the law is contained a finding by the legislature that "the Communist movement plainly presents a clear and present danger to the United States Government and to the State of Maryland." In the light of this finding, a court might hold that proof of clear and present danger need not be offered in order to convict a Communist who advocates violence.

[37] *Gitlow v. New York,* 268 U.S. 652 (1925); *Burns v. United States,* 274 U.S. 328 (1927); *Whitney v. California,* 274 U.S. 357 (1927). In upholding the constitutionality of the Smith Act, the Supreme Court has ended all doubt as to its present attitude toward such laws. *Dennis v. United States,* 341 U.S. 494 (1951).

[38] *State v. Moilen,* 140 Minn. 112, 167 N.W. 345 (1918); *State v. Tachin,* 92 N.J.L. 269, 106 Atl. 145 (1919); *State v. Gibson,* 189 Iowa 1212, 174 N.W. 34 (1919); *State v. Kahn,* 56 Mont. 108, 182 Pac. 107 (1919); *In re Moriarity,* 44 Nev. 164, 191 Pac. 360 (1920); *People v. Steelik,* 187 Cal. 361, 203 Pac. 78 (1921); *State v. Hennessy,* 114 Wash. 351, 195 Pac. 211 (1921); *People v. Gitlow,* 234 N.Y. 132, 136 N.E. 317 (1922), 234 N.Y. 539, 138 N.E. 438 (1922); *People v. Lloyd,* 304 Ill. 23, 136 N.E. 505 (1922); *State v. Dingman,* 37 Idaho 253, 219 Pac. 760 (1923); *People v. Ruthenberg,* 229 Mich. 315, 201 N.W. 358 (1924); *Berg v. State,* 29 Ok.Cr.R. 112, 233 Pac. 497 (1925); *Commonwealth v. Widovich,* 295 Pa. 311, 295 Atl. 295 (1929); *State v. Boloff,* 138 Ore. 568, 4 P. 2d 326 (1931); *Carr v. State,*

In prohibiting foreign subversive organizations and punishing their members, on the other hand, the Ober Act moves into an area where direct precedents are lacking, and constitutional issues are somewhat less clear. A foreign subversive organization is an organization controlled "directly or indirectly" by a foreign power which seeks to establish a puppet government in the United States. There is room for serious doubt that the ban which the Ober Act imposes on such organizations is constitutional. If political, social, or economic change is advocated without resort to violence or other illegal means, the advocate of change—no matter how drastic—cannot be punished. If change is sought by peaceful means, by orderly discussion, by ballot, by the established processes of lawmaking and constitutional amendment, urging it cannot be made an offense without violating the freedoms of the First Amendment.[39] Nor can the advocates be punished for banding together to advance their cause by peaceful means.

The provision of the Ober Act under discussion makes criminal any organized advocacy of the establishment of a government under foreign domination in the United States regardless of the means by which such a change is to be brought about if the organization seeking the change is under foreign control "directly or indirectly." A group of this description which seeks to effect its

---

176 Ga. 55, 166 S.E. 827 (1932); *State v. Kassay,* 126 Ohio St. 177, 184 N.E. 521 (1932); *Barton v. Bessemer,* 234 Ala. 20, 173 So. 626 (1937). The highest tribunal of New Mexico seems to be the only state supreme court which has invalidated a law of this type, *State v. Diamond,* 27 N.M. 477, 202 Pac. 988 (1921).

[39] *Fiske v. Kansas,* 274 U.S. 380, 386 (1927); *Stromberg v. California,* 283 U.S. 359, 369 (1931); *Herndon v. Lowry,* 301 U.S. 242, 258 (1937); *Schneidermann v. United States,* 320 U.S. 118, 137 (1943); *State v. Diamond,* 27 N.M. 477, 202 Pac. 988 (1921); *State v. Tachin,* 92 N.J.L. 269, 106 Atl. 145 (1919). In view of the fact that the section of the Ober Act here discussed bears some resemblance to sec. 4 of the Mundt-Nixon Bill, it is interesting to note that that part of the proposed national law was pronounced unconstitutional by Charles Evans Hughes, Jr., and Seth Richardson. *Hearings before the Committee of the Judiciary, United States Senate, Eightieth Congress, Second Session on H.R. 5852* (1948), pp. 416, 444.

173

aim by a constitutional amendment is illegal under this sweeping proscription. The test that Ober himself offered for the determination of the constitutionality of legislation restricting speech lends no support to this provision. "Everyone is at liberty," he declared, "to advocate change in our government by the orderly methods prescribed by the Constitution. The moment he urges the substitution of the bullet for the ballot he becomes an enemy of society and should be treated as such." [40] The Ober Act here makes no distinction, however, between change by bullet and change by ballot. Members of foreign subversive organizations are criminals, whether they want to shoot or want to vote.

It may be argued that organizations under foreign control do not enjoy the rights of free speech and assembly and that consequently restrictions which could not be constitutionally imposed on groups directed by American hands may be laid on those that take orders from abroad. Aside from the constitutional questions that such an argument raises, this theory has dangerous implications. It is the right of Americans to assemble that is being interfered with when foreign-controlled organizations are banned. A denial of their right to join bodies commanded from abroad might at some future time be turned against organizations completely unrelated to the Politburo.

But these considerations are not necessary to the resolution of the constitutional question posed by the provision of the Ober Act under consideration. It is probably defective because of vagueness if on no other ground. What constitutes foreign control is not indicated in the law, and no help toward settling this problem is offered when the law bans organizations which are *indirectly* controlled by a foreign power as well as those subject to direct control from abroad. Without some standard written into the law by which one can judge whether a given organization is controlled directly or indirectly by a foreign power, an essential element of due process is lacking.

The criminal provisions relating to foreign subversive organizations have probably been erased from the statute in effect by the decision in *Gerende v. Board of Supervisors of Elections*. But it is

[40] *American Bar Association Journal*, 34 (August, 1948), 745.

at least interesting to see how the law read before the judges made their emendations.

The Ober Act does not seem to be vulnerable to the criticism that it establishes guilt by association, though its opponents have stressed this objection. To convict a member of a proscribed organization under the law, the fact of membership plus knowledge of the organization's illegal purpose must be established. The requirements for conviction are the same as those which must be established under any conspiracy statute. That these two elements constitute personal guilt is too well settled to admit of doubt that the courts will uphold the provisions punishing the rank-and-file members of prohibited organizations.[41]

There are other issues besides those of constitutionality which demand attention. Punishment of the small fry is likely to be pointless and ineffective at best. Any good derived from it may be far outweighed by the possibility of grave injustice to the innocent and the innocuous. That the danger of injustice in the application of the law against the ordinary member of a prohibited organization is not illusory can be demonstrated from experience in those states which have vigorously enforced their criminal syndicalism laws. Where patent abuse in the application of such laws has occurred, one generally finds that prosecution was undertaken under the "membership" provisions.[42] In Maryland where the jury judges the law as well as the facts, the danger of abuse is more acute than elsewhere, for here the power of an appellate court to reverse the decision of a trial court is extremely restricted.[43]

If ordinary members are to be punished, the unwary should

[41] "Guilt by Association—Three Words in Search of a Meaning," 17 Univ. of Chicago Law Review, 148–162 (1949).

[42] Eldridge F. Dowell, *A History of Criminal Syndicalism Legislation in the United States* (Baltimore, 1939), pp. 85 ff.; Zechariah Chafee, Jr., *Free Speech in the United States* (New York, 1941), pp. 475–481, 513–514; G. W. Kirchwey, *A Survey of the Workings of the California Criminal Syndicalism Law* (New York, 1926). A sample case would be *State v. Boloff*, 138 Ore. 568, 4 P. 2d 326 (1931).

[43] S. K. Dennis, "Maryland's Antique Constitutional Thorn," 92 University of Pennsylvania Law Review, 34–52 (Sept., 1943).

get added protection in the form of a provision clearly requiring proof of personal knowledge of the illegal purpose of an organization for conviction. Knowledge that the attorney general or some other state official has declared a given organization subversive should not be considered to establish *scienter*.[44] Finally, the penalty imposed on the ordinary member should be reduced. As the act stands, it authorizes penalties up to $5,000 and/or five years' imprisonment.[45] Let us attack mosquitoes with swatters, not with a sixteen-inch cannon. Ober himself intended the provisions applicable to mere members as a shotgun behind the door, rarely if ever brought into use. Subversive groups, he believed, would wither away once their leaders were convicted. But the author's intentions do not determine how the law will be enforced. Zealous prosecutors might decide that the legislation meant what it said.

The lower court which found the Ober Act unconstitutional pointed to a serious hardship which could follow from the enforcement of the law against the members of labor unions. If a union, found subversive because it was dominated by Communists, had a union shop agreement with Employer X, the employees of X would find themselves face to face with a weird dilemma. Withdrawing from the union would mean unemployment; remaining in it would bring conviction for subversion. The inconveniences attached to either course of action need no comment.

The hardship that can be imposed on ordinary members is the most objectionable aspect of laws which condemn groups and movements, as the Ober Act does. The unique feature of the Maryland law is its outlawing of organizations. There seems to be no other law anywhere in the United States (except the New

[44] One who believes that courts will inevitably construe the word "knowing" in a statute of this kind to require proof of personal knowledge should consult the decision of the Supreme Court of California in *People v. McClennegen*, 195 Cal. 445, 234 Pac. 91 (1925) ("proof of the act of joining an organization shown to be such as the statute denounces is a sufficient showing of the knowledge of the purposes of the organization").

[45] Most members would probably be subject to the sterner penalties of $20,000 and/or 20 years' imprisonment. If they paid dues, they would be, for having contributed to the support of an illegal organization.

176

Hampshire copy of the Ober Act) which comes as close to banning the Communist Party.

The loyalty program envisaged by the Ober Act is similar in some respects to that of the national government. Here again the act did not follow an uncharted path. Twenty-nine states had earlier imposed some sort of loyalty requirement for public employees, eight additional states (including Maryland) enacted a loyalty law in 1949, and Mississippi joined the ranks in 1950. In most of the states all that is demanded is the execution of a declaration of loyalty by those holding a public position. Only in Maryland, Mississippi, and New Hampshire does the law impose a statewide loyalty program involving more than securing affidavits from the employees affected.[46]

Courts which have passed on loyalty measures offer little comfort to the opponents of such devices.[47] The judiciary has in most instances declined to intervene to prevent the execution of loyalty programs or to stay dismissals for disloyalty. Maryland's Court of Appeals and the United States Supreme Court have upheld the loyalty declaration which the Ober Act requires of candidates for public office. It is unlikely that any part of the law's loyalty program can be successfully challenged on constitutional grounds,

[46] In New York a more elaborate test of loyalty is prescribed for teachers by the Feinberg Law (c. 360, *Laws of the State of New York of 1949*), which makes membership in organizations found subversive by the state board of regents prima facie evidence of unfitness to teach. Los Angeles County, California, requires its employees to declare that they are not members of any one of 145 specified organizations. *Parker v. Los Angeles,* 338 U.S. 327 (1949), *Steiner v. Darby,* 88 Cal. App. 2d 481, 199 P. 2d 429 (1948).

[47] *Friedman v. Schwellenbach,* 159 F. 2d 22 (1946), cert. den. 330 U.S. 838 (1947); *Bailey v. Richardson,* 182 F. 2d 46 (1950), 341 U.S. 918 (1951); *Garner v. Board of Public Works of Los Angeles,* 341 U.S. 716 (1951); *Thompson v. Wallin,* 95 N.E. 2d 806, 301 N.Y. 476 (1950); *Thorp v. Board of Trustees,* 79 A. 2d 462, (N.J.) (1951). That the procedure followed under a loyalty program may deny due process is suggested in *Joint Anti-Fascist Refugee Committee v. McGrath,* 341 U.S., 123 (1951). State courts have sometimes voided loyalty oaths on the ground of conflict with state constitutions. *Imbrie v. Marsh,* 71 A. 2d 352 (1950); *Tolman v. Underhill,* 229 P. 2d 447 (1951).

although the courts might refuse to sanction arbitrary applications of it in individual cases.

The loyalty statement prescribed by the Ober Act has met with strenuous objections. Teachers' organizations have attacked the loyalty declaration most vigorously, displaying the reaction which a hostess might expect if she asked her guests to take an oath that they would not steal the silverware. The writer is unable to discern any threat to academic freedom or any infringement of a right that can reasonably be asserted in barring from public employment those who are unwilling to say that they do not advocate the overthrow of government by force or the establishment of a puppet government in the United States. It may be granted that some loyalty oaths are highly objectionable. The oath demanded of Rhode Island's teachers obliging them to teach a specific theory of government, the oath required of Georgia's officeholders disavowing "sympathy" for any of the doctrines of communism would be cases in point. Such oaths, strictly interpreted and applied, restrict free inquiry. But the declaration demanded by the Ober Act restrains no one from seeking or speaking truth. In determining whether any given pledge of loyalty is to be condemned, the important considerations are the questions what the affiant is asked to be loyal to and what he is asked to refrain from doing.

The use of a loyalty oath to bar individuals or parties from the ballot is another thing. Democracy fails fully to live up to its claims when voters are denied the chance to vote for Communists or anybody else for public office. And, from another point of view, permitting the Communist Party to offer candidates for elective office has the salutary effect of refuting Communists' claims and quieting anti-Communists' fears that the party has a powerful following. The returns in the ballot box will only disclose how few the Communists among us are.

The Ober Act provides for a flexible loyalty program, granting to the several thousand appointing officers within the state the power to establish procedural rules for determining loyalty. The authority conferred on those who appoint to public jobs is in fact the power to determine the loyalty of the men and women holding or seeking such positions. The act guarantees a hearing and the right of appeal to job holders before they can be discharged for disloyalty but gives no guarantee of any sort to applicants for positions in the service of the state. In the discretionary authority which it confers on appointing authorities, high and low, the act introduces some danger of petty tyranny. If a program of this delicate nature is to be employed, it should be subjected to close supervision by a responsible officer of high rank. Allowing each appointing officer to adopt his own procedures for testing loyalty and to determine who is loyal and who is not may produce confusing variation, erratic and uncertain standards, error and injustice.

By granting appointing authorities the power to prescribe the procedures by which their agencies would determine the loyalty of present and prospective employees, the Ober Act was designed to avoid the imposition of needless effort. It was recognized that the consequences of employing a Communist street sweeper would not be serious enough to justify any elaborate inquiry into the subject of his loyalty. In fact, the law permits public agencies to employ common laborers without conducting any investigation of them. The exemption might well have been extended to other classes of public employees holding "nonsensitive" positions in which a Communist, however zealous he might be, could do no harm. In this "nonsensitive" category would fall the bulk of the positions at the level of state government and below except for those in the militia, the state police, education, and the agencies which administer justice.

The imposition of rough standards of loyalty forged by political leaders upon private educational institutions is an ominous possibility under the Ober Act. No private school may receive state funds unless it has adopted procedures to determine whether subversive individuals are in its employ and has taken steps to terminate such employment. A lever is thereby provided by which small-minded politicians may impose their standards of loyalty upon some of the schools of the state if they are disposed to do so. The only penalty imposed upon an institution which refuses to carry out this provision of the law is denial of financial support from the state treasury. To Johns Hopkins University, which derives about 1 per cent of its income from the state, the penalty which the law imposes directly would not be severe; to St. John's

College, which depends on the state treasury for one-seventh of its revenue, the result would be catastrophic. That the law carries indirect and intangible penalties; that an institution might suffer in other ways than by loss of a subvention in consequence of a difference of opinion with political leaders on the matter of what constitutes loyalty ought not to be overlooked. In the writer's opinion the present political leaders of the state have too much respect for the great private schools of Maryland to seek to place them under any sort of political control. It may not be always thus.

The seriousness of the defects mentioned should not be exaggerated. The weight to be accorded to the criticism directed at most provisions of the law depends on the degree of probability that the abuses permitted by such provisions will actually occur. Fear of abuse has been voiced by such responsible groups as labor unions, the National Association for the Advancement of Colored People, the Johns Hopkins chapter of the American Association of University Professors, the Maryland Library Association, and the Young Women's Christian Association. The record to date in no way confirms their fear. There has been no witch hunt, no censorship, no character assassination, no persecution under the law. The special assistant attorney general in charge of enforcing the act has refused an invitation to censor textbooks. General unwillingness to assume the power to investigate applicants for state employment has been manifested by those to whom such authority has been granted. There are no signs observable that the immediate future will bring a rigorous policy of enforcement.

Public opinion aroused by the Korean conflict or an extension of it might in the future force a change of policy. Men who are less scrupulous about avoiding abuse of the power conferred by the act might be installed in office. Therein lies a danger which is not wholly illusory. Some complaints have already been voiced that the Ober Act is not strong enough. Some legislators reveal impatience with the circumspection with which the attorney general's office has gone about enforcing the act. War—especially a war of retreats, defeats, and heavy casualties—could quickly create a temper which will brook no moderation in the application of the law.

The need for the Ober Act was never satisfactorily demonstrated by its proponents. According to the Ober commission's figures, the Communist Party in Maryland was a puny organization of 2,700 members. According to figures offered by J. Edgar Hoover in July, 1950, Communist adherents in Maryland number only 754. When the party last appeared on the ballot in the state in 1940, it polled 1,200 votes. The only Communist known to have been on the public payroll was a kindergarten teacher in the Baltimore school system, who was dismissed in 1948. Since the passage of the Ober Act, three "probables" have been found in the school system, all of whom were removed without recourse to the Ober Act.

As the Ober commission understood its task, determining whether there was a need for a law was no part of it. Anticipating the objections that ignoring this question would provoke, the commission sought to make clear the scope of its work in this passage in its report, "It should be stated at the outset that the Commission was not appointed to act as a fact-finding commission, but that its duties are confined to the preparation of a legislative program designed to meet the facts as found by the Legislature." [48] Had the legislature done some serious fact finding, perhaps no objection could be raised to this explanation. But all that the legislature actually did was to pause in the middle of its special session of 1948 (which was devoted to other matters) just long enough to pass without discussion the resolution creating the Commission on Subversive Activities. The facts which it found in that resolution were copied from Section 2 of the Mundt-Nixon Bill and, at best, fail to establish the extent of the Communist menace in Maryland.

In its report the Ober commission, nevertheless, cites facts and expresses opinions which have some bearing on the question of whether the law is needed. It describes the expansion of the Russian sphere of control in Europe and Asia since World War II; it points to the powerful Communist parties in France and Italy; it demonstrates the servile adherence of American Communists to the party line; it cites cases of Communist espionage, Communist domination of labor unions, and Communist infiltration in educational institutions in other states.

[48] *Report,* p. 8.

When it turns to the subject of dangerous Communist activity in Maryland, however, the commission's report has nothing to say beyond a vague reference to the Hiss-Chambers espionage activity of more than a decade ago, some episodes of which took place within the state. The commission further expresses strong suspicion that subversion has sidled unnoticed into the schools. Without citing facts or authority to substantiate the conclusion, the Ober commission asserts that it has been "informed that there is substantial infiltration in some Maryland [educational] institutions." [49] It sent questionnaires to the private colleges and universities in the state to determine whether they were suffering from infiltration. The negative replies received from these institutions are discounted by the commission with the comment, "One of the curious factors that constantly appear in the study of Communism is that, due to its secret conspiratorial methods, the victims of infiltration are the last to discover it." [50]

The legislature of Maryland and the Ober commission have declared the Communist movement to be a clear and present danger to the United States. And so it is. It is possibly the greatest danger this nation has ever faced. But the Ober commission has exaggerated the strength and the influence of domestic Communists. The handful of Communists at home could rise to the stature of a real menace only in the event of war between the United States and Russia or of a major depression.

That Russia has a fifth column in the United States in the ranks of the Communist Party is hardly open to question. That American Communists are capable of some serious mischief in time of war is almost equally certain. On these considerations is built the strongest case that can be made for the Ober Act, a case which is buttressed by the war in Korea. The Ober Act may afford protection against espionage and sabotage as well as against lesser impediments to the efficient prosecution of a war. Yet doubt remains as to whether state or national agencies are better equipped to provide such protection.

A depression in the United States might turn its victims to communism and make the Communist Party an important political

---

[49] *Ibid.*, p. 47. [50] *Ibid.*, p. 51.

force. Here again is a threat against which the Ober Act may offer some protection. Obviously the law does not attack the cause of the danger. Even if efficacious, it would be a highly undesirable method of supporting existing economic and social arrangements. From every point of view it is better to drain the swamps in which Communists breed than to try to exterminate the Communists themselves.

The most basic criticism that can be made of the Ober commission's report is that it nowhere comes to grips with the problem of what causes Communists. It fails to recognize the fact that the Communist movement draws recruits chiefly from those who suffer injustice under the prevailing economic and social order. Measures designed to remedy injustice and to prevent needless suffering have no place in the anti-Communist program offered by the Ober commission. In fact, the commission dismisses such measures as the utopian schemes of impractical men who are "bold enough to suppose that we can attain the millennium in our time." [51] Of course, it is not a question of attaining the millennium now—or ever. Opening the doors of the University of Maryland to Negroes or eliminating some of Baltimore's slums would hardly amount to millenarian reforms. But they would strike at grievances that make men rebel against the existing social system. Because such reforms go to the causes of the evil to be attacked, they should commend themselves to the most hardheaded realist as a form of insurance against communism.

[51] *Ibid.,* p. 58.

IV. MICHIGAN

State and Local Attack on Subversion

By ROBERT J. MOWITZ   *January, 1951*

MICHIGAN is no newcomer to the ranks of those alarmed by subversive activities. Its statute books contain the normal safeguards against all sorts of criminal violence, whether inspired by domestic politics, international intrigue, or the more customary motivations of malefaction. Moreover, it specifically outlaws treason and misprison of treason, sedition, criminal syndicalism, the display of red flags, and the wearing of masks and disguises by those intent upon defying the state's authority. It requires its teachers and public servants to attest to their fidelity.*

Yet Michigan remains unpersuaded that it is secure against subversion. In 1947 its legislature enacted a sweeping and, according to the attorney general, an unconstitutional statute aimed at individuals and organizations which serve "directly or indirectly the purposes, aims or objects of a foreign power." In succeeding years the legislature has continued to evince a lively distrust of the

[Mr. Mowitz is Assistant Professor of Public Administration in Wayne University.]

* The author would like to acknowledge his indebtedness to Josephine Sclafani, William Monat, and Henry Morin, graduate students, for their invaluable assistance in this research, and to those public officials and others who have granted the author interviews.

ability of the state's institutions and statutes to withstand the assaults of Communist doctrine without the aid of additional legislation. Investigations of subversion have become almost a staple activity; and in 1950 the legislature resisted the governor's advice that further lawmaking be postponed until a gubernatorial commission of legal experts could analyze the pertinent constitutional problems.

Finally, in the apparent belief that despite the long-continued concern of the legislators a Communist conspiracy might be menacing the public services of the state's largest city, Detroit in 1950 initiated what is perhaps the first full-scale "loyalty program" on the municipal level in the United States. The threads of local politics, colored by the international conflicts of the era, have been woven into a tapestry that deserves close attention. The model that Detroit is providing may be seized upon in other cities. What is now only an isolated phenomenon may tomorrow become a pattern.

CRIMINAL SYNDICALISM

Our story in Michigan starts in 1919. In that year the Michigan legislature became one of nearly a score that, in the brief span between 1917 and 1920, enacted a statute identifying the crime of criminal syndicalism and prescribing its punishment.[1] Criminal syndicalism was defined as "the doctrine which advocates crime, sabotage, violence or other unlawful methods of terrorism as a means of accomplishing industrial or political reform." Those who advocated this doctrine, whether by speech or otherwise, were declared to be felons, as also were those who organized or were members of or even merely assembled with any group that spread the noxious doctrine.

The law was in terms an embracive one. And clearly it was intended to be so, for the legislators beat off attempts to except from its reach the already established farmers' organizations and the constituent unions of the American Federation of Labor.[2]

[1] *Pub. Acts* 1919, No. 255; *Pub. Acts* 1931, No. 328; *Mich. Stat. Ann.* sec. 28.235, 28.236 (1935).

[2] During legislative consideration of the bill an amendment was in-

The chief focus of alarm immediately after World War I, however, was neither the farmer nor the laborer. It was the bearded foreigner, the bomb-laden anarchist who ostensibly inspired the Palmer Red raids of that period. The initial reaction of law enforcement officials to the criminal syndicalism law was one of quiet satisfaction that these foreign menaces might now be controlled. Previously there had been a puzzling inability to detain the evil fellows. Apparently everyone knew that they were dangerous to American democracy. But, unfortunately, it rarely seemed possible to prove that they ever did anything. They merely talked—or, in the words of the statute, "advocated" and "taught" their beliefs. If they had moved from expressing an opinion to acting upon it, the police would have been amply armed by law to deal with them. The rascals stubbornly failed to behave criminally. Now the 1919 statute would plug the gap; it would make possible the apprehension of the talkers as well as the doers. "Radicals who have enjoyed comparative immunity under the espionage act and the immigration laws will find themselves up against something with plenty of teeth when Act 139, the new state criminal syndicalism law, becomes effective Thursday," declared a spokesman for the police.[3]

Not until three years had passed, however, was an occasion found to use the new law. In August of 1922 C. E. Ruthenberg and sixteen others were arrested on the charge that they had voluntarily assembled with the Communist Party of America, a group formed to advocate the forbidden doctrine. Ruthenberg was a prominent Communist of that period who, as a member of the central

---

troduced providing that "this act shall not be construed to apply to any organization which now is, or which may hereafter be organized under the laws of the American Federation of Labor or of any National or International Union affiliated therewith, or of any farmers organization, organized under the rules of any farmers organization now operating in the state." The motion to amend the act with this section originally prevailed but was immediately reconsidered and withdrawn. *House Journal*, 1919, p. 1115.

[3] *Detroit News*, August 13, 1919. Early in 1920 a mass roundup of Reds took place in Detroit, but the action was carried on by immigration officials and provided no judicial test of syndicalism legislation (*ibid.*, Jan. 9, 1920).

executive committee, was a "fraternal delegate" to a surreptitiously held local convention in Bridgman, Michigan. Secretively as the Communists had assembled, their plans were known to federal officers, who laid the matter before the sheriff of Berrien County. That official, accompanied by deputies and the federal agents, promptly raided the convention and without further formality threw Ruthenberg and his companions into the local jail.

The episode evoked a minor protest against the law as an assault on freedom [4] and even led to the introduction of a repealer bill supported by the American Federation of Labor.[5] But the protest was not sustained; the repealer bill died in committee; and the trial of Ruthenberg proceeded quickly to conviction. In 1924 the Michigan Supreme Court upheld the constitutionality of the criminal syndicalism law, saying that it neither contravened the right of the people to assemble peaceably nor impaired freedom of speech, for, said the court, the statute merely "reaches an abuse of the right to freely speak, write and publish sentiments." [6] The court specifically held that no overt act was necessary as an ingredient of criminality under the 1919 law, so that the prosecution was relieved of the necessity of showing that either the Communist Party or any of its adherents had committed or intended to commit in the immediate future any violence within the State of Michigan.

Oddly enough the Ruthenberg incident is the only decisive one

[4] *Detroit News,* Nov. 12, 1922. Report of a speech by Dean Charles N. Lathrop, executive secretary of the social action department of the National Council of the American Episcopal Church, attacking the state "anti-Red law" as an assault on freedom.

[5] *House Journal,* 1923, p. 485. The repeal bill introduced by Mr. Bartlett was referred to the Committee on the Judiciary, where it remained. The repeal measure was backed by the Michigan Federation of Labor, which stated that "the full support of the labor organization in the state will be behind the repeal bill." *Detroit News,* March 28, 1923.

[6] *People v. Ruthenberg,* 229 Mich. 315, 201 N.W. 358 (1924). The court's decision followed those of others passing on similar state statutes, especially *People v. Lloyd,* 304 Ill. 23, 136 N.E. 505 (1922), and *People v. Steelik,* 187 Cal. 361, 203 Pac. 78 (1921). On later appeal to the United States Supreme Court, writ of error dismissed, 273 U.S. 782 (1927).

under the criminal syndicalism law during three decades of state perturbation about Communist plots.

In 1929 three Negroes, representatives of the Good Citizenship League, were arrested on the charge that they possessed literature that would inflame Negroes against white citizens. The police raided a children's home conducted by the league and "removed six children, including one white baby." [7] The case against the defendants seems never to have been pressed.

A few years later, during the farm belt's resistance to mortgage foreclosures at the depth of the depression in 1933, seven farmers were accused of having led a demonstration that resulted in threats to an auctioneer, the burning of a barn, and the destruction of livestock. [8] Despite the actual commission of lawlessly violent acts, the defendants were charged only with criminal syndicalism. Their arrest led once again to an effort to repeal the law. [9] Though the legislative move was unsuccessful, the prosecuting attorney soon moved to quash the charges, and the defendants went free without trial. [10]

Finally, in 1936, the law was brought into play again, this time against twenty-two members of the Black Legion, a secret society that freely used terrorism against Catholics, Jews, Negroes, and the foreign-born. [11] Three years after the indictment of the alleged conspirators the assistant attorney general moved to dismiss the charges because, as he publicly declared, the witnesses had by then left the jurisdiction or were now unwilling to testify. [12]

Thus we see that the law aimed at the "Red" menace has also

[7] *Detroit News,* June 12, 1929.

[8] *Detroit News,* March 13, 1933.

[9] *House Journal,* 1933, pp. 548–549.

[10] *Detroit News,* January 4, 1934. For other news articles relating to this incident see *Detroit News,* 1933: March 14; May 5, 6, and 7; June 6; November 17.

[11] *Detroit News,* August 21, 1936. This issue includes a detailed account of the violent activities of the organization, including murder. See also *Detroit News,* August 22, 1936. An excellent account of the activities of the Black Legion can also be found in *Wilson v. the City of Highland Park,* 284 Mich. 96, 278 N.W. 778 (1938).

[12] *Detroit News,* May 18, 1939.

struck glancing blows at others. With the single exception of Ruthenberg and his cohorts a quarter of a century ago, however, the statute has not added to the state's prison population. The experience of Michigan up to the present strongly suggests that the criminal syndicalism law contributed little of value to the penal code's protections against public dangers.

RED FLAGS

Perhaps the outlawry of criminal syndicalism has had symbolical significance, even though it has had little practical effect on political behavior. The Red Flag law, enacted in 1931, leaves nothing to speculation on that score. It unabashedly and specifically deals with symbols alone.

The 1931 statute provides that the displayer of a red flag "in any public assembly, parade or demonstration" shall be deemed a felon because he has thus used "an emblem of anarchy." [13]

The fact of the matter is that even before this legislative enactment, one who showed a red banner in Michigan might well find himself in jail as a result. As long ago as 1908 the Michigan Supreme Court had had to consider whether a Socialist parade under a red flag constituted a disturbance of the peace and was therefore punishable under an ordinance of the city of Hancock. On that occasion there was no evidence that the paraders had been boisterous or violent. But the court took judicial notice of the possibility that the good citizens of Hancock would become violent and disorderly when they saw the piece of red bunting. The paraders, thought the court, must have known that their flag would "excite fears and apprehensions, and that by displaying it they would provoke violence and disorder." Hence, though the public peace and tranquility had been destroyed by their opponents alone, the paraders were found guilty of aiding, countenancing, and assisting in making a riot, noise, and disturbance.[14]

This precedent, of course, smoothed the path when the constitutionality of the Red Flag statute was challenged before the Michigan Supreme Court. In 1935 the court declared the law

[13] *Pub. Acts* 1931, No. 328, sec. 48; *Mich. Stat. Ann.* sec. 28.237 (1935).
[14] *People v. Burman*, 154 Mich. 150, 117 N.W. 589 (1908).

valid, again resting its decision on the asserted propensity of Americans to become violently enraged when faced with a red flag. In this instance the flag in question was unmistakably Communist in character—red, with a white sickle and hammer. It was flown, however, not amid the hostile urban crowd, but upon the secluded grounds of a children's recreational camp. This was not a distinguishing factor. A public assembly did exist, the court said, because the children were observed assembled beneath the flag.

A more vexing problem seemed to exist because of the statutory identification of the red flag as a symbol of anarchy—"the state of society where there is no law or supreme power; a state of political disorder." Now, whatever else we may quite properly think about the Communist political system, we can scarcely characterize it as one in which "there is no law or supreme power." How, then, could a statute specifically aimed at anarchists be equally applied to Communists? The court had little difficulty with the question. It acknowledged that a marked distinction exists between anarchy and Communism. It even conceded, *arguendo*, that one might advocate the adoption of either by entirely legal means. In the end, though, the court concluded that the red flag has become identified with those who do in fact advocate overthrow of our present form of government by force. "Because the red flag is the insignia of such doctrines and teachings, its use in the manner forbidden by the statute will cause a breach of public peace and endanger the lives and property of citizens generally." [15] And this, added the court, remains true even though the displayer of the flag may himself be an opponent rather than an advocate of the abhorrent principles the color red has come to symbolize.

SEDITION

By 1935 the Michigan legislature had seen its statutory handiwork withstand constitutional attack. It had successfully adopted a law that forbade advocating, teaching, or advising that violence might ever be a proper method of achieving economic or political change. It had made it a crime to associate or voluntarily to assemble with any group that did so advocate or teach, no matter

[15] *People v. Immonen,* 271 Mich. 384, 393, 261 N.W. 59 (1935).

how remote and conditional might be the events that were feared. And it had prohibited even a mute, textile symbol of radicalism— not only, apparently, because it would stir people to revolutionary acts, but because it would arouse patriots to attack radicals.

At this point the legislature resisted the impulse to relax. Instead, in 1935 it added yet another statute, "to promote respect for the constitution, laws, and institutions of this state and the United States; to prohibit and provide penalties for advocating the overthrow of our government by force." [16] This law provides in Section 1, "Any person who advocates, aids, or takes any active part in the overthrow by force or violence of the government of the United States and/or of any state of the United States is guilty of a felony and upon conviction thereof, shall be punished by imprisonment in the state prison for not more than five years, or by a fine of not more than five thousand dollars, or by both such fine and imprisonment, in the discretion of the court." Section 2 provides that the act shall not be construed to prohibit or abridge the lawful right of free speech, impair liberty of the press, or interfere with the right of peaceful picketing or striking in industrial controversies.[17]

So far as the records disclose there has been no application of this statute since its enactment fifteen years ago. It fills no discernible gap in the statute books, for both the advocacy and the action it forbids were already proscribed by existing laws.

FOREIGN AGENTS

The most recent legislation to deal generally with subversion in Michigan reflects a new trend. The so-called Callahan Act, adopted by the legislature in 1947 and ratified on referendum at the general election in 1948, undertakes to guard the state against foreign influence rather than domestic disorder.[18]

[16] *Pub. Acts* 1935, No. 168, p. 266; *Mich. Stat. Ann.* sec. 28.241.

[17] Legislative action on the bill reported in the *Senate Journal*, 1935, pp. 487, 519, 835, 893, 1406. See also *Biennial Report of the Attorney General of the State of Michigan for the Period Ending June 30, 1936*, pp. 138–142. This opinion upholds the constitutionality of the proposed bill.

[18] *Pub. Acts* 1947, No. 270, pp. 418–419; *Mich. Stat. Ann.* sec. 18.58.

The law's declared purpose is to regulate and control the operations of foreign agents in order to enhance the state's security. A
foreign agent is either an individual or a group (which includes
political parties) "subsidized by a foreign government or serving
directly or indirectly the purposes, aims, or objects of a foreign
power" by (1) being inspired from abroad to control or overthrow
our government; (2) acting concertedly with similar organizations
or political parties in foreign countries; (3) having been of foreign
inspiration and now pursuing the objects of a foreign power and
by having been "declared subversive by the Congress of the United
States of America, or the Attorney General of the State of Michigan"; (4) being a "publishing enterprise, radio station, and/or
similar institution for influencing public opinion" under the
control of an organization identified as a foreign agent; or (5)
being a labor union or any other sort of society under control of
any agency "serving the objects and purposes of a foreign power."

All foreign agencies, so defined, are directed to report their
membership, finances, and activities to the attorney general; and
these reports are then to be made available for public inspection.
Whatever such an organization may publish must be labeled as
having been "published in compliance with the law of the State
of Michigan governing the operation of foreign agencies." Disregard of any provision of the law constitutes a felony.

Although the new statute was adopted with little numerical opposition in the legislature itself, public controversy developed
following legislative action.[19] This controversy stemmed in part
from the unwillingness of Attorney General Eugene F. Black to
take steps to enforce the legislation. His explanation of this stand
was that the legislature had not appropriated sufficient funds to

[19] Prior to signing the bill, Governor Kim Sigler held a public hearing
at which spokesmen for labor unions, churches, racial groups, and civic
organizations objected to the bill as "an invasion of free speech, a step
toward totalitarianism, an open door to 'smear campaigns' and an attack
on labor organizations in general." The chairman of the Detroit subversive activities committee of the American Legion appeared in support
of the bill as an enforcement weapon against "underground intrigue"
of Communists and their front organizations. *Detroit News,* June 19,
1947.

permit his department to carry out the task, and that he considered the law to be an unconstitutional invasion by the state of powers exclusively held by Congress.[20]

Senator Matthew F. Callahan of Detroit, who sponsored the law, was joined by spokesmen for the Veterans of Foreign Wars and the American Legion in demanding that the attorney general enforce the law against foreign agencies, but the attorney general stood his ground and refused to act.[21]

[20] *Detroit News,* Sept. 5, Oct. 1, Oct. 5, 1947.

[21] *Detroit News,* Sept. 5, Oct. 5, 1947. The report on October 5 quoted Senator Callahan as stating that the attorney general's position was a step toward "the dissolution of organized society. If the head of any department, and this includes the Attorney General, may exercise his own judgment as to which laws he will enforce, then instead of government there will be nothing but anarchy."

It should be noted that during this period Senator Callahan was chairman of the senate Select Committee on Un-American Activities. This committee was created by senate resolution no. 24, adopted Feb. 13, 1947, and amended and extended by senate resolution no. 44, adopted May 26, 1947. *Senate Journal,* 1947, pp. 182, 207, 212, 1247. Senator Callahan's original resolution, No. 24, called for the appointment of a committee to investigate charges of Communist activities at Wayne University. By the time it was adopted the resolution had been amended so as to broaden the scope of the inquiry to include the investigation of Communist activities throughout the state. In spite of the broad scope of its inquiry, the committee seems to have been preoccupied with alleged Communist activities among student groups, particularly A.Y.D. See *Detroit News,* April 4, 18, 1947. The most conspicuous accomplishment of Callahan's Un-American activities committee was to recommend to the senate that a student at Michigan State College be tried for contempt of the senate for his refusal to tell the committee whether or not he was a member of the Communist Party (*Senate Journal,* 1948, p. 208). The trial was held before the senate on May 20, 1948, and the student was found guilty of contempt for refusing to answer the questions about Communist affiliations put to him by the committee. (The transcript of this proceeding is reported in *Senate Journal,* 1948, pp. 306–316, 331–336.) The sentence imposed was to spend the remainder of the legislative session in Ingham County Jail, but the sentence was suspended by the senate. (If the student had gone to jail it would have required merely staying overnight, since the legislature adjourned at noon the following day, May 21, 1948. The

The attorney general was not alone in his opposition to the Callahan Act. A "Committee for Repeal of the Callahan Act" was organized consisting of "a hodge podge of civic leaders and members representing virtually every political faith and ideology from right wing A.F.L. and C.I.O. leaders to left wingers and others." [22] This committee proceeded to organize a drive to obtain signatures upon an initiative petition requesting a referendum to repeal the law. By October, 1947, over one hundred thousand signatures had been obtained, well over the required 83,000. Since the next general election in which the propositions could be placed before the voters would not be held until November, 1948, and since the legislature was to meet in an extra session January, 1948, and thus have an opportunity to amend or repeal the law, the state board of canvassers held up certification of the proposition. The Callahan Act was neither repealed nor amended during the extra session, so the question of repeal was certified to be placed upon the ballot.[23] The vote on the question of whether or not to repeal the Callahan Act was 890,435 to allow it to stand and 585,469 to repeal.[24]

---

student was eventually expelled from Michigan State College by college authorities on the grounds that he had attended a meeting at which Carl Winter, a member of the Communist Party, spoke. This attendance at the meeting was said to violate a probation upon which the student had been placed. *Detroit News,* Dec. 20, 21, 1948; Jan. 4, 12, 13, 14, 1949).

[22] *Detroit News,* Sept. 4, 1947.

[23] *Detroit News,* May 15, 1948. In a final maneuver the "Committee for Repeal of the Callahan Act" requested the supreme court to rule the question off the ballot on the grounds that the law was unconstitutional and a vote on the issue would be a waste of money. Attorney General Black refused to appear before the court to argue the case for the state, and Senator Callahan entered the legal battle to bring the question of repeal to a vote. The supreme court turned down, without comment, the request to have the question removed. *Detroit News,* July 10, August 14, 26, 1948.

[24] *Michigan Manual,* 1949–50, p. 306. It may be of interest to note that Senator Callahan was defeated in the Republican primary in 1948 in his attempt to be renominated to run for his senate seat. The Democratic candidate won that seat in the November, 1948, election.

The law, securely on the statute books after the referendum of 1948, has been a complete cipher in operation. To date not a single individual organization in Michigan has registered as a foreign agency. Largely, no doubt, this is attributable to Attorney General Black's expressed disbelief in the statute's validity and the formal opinion of the succeeding attorney general, Stephen J. Roth, delivered on February 9, 1949, declaring the Callahan Act to be unconstitutional and void.[25] Even though the legislature by concurrent resolution requested him to test the question of legality by judicial proceedings of some sort, Attorney General Roth refused to enforce the law. He told the legislature that he had no information on which he could proceed against any individual; and that, even if such information were at hand, he could not commence an action under the statute without exposing himself to possible civil and criminal penalties he was unwilling to risk.[26]

---

[25] *Opinion of the Attorney General,* No. 895, Feb. 9, 1949.

[26] The concurrent resolution of March 4, 1949, appears in *House Journal,* 1949, pp. 307, 398. The attorney general's reply is reported in *House Journal,* March 9, 1949, p. 437, as follows: "In view of the history of this legislation I understand and respect the concern of the legislature over its constitutionality. Unfortunately, I know of no reasonable steps I may take which would secure an authoritative decision of the Supreme Court of the state. I have no information on which I may proceed against any individual. And if such information were supplied by a complainant, I could not proceed against such an individual unless I disregarded entirely the fact that, in my opinion, I would therefore subject myself to possible civil action for damages and to criminal prosecution for violation of the Federal Civil Right Statutes. That I have no desire to subject myself to either or both of these possible penalties will be readily understood.

"A test of the constitutionality of the said statute could probably be achieved by the institution of mandamus proceedings against myself for failure to enforce the Act. I say 'probably' because the Supreme Court might first consider whether, in the absence of an appropriation to make possible the collection of information preparatory to enforcement, the Attorney General should be required to perform the duties imposed upon him by the Act. An appropriation adequate to the task would run into seven figures.

"As I see it, therefore, the initiation of proceedings to test the con-

This portion of Michigan's statutory screen against subversion is, therefore, of no present use. If foreign agencies, as defined in the statute, are functioning in Michigan today—and the attorney general professes to have no information that they are—they may apparently do so without making reports about their funds or their members. This is not to say, however, that they may act however they wish. Whatever they say or do remains fully amenable to Michigan's laws against misconduct and forbidden speech.

TEACHERS' OATHS

The preceding discussion has dealt with the laws that relate to the public at large. Additional laws and regulations affect public employees.

Since 1931 teachers in the public schools of Michigan have been required by law to indicate formally their allegiance to the constitution of the United States and the constitution of the State of Michigan.[27] The law makes it unlawful for those who control "any state educational institution or any educational institution supported in whole or in part by public funds, to employ or continue to employ therein as a teacher any person unless or until such person shall make and subscribe the following oath or affirmation: 'I do solemnly swear (or affirm) that I will support the Constitution of the United States of America and the Constitution of the State of Michigan and that I will faithfully discharge the duties of the office of teacher according to the best of my ability.'"

By a later statute the oath became embodied in each teacher's contract; [28] and in 1935 the requirement of an oath was extended

---

stitutionality of the said Act must be assumed by someone other than myself."

[27] *Pub. Acts* 1931, No. 16, p. 28. *Pub. Acts* 1931, No. 19, p. 30.

[28] *Pub. Acts* 1931, No. 19, p. 30, added the requirement that the oath be embodied in and made a part of each teacher's contract and "at the time of the signing of such contract and any renewal thereof each teacher shall make and subscribe" to the oath. The University of Michigan and Michigan State College of Agriculture and Applied Science along with temporary employees were specifically exempt from the provisions of the statute.

196

to the faculties of all colleges that enjoy any measure of tax exemption.[29] Disregard of the oath requirement leads to forfeiture of tax exemption for the private institution and withholding of state funds for the state schools.

The constitutionality of this type of legislation was upheld by the Michigan Supreme Court as being within the province of legislative discretion to require teachers of the youth of the state to manifest their allegiance to the federal and state constitutions.[30]

In some quarters these generalities were not regarded as sufficient. In 1948 an attempt was made to require a specific non-Communist oath of the teachers. An amendment was introduced

[29] *Pub. Acts* 1935, No. 23, pp. 34–35, *Mich. Stat. Ann.* sec. 15.701 provides: "It shall be unlawful for any citizen of the United States to serve as a teacher, instructor or professor in any Junior College, College or University whose property, or any part thereof, is exempt from taxation unless and until he or she shall have taken and subscribed the following oath or affirmation: 'I do solemnly swear (or affirm) that I will support the Constitution of the United States of America, the Constitution of the State of Michigan, and that I will faithfully discharge according to the best of my ability, the duties of the position (title to be inserted) to which I am now or may be subsequently assigned.' " The law further provided "that this requirement shall not be construed as prohibiting such officer, person or board from employing for limited periods instructors or lecturers who are citizens of foreign countries."

[30] *Sauder v. District Board of School District Number 10 Royal Oak Township, Oakland County,* 271 Mich. 413, 261 N.W. 66 (1935). The holding is not entirely clear because the litigation revolves around a narrow technicality concerning the relationship of the oath to the contract of employment. See also *June v. School District Number 11, Southfield Township, Oakland County,* 283 Mich. 533, 278 N.W. 676 (1938); *Scalf v. L'Anse Township Single School District,* 276 Mich. 662, 268 N.W. 773 (1936). In each case the oath had been signed by the teachers, and the litigation resulted from an attempt to collect on contracts which the school board held to be invalid on technical grounds.

The tie-in of the teacher's oath with the contract has now been eliminated, and the current law merely provides that teachers' certificates have attached to them or superimposed upon them the oath of allegiance signed by the teacher. A duplicate of such oath is filed with the superintendent of public instruction. *Pub. Acts* 1941, No. 133; *ibid.,* 1939, No. 54; *Mich. Stat. Ann.* sec. 15.680.

by the Committee of the Whole in the house of representatives to amend a senate bill providing for appropriations from the general fund for school aid. The amendment would have required that every person rendering teaching services produce a statement in writing in answer to the following questions: "Are you now, or have you been within the 12-months next preceding this statement, a member of or affiliated with the Communist Party? Are you now, or have you been within the 12-months next preceding this statement, a member of, or affiliated with any organization that believes in or teaches the overthrow of the United States Government by force or by any illegal or unconstitutional methods?" The statements in answer to this question were to be kept on file with the school districts and the state superintendent of public instruction. The files were to be open for inspection by members of the legislature. Teachers who did not answer the questions would receive no pay, and those guilty of false statement would be guilty of a misdemeanor.[31] This amendment was defeated in the senate, and the house acquiesced.[32]

In 1949 a bill was introduced to prevent Communist Party members from being employed as schoolteachers in Michigan and was referred to the Committee on Education, where it apparently remained.[33]

So the matter rests at present. Today attention in being directed more broadly at the problem of "loyalty" among public employees. Teachers, as a part of that group, will be touched by whatever may develop on that front. At the moment there seems to be no acute sentiment in Michigan that schoolteachers are especially prone to subversion.

STATE EMPLOYEES' LOYALTY

In 1940 the voters of Michigan adopted an amendment to Article VI of the state constitution to guarantee a merit system in

[31] *House Journal*, 1948, p. 225. In reply to a request of one of the legislators, the attorney general advised that the oath required by the amendment would be constitutional. *Opinions of Attorney General*, No. 764, April 26, 1948.

[32] *Senate Journal*, 1948, pp. 238, 337.

[33] *Senate Journal*, 1949, pp. 620, 693.

state employment. Appointments were thenceforth to be based solely on the candidates' qualifications, and no promotions, demotions, or removals were to be influenced by partisan, racial, or religious considerations.

One of the first actions of the newly constituted Civil Service Commission was to differentiate between "partisan" and other sorts of political considerations. Its Rule 1B, promulgated in 1941, read as follows:

> *un-American Activities*—no person who has engaged in un-American Activities as defined by the laws of the United States or by the laws of Michigan, or who belongs to any group or organization advocating such activities or the overthrow of the American form of government, shall be eligible for, or remain in, any position or employment in the State Civil Service.

The commission fortified this rule in 1943 by requiring that each new employee swear to an oath of office to support and defend the constitution of the United States and the constitution of the State of Michigan. In addition employees were required to sign an affidavit that they did not advocate, nor were they a member of any political party or organization that advocated the overthrow of the government of the United States or the government of the State of Michigan by force or violence. In May of 1950, a new application form was adopted, and each applicant for examination must now answer "yes" or "no" to the following question: "Do you advocate or hold membership in any organization which advocates the overthrow of the American form of government by force?" [34]

[34] Form CS-102 (revised 5/50). The use of the oath of office and affidavit was discontinued about Jan. 1, 1948, in anticipation of a new application form. Because of the delay in obtaining the new form, the oath and affidavit form were distributed to appointing authorities Jan. 18, 1949, with the request from the state personnel director that employees hired after Jan. 1, 1948, and all new employees complete the form. (Letter dated Jan. 18, 1949, from Arthur G. Rasch, State Personnel Director, to All Appointing Authorities.) A newspaper report of the resumption of the use of this form was to the effect that 22,000 state employees were being asked to sign anti-Communist affidavits. See *Detroit News*, Jan. 22, 1949.

Although the affidavit required of state employees may be loosely referred to in the press as a non-Communist oath, the Civil Service Commission was advised by its legal adviser in 1949 that membership in the Communist Party of the United States would not in and of itself bar a person otherwise qualified from entering state service or constitute sufficient reason for removal.[35] In its counsel's opinion, the Civil Service rule regarding un-American activities requires that such activities be defined by the laws of the United States or by the laws of Michigan. Since membership in the Communist Party had not in 1949 been defined by law as an un-American activity, the Civil Service Commission could not disqualify or proceed to remove a member of that party without some evidence of misconduct by him personally. Whether the opinion so stated in July of 1949 would be modified by events that have occurred in succeeding months (including the successful prosecution of Communist leaders under the federal Smith Act) has not yet been clarified.

In any event, during 1950 the initiative shifted from the Civil Service Commission to the state senate.

For a considerable time the Michigan Unemployment Compensation Commission had been subjected to legislative criticism because some of its officials were said to have been members of the left-wing Public Workers Union. When Unemployment Compensation Commissioner Robert M. Ashley, who had been nominated for reappointment by the governor, appeared before the senate Business and Rules Committee for questioning, Republican Senator Colin L. Smith of Big Rapids broached the possibility of creating a loyalty board for the M.U.C.C. Commissioner Ashley promptly replied, "I think it would be a very good idea." [36] Commissioner Ashley was confirmed.

By May 2 Senator Smith had progressed to preparing a resolution calling not for a check of M.U.C.C. employees, but for an inquiry into whether all state officers should be investigated. "There are reports that the efficiency of State employees may have been lessened because of subversive or other influences,"

[35] Opinion prepared by Robert H. Dunn, legal adviser, Civil Service Commission, July, 1949.

[36] *Detroit News,* April 14, 1950, p. 63.

Senator Smith remarked.[37] Senate resolution 14, which he introduced on that date, called for a committee to study "the advisability of creating a Loyalty Board concerning State employees."
In due course the resolution was adopted, and Senator Smith
became the committee's chairman.

The committee held its first hearing on July 8, 1950. At that
time the setting up of a loyalty board was urged by spokesmen
for the American Legion, Veterans of Foreign Wars, Disabled
American Veterans, and Knights of Columbus, and once again by
Unemployment Compensation Commissioner Ashley. The state
adjutant of the Disabled American Veterans advanced a truly
novel idea: he suggested that the loyalty board might even advan-
tageously "screen legislative action," since some proposed laws are
"socialistic, but are excused as progressive." [38] None of the witnesses, it was reported, "said they had any evidence of disloyalty or
subversive activities among State employees, but argued that the
Communist technic was to infiltrate Government agencies." [39]

Governor G. Mennen Williams entered the picture on July 15,
when he called on the Civil Service Commission to report to
him the means it proposed to use to guarantee that state jobs
would be held only by loyal Americans. He did so, he said, in
order "to see whether I can be of any assistance in coordinating
your efforts with outside agencies, such as the State Police or the
Federal Bureau of Investigation." The Civil Service Commission
seemed not to be greatly perturbed by the gravity of the situation.
Its deputy director said, "You could count on the fingers of one
hand all those reported as members of suspected organizations";
and he added that Civil Service records showed not a single "outright Communist" on the state payroll.[40]

As events in Korea intensified public antipathy toward Communists the Smith committee broadened its interests. The question
of whether Michigan needs an employee loyalty program was at
least temporarily shunted aside while the committee considered

[37] *Detroit News*, May 2, 1950, p. 2. For text of resolution, see *Senate
Journal*, May 2, 1950, p. 166.
[38] *Detroit News*, July 8, 1950, p. 2.
[39] *Detroit News*, July 9, 1950, p. 16.
[40] *Detroit News*, July 16, 1950, p. 12.

whether or not it should recommend formal outlawry of the Communist Party.[41] As a result of its deliberations the committee proposed—and the legislature unanimously approved—a constitutional amendment which recognizes the crime of "subversion," declares that subversion is an abuse of the constitutional guarantee of free speech, and withdraws that guarantee as a possible defense in any trial for this offense.[42]

The Smith committee's second proposal was somewhat more related to the study that it had been appointed to make. On July 25 Senator Smith suggested the creation of a secret subversive squad in the State Police, to be engaged by and solely responsible to the State Police commissioner. The proposed squad would check both classified and unclassified state employees and "any group in the State of Michigan." [43] Governor Williams has opposed the whole idea of a special "Red squad" of this type, on the

[41] *Detroit News,* July 27, 1950, p. 12.

[42] Enrolled Senate Joint Resolution G, Extra Session of 1950. The text of the proposed amendment is as follows: "Section 22. Subversion shall consist of any act, or advocacy of any act, intended to overthrow the form of government of the United States or the form of government of this State, as established by this constitution and as guaranteed by Section Four of Article Four of the Constitution of the United States of America, by force or violence or by any unlawful means.

"Subversion is declared to be a crime against the State, punishable by any penalty provided by law.

"Subversion shall constitute an abuse of the rights secured by Section Four of this article, and the rights secured thereby shall not be valid as a defense in any trial for subversion."

On August 17, 1950, both houses approved the amendment without a dissenting vote. The only persons reported to have appeared at a hearing in opposition to the amendment were a spokesman for the Michigan Communist Party and an official of the Michigan branch of the Civil Rights Congress. *Ibid.,* August 18, 1950. The "subversive amendment" was approved by the voters at the November, 1950, elections. Although canvassed returns are not available at this time, the "subversive amendment" appears to have won by a narrower margin than the proposal authorizing the sale of colored oleomargarine which was submitted on the same ballot.

[43] *Detroit Free Press,* July 26, 1950.

ground that such a unit "would transform the state police into a 'Gestapo.'" He advocated as a substitute for the Committee's Red squad a special security squad, whose duty it would be "to guard against industrial sabotage or sabotage of military installations in Michigan, to investigate violations of the criminal syndicalism and other statutes and to cooperate with the Federal Bureau of Investigation in its anti-Communist and anti-subversive activities." So far as the governor could see, no new legislation would be needed to authorize an organization of that type.[44]

The question as to whether there were any obscure Reds in the unemployment compensation administration seems to have been pretty thoroughly overshadowed by broader considerations. Even if there were objectionable individuals in that agency (and the Civil Service Commission seemingly regarded this as highly doubtful), it is unlikely that sabotage of the type of work in which they are engaged could have seriously jeopardized the security of the State of Michigan. But the debate that was stimulated by this somewhat unrealistic issue resulted in legislation of a sweeping nature.

Ignoring the recommendations of Governor Williams, the legislature proceeded, in September, 1950, to enact a law authorizing the commissioner of the State Police to create a subversive activities investigation division within his department.[45] The law grants extraordinary powers to the commissioner, including the power to maintain confidential files; to appoint or retain persons outside of or with the department "as he may deem necessary, to carry out the act at such compensation as he may determine"; and to decide whether or not expenditure of money appropriated for the purpose of carrying out investigations should be made public.[46] Still unconvinced that adequate laws were available, the legislature enacted still another law outlawing activities designed to overthrow the government by force.[47] This latest addition appears to be no more than a restatement of the original criminal syndicalism law of 1919 with the notable addition of a possible life sentence for those found guilty. The Democratic governor signed both of these laws passed by the Republican legislature.

[44] *Detroit News*, August 1, 1950.   [45] *Pub. Acts* 1950, No. 40.
[46] *Ibid.*, secs. 1–6.   [47] *Pub. Acts* 1950, No. 38.

Active as the State of Michigan had been in erecting a wall of laws against subversion, its tempo was not fast enough to satisfy the voters of its metropolis, Detroit. In September, 1949, they decided that a commission should be established to rid the city payroll of "disloyal" employees. Detroit thus became the first municipality in the United States to launch a full-scale loyalty program to test public servants' beliefs and associations as well as their actual discharge of assigned responsibilities.

The charter of the city of Detroit, adopted in 1918 in a wave of reformist sentiment, undertakes to guarantee a merit system in public employment. In an apparent effort to strike at the spoils-and-patronage tradition by preventing political identification, the charter forbade questioning any applicant for or incumbent in a public job about his political affiliations or opinions.[48] In the course of time this provision came to be viewed not as a safeguard against discrimination, but as a screen that shielded subversive persons from exposure. After a campaign that warrants separate description, the voters amended the charter to provide, in part:

> The prohibitions against inquiry into political opinions or affiliations as now set forth in the charter of the City of Detroit shall not in any way apply to inquiry or questions as to membership in, active association with, or belief in the principles of any organizations, groups, associations or political parties controlled directly or indirectly by a foreign power, or which advocate the overthrow of the American form of government by

[48] *Charter of the City of Detroit*, tit. 4, c. 2, sec. 21: "No question in any form of application or in any examination shall be so framed as to elicit information concerning the political or religious opinions or affiliations of any applicants, and all disclosures thereof shall be discountenanced. No discrimination shall be exercised, threatened or promised by any person in any manner responsible for the carrying out of the provisions of this chapter against or in favor of any applicant eligible or employee in the classified service, because of his political or religious opinion or affiliation, and no recommendation of an applicant eligible or employee involving a disclosure of his political or religious opinions or affiliations shall be considered or filed by the commission or by any officer concerned in making appointments or promotions."

force or violence, or have been termed subversive by the Attorney General of the United States or the Federal Bureau of Investigation.[49]

Whether this amendment will succeed in its purpose is a question still in litigation. At any rate, the electorate indicated that the charter is no longer to be the refuge of subversives who decline to expose themselves.

Long before the 1949 amendment, however, there had been active public concern about the loyalty of Detroit's municipal workers. In 1938 the chairman of the American Legion's State Committee on Subversive Activities, supported by a member of the Detroit Police Red Squad, had testified before the Dies committee that Detroit's government was a congenial nesting place for Reds. The mayor promptly ordered all department heads to "stamp out" communistic influences by vigorously searching for un-American activities and immediately disciplining those who were found to be engaging in them.[50] So far as can now be learned, the campaign produced no results. Either the communistic and other un-American influences did not exist, or they were so subtle as to defy detection, or the mayor's subordinates ignored his instructions.

In 1941 the common council, responding to the mounting tensions that preceded World War II, enacted a requirement that all city employees swear their allegiance to the United States and at the same time state under oath, "[that] I do not advocate the overthrow of the government of the United States by force or violence; that I am not a member of any political party or organization that advocates the overthrow of the government of the United States by force or violence; and that during such time as I am an employee of the City of Detroit I will not advocate nor become a member of any political party or organization that advocates the overthrow of the government of the United States by force or violence.[51]

This oath requirement remained in force throughout the war

[49] *Charter of the City of Detroit,* tit. IX, c. IX, sec. 8 (1949).

[50] *Detroit News,* Oct. 14, 1938.

[51] *Compiled Ordinances of the City of Detroit,* 1945, c. 11, Ordinance 213 D, effective Sept., 1941.

years and continues in effect today. Only one person has refused to take the oath—a member of the sect of Jehovah's Witnesses, who refused on religious grounds. Civil Service Commission officials agree that the oath requirement has not induced disloyal persons to confess their disloyalty; they also agree that no one who has taken the oath is known to have committed sabotage or engaged in overt acts against the city which might have jeopardized its security.

Embracive as the required oath seems to be, there was occasional agitation for its amplification. Thus, for example, the local representatives of the American Federation of State, County and Municipal Employees urged the mayor in 1948 to obtain specific non-Communist pledges from all city employees who operated public utilities or were responsible for other principal activities.[52]

It was not until the summer of 1949, however, that agitation for a more thorough examination of public employees' loyalty became intense. Possibly it is entirely coincidental that municipal elections were then in the immediate offing.

THE BALL STARTS ROLLING

As often happens in human affairs, the first step toward an important development was a small one. It involved an individual of no prominence and an episode of minor dimensions. George Shenkar, inconspicuously earning $3,298 a year as a junior mechanical engineer on the staff of the Detroit Water Commission, in December, 1948, sought promotion to the rank of assistant mechanical engineer. The Civil Service Commission disapproved his promotion because Shenkar, while an undergraduate at Wayne University, had been chairman of the Marxian Study Club, an

[52] *Detroit News,* March 16, 1948. It will be noted that most of the references to news items are from the *Detroit News.* The three newspapers in Detroit with the largest circulation are the *Detroit News, Detroit Free Press,* and the *Detroit Times.* The *Detroit News* led the campaign for the adoption of the charter amendment and devoted a good deal of space to the various items relevant to it. However, in most cases where the *Detroit News* is mentioned as a source, reports of the same event can be found in either the *Detroit Times* or *Free Press.*

outlawed student organization, and was reputed to be a Communist.[53]

Shenkar appealed to the common council. That body on June 29, 1949, rejected his appeal on the ground that a municipal employee who declined to state whether or not he was a Communist was not entitled to promotion. The council went further and sought the advice of the corporation counsel as to whether Shenkar could be dismissed.[54] It was not until more than a year later that Shenkar was finally discharged, after he had first been exiled from the main office to the sewage disposal plant; and when he was dismissed, the assigned grounds were insolence and insubordination rather than communism. But this petty case provided the spark that started the blaze of the loyalty program. Regardless of their motivation, all those who in the past had felt the need for or who had urged the investigation of the loyalty of city employees found in the Shenkar affair ammunition to support their insistence upon further inquiries.

Three days after Shenkar's request for promotion had been denied because of his alleged Communist affiliation, Donald Sublette, secretary of the Detroit Civil Service Commission, made the startling assertion to the common council that at least 150 Communists or their sympathizers were employed by the city. Especially denouncing the United Public Workers of America (then an affiliate of the C.I.O., but later to be expelled by that body), Sublette was quoted as saying: "For sabotage purposes, for disruption of production, for effective bacteriological warfare, and for many other things, local governments are far more im-

[53] In the file of the Civil Service Commission on Shenkar was a copy of a brochure of the study club, containing a list of organizations with which Shenkar was affiliated; and included in the list was the Communist Party (*Detroit News*, Dec. 21, 1948). The author was permitted to examine a photostat of the brochure in the Civil Service file. As it appeared in the photostat, the brochure was a mimeographed "throw-away" typical of student organizations. Following Shenkar's name there was a statement of his military service; and the Communist Party of the United States was shown as one of his affiliations.

[54] *Detroit News,* June 29, 1949.

portant in the Communist take-over plan than the Federal government." [55]

It is perhaps worth digressing for a moment to consider the
basis of Mr. Sublette's estimate of Communist infiltration into
municipal employment, for there is no doubt that his widely
publicized guess had considerable influence on Detroit's thinking.
Mr. Sublette told the council that he assumed that Detroit had
about the same percentage of Communist employees as were to
be found in the federal service. According to him, the F.B.I. had
fixed the latter at one-half of 1 per cent. Since Detroit had 30,000
municipal employees, a simple arithmetical computation established the presumed number of Communists and Communist
sympathizers as 150. The fact of the matter is that after three
years devoted to checking some 3,000,000 employees, the federal
loyalty program had disclosed Communist ties in not 0.5 per
cent of the cases, but by the most generous estimate, in less than
0.05 per cent of all those checked—one-twentieth of 1 per cent
rather than one-half of 1 per cent.[56] If Mr. Sublette had related his
arithmetic to the true facts of the federal program, he would have
estimated fifteen rather than 150 suspects on the Detroit rolls.
The smaller estimated number might well have been closer to
the mark. For today, months after the figure 150 was first projected,
the Shenkar case remains the only one in which publicly presented
evidence suggests the presence of a Communist on the city's payroll.[57]

[55] Detroit News, July 3, 1949.

[56] Walter Gellhorn, Security, Loyalty, and Science (Ithaca, N.Y.:
Cornell University Press, 1950), p. 169.

[57] Subsequent to the above writing, the loyalty investigating committee has submitted charges of disloyalty against a garbage collector
employed by the Department of Public Works. The employee so charged
is an official of the United Public Workers, who had been granted a leave
of absence since 1947 to carry on union activities. Soon after it was announced that the charges of disloyalty had been made, the Civil Service
Commission proceeded to dismiss the employee on the technical ground
that he no longer maintained his Detroit residence. This action would
have ended the case, but the Civil Service Commission later reversed
itself and gave the employee an opportunity to return to his position

In any event the Sublette estimate, whether or not well founded, stimulated an immediate reaction. It was made on July 3. By July 5, after an interlude to celebrate Independence Day, there was a stampede on the part of public officials to get into the act. Leading the charge was Mr. Sublette himself, taking skillful advantage of the sensation he had created with his previous statement and now urging that a loyalty check of the 30,000 city employees be made. Police Commissioner Harry S. Toy—who was later to become somewhat unfavorably known for his effort to set up a loyalty program for newspaper reporters—declared that he had already required police officers and civilian employees of the Police Department to take non-Communist oaths. The Civil Service Commission remained cool in its response to its secretary's assertions. It said that it had no list of Communists or Communist sympathizers in the city employment but added that a loyalty check was a matter of policy to be determined by the mayor and the council. Mayor Van Antwerp, after conferring with Mr. Sublette, announced his intention of ordering the dismissal of Shenkar for his refusal to deny that he was a Communist.[58]

On July 6 Mayor Van Antwerp appointed a special investigating committee composed of the police commissioner, the corporation counsel, and the president of the Civil Service Commission. The purpose of the committee was explained in an executive order issued the following day to department heads.

In view of the serious situation created by the charges of infiltration of Communists and communistic sympathizers into the service of the Detroit city government, I have named a committee of three to make an immediate and thorough investigation and to report to me as quickly as possible with recommendations to eliminate these disloyal employees, wherever found, and to prevent others of like nature from entering the City Service now or at any future time.[59]

as a garbage collector. If the employee reports for work within a "reasonable" time, his status as a city employee will be restored, and the loyalty proceedings can continue. If he refuses to report for work, the case will automatically close.

[58] *Detroit News,* July 5, 1949.
[59] *Executive Order No. 16,* July 7, 1949.

THE MOVE FOR CHARTER REVISION

But now the *Detroit News* began to express doubt whether a loyalty check could be effective so long as the charter forbade the questioning of political affiliations. On July 7, 1949, it published a front-page editorial as the first gun in an aggressive campaign to procure adoption of a city charter loyalty amendment. "Shut the Door to Commies by Changing the Charter," urged the *News*. The present charter provisions, said the editorialist, forestalled the questioning that would ferret out "Communists, fellow-travelers and other potential traitors." All this could be quickly cured by an amendment that "could cut through the legal question and provide at once and in an orderly way for a loyalty screening of City employees. It could provide a loyalty board appointed by the Mayor. It could state in clear language that membership in any organization listed by the F.B.I. as subversive shall be cause for dismissal from the City Service." [60]

Anxious for action rather than tedious discussion, the *News* urged the city council to adopt the suggested amendment for submission to the voters in the September primary. It called on its readers to support its editorial stand in letters to the mayor and council. To facilitate the expression of public opinion it printed below the editorial a coupon containing the following message:

> I, as a faithful Detroit voter, believe the City should protect itself and its people from plotting by subversive employees of the city.
>
> I support the suggestion of the Detroit News that the City Charter be amended to provide for a loyalty board to determine the qualifications for public office of any City Civil Service employee.
>
> I ask you and the City Council to put such an amendment on the ballot at Primary election, September 13, 1949.

Action was what was wanted; and action was what the *News* got. On the very day its editorial appeared, the newspaper was able in its later editions to quote Mayor Van Antwerp as exclaim-

[60] *Detroit News,* July 7, 1949.

ing, "The moment I saw the front page editorial in the Detroit News today, I called Kelly [the Corporation Counsel] and told him to prepare the amendment."

The common council next met on July 12. By that time the Mayor could report not only that he had appointed his three-man loyalty investigating committee [61] but also that he had received "many hundreds" of the *News* coupons. He also submitted to the council a proposed charter amendment providing for a loyalty board and urged the council to take action in time to submit the amendment to the voters in the September primary election.[62]

At this point there first became apparent the conflict of political ambitions that helped to shape later events. Council President George Edwards and Mayor Van Antwerp were rival candidates for mayor in the approaching September primary. The council president was absent from the city on July 12, but he took pains to make his influence felt. He sent a message to the council in which he first expressed the opinion that the city was already amply empowered to protect itself against disloyal acts such as sabotage. He added, however, that he had long previously urged the Civil Service Commission to screen all city employees for loyalty. The commission's failure to do so, he asserted, reflected the fact that it was part of a "fuddy duddy" administration that was dependent upon newspaper editorials for a cue to action. In any event, Mr. Edwards indicated his support of a charter amendment, simply to make the city's protection doubly assured and also to protect city employees from an unbridled witch hunt.[63]

The American Federation of Labor Public Employees Union was officially heard from on the same day in messages reported in the council's *Journal*. The American Federation of State,

[61] The mayor's committee had been named, according to his executive order of July 7, primarily to consider methods. According to the *Detroit News,* July 11, 1949, however, it had actually commenced investigating 34 persons "on suspicion of Communism." The names had been submitted to the committee by department heads and by the Police Department's Anti-Subversive Squad.

[62] *Journal of the Common Council,* July 12, 1949, p. 2066.

[63] *Ibid.,* pp. 2066–2067.

County and Municipal Employees Union, Council No. 77, reluctantly accused a rival union (United Public Workers) of Communist domination. The solution to the loyalty problem was
simply to require the filing of non-Communist oaths by the leaders
of all unions representing city employees, without disturbing
individual employees by possible witch hunts. Still, this labor
organization did not condemn a loyalty investigation of city
employees but contented itself with cautioning that it should be
done carefully.[64] The second message from an A.F.L. affiliate was
from the Water Board Employees Union, Local 207. This was
merely an affidavit signed by the officers of this union that they
were not Communists.[65]

The United Public Workers of America also received space
in the *Journal* but not by its choice. A resolution was passed by
the council to subpoena Yale Stuart, president of the Detroit
Joint Board of the U.P.W., to appear and testify regarding the
proposed loyalty program.[66]

The deadline for submitting charter amendments to appear
on the September primary ballot was July 15. If there was to be
an opportunity to vote on the amendment at the primary, it was
therefore necessary for the council to act on or before that date.
On July 15 a charter amendment was approved for submission
to the voters by all council members present.

At least three councilmen played direct roles in the drafting
of the charter amendment. Councilman Charles Oakman proposed the initial draft. Councilman Edward Connor objected to
certain provisions of this initial draft, but these differences were
compromised with Oakman by changing the wording of some
of the sections.[67] Council President George Edwards, who returned to Detroit for this meeting, submitted his own version of

[64] *Ibid.*, p. 2104.   [65] *Ibid.*, p. 2105.   [66] *Ibid.*, p. 2073.

[67] The *Detroit News*, July 14, 1949, reported the revisions resulting
from this compromise. "Past or present membership" in a subversive
organization as a cause for dismissal was objected to by Connor as punishing persons for acts not proscribed at the time committed. Therefore,
the words "past or present" were deleted. Another change was a section
making "belief in the principles of" subversive organizations cause for

the amendment at the last minute, and in the end his version was the one adopted. The principal innovations in the Edwards version seem to have been the requirement of secrecy concerning suspects until written charges were preferred and a provision whereby membership in any organization described as subversive by the attorney general of the United States or by the F.B.I. could be considered grounds for charges of disloyalty. Regardless of who should get the credit for having drafted the amendment, the thing was done and submitted in time to be placed on the September ballot. Or so it seemed.

A complication developed early in August. Michigan law requires that charter changes proposed by the common council be submitted to the governor for his approval before they can be placed on a ballot.[68] The governor may veto a proposed amendment by returning it to the common council without his signature and with a list of his objections. His unfavorable action may be overridden by the local council by a two-thirds vote on reconsideration of the amendment. It is considered a matter of routine for the governor to approve proposed charter changes.

At a regular session held August 9, 1949, the common council was informed that the governor had returned the loyalty charter amendment without his signature.[69] The proposed amendment had been sent back along with a message from the attorney general to the governor's legal adviser stating that in the opinion of the attorney general the loyalty charter amendment was unconstitutional. The attorney general based his opinion upon a provision of the proposed amendment that permitted a finding of disloyalty against employees who held membership in organizations labeled subversive by the attorney general of the United States or the

---

dismissal. Connor argued that this might be the basis for "thought control." A third change specifically defined the term "associated with" a subversive organization as meaning "working with that organization." This change was to protect those who were innocently linked with Communist front organizations.

[68] *Mich. Stat. Ann.* sec. 5.2101 (1935).

[69] *Journal of the Common Council,* August 9, 1949, p. 2352.

Federal Bureau of Investigation. This was considered to be an unconstitutional delegation of legislative power.[70]

The assistant corporation counsel of Detroit told the common council that he disagreed with the attorney general's opinion. He pointed out, too, that in order to have the amendment voted upon in the September primary it would be necessary to override the governor's veto by a two-thirds vote, rather than to play with the possibility of changes to meet the attorney general's objections. For if the perhaps unconstitutional section were now altered, the council would in effect be proposing a new amendment; and if this were done, it would be too late to present the amendment in September, since the date for filing amendments had already passed.[71]

The common council did not immediately resolve this new problem. Councilman Connor moved to refer the whole matter back to the corporation counsel with instructions to get together with the attorney general to prepare a new charter amendment eliminating unconstitutional sections. His proposal was defeated by a four to three vote.[72] Another resolution was introduced by Councilman Oakman for a vote to override the veto of the governor. This was defeated by a vote of 4–4, a two-thirds vote being necessary to override.[73] It was finally decided to adjourn until August 12, when the corporation counsel was formally to present his opinion concerning the validity of the governor's veto.

The reaction of the *Detroit News* to the governor's veto and the council's refusal to override it was bitter. The three councilmen, Edwards, Edgecomb, and Connor, who voted for a restudy of the loyalty issue based on the attorney general's opinion and who also voted against overriding the governor's veto, were singled out as a clique by the *News* in its editorial of August 12. The editorial pointed out that Councilman Edwards had submitted the version of the amendment, which was now considered unconstitutional by Attorney General Roth.[74]

---

[70] *Ibid.*, p. 2352. The attorney general pointed out that these were the very grounds upon which he had declared the Callahan Act unconstitutional. See discussion above, p. 195.

[71] *Idem.* [72] *Ibid.*, p. 2353. [73] *Ibid.*, p. 2354.

[74] *Detroit News*, August 12, 1949. The tone and content of this edi-

Beset as it was by public clamors, the council now seized gratefully upon a technicality. The proposed charter amendment had been returned to the council on August 9, not by a letter from the governor personally with a statement of his objections, but by a letter from the governor's legal adviser. True, the governor had publicly endorsed his subordinate's act on his behalf. But since he had not himself signed the message of disapproval, the council was able to accept the assistant corporation counsel's opinion that the attempted veto was invalid and could safely be ignored.[75]

Whatever doubt or confusion may have remained was finally dispelled at the common council's meeting on August 16. On that date the council unanimously reaffirmed its original action looking toward a September vote on the proposed charter amendment. This reaffirmation had the effect of overriding the governor's veto, if a veto did exist.[76] Thus the last obstacle in the way of presenting the charter amendment to the voters in the September election was removed.

The proposal that finally went before the electorate had the following features:

(1) It created a loyalty commission of five ex officio members: the mayor (chairman), the city treasurer (vice-chairman), the city clerk (secretary), the president of the common council, and the police commissioner.

(2) For the purpose of bringing charges before the loyalty commission, there was to be established by ordinance a "loyalty

---

torial might lead one to infer that a conspiracy had taken place between George Edwards and Attorney General Stephen Roth to have the proposed amendment declared unconstitutional. The *Detroit Times* in an editorial of the same date took the position that since the council could override the governor's veto by two-thirds vote, neither the governor nor the attorney general should be used as scapegoats by the common council.

[75] *Journal of the Common Council,* August 12, 1949, pp. 2401–2402. The reasoning of the opinion was that the act of veto is a personal one that cannot be subdelegated to a subordinate.

[76] *Ibid.,* pp. 2472–2473.

investigating committee." Its investigations were to be private, and all publicity was to be withheld until the committee had made a positive finding of disloyalty. Then its finding was to be embodied in a written charge, for further consideration by the loyalty commission after a formal trial hearing.

(3) Disloyalty was stated to be cause for dismissal, "all provisions of the charter to the contrary notwithstanding," but subject to whatever processes of judicial review might have been established by law. In determining whether an employee is disloyal, the commission was instructed to "consider as prima facie evidence membership in or active association with an organization controlled directly or indirectly by a foreign power, or membership in or active association with an organization which advocates overthrow of the American form of government by force or violence. In determining disloyalty the committee may consider any other evidence of reasonable force, including membership in or active association with an organization officially termed subversive by the Attorney General of the United States or the Federal Bureau of Investigation."

(4) The charter's prohibitions against political questioning were to be inapplicable to loyalty proceedings.

On September 13, 1949, the electorate approved the charter amendment by a vote of 263,989 to 78,160. The interest in the issue is attested by the fact that the votes cast pro and con totaled only 11,000 less than those cast for the four leading contenders in the mayoralty race.

ACTION UNDER THE REVISED CHARTER

Legislative responsibility did not end with approval of the amendment. Since charges of disloyalty could only be brought before the Loyalty Commission by the Loyalty Investigating Committee, and since the latter had first to be created by ordinance, the newly authorized Loyalty Commission could take no action to cleanse the city of disloyal employees until the common council had established the Investigating Committee. In spite of the urgency to get a loyalty charter amendment on the September ballot, the council did not complete action on the necessary enabling ordinance until December 13, 1949. On that date it provided for a Loyalty Investigating Committee of seven members, to be appointed and be removable by the mayor (subject to council approval) and to serve without compensation. The investigating and accusatory functions prescribed by the charter amendment were once again spelled out. In addition the Investigating Committee was given discretionary power to require each city employee to execute yet another loyalty oath in a form set forth in full detail in the ordinance. No separate staff was provided, but the committee was authorized to call on other municipal agencies for "such assistance as may reasonably be required," and the police commissioner was directed to assign "such members of the Police Department as the Investigating Committee may from time to time require." [77]

The appointment of members to the Loyalty Investigating Committee was completed at the end of January, 1950,[78] and the group met for the first time on February 5. After this first meeting it was announced that the Loyalty Investigating Committee had decided that it would not require city employees to renew their oath of allegiance, as was suggested in the ordinance setting up the committee. The purpose of this policy, according to the chairman, was to have the committee function "without disturbing the lives of city employees unduly." [79]

From February until July, 1950, the Loyalty Investigating Committee remained dormant. A judicial test of the loyalty program

[77] Ordinance No. 394-E; *Journal of the Common Council,* December 13, 1949, p. 3626.

[78] *Journal of the Common Council,* January 31, 1950, p. 186. The following members were appointed to the committee: George Schudlich, attorney; Rev. Raymond S. Clancy, director of Social Action for the Archdiocese of Detroit of the Roman Catholic Church; Charles Nugent, University of Detroit, law instructor; George Elliot, business agent of Local 19, Carpenters Union, A.F.L.; Rev. Malcolm Dade, pastor of St. Cyprian's Church; Edward Frey, president of the Detroit Municipal Employees Association; Mrs. Margaret Abernethy, member, Wayne County Board of Supervisors.

[79] *Detroit News,* Feb. 5, 1950.

had been initiated. Instead of issuing a temporary injunction to maintain the status quo pending judgment, Judge Ira W. Jayne of the Circuit Court, before whom the case was being heard, had an agreement with the corporation counsel that the city would not proceed with its investigation of employee loyalty until the lawsuit was decided.[80]

The outbreak of the war in Korea and the United Nations' action to halt aggression stimulated renewed interest in the city loyalty program. Edward Frey, executive secretary of the Loyalty Investigating Committee, urged the mayor to call an early meeting of the committee so that it could "at least set up a method of procedure and be in readiness for any eventualities." [81] Finally, on July 20, the Loyalty Investigating Committee was advised by the corporation counsel that it possessed authority to act with respect to every city employee except the one, Eugene Green, whose challenge of the constitutionality of the amendment had not as yet been decided.[82]

At this writing, the Loyalty Investigating Committee is pre-

[80] *Ibid.*, Feb. 15, 1950.   [81] *Ibid.*, July 14, 1950.

[82] *Ibid.*, July 20, 1950. Green, a Department of Public Works employee, filed his action through Ernest Goodman, attorney for the United Public Workers. The author has had an opportunity to examine the briefs in the case. The city's brief alone runs over 100 pages. In addition to the brief of Mr. Goodman, the American Civil Liberties Union was permitted to file a brief as *amicus curiae,* challenging the constitutionality of the amendment. In general, the briefs attacking the loyalty amendment claim a violation of the due process clause of the Fourteenth Amendment of the federal constitution. They argue, too, that the language used is so vague as to imperil freedom of speech and association. Since an employee may be discharged if he joins an organization "controlled directly or indirectly by a foreign power," the American Civil Liberties Union brief questions (among other things) whether a Detroit employee could safely belong to a mutual insurance company chartered in Ontario, the Catholic Church, or the British Society of Astronomers. The city's brief, on the other hand, argues that the right to city employment is not a vested right and that the city has the unrestricted power to attach conditions for employment. The city's brief further provides several grounds upon which the judge could throw out the case without deciding the constitutional issues, and such an alterna-

sumably engaged in drafting its procedures and investigating reports submitted to it by the police Red squad. According to reports, the Police Department had accumulated the names of "more than fifty" city employees "believed to have Communist leanings." [83] If experience elsewhere is duplicated in Detroit, this list of suspects is likely to shrink to a much smaller number when subjected to critical examination. The time may come when the absence of wholesale dismissals will stir charges that the Loyalty Investigating Committee has been engaged in "whitewash." For if the public becomes fearfully convinced that the public services have been infiltrated by dangerous persons, its anxiety may not be easily allayed, no matter how conscientiously the matter has been explored and no matter how empty the charges have been shown to be. The specter of Mr. Sublette's "150 Reds" may yet rise to harass Detroit's investigating agency.

EVALUATING THE LOCAL FACTORS

It is difficult to list all the major factors that played a role in the development of the Detroit loyalty program. It is still more difficult to attempt to assess each of these factors in true relationship to the others that conditioned the development of the loyalty program. What follows is an attempt to summarize some of the major elements involved, but their relative significance will probably remain a matter of opinion and conjecture.

That local politics played an important role in the adoption of the charter loyalty amendment seems obvious. Since Detroit uses the nonpartisan ballot in municipal elections, the identification of candidates with issues and their responsibility for positions on policy is personal rather than partisan.[84] The three major

tive is also provided in the Goodman brief. There will, no doubt, be an appeal as soon as the decision of Judge Jayne is available, no matter how he decides the case.

[83] *Detroit Free Press*, Jan. 26, 1950. A police sergeant, attached to the Subversive Bureau, is quoted as saying that the list includes city workers who have been "recognized by investigators at Communist front meetings."

[84] The opponents of the nonpartisan ballot maintain that it destroys

aspirants for the office of mayor in 1949 were incumbent Mayor Eugene Van Antwerp, Council President George Edwards, and City Treasurer Albert Cobo. The September primaries narrow the field to two candidates for the November election. Candidate Edwards was commonly considered to be the most liberal of the top three contenders, and the one who would be expected to be the champion of civil rights. The pressure on the city council to submit a loyalty amendment to the voters in the September primary forced Edwards either to support the proposed amendment and therefore jeopardize some of his liberal support, or to block the proposed amendment and thus expose himself to charges of being "soft" toward Communism.

As has been seen, Edwards' response was that he felt that a loyalty charter amendment was unnecessary, that he had recommended loyalty screening of public employees even before the current agitation, and that he would support a loyalty amendment in order to make doubly sure that both the city and its employees were protected. That his support of the loyalty amendment somewhat complicated the position of an important segment of Edwards' political support is indicated by a resolution passed by the C.I.O. Council of Wayne County. The C.I.O. resolution denounced Communists but at the same time opposed the amendment on the ground that the loyalty board would be a "means through which civil liberties are placed in jeopardy." The resolution went on to support the candidacy of George Edwards for mayor, even though he claimed authorship of the proposal just denounced.[85]

---

party responsibility for the conduct of the city government, that it enhances the power of the newspapers in local politics, and that it is a subterfuge for obtaining the election of Republicans in a normally Democratic town. Proponents of the nonpartisan ballot believe that it keeps machine politics out of the management of the city government.

[85] *Detroit News,* July 21, 1949. The resolution also said in part: "We are not satisfied as citizens with hysterical screaming against the Communist Party to cover up the lack of initiative on the part of Detroit's Mayor and a number of City Council members." It cited transportation, taxes, sanitation, schools, and recreational and other facilities as important election issues. *Ibid.*

The *Detroit News,* which backed the candidacy of Albert Cobo, the eventual winner in the November election, printed an editorial ten days before the primary expressing doubt about the sincerity of Edwards' support of the loyalty amendment. The editorial was entitled "The Whole Truth" and read as follows:

> Councilman Edwards expresses pleasure that his rivals for the mayoralty nomination "have endorsed" the Loyalty Board Charter Amendment. "I wrote it," says Mr. Edwards.
>
> And so he did, or at any rate he dashed into town on the last day for putting an amendment on the ballot with a proposed draft that someone had written.
>
> His vote was needed. The Council perforce adopted his draft, since it was that or nothing. Besides, the draft differed from the original mainly in setting out certain procedural detail primarily intended to be left to later council decision.
>
> So it was Mr. Edwards' very own amendment that he subsequently discovered with every show of eagerness to be "unconstitutional." He refused to vote to override Governor Williams' veto, being readily persuaded by the flowing reasoning of Attorney General Roth, the former C.I.O. Attorney, that his very own handiwork was no good.
>
> Mr. Edwards did finally get around to indorsing his own amendment, when on second thought, he went along with the Council majority in overriding the veto. *But* that was after it *was sure that the amendment would be on the ballot anyway.*[86]

What effect the Detroit loyalty program had upon the political future of George Edwards is of course impossible to determine. But the timing of the campaign for a loyalty program leaves little doubt that it was intended to have—and probably did have—considerable impact on Edwards' immediate fortunes.[87]

[86] *Detroit News,* Sept. 3, 1949. The *Detroit News* persisted in taking Mr. Edwards to task for including in the charter amendment the provision that the subversive lists of the U.S. attorney general and the F.B.I. should be used in identifying disloyal organizations. However, the *Detroit News* itself in its initial editorial of July 7, 1949, had specifically suggested that a charter amendment "could state in clear language that membership in any organization listed by the F.B.I. as subversive shall be cause for dismissal from the City Service."

[87] Edwards was runner-up to Cobo in the mayoralty primary race and

That politics conditioned the behavior of members of the common council during the summer of 1949 also appears obvious. Six of the councilmen were running for re-election and were facing a field of 105 candidates on the primary ballot. With such a long nonpartisan ballot, the advantage goes to those individuals whose names can be recognized by the voters. The publicity given to the activity of the council in adopting a proposed charter amendment and overriding the governor's veto of their proposal was no doubt welcome. Moreover, it gave the incumbents an opportunity to display publicly their zeal in combating the "red menace." While it is impossible to determine the precise extent to which the members of the common council politically benefited from their activities, all six councilmen who ran for re-election were successful in their candidacies.[88]

The particular target of the council throughout the whole affair was the United Public Workers of America and its local leader, Yale Stuart. Stuart had appeared at a somewhat heated hearing before the council, upon its request. He flatly refused to swear that he was not a Communist. He did, however, join with Councilman Miriani in swearing to the oath of allegiance required of municipal employees, though he was not himself employed by

---

was defeated by Cobo in the November election. The position of organized labor on both the loyalty charter amendment and candidates for mayor was not consistent. The C.I.O. opposed the loyalty charter amendment. The Michigan Federation of Labor did not support the loyalty amendment, but locals of the American Federation of State, County and Municipal Employees did support the loyalty amendment. The position of the C.I.O. during this period was complicated further by the fact that the C.I.O. was preparing to oust the U.P.W. as an affiliated union for its extreme left-wing position, and the C.I.O. leadership did not want to be in the position of supporting the very union that it was preparing to oust. Subsequently the U.P.W. lost its affiliation with the C.I.O.

[88] Five of the re-elected couuncilmen, Oakman, Kronk, Smith, Miriani, and Garlick, received the support of the *Detroit News* for their consistent fight for the loyalty amendment (*Detroit News*, September 9, 1949). On the other hand, Councilman Connor, whom the *News* associated with George Edwards in attempting to withdraw his support in the face of the governor's veto, also was re-elected.

the city.[89] On an earlier occasion he had formally written the common council, stating in part:

You are attempting to divert public opinion from the fact that you are cutting the wages of the sanitation department employees; that you are playing politics with the wage adjustments of thousands of the city's clerical, hospital, skilled and semi-skilled employees; that you are practicing unlawful discrimination against minority groups like the Negro and Jewish workers in city government; that you are violating your oath to uphold the city charter by your discriminatory and intimidatory acts.

Your excursion into red-baiting is quite evidently not an attempt to reach the truth or to safeguard the security of our city. It is a camouflage for your political purposes in the midst of a campaign year, an effort to catch votes without regard for the rights of city employees or the decencies ordinarily observed towards any citizen.[90]

His rhetoric did not move the members of the council. Armed by a memorandum prepared for one of the councilmen by "a Nationally recognized research organization on subversive activities," they were persuaded that the U.P.W. was Communist-dominated and that Stuart provided Red leadership at the local level.[91]

A good argument could be made for the contention that the loyalty program was specifically aimed at getting rid of the U.P.W. as a union representing Detroit employees. During the summer of 1949 one of the largest locals of the U.P.W. was Local 312, which consisted of maintenance employees of the municipally owned

[89] *Journal of the Common Council,* August 19, 1949, p. 2540.

[90] *Ibid.,* July 15, 1949, p. 2137.

[91] The *Journal of the Common Council* for July 15, 1949, pp. 2137–2138, includes a memorandum on the United Public Workers of America prepared for Councilman Charles G. Oakman by "Counterattack," identified in the journal as being "a Nationally recognized research organization on subversive activities, composed of former F.B.I. agents." This memorandum identified the U.P.W. as one of the "most completely Communist controlled unions in the United States" and proceeded to give a brief dossier of its officers, including one on Russian-born Yale Stuart, who had lost an arm with the Lincoln Brigade in Spain.

Detroit Street Railway.[92] Other departments containing U.P.W. membership included the Department of Public Works, Water Board, Plan Commission, and Public Lighting Commission.[93] From the very beginning of the campaign to adopt the loyalty program, the U.P.W. was singled out for pointed attack. Since the U.P.W. had organized large groups of city employees, it was possible to imply, through a process of association, that Communists and Communist sympathizers were infiltrating into the city government. Moreover, when the U.P.W. took the initiative in bringing legal proceedings in an attempt to block the progress of the loyalty program, it became easy to suggest that the raising of civil rights issues was merely a tactic employed to protect Communists. This was well illustrated early in the campaign. As was mentioned above, Mayor Van Antwerp responded to Mr. Sublette's charges of Communists and Communist sympathizers on the city payroll by establishing a special committee to investigate employee loyalty. Fifty city employees, represented by the U.P.W.'s local counsel, immediately began proceedings to restrain the mayor from continuing his investigation. A temporary injunction was issued, and the mayor and city officials were ordered by the court to show cause why a permanent injunction should not be issued.[94] In an editorial the *Detroit News* pointed to this action as an example of the Communist Party's making use of democratic processes to subvert democracy.[95] Police Commissioner Toy's rejoinder to the court injunction was to order the investigation of the fifty plaintiffs in the court action.[96]

[92] Although official membership figures are difficult to obtain, a Civil Service official has estimated that between 1,800 and 2,200 members make up this local. Local 312 seceded from the U.P.W. just prior to the time when the U.P.W. was ousted from the C.I.O. Now no longer a U.P.W. affiliate, Local 312 is today directly linked with the C.I.O.

[93] Civil Service officials estimate that today there are no more than 500 dues-paying members of the U.P.W. on the total city payroll.

[94] *Detroit News*, July 12, 1949.

[95] *Detroit News*, July 14, 1949.

[96] The signers of the petition were members of the U.P.W. Ultimately Circuit Court Judge Jayne upheld the power of city officials to inquire into whether or not employees were living up to their oath of allegiance. *Detroit News*, July 20, 1949.

Undoubtedly the identification of communism with the U.P.W. and the U.P.W. with opposition to the loyalty program assisted in the adoption of the program. On the eve of the September election this reasoning had been stretched to the point where a vote against the proposed amendment was reasoned to be a vote for communism in Detroit. In a radio address delivered on September 12, the day preceding the election, Donald Sublette urged Detroiters to approve the loyalty amendment, saying that failure to do so would be interpreted by the world as a vote for communism:

> Very unfortunately, the Loyalty Amendment has been belabored by persons raising technicalities to the point where the issue has been so twisted that a "no" vote conceivably cast in good faith, is going to be represented to the world as a vote for Communism in Detroit. There is a school of thought that the amendment is much ado about nothing, that it is needlessly cluttering up the Charter, and that there is no Communist menace in Detroit or in the United States. Citizens following this line of thought will therefore cast "No" votes in good conscience. Those votes will be seized upon and broadcast throughout the world as votes for Communism in Detroit.[97]

Following the referendum on the amendment, the *Detroit News* editorial had a somewhat disenchanted tone over the fact that the loyalty amendment had won by only a three to one majority, but the U.P.W. again figured in the *News* explanation of why the majority favoring the amendment was not larger—"That the vote against the amendment was that large must be attributed to the campaign of misrepresentation waged against it by the C.I.O., especially by the U.P.W.—C.I.O. . . . It is noteworthy that the latter union, officially described as infiltrated by the Communists, is threatening further court action to delay applications of the amendment. . . ."[98]

[97] *Detroit News,* Sept. 12, 1949. The *Detroit News* editorial of Sept. 11 carried the heading, "All Americans Will Be Watching Detroit's Vote on Communism." The editorial went on to cite the Communist infiltration of the U.P.W. as a step toward infiltration, for sabotage purposes, in city departments. *Ibid.,* Sept. 11, 1949.

[98] *Ibid.,* Sept. 15, 1949.

An editorial in the *Detroit Free Press* for September 10, 1949, supporting the charter amendment, presented the more thoughtful and sober side of the whole question of Detroit employee loyalty. The editorial stated in part:

> We do not doubt that there are subversives on the public payroll who, in time of emergency, might be dangerous to the national or local security. We do doubt, however, that there are very many in this category and we are inclined to minimize the danger at this time.
>
> However, we must admit that the danger is potential and safeguards should be erected. We believe, further, that the proposed amendment will offer protection against witch hunts. That it is certain to be tested in the court upon its first application is obvious. Its constitutionality can be determined at that time.
>
> The amendment was brought up at this time, not so much because of any real threat to the community, but as a political measure to foster the fortunes of certain candidates for office. It would have been better, we think, had the amendment been offered at some other time when its necessity and effectiveness could have been more soberly examined by the voters without political implications.

It is unquestionably true that the political overtones of the campaign for the adoption of the loyalty program did not encourage thoughtful public consideration. Fundamental problems are involved in balancing the demands of public safety and security on the one hand and the individual rights of public employees on the other.[99] They deserve more dispassionate examination than perhaps they received. The tremendous mass produc-

[99] The Detroit Chapter of the Michigan Committee on Civil Rights attempted to dissuade the common council from hasty action and recommended careful study of the need and requirements of a loyalty program. In letters to the common council dated July 14, 1949, and August 18, 1949, this organization pointed out how the council's action was unwittingly making the Communists and fellow travelers the defenders of civil liberties. The committee urged the council to appoint a special study commission, including in its membership representatives from responsible community organizations, to make a study and hold hearings on the loyalty question before proceeding to set up a program.

tion facilities located in and immediately around Detroit are essential to the national economy and a vital part of a war economy. The municipal services provided by the city, either directly to industry or indirectly through serving the general population of the community, are necessary if industrial output is to be maintained. There can be little argument with the contention that a municipality has not only the right but also the responsibility to assure that the staffing of public agencies will be such that the public health and safety will not be endangered.

Of course, one cannot now definitively say whether the Detroit loyalty program will achieve its declared purpose of guarding the city against politically inspired sabotage. It is also impossible to say that the loyalty program will seriously circumscribe the political freedom of city employees. The extent to which "guilt by association" will be employed as a measure of disloyalty will depend more upon the status of international affairs than upon the words or logic of the charter amendment and the ordinance. This point is well revealed in the history of the Detroit loyalty program itself. The fever of the common council in rushing a proposed charter amendment before the electorate in the September primary seemed to cool down once the primary was over. Three full months elapsed before the council passed the necessary enabling legislation to set up the Loyalty Investigating Committee. Then the Investigating Committee which was not organized until February, 1950, remained dormant until July, 1950, when the Korean War stirred it into the beginnings of action. Until the outbreak of the Korean War, it would be possible to analyze the Detroit loyalty program as primarily a political gesture. After that explosion in international relations, the loyalty program may take on a new meaning regardless of its original motivations.

The effect of the Detroit loyalty program on individual employees will be known only when (and if) specific findings of disloyalty are made by the Loyalty Investigating Committee and upheld by the Loyalty Commission. The Loyalty Investigating Committee, the body that is authorized to bring charges of disloyalty, is composed entirely of lay personnel. It may be presumed, therefore, that the evidence provided to the committee by the Police Department and other sources will have to meet standards imposed by an approximation of public sentiment, reflected through the varied interests and backgrounds of the Investigating Committee's members. The effectiveness of the loyalty program both from the point of view of protecting public security and employee rights will largely depend upon the quality of those who compose the Loyalty Investigating Committee. Since all but one of the members of the final review board, the Loyalty Commission, are elected (the single exception being the police commissioner, a mayoral appointee), political responsibility and respect for public opinion can be expected to be reflected in their determinations. In any event, regardless of procedural requirements contained in both charter amendment and ordinance, a finding of disloyalty in any particular case is likely to be colored by shifts in public attitudes concerning the characteristics of disloyalty. This no doubt involves risks for both the public employee and those making the determination.

THE ANTICLIMAX

An appropriate conclusion to this study of the Detroit loyalty program is a review of the disposition of the Shenkar case. It will be recalled that this was the overt incident that stimulated the active campaign for a loyalty program. Although Mayor Van Antwerp on July 5, 1949, had ordered that Shenkar be dismissed, his command was ineffective because, as was later determined, only the Water Commission could issue the necessary order. Instead of being fired, Shenkar was granted a six months' leave of absence for the purpose of pursuing graduate work. The mayor approved the leave of absence, stating that this method would be the "surest and safest way to secure a permanent discharge for Shenkar." [100]

Though the Shenkar incident was referred to throughout the campaign for the loyalty charter amendment as evidence of the

[100] *Detroit News,* July 15, 1949. In an editorial of July 14, the *Detroit News* accused the administration of using the leave of absence as a device for ducking the issue until after the election. The reason Shenkar was not discharged at this time seems to have been the fear on the part of the administration that his ouster might be invalid in view of the charter provision against political discrimination.

need for a loyalty program, events afterwards seemed to prove a different proposition entirely. The leave of absence postponed action on Shenkar's case until January, 1950. Meanwhile, it was reported, the Civil Service Commission had debated whether an unidentified person should be reinstated after a leave of absence, when there were strong suspicions of his Communist activities. At the commission's meeting on December 30, 1949, Secretary Donald Sublette was said to have urged against rehiring this person. Sublette was quoted as saying: "Several government agencies have investigated this man. If not actually a Communist, he belonged at one time or another to several Commie front organizations." [101] While the commission was still trying to make up its mind, the Water Commission took the matter into its own hands by dismissing Shenkar on January 10, 1950, for insubordination and for making "insolent, disrespectful, and libelous" statements about the Water Commission and the city administration. These statements of Shenkar were termed "incompatible with the harmonious relations between employer and employee." [102] The corporation counsel's office, it was explained, had advised the Water Commission that Shenkar could not be discharged under the loyalty amendment, because the law did not become effective until Febru-

[101] *Detroit News,* Dec. 30, 1949.

[102] *Detroit News,* Jan. 10, 1950. According to a written memorandum given to the general manager of the Water Commission by its personnel director: "Shenkar appeared at the main offices of the Water Department on September 12, 1949 and distributed among staff members 'The Twilight of World Capitalism' by William Z. Foster, and the 'Deadly Parallel' by the Civil Rights Congress. He also gave out copies of an open letter.

"The letter shows beyond question that Shenkar has gone to great length in publishing documents indicating disrespect and lack of confidence in the Water Commission. His attitude toward City service is contemptuous and tends to destroy the harmonious relationships that should exist between employer and employee.

"After distributing the material at the main office, Shenkar went to the Sewage Treatment Plant and asked permission to make distribution there. This was refused. He then stood in the driveway of the plant and distributed to employees as they left work."

ary 1, when the Loyalty Investigating Committee would begin operations. Insubordination, therefore, was used as a plausible as well as legally defensible basis for removal.[103]

The firing of Shenkar for insubordination illustrates, perhaps naïvely, that a loyalty program can function perfectly well without the legal foundations so laboriously built in Detroit. Realistically, it can operate with equal effect under the guise of a merit system that protects employees from political discrimination. As long as discretion is granted to appointing officers and personnel agencies, it will be possible to impose standards of "loyalty" within the area of this discretion. The standards thus imposed may be covert and perhaps even unconscious. Disqualification from public service because of failure to qualify on "character" or "moral" grounds may provide wide latitude for discretion. A dismissal for the "good of the service" or "insubordination" may, as in Shenkar's case, achieve the same result as would a "loyalty program"—and often it can be accomplished more deftly than happened in this instance in Detroit. In saying this, one does not argue that discretion should therefore not be granted. One merely observes that changing standards of what is proper conduct on the part of municipal employees may creep into public personnel systems without necessarily changing the mechanism to deal specifically with the new standards.

[103] *Ibid.,* Jan. 10, 1949. In an editorial on Jan. 17, the *Detroit News* declared that the Water Commission had used the wrong weapon in discharging Shenkar. The editorial went on to comment that Shenkar's identification as a Communist started off the campaign for the amendment and that failure to proceed against him under it "must win adherence to the Commie claim that it is no good, constitutionally or otherwise."

V. NEW YORK

A Generation of Legislative Alarm

By LAWRENCE H. CHAMBERLAIN *January, 1951*

AMERICAN legislatures have long exhibited an interest in loyalty and the threats or purported threats which disloyal persons pose. Both the national Congress and the several state legislatures have repeatedly concerned themselves with one or another facet of this perennial problem. From early Federalist gestures against seditious plots down to present-day campaigns against subversive activities there has been an almost continuous legislative concern with this fascinating subject. The intensity has varied from time to time, and the terminology has changed slightly, but the pattern of 1950 differed very little from that of 1798.

The State of New York has not permitted itself to be outdone in this respect. As early as 1780 one finds a record of a legislative investigation of alleged Loyalist activities in New York. Similarly, during recent years loyalty investigations there have kept pace with those in sister states. During the thirty years since World War I New York has been the scene of two major loyalty investigations and a couple of minor ones. In addition to investigating threats to democracy the legislature has enacted a number of laws intended to reduce the vulnerability of our supposedly fragile institutions. Investigations, loyalty oaths, and purges—all familiar features of a society where fearful people have little faith in the strength or durability of their own institutions—have become more or less permanent fixtures.

[Mr. Chamberlain is Dean of Columbia College.]

231

During the period here under scrutiny—from World War I to the present—two major legislative investigations have been devoted to the problem of subversive activities. Within the same period a third investigation was authorized and prosecuted upon a limited scale. Investigative activity has been supplemented by lawmaking; a number of laws dealing with varying aspects of seditious activity or utterance have been proposed, and several have been passed. Some have been repealed; others have been challenged in the courts. At the moment no legislative investigation is in existence or impending, but legislative effort to erect safeguards against subversion by statutory enactment remains very much alive. The Feinberg Law, which was approved by large majorities in both houses in 1949, only to be contested in the courts for almost two years, has recently been upheld by the New York Court of Appeals. The law established procedures for detecting and removing public schoolteachers who are Communists or who espouse doctrines of violence or overthrow of government by force.

Each new development has left a record of its operations in the contemporary press. Each investigating committee has added to the cumulative record by its hearings and its formal reports. What does the total record reveal?

THE LUSK COMMITTEE

The account of modern-day legislative investigations of subversive activity in New York begins with the activities of the Lusk committee in 1919–1920.[1] This joint legislative committee, which took its name from its chairman, Senator Clayton R. Lusk of Cortland, New York, was created in March, 1919, during a period of general political and economic unrest. In the months following the cessation of actual hostilities in Europe conditions here at home had worsened. The superficial unity which a fighting war had imposed upon a reluctant and basically undisciplined population deteriorated rapidly when pressure was released by the armis-

[1] This chapter is a condensation of a more comprehensive, fully documented report published as *Loyalty and Legislative Action* (Ithaca, N.Y.: Cornell University Press, 1951).

tice. Many factors contributed to the generally disorganized social situation to produce a state of mind that bordered on demoralization. Labor strife was perhaps the chief disturbing element, but the issue was complicated by the political overtones that accompanied much labor activity in this period. The combination and interaction of indigenous labor pressures and foreign-inspired efforts produced an atmosphere that was potentially explosive.

A committee of the United States senate had already made some headlines by its probings into alleged radical activities then being carried on by various labor and foreign groups. The resolution creating the Lusk committee reflected the uneasy state of mind that existed inside and outside the legislature. Almost no dissenting voice was raised when the committee was established.

Shortly after the Lusk committee was created, its chairman made a decision which vitally influenced the entire history of the investigation. After consultation with state Attorney General Charles D. Newton, Senator Lusk decided that the committee's investigatory work should be carried on by the attorney general, who would serve as committee counsel. From the outset, therefore, Attorney General Newton and his assistant, Deputy Attorney General Samuel A. Berger, who also held the post of assistant counsel to the committee, were in a strangely contradictory position because they were simultaneously charged with performing two separate functions. At no time during the life of the committee did its leaders succeed in reconciling this fundamental contradiction.

One of the most remarkable features of the Lusk committee's activity was the almost unlimited scope it construed its authority to cover. Nothing in the language of the authorizing resolution suggested the sweeping powers which the committee arrogated to itself. Two sentences in the brief concurrent resolution set forth both the purpose of the investigation and the specific directive under which it was to function:

> Whereas, It is the duty of the Legislature of the State of New York to learn the whole truth regarding these seditious activities and to pass when such truth is ascertained such legislation as may be necessary to protect the government of the State and to insure the maintenance of the rights of its citizens,
> Now, Therefore, Be It Resolved, That a joint committee of

the Senate and Assembly be, and hereby is, created . . . to investigate the scope, tendencies, and ramifications of such seditious activities and to report the result of its investigation to the Legislature. . . .

The authorizing portion of the resolution has been reproduced in its entirety. There is nothing else in this language that could be construed to direct or authorize the committee to do more than elicit information for the use of the legislature. Yet at no time during its existence did the Lusk committee limit its activity to fact finding. From the first raid on June 12, 1919, to the final one on January 4, 1920, the committee functioned as a police force with all of the familiar apparatus of John Doe search warrants, seizure of property, and surprise arrests. Although the authorizing resolution had granted to the committee the power of subpoena, Senator Lusk and Attorney General Newton made little use of such comparatively mild procedures.

The Lusk committee functioned for approximately a year. Although it was created in March, 1919, it did not organize until May. On June 12 the committee conducted its first raid and held its first public hearing. The pattern established in this initial action was repeated in each subsequent instance.

The raid of June 12 was directed against the headquarters of the representative of the Russian Socialist Federal Soviet Republic, popularly known as the Russian Soviet Bureau and the Soviet Mission. Subsequently, the committee conducted simultaneous raids on June 21, 1919, on the Rand School of Social Science, the headquarters of the left-wing section of the Socialist Party, and the New York City headquarters of the Industrial Workers of the World. On August 14, 1919, a raid was made on the headquarters of the Union of Russian Workers, and on November 8, 1919, a gigantic city-wide raid was carried out against seventy-three "Red Centers." On December 28, 1919, the committee shifted its attention northward and conducted simultaneous raids against headquarters of the Communist Party in Utica, Rochester, and Buffalo. Returning to the scene of its earlier operations, the Lusk committee conducted its final raids on January 3 and 4. On this occasion the plants of four radical publications were visited and put out of business by the seizure of paper, printing presses, and office equipment.

The committee's methods varied little. Each raid was conducted along lines commonly employed by police squads in cleaning up vice rings such as gambling dens, houses of ill fame, or prohibition era speakeasies. A sudden dramatic coup by armed men equipped with John Doe warrants was the initial move. All persons found on the premises were taken into custody, and everything from stationery to office furniture was loaded into trucks and carted away.

Without the co-operation of the local magistrates' courts the committee could not possibly have operated as it did. But there was no difficulty on this score. From the chief magistrate down there was wholehearted support. Search warrants were issued in terms of complete generality; the committee was permitted to seize everything it could lay hands upon, and it was accorded full freedom to dispose of its booty as it saw fit. After sharp public criticism the magistrates' courts did make a feeble gesture toward requiring the committee to report officially upon its seizures. Even then, however, the magistrates' response to public criticism was little more than a gesture, because the committee continued to do as it pleased with the documents, equipment, and office furnishings which it seized. As a matter of fact, with each successive raid the committee employed tactics even more extreme than before.

Unlike other legislative investigations that have preceded and followed it, the Lusk committee depended chiefly upon the police raid for obtaining evidence. Either simultaneously with or immediately following each raid, the committee chairman or counsel, and usually both, would stage a public hearing for the press. Members of the committee staff or hand-picked witnesses would then read into the record selected bits of evidence. Thus the public hearing became merely a publicity device, calculated to dramatize what had already been done rather than to add to the committee's understanding.

All public hearings may have some elements of staging about them. Supposedly a procedure for eliciting information, a public hearing also has great potentialities as a propaganda device and as a means of high-lighting a committee's work; and often the line separating these purposes is unclear. For Senator Lusk and his associates, however, the public hearing was employed exclusively to stir the emotions while leaving the intellect untouched.

During its year of activity the Lusk committee sprayed venom over a wide area. Among those swept up in its wide-ranging forays were foreign language groups, labor unions, social service agencies, civic reform associations, and pacifist societies. The committee seemed particularly suspicious of labor activities and peace movements, but it was quick to daub the label of "subversive" upon all who resisted or criticized its objectives or methods.

Of the numerous objects to come under its disapproving eye, two were singled out for particularly intensive and prolonged harassment: the Soviet Bureau and the Rand School of Social Science. Senator Lusk and his committee launched their campaign by invading the New York City headquarters of the Russian Soviet Bureau. Armed with extremely broad search warrants, the committee operatives, supported by state police and private detectives, made a clean sweep. Among the papers seized was a file labeled diplomatic correspondence belonging to Ludwig C. A. K. Martens, the Soviet representative in the United States. For some weeks the committee carried on a sort of guerrilla warfare with Martens and his associates. Before the matter was ever settled or even clarified, however, the investigators had shifted their attention to other fields.

Initially, the committee charged the Soviet Mission with attempting to foment violence as an agent of Communist Russia. Yet, simultaneously, it rejected the mission's claims of diplomatic immunity on the ground that it was an impostor rather than a bona fide representative of a foreign power. Similarly, the committee's attitude concerning the nature of the mission's assignment was confusing. The mission through its spokesman, Mr. Martens, emphasized its primary interest in establishing business relationships with American industrial concerns. Sizable contracts were negotiated with the Ford Motor Company and the Swift Meat Packing Company, not to mention scores of other concerns. The Lusk committee was not impressed. It insisted that these commercial activities were merely convenient façades behind which the mission was carrying out its real objective of undermining the government. At a later moment, however, the committee shifted its position and attempted to place the onus on these companies for engaging in business with a foreign agent.

In the end the committee merely dropped the whole Soviet Mission action because its attention was momentarily attracted by a more interesting morsel—the Rand School of Social Science. After the Soviet Mission had been attacked, harried, and dropped, no one, including the committee itself, if one can judge from the comment in its final report, could draw any conclusions from or reach any constructive evaluation of the fruits of this erratic, sensational, and completely haphazard "investigation."

Perhaps no other incident reveals the operating premises and working methods of the Lusk committee more fully than the episode of the Rand School of Social Science. This organization was founded in 1906 to advance the welfare of laboring people. From the beginning the Rand School frankly espoused pacifist, evolutionary socialism. At no time did it endorse or support the Communist Party or its principles. Yet the Lusk committee quickly singled the Rand School out for special attention. Beginning with a raid which gutted the school property, the committee followed up with charges of an alleged conspiracy to incite an uprising among Southern Negroes. Shortly thereafter the committee counsel, functioning as attorney general, sought to close the school by legal process. When a number of prominent civic leaders came to the school's defense, the committee's attention became deflected to another victim. It is worth noting in passing that the Rand School remains today a respected member of New York City's educational community.

The committee betrayed its unsuitability for its task by the clumsy, crude quality of its judgments. Utter lack of discrimination led it to lump all liberal and radical institutions or organizations together. But its initial lack of sensitivity was not as reprehensible as its willingness to twist facts in order to smear its victim. Illustrative of this slick practice is the way the committee attempted to exploit the Domingo manuscript. This manuscript had been found among the papers seized when the Rand School was raided. Its author, W. A. Domingo, a Negro writer and lec-

turer, had addressed himself to the problem of arousing the Negroes of the South to the necessity of improving their social and
economic status. In his paper he listed such specific suggestions
for achieving this objective as "condemn all acts of injustice to
the Negro; give Negroes more prominence in the discussion; do
everything to attract Negroes to our [Socialist Party] meetings;
launch a special proposal among Negroes to show them the benefits they will derive from the economic changes we propose; sub-
sidize radical Negro newspapers; send radical white speakers to
spread radical propaganda among the Negroes, especially in the
South; avoid stressing problems of race and emphasize the advantages to all of the cooperative commonwealth."

Senator Lusk told the press that he regarded "this evidence of
a detailed plan for spreading of Bolshevist propaganda among
Negroes of the South as the greatest menace the evidence before
the committee so far has disclosed." If this statement was uttered
in good faith either of two possible conclusions could be drawn:
(1) the committee was incapable of distinguishing between dangerous and harmless activity and was therefore unfit for the task
assigned to it; or (2) nothing which fell within the purview of the
committee was serious enough to merit investigation. Yet by twist-
ing and magnifying the contents of a harmless political tract the
committee concocted out of thin air the fiction that the Rand
School was already embarked on a conspiratorial project for ad-
vancing Bolshevist plans. Not only was the manuscript harmless
—there was never any evidence that the Rand School had ever
been in any way connected with it. Press reports of the period,
however, bear witness that the committee chairman was completely successful in establishing a connection between the two.

The Lusk committee terminated its work by issuing a voluminous report and drafting four bills embracing its legislative proposals. The four-volume report, totaling more than 4,000 pages,
dealt only incidentally with the actual work which had occupied
most of the committee's attention. Less than 400 pages were devoted to the "investigations" conducted by its operatives. Hundreds of pages merely reproduced parts of books, articles, and
various fragmentary documents. Some of this material described
the doctrines or activities of Socialist, Communist, and Anarchist

organizations all over the world. Another sizable segment was given over to the literature of various organizations or groups whose activities the committee regarded as dangerous. In this heterogeneous category were labor unions, peace movements, and agencies concerned with protecting civil liberties. Singled out for particularly denunciatory treatment was industrial unionism. In a section entitled "Revolutionary Industrial Unionism," such organizations as the International Ladies' Garment Workers Union and the Amalgamated Clothing Workers were described as "subversive" because their objective was to encourage "an intense hatred for all other classes of society." Referring specifically to the Amalgamated Clothing Workers, the committee reported, "Like all of the other subversive organizations its tactics are those of the class struggle."

Similar treatment was accorded various peace movements. Many well-known persons who were then active in these organizations were investigated. Such individuals as Jane Addams, Louis P. Lochner, and David Starr Jordan, to mention but a few, were among the prominent figures in public life whose peace activities drew the committee's fire. In the eyes of the committee the American Civil Liberties Union was anathema. It noted in its report that that organization "today is as active as ever working up sympathy for revolutionaries, influencing public opinion, and generally spreading subversive propaganda."

Two volumes, approximately half of the entire report, were concerned with what the committee termed "constructive movements and measures in America." Here were reproduced materials collected from the forty-eight states describing citizenship training programs, proposals for labor-management co-operation, compulsory arbitration, and the co-operative movement. There is little in this conglomerate compilation that bears any relation to the actual work carried on by the committee.

The Lusk committee responded to its mandate to propose legislation by submitting four draft bills. Two bills bore directly upon the subjects which had occupied the committee's attention. One proposed that before a teacher could be employed he must obtain a "certificate of character" which would attest that he was of good moral character and would support the constitution and laws of the state and the United States and was desirous of the welfare of the country. The certificate could be revoked by the commissioner of education if he found that the person offended on any of these grounds.

The second bill provided for the licensing of any individual, group, or organization before it could establish or conduct a school or offer instruction. The state board of regents was empowered to revoke the license when in their judgment the school was being conducted "in such manner as to be detrimental to public interests or . . . in a fraudulent or improper manner."

Both bills were passed in the 1920 session of the legislature but were vetoed by Governor Alfred E. Smith. The following year the legislature re-enacted them, and the new governor, Nathan L. Miller, signed them. Action was immediately initiated against the Rand School under the school license law. Before the case had been finally settled in the courts, after a lower court victory for the administration, Governor Smith was re-elected in 1922. He immediately urged repeal of both laws; and when the legislature responded favorably, the Rand case was dropped.

The other two Lusk bills were admirable in aim. They proposed the establishment of a teacher training program and the introduction into factories and other places of employment of courses in English, civics, and history. Provisions for financial support of these praiseworthy plans were so inadequate that some question must be raised concerning the seriousness with which they were suggested. Amid the intense interest aroused over the other proposals, these bills were permitted to die.

Despite its bulky report the Lusk committee passed from the scene without rendering an adequate accounting of its findings and conclusions. Of the approximately 400 pages of its report that touched upon its own investigative activities, only fragmentary segments here and there dealt factually with the actual activities of the organizations investigated. To anyone who has followed the day-by-day operations of the committee and its staff this does not cause surprise, because—as has already been noted—the investigators never really finished with any of their successive projects. A spectacular raid followed by a few sensational disclosures —or claims—would be played for headlines for two or three days, then dropped in favor of another adventure. It was by way of this familiar formula that the Lusk committee made its exit.

Early in 1920 the New York State assembly attracted nation-wide attention when it voted to unseat five of its members who belonged to the Socialist Party. For the next two months Messrs. Newton and Berger, who had been devoting their time to the Lusk committee, shifted their energies to the Socialist trial. Other members of the committee staff were diverted to deportation proceedings then in progress. The committee took some pride in noting in its final report that as a result of its work seventy-five persons had been arrested, of whom eight had already been convicted and three deported while the remainder awaited trial. As a statistical measure of law enforcement this may be an impressive record—but not for a legislative investigating committee.

Between the events of the Lusk era and the second full-scale investigation twenty years later, the most significant New York State legislative action in the field of un-American activities is represented by the Ives Loyalty Oath Law, the abortive McNaboe investigations, and the Devany Law. Each of these will be discussed briefly.

THE IVES LOYALTY OATH LAW

In 1934, Assembly Majority Leader Irving M. Ives introduced a bill requiring all teachers to take a loyalty oath. Actually, all newly appointed public schoolteachers in New York City had been required to take such an oath for many years. An oath which dated back to World War I had crept into the regulations of the New York City board of education, although no statutory authority could be found for such a rule. The Ives bill did not explicitly identify the teachers to whom it applied, and Governor Lehman emphasized this as one of the defects which prompted him to veto the bill.

Later in the same year, an extraordinary session of the legislature provided Mr. Ives with another opportunity to advance his bill. An amended bill required teachers in all public schools and in private schools operating on tax-exempt property to subscribe to the following oath: "I do solemnly swear (or affirm) that I will support the Constitution of the United States and the Constitution of the State of New York, and that I will faithfully discharge, to the best of my ability, the duties of the position to which I am now assigned."

Although the bill was vigorously attacked by teacher groups and the American Civil Liberties Union on the grounds that teachers should not be singled out for special treatment, the assembly approved it, 129 to 8, and the senate, 40 to 2. Governor Lehman signed the bill, explaining that some of his original objections had been met and "because of the very strong sentiment there is in its favor among the teachers themselves." The statute remains in force today.

THE McNABOE INVESTIGATIONS

The individuals and groups who had sponsored or supported the loyalty oath bill apparently did not gain from its enactment the sense of security that they had expected. Otherwise it is difficult to account for the revival and intensification of sentiment for additional protective measures a year or two later. Beginning in 1935 and continuing at an accelerated rate in 1936 a number of new bills were introduced into the legislature. Among the new proposals were: requirement of a loyalty oath from all students before they could be admitted to any high school or college supported in whole or in part by public funds; elimination or prohibition of state financial aid to any institution where "destructive doctrines such as communism, bolshevism and other radical theories are taught and encouraged"; a requirement that the American flag should be displayed in every public school classroom; a requirement that all school buses be painted red, white, and blue. Only the flag bill reached final stages of action. After the bill had been modified so as to apply to schoolhouses rather than individual schoolrooms it became law.

The 1936 session also witnessed another investigation, although this one turned out to be abortive. The first McNaboe investigation came about as a result of a resolution introduced by Senator John J. McNaboe of New York City. The resolution alleged that the schools of the city and state were permeated with professional paid agitators who were saturating the students with "seditious and treasonable" propaganda. Despite some opposition Senator

McNaboe succeeded in putting his resolution through, and the investigation was authorized in July, 1936. A joint committee with bipartisan membership was created with Senator McNaboe as chairman.

This committee never functioned. It expired early the following year when the legislature rejected Senator McNaboe's request that its life be extended. During the six months of its legal existence the committee failed to hold a single meeting. Its chairman showed considerable aptitude in drawing headlines by charging that many of the state's institutions of higher education were steeped in communism. At one time or another he directed his fire against Cornell, New York University, and Teachers College, Columbia University. He shifted to the American Civil Liberties Union and then to the New York City public schools. Mayor La Guardia seemed to incur particular disfavor. Not content with his one-man campaign of billingsgate against the ostensible objects of his investigative assignment, McNaboe also feuded with his fellow committee members who objected to being associated with an agency in whose activities they had no voice. Just how much of its original appropriation of $15,000 was actually expended is not known. Senator McNaboe, the only person who presumably might be able to answer that question, contradicted himself flatly. Upon one occasion he declared that party patronage demands had completely exhausted the appropriation, but later he asserted that because of behind-the-scenes politics not a penny had been spent.

Senator McNaboe was not without resourcefulness. When the legislature declined to extend his un-American activities investigation during the 1937 session, he shifted his area of emphasis. Before the legislature adjourned it had authorized his new proposal to investigate the administration and enforcement of the criminal law with special emphasis upon treatment of persons on parole. By exceedingly nimble footwork Senator McNaboe managed to transform his new assignment into the one originally authorized in 1936. The change was made easier by the extremely broad language of the authorizing resolution.

The second McNaboe investigation extended over 1937 and 1938. During the first year the committee adhered to its au-

thorized assignment. Numerous hearings were held on matters
pertaining to the treatment of abnormal patients, psychiatric
problems, and parole of prisoners. Early in 1938 the legislature
extended the committee's life and gave it an additional appropriation of $40,000. Shortly thereafter Senator McNaboe turned
his back on this line of investigation and plunged abruptly into
the field of un-American activities.

One cannot be sure what produced the sudden shift. Possibly
such a plan had been in his mind from the beginning. Another
possible reason can be advanced. When early in 1938 a Communist had been appointed to a position on the staff of the Man-
hattan Borough president's office, McNaboe introduced into the
legislature a bill barring from civil service and teaching positions
any person who espoused the overthrow of the government by
force. Both houses approved the bill, but it met with a sharp veto
by Governor Lehman. It is possible that Senator McNaboe was
prompted to direct his attention to the threat of communism by
this setback to his legislative program. This hypothesis is supported by the bitter attack that McNaboe made upon those whom
he held responsible for the veto.

The investigation itself calls for little comment. For a period
of approximately six weeks during the early summer of 1938 the
committee held a number of public hearings upon one or another
aspect of un-American activity. Officials representing the German-
American Bund and the Communist Party were interrogated by
the senator and his associates, but the record of the hearings casts
doubt upon the fruitfulness of the proceedings.

None of Senator McNaboe's colleagues approached him in personal vindictiveness toward witnesses, but neither he nor they
seemed to have any conception of how to plan, organize, and conduct a hearing so as to obtain information that might be useful
to the legislature. They insisted upon handling the questioning
themselves rather than selecting a counsel or staff. The result was
almost a travesty. Witnesses were badgered and insulted by committee members who either did not wish or did not know how to
elicit pertinent facts from them. Questions were phrased in such
a manner as to defy answers; many of them had no bearing upon
the subject on the agenda; witnesses' answers were frequently mis-

interpreted—whether by design or lack of acuteness on the part of the interrogators is not known.

The McNaboe committee completed its work with a two-volume report approximately two-fifths of which dealt with the committee's original assignment—enforcement of the criminal law. The remaining three-fifths reproduced some 325 pages of verbatim testimony amassed during the hearings, supplemented by a thousand pages of exhibits. This latter material was made up principally of copies of the *Daily Worker* and various Communist shop organs put out by party units in schools, colleges, and hospitals throughout the state. Included also were pamphlets, speeches, and miscellaneous writings by Communist Party officials.

All of this material is simply lumped together without explanation or comment. It is impossible to know what purpose the committee had in mind in reproducing it. Hundreds of similar documents were at that time being circulated freely. In the absence of some kind of orderly introductory discussion the incorporating of all these exhibits adds nothing to a report which in itself presents so little information. The McNaboe committee report seems entirely in character with the investigation itself.

THE DEVANY LAW

Senator McNaboe was to have one final inning before he retired from the scene. In the 1939 session of the legislature he reintroduced his bill barring Communists from civil service positions in government and the schools. The language of the bill was so vague that many persons who in no sense adhered to the principles of the Communist Party would have been vulnerable to attack. Many legislative leaders disassociated themselves from the McNaboe bill, but there was considerable undercurrent of support for some legislation of this type. It was generally agreed that a more moderate, carefully drafted bill would be approved by many legislators of both parties who favored placing some loyalty restrictions upon civil service employees.

When Senator McNaboe could not be persuaded to modify his bill, a substitute was introduced in the assembly by John A. Devany. The Devany bill excluded from public office persons advocating or teaching that the government "should be overthrown by force, violence, or any unlawful means." After several amendments had been incorporated to clarify its application and to strengthen procedural safeguards against its abuse, the bill was passed by the assembly. After some negotiation the Devany bill received the necessary approval in the senate. Amid considerable speculation as to his intentions Governor Lehman signed the bill, with the explanation that most of the objectionable features had been removed.

The Devany bill clearly proposed to bar from civil service and from employment in publicly supported educational institutions anyone who advocated, advised, or taught the doctrine that government should be overthrown by force. It likewise prohibited such employees from writing or publishing articles which expressed these views, and, further, it expressly forbade the joining of organizations for this purpose. That the law might be so administered as to constitute a serious breach of academic freedom or civil liberties was a potential danger which could neither be denied nor scoffed at.

It was at this point that important procedural safeguards were introduced which made the Devany bill much superior to its predecessor. Under its provisions any person dismissed or declared ineligible for any of the above reasons was entitled to petition the state Supreme Court for a hearing and a stay of proceedings until conclusion of the hearing. The law further stipulated that "the burden of sustaining the validity of the order of dismissal or ineligibility by a fair preponderance of the credible evidence shall be upon the person making such dismissal or order of ineligibility."

The Devany Law combined dangerous substantive restrictions with unexceptionable procedural guarantees. Thoughtful advocates of academic freedom would have felt much better with no legislation at all, but they could derive some comfort from the careful language of the procedural section. So long as the courts continued to function responsibly, they reasoned, the danger of arbitrary removals could be kept at a minimum. It is pertinent to anticipate subsequent developments in order to observe that the extensive removals that resulted from the Rapp-Coudert investigation of 1940–1941 were not made under the authority of the Devany Law.

THE RAPP-COUDERT INVESTIGATION

The Rapp-Coudert investigation represented the joining together of two separate issues upon which there was more or less general interest in the year 1939. In a way these two issues were related, although it is quite clear in retrospect that the existence of this relationship had nothing to do with the decision to join them together as a single subject for investigation. This decision was fortuitous, and, as the following account will explain, unfortunate.

Dissatisfaction with existing formulas for allocating state financial aid to public schools within the state lay at the base of the decision of the state legislature to investigate school finances. Changes and shifts in population had rendered obsolete the existing arrangement. New York City schools were under particular pressure, because, as school costs increased through rising prices and expanded school populations, financial resources shrank as a result of falling real estate values—the chief and, except for state aid, almost the sole source of tax revenue for educational purposes.

The demand for greater state financial aid—both proportionately (as compared to rural sections of the state) and absolutely —was pressed with increasing vigor by New York City interest groups. Simultaneously, there was an equally clamorous demand for reducing educational appropriations. By 1940 pressure on the legislature on both sides of the issue was considerable, and it was in response to this pressure that Assemblyman Herbert A. Rapp, late in the session, introduced a resolution proposing a legislative investigation of state aid to education. Mr. Rapp's resolution had been approved and was awaiting formal action when the developments which led to the second part of the investigation got under way.

In the two years preceding, New York citizens had been alternatively amused and disturbed by a combination of incidents. The antics of the McNaboe committee have already been described. The honest concern which charges of Communist infiltration of schools aroused was diluted by the extravagant accusations and burlesque tactics employed. Simultaneously, deep-seated dissatisfaction had arisen over the presidencies of two of the city

247

colleges. After extended discussion and some not very praiseworthy maneuvering by members of the board of higher education, the heads of both City College and Hunter College vacated their posts, but the incidents did not pass without stirring up a great deal of gossip and speculation. Veiled charges were exchanged rather indiscriminately until the atmosphere was confusing; but floating about in the background were such inflammatory phrases as "anti-Semitism," "church interference," and "liberal-conservative schisms."

During the winter of 1939–1940 a new incident occurred which helped bring to a head the disaffection which had accumulated during the two preceding years. When the announcement was made public that the eminent British philosopher and mathematician Bertrand Russell had been appointed professor of philosophy at City College, the reaction was instantaneous and violent. Opposition led by and expressed through the Roman Catholic Church was especially vigorous because of Mr. Russell's unorthodox views and practices concerning the institution of marriage.

Action opposing the Russell nomination occurred on many fronts, among them the state legislature. There on March 22, 1940, the senate passed the Phelps resolution protesting Russell's appointment. Only a few moments later Senator John J. Dunnigan of New York City introduced a resolution proposing an investigation of the New York City schools. Both the language of his resolution and his own accompanying remarks made it clear that he was primarily concerned with allegedly "immoral" and "ungodly" conditions in the schools, although the resolution also mentioned "un-American" activities.

After some days of legislative negotiation the Rapp proposal for investigating school finances and the Dunnigan proposal were combined and the so-called Rapp-Coudert joint committee emerged. It was directed to look into the entire broad question of allocating state education funds among schools throughout the state and also to investigate the administration and conduct of the public school system of New York City, including the "extent to which, if any, subversive activities may have been permitted to be carried on in the schools and colleges."

From the legislative point of view there seemed to be no objection to combining two such disparate subjects. Indeed, if the matter was ever considered, it seems likely that at the outset positive advantages might be expected to accrue.

Reaction on the part of the Teachers Union, the outspoken critic of the investigation throughout its existence, and soon to become the chief object of its attentions, was instantaneous. The point singled out for chief emphasis was the incongruity of combining finances and subversive activities. The union insisted that the investigation was an ill-concealed move to cut educational appropriations behind the false front of driving out Communists. By combining finances and subversive activities, reactionary officials could put a double squeeze on school appropriations and upon the Teachers Union, the one organization with the courage and strength to expose or resist.

There is no clear evidence that such ill-conceived motives lay in the minds of those concerned—either in the legislature or in the committee staff that planned and executed the inquiry. Indeed, Paul Windels, committee counsel, later publicly deplored the fact that the two functions had been joined. In retrospect, however, it seems likely that this decision was the single most unfortunate one in the entire inquiry.

The Teachers Union quickly seized upon this vulnerable weakness in its effort to discredit the integrity of the entire investigation. Representatives of the union were extremely articulate. They lost no time in launching their attack. Long before the investigation actually got under way the union had broadcast widely through the public press as well as through its own news organs and numerous pamphlets and leaflets that the investigation was not conceived in good faith.

This development had numerous repercussions. Many private citizens with no special allegiance to either side but with an honest desire to see justice done were confused and uncertain. They hesitated to accept the union's allegations at face value, yet they could find little contradictory evidence against which to balance union claims because at this time—and, for that matter, later— the committee made almost no effort to state publicly its position.

The committee itself was affected adversely by public reaction. In the early days of the committee's existence it had expected to receive the support of various liberal leaders and groups. But most of these people, for reasons already explained, withheld their support. Some aligned themselves with the Teachers Union; most merely suspended judgment in the hope that the committee would clarify its function. To the committee the failure to receive the kind of wholehearted support it had expected amounted to an outright rebuff. Its reaction was one of surprised resentment that did not aid the investigators in maintaining the judicial calm necessary for achieving their objectives.

It is not to be supposed that all of the committee's difficulties stemmed from the unhappy decision to merge two separate investigations, nor is it assumed that the Teachers Union would have been less violent in its opposition to an investigation of alleged subversive activities if the financial assignment had not also been included. But the belief is entertained that the general public might have been less disposed to jump to conclusions had the single issue of communism in the schools been up for consideration.

Assemblyman Rapp, who had been designated chairman of the original committee, retained his post when the two investigations were merged. But Senator Frederic R. Coudert, Jr., of New York City became vice-chairman of the committee and chairman of the special subcommittee to investigate subversive activities in New York City schools. This subcommittee was popularly known as the Coudert committee and will be so designated in this report. After the first few weeks Mr. Rapp took no part in the subcommittee's work, and none of the other members of either the entire committee or the subcommittee were ever active forces in the investigation.

Senator Coudert selected Paul Windels, a prominent New York City lawyer, as committee counsel. Windels in turn recruited a professional staff of some six or eight assistants. Throughout the investigation Mr. Windels and his chief aide, Phillip Haberman, Jr., functioned as the key figures in matters both of policy and procedure. Senator Coudert retained close touch with proceedings and took part in most of the public hearings. He served as principal spokesman for the committee and always accepted full responsibility for its decisions and actions, but he was not active in day-by-day operations.

During the lifetime of the Coudert committee a vast number of issues arose. No investigation promotes tranquility, but it is doubtful if many were so utterly embedded in controversy as this. Subversive activity defies objective definition. What to one person or group seems subversive is to another simply liberal. At either end one finds extremists; but even at the center opinions vary as to where one draws the line between subversive and nonsubversive activity. The controversial character of the investigation multiplied and magnified the number of troublesome items, and it is impossible in a brief summary to dwell in detail upon many of them.

From the welter of disputed points three major ones stand out. Each is unique, yet individually and collectively these three serve to illustrate the differing viewpoints from which the entire episode could be appraised. The first issue singled out for discussion is the committee's decision to concentrate on the Teachers Union, its consequent request that the union surrender its membership lists, and its resort to force when the union refused to comply. The two others grew out of procedural problems: the first, the rights accorded witnesses during the private hearings; the second, committee conduct during the public hearings. Each of these points will be treated briefly.

Although the committee was created in March, little was done during the spring and summer, and it was not until September, 1940, that actual investigative work began. During this preliminary period, however, Mr. Windels and his staff were not idle. In their tentative exploratory moves they attempted to establish a plan of campaign and to map out the chief areas to be investigated. Numerous sources were consulted, but perhaps of even greater influence at this stage were suggestions volunteered by interested persons. From many sides came urgent demands that the Teachers Union should be the first organization that the committee should examine. By its own vigorous and frequently blatant attacks upon the committee the union did nothing to counteract this line of pressure. Some members of the committee staff have expressed the opinion that the Teachers Union was deliberately attempting to get itself investigated and that its campaign of vilification was planned with this objective in mind. This view is conjectural at best, and evidence to support it is lacking. Furthermore, it is difficult to see what advantage the union might have sought to gain.

The committee staff did, however, decide to concentrate its initial attention on the Teachers Union, and with very minor exceptions the investigation of the Coudert subcommittee never shifted away from its original focus of interest. The fortunes of the Teachers Union are thus so closely tied up with the successes and failures of the Rapp-Coudert investigation that the relationship must be examined in some detail if anything approaching an informed impression of the entire episode is to be achieved.

The Teachers Union, Local 5, A.F.L., had been in existence since 1916. Originally all teachers functioned in a single union. In 1935 a college section of Local 5 was formed. By 1938 this section had grown to the point where it withdrew from the parent local and received its own charter as Local 537, the College Teachers Union. The two unions functioned separately but co-operated closely during the period here under discussion. At no time had more than a small fraction of the total teaching staffs of the city schools been organized; nevertheless, there had been periods when union influence was of major importance with New York City school authorities. During the 1930's factionalism had badly disrupted the internal functioning of the union. The friction grew increasingly intense until the original leadership withdrew and the more radical group took over. The struggle for control was more than a contest for power between two ambitious groups, although this consideration was not absent. Communism was a factor in that some of the left-wingers were avowed Communists, and others were strongly suspected of belonging to the party. Not all adherents or supporters of the left-wing faction were Communist Party members, however. The salient fact is that the union's internal disorders were compounded of several causes; to attribute them to one is to oversimplify.

Throughout the late thirties the union did grow increasingly belligerent. Its changing tone is well reflected in the pages of the *New York Teacher,* its official journal. The union became more politically oriented in its interests, and a note of stridency, previously absent, crept into almost all of its comment. On such issues as tenure, compensation, and security the union pressed vigorously for the interests of its members and lost no opportunity to heap bitter denunciations upon the school administration and the state legislature.

Whether all this campaign of attack was conducted or inspired by Communist strategy is not clear. Certainly, not all who directed criticism against existing educational practices were Communist. This much is known: some of the most able, outspoken defenders of the union when the investigation got under way were clearly not Communists. Yet these persons—and there were several—fought just as bitterly every effort of the investigators as did any of the persons who admitted to being Communists.

In the opinion of the writer the fact that numerous non-Communists participated actively in attacking the Coudert committee and thereby incurred the suspicion of the investigators is of the utmost importance to anyone attempting to understand the investigation, its procedures, and its results. The issue is crucial because around it revolves the basis for appraising the investigation.

Although at the beginning of its work the committee might not have concluded at once that the Teachers Union and the Communist Party were identical, clearly, it fully accepted that view at some early stage of its operations. Once the basic premise was established, the committee's entire course of action was virtually determined. It assumed that it could most effectively execute its mandate to ascertain "the extent to which, if any, subversive activities may have been permitted to be carried on in the schools and colleges" by centering its fire on the union.

The committee immediately called upon the union officials for the membership lists. When this request was refused, Mr. Windels successfully resorted to legal process to obtain possession. The decision to scrutinize union membership lists placed the committee in a questionable position; when the union refused to reveal its members and the committee employed compulsory means, the damage was done. This incident occurred early—

before most people not directly connected with the inquiry had determined their own position about it. Many persons reacted unfavorably because the committee's action seemed both un-justified and unnecessary. The confidential character of union membership had long been accepted as a right of organized labor; any effort to invade that right was bound to excite allegations of labor baiting and antiunion tactics. This is exactly what happened, and the committee unwittingly found itself placed on the defensive by persons who would have rallied to its support if it had not directed its attack against the entire union membership.

There is evidence that suggests that the committee's decision to go after the lists was taken in utmost good faith, reflecting an assumption that the membership rolls would be the only precise indicators of the existence or extent of subversiveness. But the committee did not make clear just how possession of these lists would advance its work. Nothing in the union's membership lists did, in fact, throw any light upon the identity of members of the Communist Party because under union rules information concerning party affiliations, religion, nationality, etc., was intentionally omitted. Moreover, since the committee had no access to Communist Party membership records, it could not possibly claim that union lists would yield important data through a comparison of the two lists. Why then did the committee want the lists? In the absence of a specific answer by the committee, its adversaries could allege with some plausibility that the investigators were using the Communist bogey as a front for a drive to destroy the union by intimidating its members.

Apparently the lists gave the investigators no relevant information not already in their possession. But neither did the worst fears of the union or its champions materialize. One of the chief arguments advanced for resisting Mr. Windels' demand was the prediction that the lists would immediately be made public. This both Mr. Windels and Senator Coudert denied. They scrupulously kept their word. To this day the membership of the union has never been divulged. At the time the request was made, however, the committee's motives were suspect and its good faith unproved. At a strategic moment in the battle for public support the membership list incident threw the balance strongly against the committee.

After Mr. Windels had organized his staff he set it to work establishing a pattern of procedure that varied but little throughout the investigation. A research group devoted much time to collecting, analyzing, and digesting a wide variety of documentary data. Included in this exceedingly voluminous material were books on Marxian theory, histories of Communist activity all over the world, periodical and newspaper literature issued by Communist organizations both domestic and foreign. Through its analysis of documentary material the committee hoped to detect the general framework of the party's operations, its strategy, and its chief points of concentration, but there was also present the hope that from an intensive screening of this material clues to the identity of participating Communists would be discovered.

Supplementary to its documentary research the committee carried on an extensive program of interviewing. Mr. Windels invited the public to volunteer any information which might aid the committee. The response to this general invitation was disappointing, however, and most of those who appeared before the committee did so only upon personal request. For the most part the committee was obliged to find its witnesses through the rather haphazard process of following up leads thrown out by those it questioned. Most of the early clues turned out to be worthless, but after a number of false starts the investigators were led to the trail of several members of the teaching staffs of various city educational institutions who were reported to have been at one time members of the Communist Party.

After efforts that initially were unsuccessful, several of these persons were persuaded to co-operate. William Canning was the most important witness, but several others aided. From their collective testimony the committee compiled a list of teachers or administrative employees who were allegedly Communists. The committee then issued subpoenas to many of these persons. In eliciting information it employed the private interview, the private examination, and the public hearing. Typically a witness was invited to committee headquarters where he was informally questioned by one or more members of the staff. For this step no oath was administered, and the witness's testimony was not taken down. When staff members felt that something useful for their purposes had been turned up in an informal interview, they would call in a committee member to administer an oath to the witness and a stenographer to take down what was said.

The private hearing procedure quickly became one of the storm centers of the inquiry. In order to expedite its work the committee staff adopted the policy of using one-man subcommittees during the private hearing stage. Ordinarily a member of the committee would be present at such a hearing, although it was not uncommon practice for the committee member to withdraw after he had administered the oath to the testifying witness. Where this occurred the only persons present would be the interrogator, who was a member of the committee staff, a stenographer, and the witness.

Repeated efforts on the part of the Teachers Union to win for its members the right to be accompanied by counsel met with no success. Furthermore, despite strong protests from the union, its members, and such organizations as the American Civil Liberties Union, the witness was not permitted to obtain a transcript of his testimony. This ruling was the root of most of the trouble; it caused the committee and its staff more grief than almost any other point. But there was no retreat. By its refusal to relax its inflexible policy on this relatively minor point the committee incurred unnecessary enmity and hampered its own work.

During the early stages of its private hearings the committee met with organized resistance. A group of some twenty members of the Brooklyn College staff, several of whom have never been remotely suspected of being Communists, refused to testify before the one-man subcommittees. The chief reason they gave for their unwillingness to appear was the danger they would incur of being inaccurately recorded with no opportunity to correct the written record.

The group challenged the legal power of a single man to compel testimony, and it was several months before a second legislative resolution sustained the committee. Thereafter, witnesses reluctantly acquiesced, but the Teachers Union made great capital of the "star chamber," "inquisitorial" methods allegedly employed and the Coudert committee did not benefit from such publicity.

Its adamant stand on a relatively minor point cost heavily in both time and friends. For almost four months it was faced with a sit-down strike, but this campaign of passive resistance was not so damaging to the committee's prestige as was the bad publicity it received for its reputedly third-degree tactics. There does not appear to be any reason why the committee could not have avoided this unpleasant episode without sacrificing a shred of its effectiveness.

The committee based its refusal to permit a witness to obtain a copy of his private testimony on the grounds that such testimony was confidential and should not be made public, and, secondly, that the witness might in some way—never made plain—use his testimony to injure the committee. Not only did the committee fail to make its position sufficiently clear to convince the public; it actually retreated to a position where, in effect, it repudiated itself without gaining anything in so doing. Witnesses appearing before the committee in private hearing insisted upon taking notes upon the questions directed to them and their replies. Often the witness would carry this practice to the extreme of making his own personal verbatim record. At first the interrogators took exception to this procedure, but they discovered that it was the price exacted for co-operation, and it was not long until the practice became recognized as acceptable. But with this development the committee's stated reasons for withholding the transcript no longer had any substance. Up to the end, however, the policy of no transcript was retained.

The public hearing was not, strictly speaking, so much a fact-finding device as it was a reporting or public information instrument. Ordinarily a public hearing was not called until the committee staff had sifted through the private testimony and selected certain portions which it desired to make public. Then a formal public hearing would be called at which the witness would repeat designated portions of his previous testimony. The early public hearings were full-dress affairs with virtually all committee members present. As the first sharp edges of sensationalism wore off, committee attendance dropped until customarily only a single member took part.

Public hearings took on additional significance during the later stages of the investigation. After Canning and his associates named fifty-odd alleged Communists at public hearings, the accused individuals demanded the right to reply under similar conditions. The committee granted this request, and each person named did appear at a public hearing. Notwithstanding the fact that the accused persons had initiated the request to be heard, the committee summoned each of them by subpoena. This action, when coupled with the undeviating practice of addressing to each witness immediately after he was sworn the identical question, "Are you a member of the Communist Party?" suggested that the committee placed some legal significance upon the public appearances of those accused.

The technical ground upon which alleged Communists were suspended and later removed from their positions was "conduct unbecoming a member of the staff," one of the legal bases for removal specified in the teacher tenure law. Perjury was interpreted as falling within this provision by school authorities. Accordingly, care was taken to make sure that each person accused should appear and testify under oath whether or not he was a Communist. The meticulous timing of each person's suspension so that it followed immediately upon his sworn statement suggested strongly (1) that the perjury issue was being consciously used, and (2) that the committee had already made up its mind that all those named were actually Communists. Under these circumstances it is not strange that committee members and staff took little interest in the public hearings. Apparently they regarded the public hearings chiefly as a *pro forma* device, whereas those accused looked upon them as a vital opportunity to present their case.

Such widely divergent conceptions of the purpose of the public hearings could not fail to arouse controversy. What seemed to the committee a generously fair procedure appeared to the accused a sham imitation of a genuine hearing. The investigators emphasized the fact that since hearings were not obligatory, the beneficiaries should appreciate the generosity of the committee and not quibble over details. But the accused insisted that a public hearing was a right rather than a privilege, and they were not content with a merely formal fulfillment. They had been branded as Communists. They knew that unless they could clear themselves of the charge their jobs were in jeopardy. At this time the public hearing of the committee was the only forum in which they could present their side.

In linking individual names to his account of Communist activities in the colleges, Mr. Canning had sometimes mentioned particular individuals in connection with specific incidents. More frequently, however, he described in general terms the nature of his experiences. Among the points stressed were the innumerable meetings, the heavy demands both in time and money which the party exacted from its members, the discouragement of individual research or other scholarly work, the insistence upon active participation in party recruiting, propaganda, and organizational work. Some of the specific activities mentioned were writing for or participating in the publication or distribution of the *Teacher-Worker*, the paper issued by the Communist unit in City College; surreptitiously distributing party literature or pasting up party slogans; teaching in party indoctrination programs; marching in May Day parades, etc. Mr. Canning also alleged that classroom indoctrination was emphasized, and he gave illustrative examples of how it could be done. Although he declared that classroom indoctrination was actually carried on, he cited no specific instances.

Each of the persons named as a Communist was faced with the task of defending himself against a general set of charges rather than against particularized accusations. In the rare instances where a specific charge was made, it was the unsupported statement of one individual against another. About the only kind of rebuttal evidence open to an accused person was the presentation of general character testimonials or accounts of his professional and personal career which might challenge the credibility of Canning's evidence or at least demonstrate its inapplicability in the present case.

When the rebuttal hearings opened, however, the committee chairman indicated little interest in this kind of evidence. He and his colleagues attempted to be fair, but they repeatedly sought to expedite proceedings by curtailing the amount of time taken by accused teachers in reading into the record character references and similar data.

After the first day the chairman attempted to limit each person to five minutes. Later the time limit was extended to ten minutes. Neither limit was effective, because the accused persons were persistent and usually managed to get at least part of their rebuttal testimony read into the record before they were compelled to terminate. Senator Coudert argued that the committee need not waste its time listening to extended character references and letters of testimony from students and colleagues of the accused so long as it was willing to have such documentary evidence entered into the record by title and made available to the press if request was made.

As has already been observed, this attitude on Mr. Coudert's part strongly supports the hypothesis that he and his associates were not looking upon these hearings as sources of further information. Quite apparently they had already made up their minds concerning the guilt of those appearing before them. Additional support for this view was supplied by the almost invariable failure of the committee to cross-examine the responding witnesses as they presented their evidence.

The right of the teachers to full opportunity to present their side of the case does not seem an unreasonable request. The evidence against them had been presented in great detail, and the committee witnesses had been encouraged to dwell at length upon incidents or actions in which the respondents were alleged to have been involved. Here then was the first opportunity to give their story. The chairman's proposal that they could file their evidence where the press could examine it did not strike them as a suitable substitute for the right to speak themselves. One can hardly doubt that they were correct in assuming that if they wanted their evidence to reach the public they had better read it into the record in open court. At least this is what actually happened. No press report has been found dealing with any of the documents which were merely identified by title and turned over to the committee. Nor for that matter has the committee itself ever given any indication that it read them.

This issue of the public hearing is certainly one of the key points of the investigation, because it provided one more occasion for testing the sincerity and the judgment of the public authorities. Again Senator Coudert and his associates came off second best in the eyes of many persons because they proceeded from challengeable premises and they failed to make explicit the reasons for acting as they did.

When Mr. Canning and his associates publicly identified as Communists fifty-odd members of the teaching and administrative staffs of the municipal colleges, the Coudert committee assumed that their identity was established beyond doubt. Henceforth the committee proceeded from this assumption, and its treatment of the persons accused was determined on this basis. On its part the committee concluded that it had sufficient evidence that the people publicly named were actually party members before it permitted Canning or one of the other co-operating witnesses to mention them in a public hearing. There were instances, moreover, when these co-operating witnesses had privately named additional persons as Communists and the committee had not permitted their names to be made public because the evidence against them was too sketchy or so contradictory that strong doubt existed as to its reliability. Furthermore, in most cases *but not in all* the committee did not permit a person's name to be mentioned publicly until he had been examined privately.

All this would suggest that the committee and its staff were making an honest effort to conduct their inquiry on a high level and to avoid smearing innocent persons by making sure of their facts before pinning the Communist label upon anyone. It appears that the investigators' motives were honorable but that their execution was poor. Despite their efforts to check their evidence before reaching a final judgment they did not exercise sufficient care to make certain of the accuracy of their results.

Canning and his associates had no way of proving their claims in many of the instances when they named particular individuals as fellow party members. In a number of cases the intimacy and duration of association was such that there could be little reasonable doubt concerning the accuracy of an identification. There were other cases, however, where alleged contacts had been casual and infrequent. Most of those named had been fellow members with Canning and his associates of three other organizations that held frequent meetings throughout the period of their alleged party membership. These organizations—the Instructional Staff Association, the College Teachers Union, and the Anti-Fascist Association—were all militant groups vigorously engaged in campaigns full of controversy.

Whether through innocent confusion of identity or deliberate misrepresentation, it seems highly likely that along with a number of persons correctly identified as Communists were a number of others who should never have been named. The committee did not exercise sufficient care before accepting an unsupported opinion in view of the seriousness of the accusation and the possibility that it might do irrevocable harm to an innocent person. This point gains added substance in view of the committee's knowledge that Canning and his associates had already been proved inaccurate or unreliable in particular instances.

Usually, as has already been indicated, the suspected individual was summoned before the committee in private session before his name was made public. This procedure did give some protection to the accused in that at least he was given an opportunity to make a response before being judged. Presumably, the committee did not feel that his evidence was sufficiently credible or substantial because there is no record of an instance where a name was struck from the black list as a result of rebuttal by the owner, but at any rate the individual did have the satisfaction of getting his denials into the record of the private hearings.

Yet even this frail reed of self-defense was withheld in some instances. In an incident that should have been embarrassing to the committee one of the persons named by Mr. Canning as a member of the Communist Party bitterly denounced the committee for not permitting him to appear before it in private before spreading his name on the public record. He bluntly denied any affiliation with the party and insisted that he could have proved his contention had he been given an opportunity.

This person is one of the few named who were not subsequently removed, so his claims must be accorded some consideration. There is no way of telling why he was not summoned before the private hearing. But whether the explanation was a careless slip or a deliberate decision the committee's position is not strengthened. Its conduct left it vulnerable to the charge that in carrying out its work the rights of the individual had not been adequately safeguarded.

At a later time when this charge had been directed against its procedures, the committee replied that such arguments were irrelevant because it was not a judicial tribunal trying people but a legislative committee seeking information. On narrowly technical grounds this was correct. When viewed realistically this was not the case. In the first place, the committee was not limiting itself to eliciting information. It was at the very least attempting in effect to pin indictments upon particular individuals. Moreover, the committee had already gone on record publicly and especially in its communications to the school authorities to the effect that no Communist should be permitted to retain his job. Under these circumstances, it ill befitted the committee to defend itself from charges of ignoring due process by pleading the conventional immunities of a legislative committee.

There is no way of knowing how many cases of mistaken identity there were among the fifty-odd named. But there is strong reason to believe that there were several. Yet the committee had already so definitely made up it own mind that *all persons publicly named* were guilty as charged that it in effect prevented them from proving their innocence during the public hearings by turning what might have been a meaningful and highly significant procedure into a purely *pro forma* ritual. It did this without explaining its action, thus adding to the confusion and dismay of those who were involved in or affected by its work.

From the beginning there was some division of opinion within the New York City board of higher education concerning the action it should take against the teachers in city colleges who had been denounced by Coudert committee witnesses. Some members pressed vigorously for immediate suspension or expulsion of all persons named, but the majority of the board urged a more moderate course. As pressure built up both inside and outside the board the more positive group gained in influence, although a reduced minority continued to resist punitive steps.

Under the teachers' tenure law four grounds were enumerated under which removal proceedings against a teacher could be taken. Membership in the Communist Party was not among the listed grounds for removal, but "conduct unbecoming a teacher" was a cause for dismissal. It was on the basis of this phrase that disciplinary proceedings were initiated.

When the accused teachers refused to co-operate with the Coudert committee by declining to testify at private hearings, the senator called upon the board to direct its employees to respond. This the board did; but later, yielding to the insistent demands of its more extreme members, the board approved another resolution that it had reason to regret.

The disclosure by Mr. Canning that a number of Communists were then employed in the city colleges evoked much comment in which the board of higher education did not escape criticism for its failure to take a more vigorous stand against Communists in the schools. The moderate group on the board was weakened and for the moment silenced, and the advocates of strong measures succeeded on March 17, 1941, in winning unanimous approval of a resolution that provided: "Resolved that it is the purpose of the Board of Higher Education not to retain as members of the collegiate staffs members of any Communist, Fascist or Nazi group or society, or to retain any individuals who, or members of any group which, advocates, advises, teaches or practises subversive doctrines or activities."

The language of the resolution was not such as to lend comfort to defenders of academic freedom. The wording was sufficiently broad and ambiguous to permit the dismissal of any person who dared to speak critically of governmental institutions. Surely this was not what the board had in mind in approving the resolution, but it had permitted itself to be rushed into a decision that would make such extreme action possible. The real believers in academic freedom on the board were soon convinced by the unanimity of the criticism from educational and professional organizations that the language of the resolution was too sweeping, and they sought an opportunity to improve it. The result was a second declaration, which reiterated the policy laid down in the earlier one but added to it the confusing qualification:

and further Resolved, that it is the intention of the Board to adhere to its established policy not to discharge any member of its staffs (1) merely because of membership in a political organization unaccompanied by any of the activities or elements referred to in the resolution above or (2) merely because of any differences of opinion on political, economic or social matters.

The second resolution, adopted April 21, 1941, met a mixed reception. Some of the critics of the earlier resolution expressed satisfaction by declaring that their initial fears had been allayed. Others, however, found little to praise in the new resolution, because, under its terms, the board or its representatives could take any action they pleased and point to some part of the resolution to support their stand. If the purpose of the resolution was to promulgate a sort of political platform plank into which all groups could read anything they pleased, the board had been singularly successful in achieving its objective. But if the board had intended to establish with some precision a general policy which would serve as a guide to action in specific instances, its efforts had been wasted.

During the early stages of the investigation the board had not discharged its responsibilities in a manner calculated to inspire confidence among the teaching staffs or on the part of the general public. Let us turn now to its handling of the individual cases which came before it. The order of procedure for handling the cases varied little. After a person had been named by Canning or another committee witness he would be summoned before the Coudert committee in public hearing and asked under oath if he was a member of the Communist Party. Without exception the answer was negative. Shortly thereafter the board would bring charges against the accused, and he would be suspended from his position. If he did not happen to have tenure he would be dismissed or simply not re-employed since this action took place at the end of an academic year.

For those with tenure, after charges had been made against them and they had received an opportunity to reply, they were called to trial before a committee of the board of higher education, presided over by a board member who was a lawyer. The trials were held publicly and were conducted like a court of law. Accused was permitted counsel who could present his own witnesses and cross-examine those called by the office of corporation counsel of New York City, who represented the board during its trials.

With the exception of the first one, the procedure and the temper of the trials were moderate, fair, and generally above reproach. Counsel for both sides sometimes resorted to tactics more suited to the barroom than to the bar, but these aberrations were comparatively rare. An inspection of the typed transcripts of several of the trials reveals that procedure, testimony, and arguments showed more similarity than difference from one trial to another. Nor can any significant difference be detected in the quality and fairness or the co-operativeness shown by counsel for either side.

One member of the board of higher education who from the beginning had taken the lead in urging the board to adopt severe measures against the accused persons and who was in fact the author of the sweeping resolution already described was at his own request designated as chairman of the first trial committee. One has only to read the transcript of this trial to discover how little like a judicial officer the chairman acted. His repeated tendency to slip into the role of the prosecutor betrayed the fact that despite his obviously sincere desire to be fair he had apparently entered the trial with his mind made up concerning its outcome.

Subsequent trials were conducted in an atmosphere considerably more decorous, chiefly because of the greater restraint of the presiding officers. There was little difference in the results, however, and there is some reason to believe that the conduct and results of the first trial had more than ordinary importance because of the influence they may have exerted upon subsequent trials. Evidence on both sides was chiefly circumstantial and inconclusive. A reading of the transcripts does not establish a clear preponderance of evidence on either side. Final verdict, then, depended to a large extent upon the particular assumptions of the persons reviewing the evidence. When in the first trial, there-fore, a verdict of guilty was rendered on the evidence, it was not unlikely that subsequent trial committees confronted with sub-stantially the same evidence would reach the same verdict.

It is not necessary to allege fraud or bad faith in the conduct of the trials, and certainly no such thing is intended. Each trial was bona fide, and the trial committee made a sincere attempt to judge each individual case on its own merits without regard to what had happened in other cases. But, as the trial transcripts reveal clearly, the cases differed only in minor details and coin-cided so completely in most major points that it was difficult to avoid the tendency to judge by formula. If in one case a particular bit of evidence seemed incriminating, it would probably be sim-ilarly construed where it recurred in subsequent cases.

A verdict of guilty was rendered in every case tried during this period. The single case where the accused was acquitted was one in which the trial was not held until almost two years later. In this instance the lapse of time may have served to loosen some-what the mental set that had existed earlier.

It is unfortunate that a court of law never had an opportunity to review the evidence in any of these cases. In each instance the evidence and verdict of the trial committee was reviewed and affirmed by the entire board before the individual was dismissed, but with a single exception no outside agency ever passed upon the action. In that one case the board was not upheld. Before discussing this episode it seems desirable to comment briefly upon the reasons why the dismissed teachers did not carry their cases to the courts.

Actually a number of court actions were begun, but none ever came to trial. The board of higher education trials occurred dur-ing the period between June, 1941, and the end of the following year. When our entry into the war accelerated the expansion of the armed services, many of the persons under charges found themselves absorbed by problems of a completely new order. With other matters more immediately urgent and with the future uncertain, several of the persons who had already begun action for judicial review of the board's decision did not press their appeals. But perhaps a more important reason was financial. Almost without exception the persons involved were dependent upon their salaries for their livelihood and had no other financial resources to fall back upon. Their salaries had been suspended, and most of them had been without income for a year or more before their cases were finally settled by the board. The upshot was that no case received judicial review.

The single instance already referred to in which the decision of the board of higher education did come before another agency is suggestive. One of the teachers tried and found guilty by the trial committee entered military service before the entire board heard his appeal. His case was not different from any of the others upon which similar judgments had been passed. Upon his return to civilian life four years later his case was presented to the board, and he was found guilty and dismissed. He appealed to the state commissioner of education. The acting commissioner reviewed the evidence, including the trial transcripts, and sustained the appeal with instructions to the board to reinstate the appellant with back pay. The opinion stressed the fact that the record contained insufficient evidence to sustain a finding of guilt. When the board attempted to reopen the case some months later with the hope that the commissioner would reverse the earlier decision of the acting commissioner, the request was denied. This lone case is not conclusive, but it does show that the evidence which to the board left no room for reasonable doubt as to the defendant's guilt seemed less convincing to persons whose emotions were not involved in the whole Communist episode.

Though it is idle and perhaps risky to speculate about motives, some comment upon the situation confronting the board may throw light upon its actions. For some years the menace of communism in the city colleges had been urged upon the board. Much to the displeasure of the complainants the board had repeatedly brushed off demands for a purification of the faculties. Its position at this time is well set forth in a statement handed to the press in August, 1938:

Allegations of Communist activity in our city colleges are not news, nor is the fact of such activity unknown to our board. . . . Indeed, differences of opinion and attitude among faculty members are a wholesome sign of vitality, and as this is reflected in the teaching, it supplies students with a useful cross-section of the divergence of views in the community at large.

The board as a whole continued to take a more or less aloof attitude toward the alleged threat of subversives even after the Rapp-Coudert committee began its investigative work. In fact, so detached did the board seem to Senator Coudert and his associates that the senator felt obliged to appeal for more active support. He concluded with a thinly veiled threat that unless the board changed its attitude of halfhearted co-operation, the committee would ask the legislature to step in.

During the fall and early winter of 1940 the board did move slowly from a wholly passive attitude to one slightly more active. It was not until March, 1941, however, after some members of the City College staff had actually been named as Communists, that a marked change occurred. The sensational disclosures of Mr. Canning suddenly shifted the spotlight of unfavorable publicity to the city colleges, and the board of higher education found itself on the defensive.

Many members of the board who did not share the views of the most extreme group were now persuaded to go along because they felt that they had no alternative. They yielded to the argument that the public wanted a house cleaning and was beginning to lose confidence in the board for its failure to act. Another factor that may have influenced them was the fear that the legislature —then in session—might take matters into its own hands.

In the end the board came to view the whole Communist episode as a nasty mess that was embarrassing its work by undermining its prestige. The only sensible solution under these circumstances was to clean up the mess as quickly as possible. This was what the board did, and in doing so it may have become more concerned with getting the problem of communism eliminated than with the dilemma faced by innocent persons who might have become entangled. It would probably not have employed the same procedures in handling other personnel problems, but the excitement over communism destroyed its confidence and demoralized its judgment. Individual welfare was subordinated in eliminating a troublesome issue.

Undoubtedly the most sensational episode in the Rapp-Coudert investigation and the one from which newspaper readers probably formed their opinion of the entire investigation was the Schappes case. It is unfortunate that this should be so because Schappes's experience was in no way typical. In fact, this whole bizarre chapter was little more than a caricature of the larger situation.

Morris U. Schappes, a tutor in English in City College since 1931, had first attracted attention in 1936 when he was not reappointed. He declared that the president had struck at him because of his radical activities. After student and faculty protests the board of higher education intervened in his behalf, and he received reappointment. On March, 1941, when the word got out that the committee witness, Canning, was going to make public the names of Communist party members then on the municipal college staffs, Schappes decided to seize the initiative. He hastily called a press conference in a downtown hotel and made a statement that was most extraordinary. He declared that he had been an active party member from 1934 until 1939, when he withdrew to devote his time to scholarly writing. Schappes's strategy was obviously an attempt to divert attention from others suspected of belonging to the party and at the same time to disavow any information about its current activities. He sought to achieve the first objective by insisting that he had been the only party member on the college staff. By claiming that he had left the party some time ago he hoped to avoid further disclosure.

Whether Mr. Schappes decided of his own volition upon this remarkable tactical move is not clear. At least two persons who were associated with the union but who have never been suspected of being party members themselves have asserted that Schappes was acting on their advice in calling the press conference. Whoever the instigator was, either the scheme was ill-conceived, or Mr. Schappes bungled in carrying it out. His story was so patently phony that instead of eliminating others it inevitably involved accomplices, because it would have been humanly impossible for a single person to have carried on the numerous activities for which Schappes claimed exclusive credit. The list is too extensive to repeat, but, as one example, Mr. Schappes asserted that he alone edited, published, and circulated the *Teacher Worker,* a

monthly newspaper produced by the Communist unit on the City
College campus.

The paper, a four- to six-page publication distributed to all
members of the instructional and administrative staffs of City
College, was obviously not the work of a single person; yet Mr.
Schappes blandly declared that he alone was responsible. When
later he repeated his fantastic testimony under oath to the Coudert
committee, he was quickly indicted for perjury. Almost simultaneously he was suspended upon charges brought against him by
the board of higher education.

Schappes succeeded in forcing the board to postpone his trial
until the perjury issue was settled in the courts. After some delay
he was tried and found guilty. Two appeals to higher courts resulted in affirmation of the trial court decision, and he was obliged
to serve a prison sentence. He was, of course, dismissed from his
post.

The Schappes case represented the extreme fringe of so-called
subversive activity in the college. Yet he was convicted for lying
rather than for some more dangerously destructive action. There
is no intention to deny the seriousness of giving false testimony,
but the point should not be lost sight of that this was the only
charge proved against him that was serious enough to sustain
legal action. Since Schappes was the only person prosecuted for
perjury, one must assume that evidence of similar conduct on the
part of all others was significantly less clear-cut or conclusive. If
this assumption is correct, it would not be wise to judge the entire
case upon the Schappes evidence. To a considerable extent, however, that is what occurred. Thus a whole situation came to be
appraised on the basis of the most extreme sample. Such was the
atmosphere in which the board of higher education trials were
launched. It was more than coincidental that the sweeping resolution of March 17 came shortly after Schappes had attempted his
coup.

THE FEINBERG LAW

The latest chapter in the history of New York State legislative
actions in pursuit of subversive activities is represented by the

Feinberg Law of 1949. New York has always been a fairly accurate barometer of prevailing political pressures in the country. It would, therefore, have been surprising had the legislature failed to act, since the fear of Communist infiltration was very much in the air at this time. The federal loyalty program, at least partly a reflex of the resurgence of the House Un-American Activities Committee, had been instituted in 1947. Several other state legislatures had initiated investigations of alleged Communist activities in the schools.

But the New York legislature had other reasons for reviving a subject which had never sunk far below the surface of legislative consciousness. As was remarked earlier, the Rapp-Coudert committee had severely criticized the board of higher education for its seeming reluctance to accept responsibility for purging all Communists from the schools. The committee concluded its rebuke with the demand that periodic reports should be made to the legislature on the progress of the board's renovative activity and inserted a warning that if necessary the legislature would reassume an active role.

The Feinberg Law of 1949 represented a conviction on the part of a considerable number of lawmakers that the school authorities had failed to carry out with sufficient vigor the mandate placed upon them. With minor exceptions the removals of 1941–1942 had terminated the active purge campaign. The Devany Law had never been systematically enforced. Furthermore, under the decision in the Thompson case, in which the commissioner of education had overruled the board of higher education, it appeared that the Devany Law by itself did not provide a satisfactory basis for easy and expeditious action against Communist employees. This is the background for the introduction and approval of the Feinberg Law.

A number of anti-Communist bills reached varying stages of progress during the 1949 session. One of the most favorably regarded provided for an additional loyalty oath to supplement that already required by the Ives Law. Instead of enacting the new loyalty oath bill, the legislature shifted its attention to the Feinberg bill introduced by the senate majority leader on March 11, 1949. Section 3021 of Article 61 of the New York education law provides: "A person employed as Superintendent of Schools, teacher or employee in the public schools of the State shall be removed for the utterance of any treasonable or seditious word or words or the doing of any treasonable or seditious act or acts while holding such position."

This provision of the state education law must be considered in conjunction with Section 12a of the state civil service law (the Devany Law), which provides:

No person shall be employed in the service of the state nor as a superintendent, principal or teacher in a public school or state normal school, or college or any other state educational institution who a) By word of mouth or writing wilfully and deliberately advocates, advises or teaches the doctrine that the government of the United States or any state or of any political subdivision thereof should be overthrown or overturned by force, violence or any unlawful means.

The Feinberg bill proposed to add a new section, 3022, to "eliminate subversive persons from the public school system." The new section in effect shifts legislative emphasis from substantive to procedural aspects of the loyalty program. It imposes upon the state educational authorities—the board of regents— the duty to enforce the law already on the books and stipulates in some detail the administrative procedures to be employed. Furthermore, by incorporating a requirement of annual detailed reports, the legislature virtually serves notice on the board that failure to produce tangible evidence of vigorous enforcement will invite trouble.

The second paragraph of the new section contains the procedural requirements:

The board of regents shall, after inquiry and after such notice and hearing as may be appropriate, make a listing of organizations which it finds to be subversive in that they advocate, advise, teach or embrace the doctrine that the government of the United States or of any state or of any political subdivision thereof shall be overthrown or overturned by force, violence or any unlawful means, or that they advocate, advise, teach or embrace the duty, necessity or propriety of adopting any such doctrine as set forth in Section 12a of the civil service law. Such listings may be amended and revised from time to time. The board, in making such inquiry, may utilize any similar listings or designations promulgated by any federal agency or authority authorized by federal law, regulation or executive order, and for the purposes of such inquiry, the board may request and receive from federal agencies or authorities any supporting material or evidence that may be made available to it. The board of regents shall provide in the rules and regulations required by subdivision one hereof that membership in any such organization included in such listing made by it shall constitute prima facie evidence of disqualification for appointment to or retention in any office or position in the public schools of the state.

Two features of the new proposal are worthy of particular notice. By indicating that the board of regents might make use of existing lists promulgated by federal agencies, the legislature in effect encouraged the board to adopt the attorney general's list of subversive organizations. There is nothing to prevent the board from adding to the listings employed by the attorney general.

Once the list of proscribed organizations has been agreed upon, membership in any of these organizations shall be prima facie evidence of disqualification. In other words, even though an organization may be erroneously tabbed as subversive, once it is so designated its members are automatically stamped as subversive unless they can prove the contrary. Section 12d of the New York civil service law provides that in removal cases "the burden of sustaining the validity of the order of dismissal or ineligibility by a fair preponderance of the credible evidence shall be upon the person making such dismissal or order of ineligibility." Where alleged membership in subversive organizations is involved, however, the general rule of the civil service law is reversed. In a case involving that sort of allegation, the legislature apparently intends that the burden of proof shall not rest upon the person who ordered the removal.

Senator Feinberg's proposal elicited an immediate response. Both the *New York Times* and the *Herald Tribune* took strong stands against the bill, and numerous public figures called upon the legislature to reject such dangerous legislation. Among the groups who actively opposed the measure were the American Civil Liberties Union, the American Labor Party, the Citizens Union, the New York Chapter of the National Lawyers Guild, the New York State Council of the Arts, Sciences and Professions, the New York State C.I.O., and the United Parents Association. The answer was unequivocal. By votes of 41 to 14 in the senate and 122 to 25 in the assembly, the legislature approved the bill.

The period since the enactment of the Feinberg Law has witnessed many interesting developments. On April 22, the board of regents established a committee to devise means to administer the law and to report its recommendations at the May meeting. The committee encountered unforeseen obstacles, however, and was unable to report a plan to the board in May so the matter was postponed until the June meeting. With the law scheduled to go into effect July 1, 1949, internal differences within the committee continued to thwart agreement. Two different sets of problems divided board members. The first stumbling block centered upon the nature of the lists of subversive organizations to be promulgated. The second issue dividing the committee involved the procedure for implementing the law itself. The chief points of difference centered on the desirability of a new loyalty oath and a questionnaire to elicit from teachers information on the organizations to which they belonged. Also in dispute was the machinery for trying teachers who were charged with membership in the outlawed organizations.

Finally, after an additional month's delay, the long-awaited rules were issued. The chief points are summarized as follows:

1. The school authorities of each school district shall require one or more officials to report to them on each teacher each year, stating that there is or is not evidence that he has violated the statutory provisions referred to.

2. The school authorities shall dismiss charges or prefer formal charges within ninety days of receiving an adverse report.

3. If charges are preferred, the dismissal procedures shall be those ordinarily employed.

4. The board of regents shall promulgate a list of subversive organizations.

5. Evidence of membership in any organization on the list ten days after its promulgation shall constitute prima facie evidence of disqualification.

6. Evidence of membership in an organization before it is listed shall be presumptive evidence that membership continues, in the absence of a showing that membership has been terminated "in good faith."

7. School authorities shall make annual reports to the commissioner of education; any person found disqualified shall be reported immediately.

The rules were promulgated July 15, 1949, but the oft-mentioned list of subversive organizations, the nucleus of the whole loyalty procedure, once more failed to materialize. The board announced that the list would appear on September 16, 1949. As of January 1, 1951, the list had not yet been issued.

The board of regents has been subjected to widespread criticism from every side. Opponents of the Feinberg Law have attacked the board, first, for not providing open hearings on the merits of the law and, second, for attempting to put the law into operation. On the other side, those supporting the law have criticized the board for its failure to act more positively and expeditiously.

The truth of the matter is that the board has been the victim of circumstances over which it had no control. To enforce the Feinberg Law so as to carry out the intent of the legislature and at the same time to discharge its obligations as the top policy-making body of the state educational system was difficult if not impossible. By the law the board was compelled to take substantive actions and to establish procedures which in the opinion of some members placed in jeopardy the traditional guarantees of academic freedom. Honest differences of opinion within the board concerning the permissible limits of restrictive action complicated the matter.

Following publication of the rules already mentioned, the late Francis T. Spaulding, who was then state commissioner of education, issued a memorandum implementing the regents' rules. This memorandum, which was distributed to all school officials in the state, included the following instructions:

The officials will face a twofold duty. It will be their responsibility to help the school authorities rid the school system of persons who "use their office or position to advocate and teach subversive doctrines." On the other hand, it will be their responsibility so to conduct themselves and their inquiries as to protect and reassure teachers who are not subversive.

The officials should bear in mind the fact that while statements made in connection with an official charge of disloyalty are legally privileged, no privilege attaches to gossip and the circulation of rumor.

The writing of articles, the distribution of pamphlets, the endorsement of speeches made or articles written or acts performed by others, all may constitute subversive activity.

Nor need such activity be confined to the classroom. Treasonable or subversive acts or statements outside the school are as much a basis for dismissal as are similar activities in school or in the presence of school children.

It must be borne in mind that teachers who are honestly concerned to help their pupils to become constructive citizens are likely to raise many questions and make many suggestions about possible improvements in the American form of government and American institutions, which cannot in any just sense be construed as subversive.

Moreover, teachers who take full advantage of their own privileges as citizens may raise questions and make suggestions outside their classrooms about improvements in our form of government. In addition, they may quite legitimately inform themselves fully, and enter into discussions with other people, about forms of government different from our own.

School authorities should reject hearsay statements, or irresponsible and uncorroborated statements, about what a teacher has said or done, either in school or outside. They should examine an accused teacher's statements, writing or action in their context, and not in isolated fragments. They must insist on evidence, and not mere opinion, as a basis for any action which they may take.

The commissioner points out that under the law a teacher may be guilty of subversive activity if he writes articles or distributes pamphlets. He may also be engaged in subversive activity if he endorses speeches made, articles written, or acts performed by someone else. These actions need not occur in the classroom in order to render the teacher liable. But while the memorandum is explicit in stating the several kinds of actions which may be subversive, no guidance is given concerning the nature of articles, speeches, or acts that would be regarded as objectionable. The concluding sections of the memorandum introduce a note of caution by declaring that discussions of the American form of government and suggestions for its improvement may not be subversive, and officials are warned to reject hearsay or irresponsible, uncorroborated statements.

School officials charged with responsibility for administering the law as amplified by these instructions will hardly find here a sure guide for temperate enforcement. One can only suspect that the first part of the directive will receive greater emphasis than the latter. The record of the state commissioner of education showed him to be a person of judgment and tolerance. His attempt to implement a law that places such heavy premium upon conformity and yet to preserve an atmosphere favorable to academic freedom is probably the best that could be achieved even though it is not wholly reassuring.

The latest chapter in the yet unresolved controversy can be sketched briefly. On September 12, 1949, preparatory to the law's going into effect on September 15, Superintendent of New York City Schools William Jansen issued instructions for administering the Feinberg Law and the board of regents' rules. The following day the Communist Party obtained a ten-day Supreme Court order restraining the board of regents from promulgating its list of subversive organizations. Within the next few days similar actions were taken by the Teachers Union and various citizen groups. The initial restraining order was subsequently extended.

In two separate actions in the New York Supreme Court (a court of original jurisdiction), the Feinberg Law was declared unconstitutional. Both of these decisions were reversed in the appellate court of first instance. Twenty-one months after its enactment the Feinberg Law was upheld by the New York State Court of Appeals. On November 30, 1950, Associate Judge Edmund H. Lewis, speaking for a unanimous court, declared that

278

"when in its judgment and discretion the Legislature finds acts by public employees which threaten the integrity and competency of a governmental service, such as the public school system, legislation adequate to maintain the usefulness of the service affected is necessary to forestall such danger."

Judge Lewis considered separately each of the constitutional grounds upon which the law had been attacked—freedom of speech and assembly, due process of law, and bill of attainder—and in each instance sustained the validity of the pertinent provisions.

The board of regents prepared to go ahead with plans for putting the law into effect. The long-delayed and often-postponed list of subversive organizations would now presumably be issued and steps taken to act against school employees discovered to be members of these organizations. Meantime representatives of teachers' organizations and officials of the Communist Party had given notice that they intended to carry the case to the United States Supreme Court.

CONCLUSION

Experience in New York indicates that legislative efforts to guarantee security by weeding out disloyal teachers have not been notably successful. Neither investigations nor laws have produced satisfactory results, judged either from the point of view of those who supported such measures or from that of those who opposed them. Indeed, the failure of the exponents of repressive action to achieve security through such action is one of the most significant facts to emerge from this survey. Once the legislature accepts the idea that free institutions can survive only by ferreting out and exterminating all who are suspected of being "subversive" there is no foreseeable end to its actions. Each successive step must be more severe than the last, because the preceding step failed to allay the fears which dictated its adoption. Definitions of subversive activity must be constantly broadened, because earlier ones permitted suspected individuals to escape. A comparison of the substantive and procedural provisions of the Ives Law, the Devany Law, and the Feinberg Law reveals a steady progression toward ultimate extinction of our traditional concept of due process. The once unchallenged presumption that a person is innocent until proved guilty has been repudiated in the Feinberg Law.

The record of the investigators does not arouse greater enthusiasm than that of the laws. Investigations have varied markedly in quality. Judged from any point of view the Rapp-Coudert investigation was superior to either the Lusk or the McNaboe investigations. Yet the Rapp-Coudert investigation falls well short of winning endorsement. Despite the honesty and intelligence of its leadership the committee probably retarded the cause of freedom rather than advanced it. From the outset the committee, through its chairman and staff, made policy decisions and procedural judgments that were open to challenge by sincere non-Communist defenders of academic freedom and civil liberties. Because of its self-righteous consciousness of its own patriotism the committee did not concede to its adversaries or critics the same standard of probity that it attributed to itself. As a consequence, even the most well-conducted investigation on record failed to protect the very values that it was created to preserve.

In sharp contrast to its predecessors the Coudert committee rejected the tactics of the honky-tonk barker. Similarly the hypocrisy of the two earlier investigations was scrupulously avoided. Nevertheless, a number of serious indictments must be lodged against Senator Coudert and his associates. They failed to distinguish between Communists and members of the Teachers Union who were not Communists; they operated upon challengeable premises by singling out the Teachers Union; they concentrated upon identifying individual Communists when they should have investigated underlying causes of discontent among teachers; they jumped to conclusions without sufficient corroborative evidence; they employed procedures that were not necessary or justified under the conditions.

The preceding enumeration emphasizes points at which the committee's action was faulty. It seems quite possible, however, that the committee's most significant mistake lay in its failure to capitalize upon the fine opportunity open to it. Occurrences in the New York City school system during the preceding decade had served amply to warn the legislature that conditions were not entirely healthy. Circumstances were ideal for a deeply probing inquiry that could sort out the entangled allegations, rumors, and facts and thus take the first constructive step toward the re-establishment of a sound morale in the school system. Instead, the committee contented itself with attempting to remove symptoms by purging those who had organized to improve their status.

What conclusions may be drawn from this survey? The temptation is strong to accept the view that legislative action in this field cannot be constructive. Indeed, some thoughtful persons have expressed this opinion. Such persons reason that academic freedom and civil liberties cannot be acted upon by governmental bodies without imposing restraints that did not exist previously. They press their argument by pointing out that there is no such thing as a *good* or *beneficial* investigation in this field—that even the least objectionable investigation hamstrings rather than liberates free people. They conclude: what the legislature cannot improve it should leave alone.

There is no basis, however, for believing that legislatures will refrain from intervening in this area. The record of previous legislative action suggests that subversive activity will continue to be a fertile field. Only self-restraint can limit new investigations or laws, and legislative self-restraint has not been conspicuous in matters of this kind. The practical problem then becomes one of slowly attempting to develop standards and procedures whereby the maximum good can be obtained with the minimum damage. To state the problem is easy but to solve it is another matter. Whether our leaders have the wit and patience to do so will determine in large part the continued viability of our form of democracy.

VI. WASHINGTON

The Canwell Committee

By VERN COUNTRYMAN   *July, 1951*

IN 1947 the legislature of the State of Washington created a committee to investigate "un-American activities" in the state. This action and the subsequent work of the committee reflected a concern over communism in the State of Washington which can be traced back to the depression years of the early thirties, when Seattle Mayor John F. Dore began providing headlines for Hearst's *Seattle Post-Intelligencer,* the conservative, locally owned *Seattle Times,* and the now-defunct *Seattle Star* by sounding alarums about the "Communist menace" in Seattle.[1]

After 1935, those who shared Dore's fear of the "Communist menace" frequently identified it with the Washington Commonwealth Federation, an organization that was formed in that year as a "triple alliance of Liberals, Labor and Farm" and that functioned for nine years chiefly by endorsing Democratic candidates in state primaries and general elections and supporting individual candidates in Seattle's nonpartisan municipal elections. In 1937 Hugh DeLacy, a young English instructor at the University of Washington, was elected to the Seattle city council as a W.C.F. candidate. Although DeLacy was dismissed by the university

[Mr. Countryman is Associate Professor of Law in Yale University.]

[1] This chapter is essentially a condensation of a more comprehensive and fully documented report, published separately under the title *Un-American Activities in the State of Washington: The Work of the Canwell Committee* (Ithaca, N.Y.: Cornell University Press, 1951).

when he announced his candidacy, his appearance under W.C.F. auspices was corroborative evidence for those whose growing concern about communism was based in part on the notion that the university in Seattle harbored a number of Communists on its faculty.

New alarums were sounded at this time by Dave Beck, an international organizer for the A.F.L. Teamsters' Union, whose successful policy of "stabilizing industry" under his "voluntary N.R.A." had won him many friends among businessmen and who was well on the way to becoming the most powerful labor leader on the Pacific Coast. The water-front strike of 1934 had, however, established Harry Bridges as a challenger to Beck's dominant position, and Beck gave impetus to the rising fear of Communist action by labeling "Red Harry" Bridges an instrument of the Communists.

In 1937 State Senator James T. Sullivan, under Washington Commonwealth Federation auspices, had formed the Washington Pension Union to campaign for increased old age pensions in the state. By resorting to popular initiative in 1940 the Pension Union secured an increase in the monthly grant from $30 to $40. But, shortly before the adoption of this measure, Sullivan resigned as president of the Pension Union, charging that it was "dominated by Communists."

From 1932 to 1940 the Democratic Party had controlled both the governor's office and the state legislature. By 1940, however, the charges of communism were causing fissures in the dominant political group, and in that year Republican candidate Arthur C. Langlie was elected governor.

The Democratic Party then undertook to unify its forces. United States Senator Mon C. Wallgren was selected as its candidate for governor in 1944, and he was endorsed by Dave Beck. The W.C.F.'s Hugh DeLacy became a Democratic nominee for Congress, and the W.C.F. was dissolved. Wallgren and DeLacy were both elected, as were nearly all other Democratic candidates, in the general election in November, 1944. In the legislative session of 1945 a statute increasing old age pensions to $50 a month was enacted without a dissenting vote in either house of the legislature.

283

But the Democratic victory was short-lived. The 1946 elections were bitterly fought. The chief stakes were the seats in the lower house of the state legislature, half of the state senate, six seats in the United States House of Representatives, and the senatorial office that Wallgren had vacated. Harry Cain, mayor of Tacoma, campaigned as the Republican candidate for United States senator on his military record and on charges of Communist influence in the Democratic Party. Homer Jones, former state commander of the American Legion and Republican candidate for the Congressional office held by DeLacy, adopted a similar strategy. Other Republican candidates joined in the Communist charges, which were widely aired in the newspapers. Howard Costigan, former executive secretary of the W.C.F., also joined in the charges in his unsuccessful attempt to take from DeLacy the Democratic nomination for Congressman.

The election gave the Republicans a nearly complete victory. Cain was elected; Jones defeated DeLacy and was joined by four other Republican Congressmen; and the Republicans won a two-thirds majority in the lower house of the state legislature. The state senate was evenly divided between Republicans and Democrats, but the Republicans perfected a working coalition with eight Democratic senators which gave them complete control of the state legislature for the first time in fourteen years.

Shortly after the election, state Attorney General Smith Troy and other leaders in the Democratic Party began to urge the party to eliminate its "Communistic inclined elements." Dave Beck joined in the cry for a house cleaning, and the *Seattle Post-Intelligencer* advised the party editorially that its only salvation was to be found in ridding itself of "admirers of the Russian dictatorship."

It was against this background of local political developments that the newly chosen legislators prepared to convene. News of a possible legislative investigation of "Communists and subversive activities" first broke in the *Post-Intelligencer* before the 1947 legislative session had actually begun. On December 13, 1946, a front-page story by Fred Niendorff, *Post-Intelligencer* reporter assigned to cover the legislative session, announced that the Republicans and the coalition Democrats in the state senate had held a caucus and that one of the principal items on their agenda was such an investigation. The story quoted a caucus report on the need for the inquiry into Communist infiltration of the University of Washington, labor unions, and the Democratic Party.

THE CREATION AND COMPOSITION
OF THE COMMITTEE

When the legislature convened, a measure to authorize the investigation was introduced in the lower house by two freshman legislators, Albert F. Canwell and Sydney A. Stevens. Copied largely from a California resolution of 1945, the measure authorized a "Joint Legislative Fact-Finding Committee on Un-American Activities" to investigate activities which "indicate a purpose to . . . undermine the stability of our American institutions," including "the activities of groups and organizations whose membership includes persons who are Communists, or any other organization known or suspected to be dominated or controlled by a foreign power, which activities affect the conduct of the state, the functioning of any state agency, unemployment relief and other forms of public assistance, educational institutions of the state . . . or any political program." The committee was empowered to function after adjournment of the 1947 legislature and was directed to report to the 1949 legislature. Any possibility of a veto of the measure by Governor Wallgren was avoided by casting it in the form of a concurrent resolution, to become effective upon adoption by both houses of the legislature.

The Canwell-Stevens resolution promptly passed the house, but before it was considered by the senate that body's attention had been called to the threat of communism in another connection. Governor Wallgren had filled vacancies in the University of Washington board of regents by nominating Dave Beck, now executive vice-president of the Teamsters' Union, John King, educational director for the Washington State Grange, and John Fox, maritime union official, and the appointments were before the senate for confirmation. The appointments of King and Fox were opposed by Senator Thomas Bienz, one of the eight coalition Democrats in the senate, because, when the nominees appeared before

285

the Senate Committee on Higher Education, they both stated that they had never heard of "subversive activity" being taught on the University of Washington campus. Senator Bienz was outraged: "For years and years we members of the Senate have heard it. . . . If Mr. Fox and Mr. King haven't heard about these things, I don't think they should stay on the board of regents another two days."

The senate confirmed the appointments of Beck and King and rejected the appointment of Fox. Bienz's charges were immediately and emphatically denied by Lee Paul Sieg, who had retired as president of the university in September, 1946, and by Raymond B. Allen, former dean of the College of Medicine at the University of Illinois, who had succeeded Sieg as president of the university. A few days later a senate committee headed by Senator Bienz reported out the Canwell-Stevens resolution with a recommendation that it pass, and the senate followed the committee's recommendation.

On the last day of the legislative session the following legislators were appointed to the committee on un-American activities pursuant to the Canwell-Stevens resolution:

Representative Albert F. Canwell, Republican, to be chairman of the committee. Canwell traces his concern about Communist activity to the water-front strike of 1934, which he covered as a reporter for a small weekly newspaper in Yakima, Washington. After five years with the Yakima paper and four years as a commercial photographer, Canwell became a deputy sheriff in Spokane County and was put in charge of the county Identification Bureau, a position which he held until elected to the legislature in 1946. He attributes his conviction that a state investigation should be made, and his knowledge of investigating techniques, to his experience in the sheiff's office and to contacts which he had there with federal investigating agents.

Representative Sydney A. Stevens, Republican. Stevens, now deceased, was the proprietor of a small mattress factory in Seattle. He had no prior experience in public office. When he found himself elected, however, he "went to the legislature with the intention of doing something about Communism." He traced his interest in the subject to his work on Americanism committees of the

American Legion and to his concern about the tendency of modern youth to reject parental authority—a tendency which he attributed to Communist influences in the schools.

Representative Grant Sisson, Republican. Sisson, a farmer from Mt. Vernon, Washington, and an experienced legislator, favored an investigation of communism but neither has nor claims any special knowledge on the subject.

Representative George F. Yantis, Democrat. Yantis, a veteran legislator, was the only lawyer on the committee. He was ill at the time of his appointment and died in December, 1947, one month before the committee's first public hearing.

Senator Thomas H. Bienz, Democrat. Bienz, a retired druggist from Spokane and a member of the legislature since 1939, was one of the most enthusiastic advocates of the investigation. He traces his concern about communism to what he learned of the movement in Europe in 1937 when he was a delegate to an American Legion convention in Paris. Since that time he has read all available literature on the subject and has become more and more alarmed about it.

Senator R. L. Rutter, Republican. Rutter is a rancher from Ellensburg, Washington, who, like Canwell and Stevens, was serving his first term in the legislature. He favored the investigation but makes no claims to special knowledge of communism or special competence for investigatory work.

Senator Harold G. Kimball, Republican. Kimball is the editor and publisher of a small neighborhood weekly in Seattle. He was also serving his first term in the legislature but had taken some part in political activities in the state during the depression years. He was commander of the Seattle assembly of the National Veterans' Association, which sent a delegation to the Bonus March on Washington, D.C., in 1932. He helped form an organization called Commonwealth Builders, which later merged with the Washington Commonwealth Federation, but he refused to participate in the W.C.F. because he suspected that it was subject to Communist influence. He has attempted to keep himself informed on Communist activity in the state and believes that he was the only member of the committee who had any firsthand knowledge of the subject, although he considers Canwell a qualified investigator.

287

At the outset the committee decided that the investigating part of its job should be turned over to Canwell and a hired staff. So, while the other members of the committee returned to their homes, Canwell made a trip to Washington, D.C., to confer with the House Un-American Activities Committee, returned with the report that he had been "received with open arms and given the utmost cooperation," and opened offices in the state Armory in Seattle in April, 1947. He hired a staff of seven investigators headed by Chief Investigator William J. Houston, who left his job as chief investigator for the northwest regional office of the Civil Service Commission to take the position, and Assistant Chief Investigator John W. Whipple, who had worked with Houston in the Civil Service. Investigators Aaron R. Coleman, Ernest P. Stith, and Earl J. Tibbetts also had had civil service experience. Investigator Dana T. Robinson came from the staff of the Bureau of Internal Revenue, and Investigator Evert Pomeroy was formerly a colonel in Army Intelligence. Houston and Whipple were lawyers.

THE OPENING HEARING IN 1948

Early in January, 1948, Canwell announced that the committee would hold a public hearing on the Washington Pension Union in the Seattle Armory on January 27. The committee's investigation had disclosed "without the slightest room for doubt," Canwell said, "that a clique within the state organization of the Washington Pension Union has consistently and invariably followed every twist and turn of the Communist Party line as laid down in Soviet Russia."

The Washington Pension Union had from the first identified itself as an opponent of the Canwell committee. Shortly after the 1947 legislature adjourned, the W.P.U. had attempted to resort to popular referendum to nullify the resolution creating the un-American activities committee. Its efforts failed when the state Supreme Court held that a concurrent resolution was not subject to referendum. When the committee announced its intended investigation, the president of the Pension Union promptly ascribed the committee's "unwarranted attack" to the fact that the W.P.U.

was sponsoring an initiative to repeal a 1947 statute which had eliminated the $50 minimum for old age pensions.

There were some legal difficulties connected with the opening of the committee's hearing. The Pension Union had brought an action to enjoin the hearing and had gotten a show cause order served on committee members Stevens and Kimball. On the morning of January 27 the court granted an order temporarily restraining Stevens and Kimball from sitting "as a state committee," but Canwell opened the hearing anyway with the observation that "if there should be any doubt as to whether this committee may legally speak for the State of Washington, any statements which we may make in the course of the proceedings should be considered as the statements of us as individual members of the Legislature, rather than as official statements made on behalf of the State of Washington." Four days later the court concluded, as a matter of state constitutional law, that the legislature could not by concurrent resolution create a committee to function after legislative adjournment; but it also concluded that the Pension Union, none of whose officers had been subpoenaed to appear before the committee, was not entitled to an injunction, and the restraining order was dissolved.

Meanwhile, the committee had proceeded with its hearing. Testimony on the nature and objectives of the Communist Party of the United States came from three imported witnesses. Louis Budenz, a member of the party from 1935 to 1945, a member of the party's national committee for nine years, managing editor of the *Daily Worker* for five years, and now a professor of economics at Fordham University, testified that the party is controlled from Moscow, that it is dedicated to forcible overthrow of the government of the United States, and that it denies the existence of God. Manning Johnson of New York City testified that he was a member of the party from 1930 to 1940 and a member of its national committee from 1936 to 1939. He agreed with Budenz that the party took orders from Moscow. Joseph Kornfeder of Detroit, Michigan, a member of the party from 1919 to 1932, a member of its secret central committee from 1920 to 1923, and a member of its national committee from 1923 to 1927 and again

289

for some time after 1930, agreed with Budenz and Johnson that the party was controlled from Russia.

Budenz and Johnson also gave some testimony on the Washington Pension Union. Budenz recalled that in 1938 Morris Rappaport, then northwest district organizer for the Communist Party, reported to the national committee of the party that Communists were beginning to enter the W.P.U. and that in 1940 Rappaport or his successor reported that the Communists had "succeeded in infiltrating and dominating the Old Age Pension Union." Budenz also testified that W.P.U. President William Pennock and W.P.U. Vice-President Thomas Rabbitt were members of the Communist Party, though he added that this testimony was not based upon his personal knowledge, but upon "official knowledge" —by which he apparently meant that he was repeating what had been said to him by some other party functionary. Johnson recalled that at a meeting of the national committee in 1937 there was a decision "to infiltrate" the Washington Pension Union, and that at another meeting of the committee in 1938 "the comrades from Washington reported that they had succeeded in entrenching themselves in the organization and were playing a decisive role in the conduct of its affairs."

Budenz also examined a list of organizations issued by the attorney general of the United States in December, 1947, for use in the federal employee loyalty program, and corroborated the attorney general's judgment on a number of the listed organizations, including the Seattle Labor School. Budenz testified that he was "not very familiar with" the Seattle Labor School, but when Investigator Houston asked, "You have in your official capacity heard it referred to as a Party organization and a Party school?" Budenz replied, "That's right."

All further testimony about the Pension Union came from local people, beginning with James T. Sullivan, former state senator, founder and first president of the Pension Union. Sullivan gave this account of Communist infiltration into that organization: The Communists had nothing to do with the formation of the union in 1937. But cessation of public works projects in 1938 and 1939 caused the dissolution of the Workers' Alliance, which had been formed to represent employees on those projects. "That released a lot of the boys for duty elsewhere," and the W.P.U., with its 30,000 members, "became a very attractive bait." The 1939 convention of the W.P.U. removed Homer Huson as executive secretary of the organization and replaced him with William Pennock. Sullivan "found later" that this was accomplished "through the pressure of the Communist Party." In 1940 Sullivan withdrew from the union. N. P. Atkinson, who succeeded him as president of the union (and who was, in turn, succeeded by William Pennock in 1942), had solicited Sullivan's membership in the Communist Party on one occasion in 1939.

When Investigator Whipple asked Sullivan if he knew of his "own knowledge of the activity of . . . William Pennock, his solicitation of young people into the Communist Party?" Sullivan replied, "It was common knowledge among those of us who built the Pension Union . . . that that was the part that Pennock played amongst the young—especially when he was going to the University of Washington."

Sullivan also testified that the Pension Union donated money to the Anti-Fascist Refugee Committee, the League Against War and Fascism, the Abraham Lincoln Brigade, and the Ramsey-King-O'Connor Defense Committee, which Sullivan identified as "a committee of the Communist Party." In 1940, Sullivan added, the Pension Union convention voted to send delegates to the American Peace Mobilization. When Investigator Whipple asked, "Do you know who railroaded that through the convention?" Sullivan replied, "Well, from the looks of the audience that day, it was easy. . . . The number of old folks you could almost put inside of this small area there. There were people there that wouldn't have been drawing old age pensions for thirty years, and some of them I don't think had attended a Pension Union convention. In other words, it was just a packed meeting of Communists."

Homer Huson told the committee that although he had never been a member of the Communist Party, "a member of the Communist Party came to me [in 1937], stating that my dues were paid" and thereafter he "had the privilege to sit in their fraction meetings." In 1938, Huson said, he and Pennock were called to the office of Lou Sass, then northwest secretary of the Communist

Party, and Sass told Huson that he was to be replaced by Pennock as executive secretary of the W.P.U. because "it would give [Pennock] more prestige as running for office—some political office." Huson also recalled that he had attended W.P.U. "fraction meetings" [defined as meetings of the Communist Party members in the Pension Union] with Pennock and N. P. Atkinson in 1938 and 1939, and that by donation of funds or dissemination of literature the W.P.U. assisted the League Against War and Fascism, the Ramsey-King-O'Connor Defense Committee, the Defense Committee for Harry Bridges, and "numerous . . . other ones of the same brand."

Howard Costigan, former executive secretary of the Washington Commonwealth Federation, testified that he joined the Communist Party in 1937 and that from that time until the signing of the Nazi-Soviet nonaggression pact on August 23, 1939, the Communists were "the most ardent and perhaps the most conservative supporters of Roosevelt," so that Costigan "was at no time put in the position of taking Party discipline during that period." But when the party line switched after the Nazi-Soviet pact, Costigan "then began to recognize for the first time that the Communist Party membership were primarily interested in the Soviet's foreign policy." He tried to get the W.C.F. leaders to continue to support Roosevelt, "but I found that it was impossible, and the executive board by that time had been so thoroughly penetrated by the Communist Party, that it was necessary for me to leave the Commonwealth Federation, and I organized the Norris–La Guardia Committee for Roosevelt in 1940 in the Pacific Northwest, and campaigned against the line that DeLacy and the rest of the Executive Committee of the Communist Party, who were also the executive board of the Commonwealth Federation, were pursuing." Again in 1946 he campaigned "to try to make it clear that I was bitterly opposed to . . . the Communist Party."

Costigan told the committee that the Communists opposed the formation of the Pension Union in 1937 because they were "still busy with the Workers' Alliance" and regarded the Pension Union as a "dual union" but that now "some of the leadership of the Pension Union are, of course, Communist Party members."

William Pennock was at one time a secretary to Costigan and, although Costigan did not know whether Pennock was a member of the Communist Party, he "would just assume that he was . . . by reason of the fact that . . . he was in all top fraction meetings at various times, and met on policy." N. P. Atkinson, who preceded Pennock as president of the W.P.U., "was a far more obstreperous belligerent follower of the Communist Party line than anyone I ever ran into contact with." Thomas Rabbitt, vice-president of the Pension Union, was "ardently attempting to be trusted" by the Communist Party, and Costigan "would assume" that John Caughlan, attorney for the W.P.U., was a Communist Party member.

Ward Warren testified that he had been a member of the Communist Party for about two years beginning in 1937 or 1938, including the six months in 1938 or 1939 when he was advertising manager for the Washington Commonwealth Federation's *Washington New Dealer.* "At least ninety per cent" of the entire staff of the *New Dealer,* including the editor, were party members and attended W.P.U. and W.C.F. fraction meetings. Warren said that Pennock recruited him into the party and that they were in the same party unit. Warren also recalled that he had attended Communist fraction meetings with Atkinson, Rabbitt, and John Caughlan. By 1940, he told the committee, the Communists controlled the executive boards of the W.C.F. and the W.P.U.

H. C. Armstrong testified that he had helped form the W.C.F.; that he was state president of the Workers' Alliance in 1938; that he had been a member of the state legislature from Seattle since 1937; and that he was a member of the Communist Party from 1936 to 1940. He said that he had attended Communist fraction meetings of the Commonwealth Federation's executive board with Hugh DeLacy, Howard Costigan, Atkinson, Huson, Pennock, and Rabbitt. He testified that "John Caughlan was a lawyer very highly thought of by the Party." When asked by Investigator Houston, "As a member of the Communist Party . . . would it be your opinion that he was a member of the Communist Party?" Armstrong replied, "It would be."

Kathryn Fogg, a member of the state legislature in 1939, testified that she joined the Communist Party in 1937 or 1938 and

293

left it at some time after the party's national convention in 1938. She told the committee that she was on the state board of the Pension Union while a member of the Communist Party and that there were enough other party members on the board to control the policies of the Pension Union; and that she had attended Communist fraction meetings with Pennock, Atkinson, Rabbitt, and John Caughlan.

Harriet Riley testified that she joined the Young Communist League in 1938 or 1939; that her former husband was the King County secretary of the Workers' Alliance; and that she had attended Communist Party fraction meetings with Pennock and Rabbitt in 1938 or 1939. She knew that John Caughlan was a Communist because she and her husband had visited his offices "and the Communist theory was always discussed back and forth," and because Caughlan told her she was making a mistake in trying to get her husband to retire from the Communist Party.

Mrs. Riley testified that her husband "worked very closely with" the Pension Union in 1938 and 1939. Investigator Whipple then asked, "Just for the purpose of clarification of our own record— do you state at this time that the Old Age Pension Union was dominated and controlled during this period by the members of the Communist Party?" She replied, "Yes, sir."

A number of former Communist Party members also testified that they had attended various sorts of Communist meetings with Pension Union officers Pennock and Rabbitt and with Pension Union Attorney John Caughlan. Two other witnesses said that they had been solicited for membership in the Communist Party by Pennock, and one of them testified that his membership had also been solicited by John Caughlan.

Investigator Houston read to the committee two letters relating to Dr. Mary G. White, a vice-president of the Pension Union. One letter was from the director of the Seattle district of the United States Immigration Service. It declined to furnish the committee with the records in a naturalization proceeding begun by Dr. White in a Washington State court in 1934 but gave a summary of the testimony given in that proceeding by one Martha Johnson, who had been employed in Dr. White's home. According to this summary, the witness stated that Dr. White had urged her to vote for a Communist candidate; that Dr. White had said to a friend "that she would die for Communism and that she thought Lenin was a greater man than Christ"; that when a friend, identified only as "Lenna," spoke "very enthusiastically of the chance for Communism in the Broadway high school because the students were ripe for that," Dr. White "answered in a very non-committal way"; and that Dr. White "made allusions to the inadequacies of the existing form of government in the United States and praised the Russian form of government highly, because they took care of the people and kept them from starving, which the United States did not do." The second letter was from the clerk of the court in which the naturalization proceedings were conducted, and it stated that the judge had denied Dr. White's application for citizenship, "stating in his order, Quote, under testimony of sworn witnesses and evidence produced in open court, it was shown that Petitioner, Mary Gabrielle White, was Communistic inclined."

Closing testimony on the Pension Union came from committee Investigator Stith, who had prepared a chart "showing the stand taken by the leaders of the Washington Pension Union throughout the period from 1937 to the present time." For three hours Stith read from this chart information from which he concluded that "the leaders of the Pension Union have constantly followed the Communist Party line."

Not all of the testimony taken in the hearing was confined to the Washington Pension Union. A number of former Communists testified that University of Washington Professors Joseph Butterworth, Harold Eby, and Ralph Gundlach had attended "Communist," "fraction," or "unit" meetings. H. C. Armstrong testified that there were many Communists in the state legislature—Kathryn Fogg, N. P. Atkinson, Thomas Rabbitt, William Pennock, and Ellsworth Wills, among others—and that they held fraction meetings during the 1939 legislative session. He said that Morris Rappaport attended some of these meetings in the home of legislator Mike Smith, who, to Armstrong's knowledge, was never a member of the Communist Party. And he added that Jesse Epstein, who later became regional director for the Public Housing Administration in San Francisco, had attended meetings in Smith's home "that were described by Mr. Rappaport as being just for the comrades." Neither Wills nor Mrs. Fogg were asked to testify about this matter, but Sarah Eldredge, who testified that she had belonged to the Communist Party for about two years between 1937 and 1939 and was assigned to "the closely guarded professional unit" along with John Caughlan and Professor Ralph Gundlach, also told the committee that she "met with [Epstein] at the home of . . . Mr. John Caughlan . . . at a meeting of our closed unit."

Mrs. Eldredge also testified that Burton James and his wife, Florence Bean James, directors of the Seattle Repertory Playhouse in the University District, "who had a unit in the Playhouse and still do have, to the best of my knowledge," did not belong to the professional unit but worked in close co-operation with it.

Howard Smith also told the committee that the Repertory Playhouse "is part of the program of the Communist Party in which to educate the youth of the University of Washington and familiarize them with their propaganda. . . . In that Repertory Playhouse many members of the actors are members of the Communist Party. They have a Communist branch." Smith said he knew this to be true "because I've been in the back room in the Repertory Playhouse behind the scenes and with all their great actresses and actors, I've sat in executive secretary meetings with their actors and actresses. . . . Nobody back there could even possibly be anything but a high Party member." Smith was then asked whether Mrs. James was a member of the Communist Party and replied, "I don't know whether she was a member of the Communist Party only for the fact that because —that we talked like brothers and sisters. She's under cover." He then reaffirmed that the persons attending the backstage meetings of the Repertory Playhouse "were all Communists" and that Mrs. James was there.

The only other testimony about the Jameses or the Playhouse came from Jess Fletcher, a former president of the Seattle local of the Building Service Employees' International Union (A.F.L.), who testified that he had worked with the Communist Party from 1936 or 1937 until 1944. Fletcher told the committee that on one occasion Florence Bean James asked his local to buy a block of seats for an evening's performance at the Repertory Playhouse and that he refused to approve the purchase until she brought Morris Rappaport and Hugh DeLacy to his office and they told him, "This is a comrade and we expect you to support him."

The name of Harry Bridges also figured prominently in the committee's hearing. Louis Budenz testified that Bridges was a member of the Communist Party and had used the names "Rossi" and "Harry Dorgan," although it was not clear whether Budenz was testifying from personal knowledge of from "official knowledge." Manning Johnson said he had learned, "in my capacity as a member of the National Committee," that Bridges was a member of the Party and was known under the name "Rossi" but that he had never heard of him using the name "Harry Dorgan." Several other former Communists appearing before the committee testified that they had attended various sorts of Communist meetings with Bridges.

At the conclusion of the testimony about the Pension Union, the committee produced a surprise witness who identified herself as Agnes Bridges. She testified that she began living with Bridges in 1923, their daughter was born in 1924, and they were finally married "a few weeks before" the water-front strike in 1934 because Bridges had applied for United States citizenship and said "it would look better if he was married." She told the committee that Communist meetings were held in the kitchen of their home "sometimes once a week and sometimes twice a week," that Bridges had told her on many occasions that he was a member of the party, and that she had seen his party membership book, in which he used the name "Harry Dorgan." Difficulties developed between her and Bridges, she said, because she did not believe in communism and because he wanted their daughter to dance with Negroes. They were divorced in 1945.

On two occasions during the hearing, committee Chairman Canwell had announced that anyone wishing to appear before the committee would be allowed to do so. At the conclusion of the hearing, Canwell reported that "not one person named here has chosen to take advantage of his right to speak freely under oath in denial of any assertions made regarding him, or her." He also announced that the committee believed "that with the publicity given [Pension Union] activities, during the course of this hearing, that the people of the State of Washington will properly and adequately take care of the Communists in that particular field of activity."

The publicity to which Canwell referred had been ample. Testimony of witnesses before the committee was summarized, with liberal quotations, in newspapers and on radio broadcasts throughout the state. Each day's proceedings provided a front-page story for each of the Seattle newspapers, and the stories of Fred Niendorff in the *Post-Intelligencer* sometimes made the testimony before the committee even more startling than it had been originally. Thus, H. C. Armstrong's revelations about meetings of Communists in the legislature during the 1939 session became, in Niendorff's account, testimony that "a secret organization of Communist legislators parading under the banner of the Democratic Party meets under the capitol dome at Olympia at every legislative session and exerts strong pressure on legislation." Again, the letter from the Immigration Service on Dr. Mary White was put into a story—with a headline, "Doctor Urged Communism in School Here"—that had Dr. White proposing the introduction of communism in the Broadway high school, where the letter had her merely giving an answer "in a very non-committal way" to someone else's proposal.

Meanwhile, the Pension Union had resorted to litigation to prevent payment of the Canwell committee's expense warrants as a means of raising its constitutional objections to the committee, but the state Supreme Court eventually decided, as a matter of state constitutional law, that the legislature could create an interim committee to function between legislative sessions and ordered the Treasurer to pay the warrants.

SPOTLIGHT ON THE UNIVERSITY

Before the Pension Union's litigation had concluded, the direction of the Canwell committee's next inquiry had become apparent. Late in March, 1948, Senator Bienz, speaking before the Spokane Realty Board, declared that there were "probably not less than 150 on the University of Washington faculty who are Communists or sympathizers with the Communist Party" and that the Canwell committee would "name names when the time comes."

Within the next month the board of regents held a meeting, and issued the following statement:

> By mutual arrangement, Mr. Canwell met with the Board of Regents. He advised that his Committee was investigating at the present time alleged subversive activities by certain faculty members of the University.
>
> The Board expressed itself unanimously that it welcomes this investigation, particularly at this time in view of recent publicity regarding these alleged activities. The Board further assured Mr. Canwell that if evidence is presented through the work of the Committee, showing beyond any doubt any faculty member to be engaged in subversive activity, it would move immediately for such member's dismissal.

Shortly thereafter, Canwell announced that his committee would begin hearings on July 19, 1948, and that approximately forty faculty members had been subpoenaed. Subpoenas were also served on Mr. and Mrs. James, directors of the Seattle Repertory Playhouse, on Albert Ottenheimer of the playhouse staff, and on Rachmiel Forschmiedt, city sanitation inspector in Seattle. When the hearing opened, Canwell made an announcement on the function of counsel for the subpoenaed witnesses: "I want it understood that the position of counsel is strictly in an advisory capacity; they may freely advise their clients whether or not to answer; they may not argue before this hearing. We are not going to debate any of the issues regarding the constitutionality of this Committee, or its methods of procedure."

In this hearing, as in the preceding one, the committee produced three imported experts to testify about the Communist Party. The first of these was J. B. Matthews of New York City, who identified himself as the first national chairman of the League Against War and Fascism, as formerly "the leading Fellow Traveler in the United States" though never a member of the Communist Party, as research director for the Dies committee from 1938 to 1945, and as a man whose business now was "researching Communism."

Matthews supplied the committee with a list of some 230 currently operating "Communist front" organizations, schools, and newspapers which he had compiled, including the Seattle Labor School, and testified that there had been approximately 1,000 Communist front organizations in the United States since the Communist Party was formed. From his study of these 1,000 organizations he had compiled a list of the leading "fellow travelers" in the United States, using as his test the proposition that "any person who has sponsored or been affiliated with twenty or more of these Communist front organizations is by definition set down as a Fellow Traveler." Included among the top one hundred fellow travelers on his list were twenty-three college professors, "by far the largest number in any category." Leading the list was Albert Einstein, who was either a member of, had sponsored, or had sent messages to some forty "Communist organizations." There was also a separate list for Professor Ralph Gundlach of the University of Washington, consisting of eighteen organizations and publications which had been declared "subversive" by the United States House of Representatives' Committee on Un-American Activities, and for which Gundlach was listed as "member," "endorser," "sponsor," "signer of petition," or "book reviewer."

Before Matthews finished his testimony, which consumed all afternoon of the first day of the hearing and part of the next morning, he had ranged far afield. Because of their membership in, sponsorship of, or appearance before various organizations, or because of their specific statements or actions, Matthews condemned a great number of people, including Harold C. Urey, J. Robert Oppenheimer, Edward U. Condon, Harlow Shapley, Rexford G. Tugwell, Frederic March, Senator Charles Tobey, Professor Arthur M. Schlesinger, Jr., Dwight Eisenhower, and Dr. Irving Langmuir. He also disposed of some "fallacies widely held," including "the fallacy that men and countries go Communist because of hunger" upon which "arguments in support of the Marshall Plan were largely based," and the fallacy "that legislative investigating committees proceed irregularly without due regard for the constitutional rights of citizens." Further, he informed the committee that "one of the most intensive campaigns ever put on by the Communists and Communist front organizations in the United States" was "the campaign to take the control of atomic energy out of the hands of the military and place it in the hands of a civilian commission."

The second expert was Howard Rushmore, a reporter for Hearst's *New York Journal-American,* who testified that he had joined the Young Communist League in 1935, became a member of the staff of the *Daily Worker* in 1937, and left the Communist Party in 1939. Rushmore read to the committee from "The Program of the Young Communist International," published by the Y.C.L. in 1929, to show that the Y.C.L. at that time had counseled its members "to carry on educational and disintegrative work" in the Army and Navy, to "combat hypocritical, bourgeois morality," and to "struggle against the church and religion by means of unkind [*sic*] educational work."

Rushmore also took cognizance of the federal indictment of the twelve members of the Communist Party's national committee in New York but expressed dissatisfaction because it included only known Communists. It would be more effective, he said, to go after concealed Communists. In this connection he read at length from an "F.B.I. report" concerning a "highly secret cell of the Communist Party" in Washington, D.C., in which Alger Hiss and other federal employees were alleged to have been active. The F.B.I. report on this "cell," Rushmore added, "plus the testimony of about one hundred and fifty other persons, most of them Communist Party members," had been given to the federal grand jury which indicted the twelve leaders of the party in New York.

The third expert witness was George Hewitt of New York City, who testified that he joined the Young Communist League in 1926, went into the Communist Party in 1927, was at one time on its national committee, and left the party in 1944.

Hewitt appeared on the witness stand on three separate occasions during the hearing. His testimony was not always consistent, and in some instances it was not coherent. In his first appearance he testified that he was in Russia from 1930 to 1934; that while there he met Florence Bean James of the Seattle

Repertory Playhouse three times; and that "we were told that she was one of the 'sparks' to be used to develop on the cultural field, agitation for the Soviet Government, in the United States." When Investigator Houston asked, "Did she admit to you, or did information come into your hands, that she was a member of the American Communist Party?" Hewitt replied, "Yes, sir."

In his second appearance, Hewitt testified that he was sent to Moscow in 1929 to attend the Lenin School and that he returned to the United States in 1933. Upon his return, he "first assumed leadership in the section in Jamaica, which took in Long Island, up to Montauk Point. Then . . . they tried to get me in the State of Louisiana, which was a way of killing me off. If I had accepted leadership in the State of Louisiana, I don't have to tell anybody in this audience what would have happened to me, as a Negro. Therefore, I was sent to the Furriers' Union . . . and from there they sent me to the State Committee of the Party, where I assumed work with Isadore Begun and Morris Schappes. I was the Assistant Education Director to Begun. He withdrew and I took the place of Educational Director in the state apparatus; Schappes then took it the next year and I resumed working as the head of the Negro work in the Educational Department, in which I taught in secret schools, both of local and national matter, and I believe the state activities ended there.

"In the State of New York, in the year 1938 and '39," Hewitt said, the Communists organized "the first secret school of professionals in this country" at Briehl's farm, near Kingston, New York. Its students were university teachers, carefully selected by the national committee of the party. Hewitt definitely identified Professors Ralph Gundlach and Melvin Rader of the University of Washington as persons who had attended the school for six weeks in "about the year '39—'38 and '39."

In his third appearance, Hewitt returned to his attendance at the Lenin School in Moscow. He said that the Negro students were mistreated there, that they wrote a letter to Stalin, that Hewitt delivered the letter personally, and that "Stalin came with a resolution favoring the rebellion of the students against the corrupt leadership that was there." When asked to describe his meeting with Stalin, Hewitt replied:

I had the occasion to meet Mr. Stalin on four different times. One was at the — a regular dinner in the Kremlin with the President Kallinen, Kaganovnitch . . . Molotov. . . . There were many other luminaries. The purpose, of course, was to dazzle you with the grandeur of Soviet power. Why, for a young student to come right before the Generalissimo or the President of the Soviet Republic was indeed a great experience. There I saw the diplomatic side of Comrade Stalin, so to speak. On another occasion I saw Mr. Stalin in one of his real mean moods. That was with a criticism of Earl Browder, in which Mr. Stalin very sharply made Browder look like a penny—criticized severely Mr. Browder's theories on the Chinese question, calling Mr. Browder all sorts of names and acting in a most peculiar way for a leader of the proletariat.

It was then, on another occasion on a demonstration in a smaller city in which Stalin was invited there as the big man to enhance the feelings of these people in the City of Tula. I was on the regular stand with Mr. Stalin and for a time felt rather proud of myself. I handed this document to Joseph Stalin, the fourth time—the Comintern headquarters. This is—must be disassociated from the Kremlin headquarters, you see. It was not far from the Kremlin; they had a secret passage, of course, in the back from the Kremlin to the Comintern for the Soviet Government, because the Soviet Government was really disguised—the power of it was disguised by the Party Lines, and let no one believe that the government really was the power. It was the Communist Party of the Soviet Union that not only was the power over Russia but the power over the entire Communist World.

I had difficulty in getting into the Kremlin and I was able to bribe the girl at the switchboard with an American ten-dollar bill.

Mr. Houston: Well, now was this the time you handed this document—this document to Stalin?

Mr. Hewitt: Yes, sir.

Mr. Houston: Well, do you mean the Kremlin or the Comintern?

Mr. Hewitt: The Comintern building. You see—at a meeting in which they were discussing problems not associated with the American question—and I gave this to Stalin. He thanked me courteously and wondered how I got into the place. He told me to sit down, for it didn't concern me. Everything was, I believe, in French at the time. They had interpretations, of course, but nothing was supplied to me in English—but I did the job I was sent there by the students—to get the document to Stalin. We did it reluctantly, but we took a chance, as I stated before, which enabled us to save many of us to return to the United States, to the land of democracy.

Hewitt added that his return to the United States was brought about by pressure from Earl Browder, whom Hewitt had opposed from the floor when Browder appeared to speak to the students at the Lenin School. When he got back to the United States, Hewitt said, he was "asked to become a District Organizer in the State of Louisiana. I refused. They then decided that I must, under Party discipline, go to the section of Long Island, a well-known Ku Klux section in Long Island, Nassau in Suffolk County, in New York. . . . The purpose was to get rid of me. The Ku Klux Klan was very strong there so I thought up a scheme of outwitting them. I went to the stronghold of the Klan, and I recruited Sullivan, one of the leaders of the Glen Cove Klan, and they wondered how I did it. I said, 'Just being natural, that's all,' . . . I went from there to the Trade Union of the Party."

Hewitt was then asked again about seeing Mrs. James in Russia and replied: "One of the most popular places for people of the Cultural International Communist field—center, I would say, in Moscow was known as the Meyerhold Theatre. I was very intimate with the aides of Mr. Meyerhold. . . . It was the Repertory Theatre of Moscow, in which two very prominent Y.C.L.ers known as Konja and Eva were in charge of this place. I was very intimate with these people, went to school, and who would help in the cultural work, and included in this was their homes, discussed very loosely the Americans who would come to the Mrs. James [sic]." When asked if he had seen Mrs. James at any other place in Russia, Hewitt replied that he "had the occasion to know and see her in the Comintern headquarters, the Profintern Building which was the Trade Union."

A recess was called at this point, and when the hearing reconvened Hewitt was asked when he had returned to the United States from Russia. He replied, "The latter part of 1933." His attention was then called to the testimony he had given in his first appearance before the committee, where he had fixed the time of his stay in Russia as from 1930 to 1934. He then stated that the correct dates were 1929 to 1933 and that he definitely saw Mr. James in Moscow in 1932 over a period of "two to three weeks."

The chief testimony on Communist Party affiliation of University faculty members came from Professor Sophus Keith Winther, who testified that he joined the party early in 1935 and withdrew in November or December, 1936. While in the party, Winther said, he belonged to "a University group" whose meetings were attended by Professors Garland Ethel, Harold Eby, Herbert J. Phillips, Melville Jacobs, Joseph Butterworth, Maud Beal, and Angelo Pellegrini. Winther also testified that Jesse Epstein attended many of these meetings, and when asked if Professor Joseph Cohen was a member of the party, replied, "Yes, he was." Winther recalled that his group attempted to get Professor Melvin Rader to join the party but that Rader refused. When asked to describe the nature of the group meetings, Winther replied that "they concerned themselves with the discussion of books—reports on the various books that concerned themselves with national and international affairs."

Mrs. Winther, who testified that she was a member of the party during the same period of time as her husband, corroborated her husband's testimony on Maud Beal, Harold Eby, Angelo Pellegrini, Melville Jacobs, and Jesse Epstein. She couldn't recall whether Garland Ethel and Joseph Cohen were members of her unit, but she "talked to [Ethel] as one member to another," and she "accepted" Cohen as a Communist and had seen him at "Communist meetings."

Nat Honig, a reporter for Hearst's *Los Angeles Examiner,* submitted an affidavit stating that he had been a member of the Communist Party from 1927 to 1939, that from 1937 to 1939 he was educational director for the party's northwest district; that in 1937 he attended a party meeting in the home of Professor Melville Jacobs; that he had discussed "Communist Party business" in the office of Morris Rappaport with Professors Joseph Butterworth, Harold Eby, and Herbert Phillips; and that he had "official knowledge" that Professors Garland Ethel, Joseph Cohen, and Ralph Gundlach, as well as Mr. and Mrs. James and Albert Ottenheimer of the Repertory Playhouse, were members of the Communist Party.

A number of other witnesses testified that they had attended various types of Communist meetings with Professors Phillips, Butterworth, Gundlach, Eby, and Jacobs, and there was some additional testimony about Professor Melvin Rader. Kathryn Fogg, who had testified at the first hearing, now told the committee that she considered Rader a "fellow traveler" but "not a Communist." Sarah Eldredge had read a book by Rader entitled *No Compromise* which was published in 1939 and in which, Mrs. Eldredge said, Rader "followed the party line and put the Communist ideology in with the anti-Fascist nations and in with the democracies." Moreover, the book was "not philosophically honest because he admits that Christ existed but he doesn't admit that some people think he is God of the Communists."

Lane Summers, a Seattle attorney, testified that his son had attended the University of Washington from 1933 to 1936; that on one occasion he had made a "more or less superficial examination" of some twenty books which some of his son's professors had recommended and found all but one of them "very radical in their essence and influence"; that his son developed a "definitely aggressive . . . Communist attitude" and finally left his home and went to live first with Professor Gundlach and later with Professor Phillips; and that in 1937 his son enlisted in the Abraham Lincoln Brigade and was sent to Spain, where he was killed while fighting for the Loyalists. Summers also testified that he had many discussions with his son during which the son mentioned several of his professors, including Gundlach, Phillips, and Melvin Rader, and "definitely indicated" that they were all members of the Communist Party.

H. C. Armstrong repeated the testimony he had given at the first hearing about attending a meeting of Communist legislators in 1939 which was also attended by Jesse Epstein; and Sarah Eldredge repeated her testimony about attending a "unit meeting" with Epstein at the home of John Caughlan. Mrs. Eldredge also testified that N. P. Atkinson once told her that Mr. and Mrs. James of the Repertory Playhouse were Communist Party members, and that on one occasion, when Mrs. James was running for the legislature, Mrs. Eldredge was instructed "by the Women's Commission of the Communist Party" to secure speaking dates for her, "to build Florence Bean James at the same time I was—that I was instructed to build Jesse Epstein."

Howard Smith added that when Mrs. James was a candidate for the school board, the Communist Party's executive secretary for King County gave Smith some pamphlets to distribute for Mrs. James and told him "she's all right, she's one of our brothers and sisters from the Repertory Playhouse."

H. C. Armstrong told the committee that he had been informed by others that Mrs. James "was a comrade" and that the Communist Party considered the Repertory Playhouse "a Communist mouthpiece, almost."

Ward Warren also testified that various "top Communists . . . all notified me, or assured me, that Al Ottenheimer [of the Playhouse staff] and various other people were members of the Communist Party," and that he also "had okehs from" these same "leading Communists" on Mr. and Mrs. James.

Mrs. Isabel Costigan testified that Mr. and Mrs. James were members of the Communist Party and that it was her "understanding" that Albert Ottenheimer was a member of the party. Investigator Houston then asked, "How did the Party consider the Repertory Playhouse? Were they back of it?" Mrs. Costigan replied, "Oh, definitely, yes. The Repertory Playhouse served as a—served a number of functions. It was a means of raising money at times for Communist activities. Also it served as a point of getting young people—ambitious young people into the Communist Party—likely young people who took English courses at the University, and who were told that they probably had dramatic ability, and then were sent to the Repertory Playhouse for trial, where they were given work in bit parts at first, and brought into the social activities of the Repertory Playhouse, which were largely Communist Party activities."

A request by counsel for Mr. and Mrs. James and Albert Ottenheimer for permission to cross-examine witnesses who had testified about the Repertory Playhouse and its staff was denied.

A number of former Communists also identified Rachmiel

Forschmiedt, Seattle sanitation inspector, as a Communist. Included among these witnesses was Howard Smith, who told the committee that while he was a member of the Communist Party between 1941 and 1945 he attended 700 meetings and made notes on "everything that took place and every person that attended those meetings." Reading from these notes, Smith testified that he had seen Forschmiedt at fifteen different meetings ranging from the meeting of "a ship committee" to "a meeting in large executive committee of the Communist Party." Ellsworth Wills, who at the first hearing had named a number of the members of the Communist Party unit to which he belonged between 1935 and 1939, now added that Forschmiedt was also a member of that unit. Forschmiedt's request for permission to cross-examine Wills was denied.

Committee Investigator Ernest Stith introduced another of his charts, compiled from newspaper clippings and letterheads, and entitled, "A Comparison of the Communist Party Line and the Activities and Affiliations of Certain Professors at the University of Washington and Officials of the Repertory Play House." This chart covered everyone from the university and the Repertory Playhouse who had been named by witnesses at the hearing and a number of university faculty members who had not been named. It listed their affiliations, and it cited instances of their "following the Party line," e.g.: Mrs. Florence Bean James visited drama festivals in England and Russia in the summer of 1934; Professor Ralph Gundlach wrote an article in 1942 advocating that the San Francisco Board of Supervisors "take a firm stand in connection with racial discrimination"; Professors Gundlach and Rader signed a statement in 1943 opposing continuation of the United States House Committee on Un-American Activities; Professor Garland Ethel entered the United States Army in 1943.

The balance of the hearing was given over to the testimony of those who had been named as Communists by other witnesses. Professor Angelo Pellegrini testified that he joined the Communist Party in 1935 or 1936 and was a member for about one year. He had attended about half a dozen meetings, he said, but could recall the location of only two of them—one at his home and one at Professor Winther's. He could not recall the name of any persons who had attended meetings with him, except Winther and Morris Rappaport.

Four other university faculty members admitted past membership in the Communist Party but refused to give the committee the names of any other persons who had been in the party with them. These four were Harold Eby, a party member from 1935 or 1936 to 1946; Garland Ethel, a party member from 1934 to 1941; Melville Jacobs, a party member from 1935 or 1936 until 1945 or 1946; and Maud Beal, a party member from 1935 to 1938 or 1939.

Seven other persons who had been named as Communists refused to answer questions about their own affiliation with the Communist Party. Each of them tried, with varying success, to state reasons for his refusal to answer.

The first of these witnesses to be called was Professor Herbert Phillips. John Caughlan appeared as attorney for Phillips, and he inquired "whether certain legal objections to Mr. Phillips' appearance here may be stated to the Committee." Canwell replied: "No statements as to objections concerning his appearance here will be accepted, and any position you have here will be merely as a counselor to your client." Caughlan then asked, "[M]ay Mr. Phillips then at the outset of this inquiry, state his legal objections to his appearance here, before being required to testify?" Canwell replied: "No, he will not. We are not going to debate the issue of the legality of this Committee or its processes. That may be done elsewhere; and at present you will be confined to the instructions given." Phillips was then asked about party membership and replied, "For conscience—conscience sake, and political sake, I refuse to answer the question." Caughlan attempted to make a statement but was cut off. The question was repeated, and Phillips began, "I must say that in light of the testimony that has previously been given, that I would regard it as a violation of my principles, a violation of what I regard to be the most sacred—" He was interrupted, and advised by Canwell to answer the question "yes" or "no." He then said, "I will not answer that question." He was directed to step aside. Caughlan again attempted to make a statement and was again cut off by Canwell, who informed him, "You aren't saying anything in here," and directed him to leave the hearing room.

Professor Ralph Gundlach was called and, with his attorney, Clifford O'Brien, received similar treatment. When Gundlach was asked about party membership, he replied, "Mr. Houston, no legislative committee has the right to ask about one's personal beliefs or associations." He was directed to step aside.

When Professor Joseph Butterworth was called, his attorney, C. T. Hatten, stated that he "would like the record to show that Mr. Butterworth is testifying under legal objections, and I would like the opportunity to state what they are under the federal and state constitutions," Canwell replied, "We are not interested in your legal objections" and ordered that the interrogation proceed. When Butterworth was asked about Communist Party membership, he replied, "Mr. Chairman, because of conscience and because I should not be required to testify against myself, I will decline to answer that question." Hatten then began, "The right of cross-examination—" He was cut off by Canwell, who directed officers of the State Patrol to remove Hatten from the hearing room. After Attorney Clifford O'Brien had agreed to act as counsel for Butterworth, the question about party membership was repeated. Butterworth again replied, "Because of conscience, and because I—this body has no right to force me to testify against myself, I refuse to answer the question." He was directed to step aside.

Rachmiel Forschmiedt replied to Houston's question about party membership, "Mr. Houston, in asking me to answer that question you are asking me to violate the supreme law of the United States of America, the Constitution of the United States—" He was cut off by Canwell, who advised him that the question should be answered "yes" or "no" and that his refusal to do so would subject him to contempt proceedings. Forschmiedt began, "I am simply stating that I do not want to violate the Bill of Rights—" He was again interrupted, the question was repeated, and he replied, "I refuse to violate the law of the United States—." He was directed to step aside.

Florence Bean James of the Repertory Playhouse was called,

identified, and asked about Communist Party membership. She replied, "Mr. Houston, I resist with everything I have your right to ask that question, and I stand on my constitutional rights to refuse to answer it." The question was repeated, she again refused to answer, and she was directed to step aside. Her husband, Burton James, went through the same procedure. His replies were "I do not care to answer" and "I stand on my constitutional rights."

Albert Ottenheimer of the staff of the Repertory Playhouse, when asked about Communist Party membership, replied, "I consider that an attempted censorship of the arts, and I can't answer that kind of question under the circumstances which are permitted here." When the question was repeated he persisted in his refusal to answer "on the basis I have stated, plus moral grounds, professional ethics, and illegal grounds."

Ted Astley, a vocational counselor in the University Veterans' Guidance Center, had not been mentioned in the testimony of any witness at the hearing, but he was called and asked about Communist Party membership. The official transcript of the hearing at this point reads as follows:

> *Mr. Astley:* Mr. Houston, I will answer your question in my own manner. This is a question which cannot be asked of any citizen of the United States without a violation of the Constitution of the United States. The—[starts shouting.]
> *Chairman Canwell:* You will be quiet.
> *Mr. Houston:* Mr. Chairman, I would just like to report, for the record's sake, that the answer was totally unexpected and unresponsive to the question.
> *Chairman Canwell:* Do I understand correctly, that he is employed by the State of Washington?
> *Mr. Houston:* Yes.
> (Witness excused)

Two more university faculty members who had been named as Communists were called to testify during the last afternoon of the hearing, and they both answered all questions. Professor Joseph Cohen denied that he was or ever had been a member of the Communist Party. Specifically, he denied that he had attended party meetings with Professor Winther or anyone else, or that there was any other basis for the testimony of Winther, Mrs. Winther, and Nat Honig that Cohen was a member of the party.

Professor Melvin Rader, whom witness George Hewitt had placed in a Communist school in New York for six weeks "in about the year '39—'38 and '39," also denied that he was or ever had been a member of the Communist Party or that he had attended the New York school at any time or that he had ever been in New York prior to 1945. In 1938, Rader said, he taught at the university through the first half of the summer term until about August 1; shortly thereafter, he went with his family to Canyon Creek Lodge, a resort establishment near Granite Falls, Washington, for approximately six weeks; he might have been in Victoria, British Columbia, for a short time in September; he was in Seattle at the time of the Munich Conference [September 29, 1938]; and he began teaching at the university again about October 1. In 1939, he added, he again taught at the university through the first half of the summer term; he was in Seattle when the first copies of his book, *No Compromise,* reached there early in August; and he was in Seattle or the near vicinity "until the outbreak of the war." Moreover, in September, 1939, shortly after the Nazi-Soviet Pact, he wrote a preface for an English printing of his book in which he strongly expressed his "sympathies, solidarity, and . . . loyalty, not only to American democracy, but to the whole concept of democracy internationally and specifically to France and England."

THE NEWSPAPER APPROACH

In announcing his second hearing, Canwell had said that "evidence now in the possession of the Committee concerning certain members of the University faculty will be publicized in the same manner that the Committee publicized its evidence concerning the Washington Pension Union and other matters." That announcement proved to be an understatement. Seattle newspapers covered the second hearing in more detail than the first, with more headlines and more photographs. The *Post-Intelligencer* featured Mrs. Costigan's testimony as a disclosure that the Repertory Playhouse was used as a "recruiting center and transmission belt and financing agency for the Communist Party" and that "University of Washington students are induced into the school through Communist Professors at the University." Her testimony as reported by Fred Niendorff in the *Post-Intelligencer* offers more support for the story than does her testimony as reported in the official transcript. She is quoted in the *Post-Intelligencer* as saying that "it was the actual work of the University English Department to get young people into the Communist Party." No such statement appears in the transcript.

Professor Pellegrini's testimony was also reported in some detail in the *Post-Intelligencer,* and color was added to the story when Niendorff described Pellegrini as a "swarthy, nervous witness who came to the United States from Italy."

Howard Rushmore's testimony that 150 persons had appeared before the federal grand jury which indicted the twelve members of the Communist Party's national committee became, in Niendorff's account, testimony of "the existence of a vast Soviet spy ring in the United States, involving at least 150 employees of Federal bureaus in Washington, D.C."

The *Post-Intelligencer* also reported that, in a "dramatic encounter" with Gundlach and Rader in the corridors of the Seattle Armory, witness George Hewitt had recognized them both as former students at the Briehl's farm school in New York and that "only a half-hour before he named the pair from the witness stand, Hewitt stood face to face with Rader before the Committee's Chief Investigator, William J. Houston, and Chairman A. F. Canwell in the latter's private office."

At the conclusion of the hearing, the *Post-Intelligencer* took editorial cognizance of a "loud outcry regarding civil rights" but stated that "there is no real evidence that anyone's civil rights have been jeopardized in the slightest. . . . Perhaps the hearings, whose procedure admittedly was clumsy at times, have been unfairly pictured in the public mind through some of the inept questioning of witnesses by the chief examiner. But each person who had been mentioned by a witness as assertedly having had Communist affiliations was given the opportunity of stating whether or not he was or had been a member of the Party."

Canwell later agreed that some of Houston's questioning of witnesses was "inept" but added that Houston was "a better investigator than a lawyer." Canwell also rates Whipple, whose interrogating technique was not perceptibly different from Houston's, as "a very able lawyer." Shortly after the conclusion of its second hearing, the Canwell committee announced that Houston had been given an indefinite leave of absence to pursue employment opportunities in the East and that Whipple would succeed him as chief of the committee's investigating staff. Houston went to Washington, D.C., and secured employment as counsel for the American Federation of Government Employees (A.F.L.).

The *Seattle Times'* coverage of the second hearing was as full as and considerably more accurate than that of the *Post-Intelligencer.* During the hearing the *Times* also published articles by Professors Arthur Smullyan and Joseph B. Harrison, which criticized the committee for its refusal to allow persons under attack to call witnesses in their own behalf or to subject adverse witnesses to cross-examination and for its failure to adduce any evidence of subversive activities. The *Times* also carried two feature stories. One was on Canwell, who "presides over the Committee's hearings . . . with a firm hand, a loud gavel, and virtually no moments of indecision. . . . It is not an accident when his gavel beats an ear-splitting tattoo which prevents anyone from being heard whom Canwell does not want to be heard. . . . Canwell was an obvious choice to head the Committee because he had experience in a related line and because his financial status and occupation make it possible for him to devote the attention the job required. . . . Canwell's wife is a daughter of the late Dr. H. P. Marshall, wealthy resident of Spokane. The Canwells . . . live on a rural estate on the Spokane River. . . . The farm produces hay and livestock and Canwell considers himself a farmer." The second story was on Chief Investigator Houston, "a blustering, 44-year-old lawyer" who "earnestly believes he can detect a Communist as easily as he can tell a man with smallpox is sick. 'By the words they use, they cannot conceal their Communist beliefs,' he declared. 'Certain words have an entirely different meaning to Communists. You can always tell.' "

The *Times* also reported that on the last day of the hearing the committee refused to allow King County Deputy Prosecutor Herbert Davis and Professor Rader's attorneys, Ed Henry and Paul Coughlin, to cross-examine witness George Hewitt.

THE HEARINGS' FIRST CONSEQUENCES

A few days after the close of the second hearing, the committee asked King County Prosecutor Lloyd Shorett to bring contempt charges against Phillips, Butterworth, Gundlach, Ottenheimer, Forschmiedt, and Mr. and Mrs. James. Prosecutor Shorett filed charges against six of the persons specified by the committee but omitted Butterworth because of "complex legal aspects" arising from the fact that Butterworth had based his refusal to testify "on the ground that the constitution gives every person the right to refuse to testify against himself."

Before trial of these charges, the trial court overruled motions to dismiss, based on the state and federal constitutions, under which defendants asserted that to require them to answer the questions asked would invade their right to privacy in matters of political faith, allegiance, and association and would also violate their privilege against self-incrimination. On the first contention, the court concluded: "None of the provisions of the Bill of Rights of our national constitution were . . . designed . . . to frustrate or prevent reasonable inquiry concerning the activities of persons or organizations which indicate a purpose to foment internal strife, discord or dissension" or to "undermine the stability of American institutions." On the self-incrimination argument, the court ruled that each defendant must establish that he had claimed that privilege in the Canwell committee hearing and that if he did not claim it there he would be deemed to have waived it.

At the trials, none of the six defendants was able to establish that he had asserted his privilege against self-incrimination in the committee's hearing. The jury acquitted Phillips. Different juries convicted each of the other defendants. Gundlach, Forschmiedt, Ottenheimer, and Mr. James were each sentenced to 30 days in jail and find $250. Mrs. James was given a suspended sentence of 30 days and fined $125.

All of those convicted appealed to the state Supreme Court. The appeals of all but Burton James were dismissed for failure to fol-

315

low proper appellate procedure. In James's appeal, the conviction was affirmed, the court finding no constitutional bar to legislative inquiry into political beliefs and no sufficiently imminent threat of criminal prosecution to justify refusal to answer questions about Communist Party membership on grounds of self-incrimination. The decision was unanimous, although one of the nine participating judges considered the question about party membership incriminating but concluded that James had failed to claim his privilege against self-incrimination before the Canwell committee, and two others separately noted their "strong impression" that the Canwell committee "asked the question which resulted in the proceeding before us, not for the purpose of securing data necessary for the framing of legislation to meet the problem of dealing with . . . subversive actions, but for the harassing effect on political dissidents and for public information."

Long before these contempt proceedings were concluded, a number of the subjects of Canwell committee inquiry had encountered other difficulties. One of the first of these subjects to feel the effects of the committee's work was the Seattle Repertory Playhouse. Organized as a nonprofit corporation in 1928, and operating in a rented theater building under a lease which expired December 31, 1950, the playhouse derived nearly all of its operating revenue from ticket sales. Since 1941 most of that revenue had come from three sources: (1) advance sales of the entire house (342 seats) or of smaller blocks of seats to various organizations, (2) box-office sales, and (3) sales for a Childrens' Theatre series sponsored jointly by the playhouse and Junior Programs, Inc., a local civic organization.

Mr. and Mrs. James and the Repertory Playhouse were first mentioned in the Canwell committee hearings on January 28, 1948, in the testimony of Sarah Eldredge. Between that date and the end of July, 1948, there were twenty-two cancellations of advance sales involving 3,900 seats. In some instances the cancellations were attributed to the testimony taken in the committee's hearing; in other instances different reasons or no reasons were given. But, prior to the hearing, the normal rate of cancellation on advance sales had been four or five per season.

In the three months following the second Canwell committee

hearing in July, 1948, there were fourteen more cancellations of advance sales involving 2,600 seats, and Junior Programs, Inc., declined to renew its contract for the Childrens' Theatre. During the entire 1947–1948 season, box-office sales at the playhouse dropped off by about one-third. Total gross income, which was $40,000 for the 1946–1947 season, dropped to $33,500 in 1947–1948, and to $14,000 in 1948–1949.

Late in 1950 the University of Washington announced that it had purchased the theater building for $70,000 for use by its Drama Department. According to the university comptroller, this was "a good buy" for the university, since the property was appraised at $114,000. But, the comptroller pointed out, the price was "fair to the seller since . . . the University is virtually the only potential purchaser."

Another subject of Canwell committee inquiry to confront immediate further difficulties was Jesse Epstein, then a regional director for the Federal Public Housing Administration in San Francisco. One month after the Canwell committee's first hearing, in which H. C. Armstrong and Sarah Eldredge had testified that Epstein attended Communist meetings, a three-man loyalty board of the housing administration filed charges of disloyalty against Epstein, and a closed hearing on these charges was held in Seattle in April, 1948.

In this hearing, Epstein was allowed to cross-examine adverse witnesses, including Eldredge and Armstrong, and to submit rebuttal evidence. After the hearing, the federal agency's loyalty board announced its unanimous conclusion that "there is no doubt about [Epstein's] loyalty" and cleared him on all charges. Soon thereafter Epstein resigned from the housing administration. He is now practicing law in Seattle.

It is probable, though not demonstrably certain, that the proceedings against Epstein resulted in part from the activities of the Canwell committee. The charges of disloyalty were based on F.B.I. reports of statements given to F.B.I. agents between December, 1947, and early February, 1948. The Canwell committee began its investigation in May, 1947, and Canwell admits that he and his staff "worked closely with some federal agencies," although he declines to identify the federal agencies involved. In any event, the committee publicized the testimony of Eldredge and Armstrong in its first hearing, prior to the loyalty proceedings, and publicized the same testimony again in its second hearing after the federal loyalty board, which heard the witnesses under cross-examination, had rejected it.

Witnesses testifying at the first Canwell committee hearing also made frequent mention of the name of Seattle Attorney John Caughlan. Two months after the hearing closed, a federal perjury indictment was filed against Caughlan, charging that he had appeared in a federal district court in Seattle in August, 1946, to testify in support of the naturalization petition of one Alex Knaisky, and that he had testified falsely to "a material matter . . . being considered by the court" in that he had denied that he was or ever had been a member of the Communist Party, whereas in fact he had been a party member from 1937 to 1946.

At Caughlan's trial in September, 1948, Sarah Eldredge, Kathryn Fogg, Ward Warren, Jess Fletcher, Isabel Costigan, and several witnesses who had not appeared before the Canwell committee testified that they had attended various sorts of Communist meetings with Caughlan. One witness from Kirkland, a small town on the outskirts of Seattle, testified that Caughlan had maintained membership in the Kirkland unit of the Communist Party and that the witness had mailed unit dues stamps to Caughlan, although he had not personally collected dues from Caughlan at any time or seen anyone else do so. Caughlan denied that he was or ever had been a member of the Communist Party or that he had ever paid party dues. He testified that he had attended many party meetings but only in his capacity as attorney for the party.

The case was submitted to the jury on instructions that, to find Caughlan guilty, the jury must find beyond a reasonable doubt that Caughlan had testified falsely as to Communist Party membership and that the question of Caughlan's membership was a "material matter" in Knaisky's naturalization proceedings. Caughlan was acquitted but, because of these instructions, the verdict affords no clue to the jury's appraisal of the evidence against him.

During the course of Caughlan's trial it was brought out by cross-examination of Isabel Costigan that she was paid $500 by the Canwell committee for "research and advice." Canwell admits that

318

both Mr. and Mrs. Costigan were on the committee's payroll as "undercover agents" but rejects any suggestion that they were paid for testifying. Canwell does not recall the amount paid to Costigan by the committee, and the information is not available from public records. Normally, such information would appear in the expense vouchers submitted by the committee to the state auditor. A state statute requires all such vouchers to be "fully itemized," and the blank voucher forms supplied by the auditor's office provide spaces for such itemization. But many of the vouchers of the Canwell committee, upon which the auditor issued warrants, are for lump sum disbursements by committee investigators which are not itemized. They are merely labeled: "Confidential Investigation expense. Records available in Committee's office for official audit." Presumably the Costigans were paid with some of these disbursements—they are not named in any voucher submitted by the committee.

Canwell also asserts that his committee "had something to do with reopening the Bridges case," but here, as in the cases of Epstein and Caughlan, it is impossible to measure the effect of the committee's activities. In May, 1949, more than a year after the conclusion of the first Canwell committee hearing, a federal grand jury in San Francisco returned an indictment charging that Bridges had committed perjury in September, 1945, when he denied Communist Party membership in the naturalization proceeding in which he acquired his United States citizenship. The trial on this indictment began in November, 1949, and ended with Bridges' conviction in April, 1950. The only Canwell committee witness to testify at the trial was Manning Johnson.

After his conviciton of contempt of the Canwell committee, and before his appeal from that conviction was dismissed, Rachmiel Forschmiedt was also the subject of further proceedings. The Seattle director of public health dismissed him from his job as city sanitation inspector for "conduct unbecoming an employee of the City in that he was in contempt of the State Legislature and has been convicted thereof, and sentenced, and for the good of the service." Forschmiedt appealed to the Seattle Civil Service Commission and that body, after hearing the director testify that Forschmiedt's behavior was "embarrassing' to the City Health Department and that there were "minor things—nothing too serious" wrong with Forschmiedt's performance on his job, concluded that Forschmiedt's conviction was "inadequate to support a dismissal at this time inasmuch as an appeal has been taken by Mr. Forschmiedt . . . and this appeal is as yet undetermined," and that the evidence did not disclose any other cause for dismissal. Accordingly, it ordered Forschmiedt reinstated.

DISMISSALS AT THE UNIVERSITY OF WASHINGTON

Shortly after the close of the Canwell committee's second hearing, the university announced that it had "reviewed" the employment record of Veterans' Counselor Ted Astley and, "since it was felt that his service . . . has been generally unsatisfactory and has deteriorated over the past year, it was decided to terminate his employment as of August 31. While the review of his case was occasioned by his appearance before the Un-American Activities Committee, the present action is based on the quality of his work and can in no sense be regarded as a result of his political activities or his behavior before the Committee." A few days later, University President Raymond B. Allen issued a statement admitting that, in addition to Astley's "unsatisfactory service," there was another factor involved—"the dignity of conduct that a University may rightfully expect of its employees. Mr. Astley's objection to the question put to him by the Committee could have been adequately voiced, I think, without outward display of temper and without shouting imprecations in what was otherwise a fairly conducted proceeding. . . . In this sense then, . . . Mr. Astley's appearance at the Committee hearings had a bearing on his dismissal."

The dismissal of Astley was followed by further proceedings at the university wherein, after a lengthy hearing, Professors Herbert Phillips, Joseph Butterworth, and Ralph Gundlach were also dismissed, and Professors Harold Eby, Garland Ethel, and Melville Jacobs were required to sign affidavits disclaiming Communist Party membership and were placed on probation for two years. The issues raised in those proceedings are beyond the scope of this chapter,[2] but some of the evidence taken in those proceedings is relevant to an evaluation of evidence taken by the Canwell committee.

Professors Phillips and Butterworth admitted that they were, and had been since 1935, members of the Communist Party. Professor Gundlach was also charged with Communist Party membership but denied it. In an unsuccessful attempt to prove the charge against Gundlach the university administration introduced the testimony of four Canwell committee witnesses, and those witnesses were subjected to cross-examination in the university proceedings.

Mrs. Isabel Costigan repeated her twice-given testimony about her party membership in 1938 and 1939. She now added that she knew Gundlach to be a Communist because, while she had never attended "Communist meetings" at his home, he had attended "Communist meetings" at her home. On cross-examination, she testified that there were many "meetings for organizing for political activity and strategy and that sort of thing" in her home, all of which were not "Communist meetings"; that "It would be hard to distinguish between the meetings of the Communist Party at that time, and the others, because . . . they were liberal, progressive ideas that they were promoting"; that Gundlach was at "some of both" kinds of meetings, but "it didn't make much difference which meeting he attended" because "I knew him to be a Communist"; that Gundlach "at no time gave any indication that he was anything but a good, sturdy, stalwart member of the Communist Party"; that he never "openly told me that he was a Communist," but "he let me understand that he was a Communist"; and that "he never at any time to my knowledge deviated from the Communist line." When asked for "any specific instance" of Gundlach's following the party line, Mrs. Costigan replied: "Well, Dr. Gundlach went along to my knowledge with the peace program, which was the program of the Communist Party during the period of the Soviet-Nazi Pact, and he was at our home during the period of advocating the all-out effort for the war."

Mrs. Kathryn Fogg repeated the testimony she had given at

[2] They are fully dealt with in Countryman, *Un-American Activities in the State of Washington* (1951), chs. vi and viii.

both Canwell committee hearings about belonging to the Communist Party from 1937 to 1939 and added that she "accepted" Gundlach as a Communist, although she "didn't know him as a Party member" and "never met in a unit" with him, because he "was acting in the front organizations." On cross-examination she testified that she never saw Gundlach in a "closed hearing"; that he never told her he was a Communist; that she could not recall that anyone else had told her he was a Communist, but that "he spoke at the different front organizations—Communist front organizations—such as the League Against War and Fascism."

Howard Smith testified that he had attended a number of "plenum meetings" with Gundlach. On cross-examination, Smith testified that the meetings where he saw Gundlach were held in Seattle between 1942 and 1946; thereafter he testified that he first saw Gundlach at a meeting in 1944. Then, after explaining that he had made records of all the meetings but had given his records to the F.B.I. and was unable to get them back, he fixed the time of the first meeting as "around 1944 or 1945."

H. C. Armstrong repeated the testimony he had given in both Canwell committee hearings about belonging to the Communist Party from 1936 to 1940 and testified that Gundlach had belonged to Armstrong's party unit. On cross-examination, Armstrong admitted that he had brought a libel action against the *Seattle Star* because it had published an article calling him a Communist, and that in 1938 and again in 1941 he had signed a sworn verification of his pleadings in that action wherein it was alleged that he was not and never had been a member of the Communist Party. This case was finally settled on payment of $750 to Armstrong.

Joseph Kornfeder, another Canwell committee witness, was also called by the university administration. While on the witness stand he identified as "Communist fronts" a considerable number of organizations, including the Seattle Labor School and Consumers Union (with both of which Gundlach had had some connection). Protracted cross-examination of Kornfeder on the basis for his testimony about Consumers Union revealed that he could not name any officer or director of the organization who was a member of the Communist Party, although "if you will give me the letterhead of their national board I may be able to do so"; that he was sure "they had passed resolutions on various occasions in conformity with the Communist Party line" but could not recall the substance of any resolution, although "if you give me the resolutions that they have passed and the literature that they issue . . . I will tell you exactly where it corresponds with the Party line"; and that the only activities of the organization which he could identify were "activities against the high cost of living," which "happens to be one activity that I am in favor of."

Professor Albert Franzke of the university's Speech Department testified that he and Gundlach had worked with a number of labor unions to set up the Seattle Labor School in 1945; that Franzke was elected chairman of the school's board of directors and Gundlach was elected to the board; that in February, 1947, Franzke resigned from the board after successfully opposing an effort "to put on the teaching staff an active, full servant of the Communist Party"; that the "complexion" of the school had begun to change about six months earlier, after a "blast" against it in the *Post-Intelligencer;* and that Franzke had told a Canwell committee investigator that he would be glad to appear before the committee and testify about the school but was not called to do so.

THE COMMITTEE'S FINAL REPORT
AND DEMISE

While the university proceedings were pending, membership of the Canwell committee was being reduced. Soon after that committee's second hearing, Senator Rutter resigned. His resignation was not publicized, but he later gave two reasons for it: (1) The committee had agreed that its expenditures would not exceed $100,000, but Canwell violated this agreement by spending $140,-600; (2) in calling Witness George Hewitt to testify about Melvin Rader, Canwell violated another committee agreement that no one would be named in the hearings unless all committee members approved and unless there were five witnesses who had attended "closed" Communist Party meetings with the person named.

Further reduction in committee membership came with the 1948 elections. The terms of four members of the committee expired at the end of the year. Only one of those four was re-elected. After one term in the lower house, Chairman Canwell became a Republican candidate for the state senate. He was defeated. Committee member Stevens sought renomination as a Republican candidate for the lower house. He was defeated in the primaries. Committee member Bienz, who had been elected to the legislature as a Democrat since 1939, secured the Republican nomination for the senate. He was defeated in the general election. Committee member Sisson was re-elected to the lower house for a seventh term. Although all of the defeated candidates campaigned on their records as members of the un-American activities committee, none of their successful opponents campaigned in opposition to the committee's work.

In the same 1948 elections, Republican gubernatorial candidate Arthur Langlie defeated Democratic incumbent Mon Wallgren, the Republicans won a substantial majority in the state senate, the Democrats recaptured the house, and the Washington Pension Union's initiative measure, increasing pensions to a minimum of $60, was adopted by a four to three vote.

Perhaps because of the success of its initiative measure, the Pension Union seems not to have been greatly damaged by the charges made against its officers by Canwell committee witnesses. Some members of the union have withdrawn because of alleged "Communist domination" and have formed a Senior Citizens' League. No figures on the numbers involved are available, but the Pension Union, which claims 16,000 members, asserts that the number of members lost by this defection is more than offset by the number of new members enrolled. Elections conducted at the three annual state conventions held since the first Canwell committee hearing have resulted in re-election of the same state officers.

When the 1949 legislature convened, Senators Rutter and Kimball introduced a bill, modeled on the Canwell-Stevens resolution of the 1947 session, to continue the un-American activities committee. But the Democratic majority in the lower house introduced a different bill, which would have vested the function of investigating "subversive activity" in the attorney general and the legislative council with certain procedural safeguards for persons investigated, including an opportunity to cross-examine and to submit rebuttal evidence.

While action on these competing bills was pending, the Canwell committee submitted its final report to the legislature. This report is a twenty-seven page document, twenty-three pages of which are devoted to summarizing the committee's achievements and defending its methods. Included among the listed achievements were: (1) accumulation of "an index file of approximately 40,000 subjects dealing with Communists, their Front Organizations and activities and related materials" [the committee's files were transferred to the state capitol and placed in a locked room, the keys to which were delivered to the president pro tempore of the senate and the speaker of the house]; (2) exposure of "an active cell of Communists" in the legislature; (3) discovery that the "State of Washington is acrawl with trained and iron disciplined Communists"; (4) exposure of the "Communist seizure" of the Washington Pension Union; (5) exposure of the Seattle Repertory Playhouse as "one of the most important aboveground Communist Front organizations in the State"; (6) discovery, through "a quiet spot check of some of our public schools," that "Communist slanted books and pamphlets" are "on the bookshelves in classrooms"; and (7) disclosure of "evidence of Communist infiltration into the faculty of the University of Washington."

So far as the methods employed by the committee were concerned, the report states that the committee took "every precaution to safeguard the civil rights of individuals who became the subjects of our investigations and inquiries, the loud accusations and protests of the Communists and their friends and legal advisers notwithstanding." The committee refused to entertain constitutional objections to the questions it asked because the committee's procedure and powers "may be challenged in the courts when thought to exceed constitutional limitations. No useful purpose can be served by arguing these issues before a legislative Committee." Cross-examination of the committee's witnesses was not permitted because "Communist attorneys are notoriously skilled in disruption" and the Committee had no power to commit for contempt. Moreover, the committee "took extreme pre-

cautions to prevent any witness from making unfounded charges."
In adopting its plan of procedure the committee "followed closely
the recommendation of the Brookings Institute [*sic*] in their 'Suggested Standards for Determining Un-American Activities,'" [3]
including the recommendation that "persons charged with un-
American activities" should not be given the right to cross-examine
witnesses appearing before the committee.

In the last four pages of its report, the committee recommended
legislative action on five matters:

1. Continuation of the investigation by an "adequately
financed" committee. In this connection, the laws on contempt
and perjury should be tightened up and the penalties "made much
more severe." The investigating staff employed by the Canwell
committee, which had "developed into a highly efficient team,"
should be retained by the successor committee. And the successor
committee should "be authorized to fully investigate the manner
in which textbooks and all other reading matter in our schools is
chosen and approved."

2. Strengthening of the "anti-subversive" oath for state employees imposed by the 1947 Appropriation Act [4] "so that it will
specifically name membership in or affiliation with the Communist
Party. . . . For the purposes of this recommendation a Communist should be defined as one holding membership in the Communist Party . . . or any organization, however defined, having a
proven working affiliation with the Communist Party of Soviet
Russia. Further, . . . party affiliation may properly be imputed
where the individual undeviatingly adheres to the Communist
Party Line or has proven affiliation with three or more known
Communist-Front organizations which have been declared subversive by a qualified branch of the State or Federal government."

[3] A pamphlet prepared by the Brookings Institution in 1945 at the
request of the United States House Committee on Un-American Activities.

[4] The act required state employees, including the faculty of the University of Washington, to swear that they did not advocate forcible
overthrow of the government and did not belong to any organization
asserting the right to strike against the government or advocating forcible
overthrow of the government.

3. Requirement of a similar oath for recipients of welfare funds.

4. Prohibition of "subversive diversion" of welfare funds.

5. Enactment of legislation to provide that any person who belongs to "three or more Communist Front organizations officially declared subversive" shall have no action for libel or slander against anyone who calls him a Communist.

The legislature did not act on any of the committee's recommendations. The 1949 Appropriation Act retained an oath provision whereby state employees were required to disclaim advocacy of or membership in any organization which advocates "overthrow of the government of the United States by force or violence" but dropped the requirement of the 1947 Act that they also disclaim membership in organizations asserting a right to strike against the government.

The state senate adopted the Kimball-Rutter bill to continue the un-American activities committee. The house adopted the Democrats' bill to continue the investigation but to transfer this function to the attorney general and the legislative council with prescribed safeguards. When the house refused to accept the senate bill, Senator Kimball introduced a senate resolution which created a "Senate Fact-Finding Committee on Un-American Disloyal and Subversive Activities" with the same powers as were vested in the Canwell committee. This resolution passed the senate, and a new committee was appointed with Kimball as its chairman.

Before this committe had taken any action, the attorney general advised the state auditor that, as a matter of state constitutional law, there was serious doubt as to whether one house of the legislature could legally create an interim committee to function after legislative adjournment, so that the auditor should not honor any expense vouchers presented by the Kimball committee until "such time as the legality of the committee may have been determined by the courts."

The auditor followed this advice. The Kimball committee did not bring action to test the attorney general's position, but Kimball announced that his committee intended to "undertake studies" and to "keep up-to-date" the information collected by the Canwell committee, even though no state funds were available for such purposes. The Kimball committee issued no further public statements, and any activities it may have engaged in have not been disclosed.

FRESH LIGHT ON THE COMMITTEE'S METHODS: THE RADER CASE

Submission of its final report to the legislature was the last official act of the Canwell committee, but considerable additional light has subsequently been shed on the activities of the committee by the efforts of Professor Melvin Rader to disprove the testimony of Witness George Hewitt that Rader had attended a Communist school "near Kingston, New York, on Briehl's farm" "about the year '39—'38 and '39."

Hewitt gave this testimony on July 22, 1948, at the Canwell committee's second hearing. He also identified Rader as the man he had "met face to face less than an hour ago." This reference was apparently to the "dramatic encounter" in the corridors of the Seattle Armory and the subsequent confrontation in Canwell's office described in the *Post-Intelligencer* on July 23. It has been variously described elsewhere.

In its final report to the legislature some months later, the Canwell committee stated that Hewitt informed the committee that he recognized Rader as a former student at the Briehl's farm school; that Canwell invited Rader to his office; that Rader came to the office, but "as soon as he saw Hewitt" he turned to leave and said he would not talk without his attorney; that Canwell invited him to return with his attorney; that Hewitt again "positively" identified Rader as Rader "hurriedly left" the office; and that Rader did not return, but his attorney, Ed Henry, did come to the office and questioned Hewitt, who persisted in his identification.

Rader's version of the affair is that Canwell, Houston, and a number of other people were in Canwell's office when he entered in response to a summons from Canwell; that he does not remember seeing Hewitt and does not yet know whether Hewitt was then in the office or not; that Canwell began to ask questions, and Rader replied that he would not answer questions without having his attorney present; that Canwell asked him to send his attorney to the office; that Rader then left the office, located Attorney Ed Henry, and sent him to see Canwell. Rader also denies that he had any encounter with Hewitt in the Armory corridors as reported by the *Post-Intelligencer.*

Attorney Henry adds to this that he went to Canwell's office and found Hewitt there; that he questioned Hewitt, but Hewitt stuck to his story; and that Henry then left to confer with Rader.

There is also some conflict in the accounts of an attempt to cross-examine Hewitt on July 23, the last day of the hearing. The following facts are uncontroverted: Hewitt first testified about Rader in his second appearance before the committee during the afternoon of July 22. Rader was in attendance at the hearing under subpoena but had not yet been called to testify. On the morning of July 23, Attorney Ed Henry accompanied Rader to the hearing, and Henry's law partner, Paul Coughlin, went to King County Prosecutor Lloyd Shorett and induced him to send Deputy Prosecutor Herbert Davis to the hearing to cross-examine Hewitt. After a brief appearance by one other witness, Hewitt took the witness stand for the third time on the morning of July 23 and occupied it until the noon recess. Rader testified during the afternoon of the same day.

According to Deputy Prosecutor Davis and Attorney Paul Coughlin, the committee was still in morning session when they arrived at the Seattle Armory. During the noon recess, Davis talked with Investigator Houston and members of the committee and requested an opportunity to cross-examine Hewitt. The committee was of the opinion that Hewitt was protected from such inquiry by legislative immunity but agreed to consider the request and to give an answer later in the afternoon. According to Deputy Prosecutor Davis and Prosecutor Shorett, Davis returned to the prosecutor's office and did not go back to the Armory for the committee's answer because Prosecutor Shorett was advised by newspapermen during the afternoon that Hewitt had left for New York. According to Attorney Ed Henry, when the committee adjourned its hearing at about five o'clock that afternoon Henry asked Investigator Houston about the committee's decision on cross-examination of Hewitt and was advised by Houston that Hewitt had departed by plane for New York at two o'clock in the afternoon.

According to Canwell, Hewitt left for New York by train at three o'clock in the afternoon of July 23, and no request to cross-examine him was made until after he had departed.

Subsequently, Prosecutor Shorett agreed to press a perjury charge against Hewitt. In announcing his decision, Shorett said that it was his understanding that Hewitt was to appear before the Canwell committee again and that he would be brought to trial when he returned to the state. But when two months elapsed without further committee hearings and with Hewitt still out of the state, Shorett in early October, 1948, requested New York City police to apprehend Hewitt and hold him for extradition.

The New York police were unable to locate Hewitt. He had testified in deportation proceedings in New York City in late August, 1948, and again in mid-September. Late in September his employer, Alfred Kohlberg, proprietor of a Chinese textile importing business in New York City and publisher of the magazine *Plain Talk,* complained to United States Attorney General Clark that Communists were harassing Hewitt and advised that thenceforth he would not give Hewitt time off to testify in deportation proceedings except on court order. Early in October the United States Immigration and Naturalization Service requested cooperation from the New York City Police Department for Hewitt's protection. The Police Department responded with an offer of a special guard for Hewitt's home in the Bronx, but Hewitt declined this offer and was assured by the police of a prompt response to any call for assistance. Early in December, New York City police advised the King County prosecutor's office in Washington that Hewitt was "last seen" in New York on October 7. On December 17, Hewitt testified in the Federal Building in New York City before a subcommittee of the House Committee on Un-American Activities. On December 22, he testified in the United States court house in New York City before the federal grand jury considering Whittaker Chambers' charges against Alger Hiss. On December 22, also, the *Daily Worker* began a series of front-page stories calling attention to Hewitt's appearances in New York, pointing out that Hewitt resided at 2750 Bronx Park East and was employed in New York City, and charging that city police and the F.B.I. were conspiring to avoid arrest of Hewitt on the Washington charge. The police were still unable to locate Hewitt.

Meanwhile, Prosecutor Shorett had been elected to the King County Superior Court and, on nomination by Commissioner Dean C. McLean, the King County commissioners had appointed Charles O. Carroll to finish Shorett's unexpired term as prosecuting attorney. On February 2, 1949, the *Post-Intelligencer* printed a letter from McLean to Carroll, calling upon Carroll "to resign in the public interest." This letter recited that "certain accredited government officials presented to you what I deem to be valid reasons for the dismissal of a certain case . . . filed by your predecessor"; that Carroll was informed "by bona fide representatives of the federal and state governments that the national security was involved"; that Carroll first suggested that it would cost him "some thousands of left wing votes" to dismiss the case, but later agreed to do so; and that Carroll had finally stated that he could not dismiss the case because he was committed to Shorett not to do so.

The *Post-Intelligencer* also published a statement from Carroll in which he refused to resign and charged that McLean's letter "was authored by Fred Niendorff of the Post-Intelligencer." Niendorff had come to him, Carroll said, and asked him to dismiss the Hewitt case because the state legislature was going to be asked to appropriate more money for the Canwell committee, and "it would be a blow to the appropriation's chances to have this Canwell witness, Hewitt, standing charged with perjury." Later, Carroll added, he was called to the office of Edward T. Stone, managing editor of the *Post-Intelligencer,* "and it was demanded that I dismiss the case. I refused. Stone told me: 'We elected one prosecutor and we can defeat another. We will blast you right out of that office if you don't dismiss this case.' "

There was also a statement from Managing Editor Stone, denying that the *Post-Intelligencer* had any interest in the Hewitt case except for "the legitimate news that might be involved in any development of the case." He admitted that there had been a meeting in his office atended by Niendorff, Carroll, and McLean but said that it was held at McLean's request. At this meeting, Stone said, Carroll expressed concern over 12,000 left-wing votes, and the following colloquy ensued: Stone: "What about the votes on the other side—the right side?" Carroll: "What do you mean?" Stone: "I mean that the *P-I* has taken on many battles for the good of the community, and usually wins." At this point, Stone's statement concluded, "Mr. Carroll took umbrage at this and angrily rose to leave. He was persuaded by Commissioner McLean to remain."

The *Post-Intelligencer* for February 3 carried another story reporting that both Canwell and McLean stated that representatives of the Department of Justice were seeking dismissal of the charge against Hewitt. There was also a statement from John W. Whipple, who had succeeded William Houston as chief investigator for the Canwell committee, saying that he had attended a meeting at Carroll's home with McLean and two "government agents" and had produced evidence which persuaded Carroll that he would have difficulty convicting Hewitt.

On the same day, the Canwell committee submitted its final report to the legislature. That report, in addition to its description of an encounter between Hewitt and Rader previously referred to here, added that "the Committee's investigating staff and an agency of the Federal Government have produced evidence showing conclusively that Professor Rader did not tell the truth when he testified before the Committee"; that while Hewitt had testified that Rader attended the New York school in the summer of 1938 or 1939, "the precise summer was later established as that of 1938"; that while Rader testified that he spent a vacation at Canyon Creek Lodge in the State of Washington during the summer of 1938, "your Committee's investigators have established that Mr. Rader's first appearance at Canyon Creek Lodge was in August of 1940"; and that "the Federal agency heretofore mentioned has in its possession the testimony of two witnesses who corroborate Mr. Hewitt's statement that Professor Rader was in New York in the summer of 1938."

On February 6, the *Post-Intelligencer* reported a statement issued by the United States attorney general's office that the Department of Justice had "absolutely no interest in" the Hewitt case. The *Post-Intelligencer* reported also that Raphael P. Bonham, district director of the Immigration and Naturalization Service for the Seattle district, admitted that two unnamed immigration inspectors "thought the case against Hewitt was without merit" and presented evidence to Carroll which they thought warranted dismissal. Several months later, Canwell admitted that he and John Boyd, deputy commissioner of the Immigration and Naturalization Service, had tried to dissuade Shorett from filing the perjury charge against Hewitt in the first place. (The Immigration and Naturalization Service is a division of the Department of Justice.)

On February 10, Hewitt surrendered to New York City police but announced that he would contest extradition, and filed a petition for habeas corpus for that purpose. The Supreme Court of the United States has ruled that "when the extradition papers required by . . . statute are in the proper form the only evidence . . . admissible in a [habeas corpus] hearing is such as tends to prove that the accused was not in the demanding state at the time the crime is alleged to have been committed." And the New York Court of Appeals, the highest court of the state, has recognized that this decision is binding on state courts. But Hewitt's petition for habeas corpus did not attack the sufficiency of the extradition papers or deny that Hewitt was in Washington at the time of the alleged perjury. The petition alleged that Hewitt's testimony before the Canwell committee was true, hence that he was not guilty of perjury—a matter which the United States Supreme Court has ruled must be left "to the trial of the case in the courts of the demanding state."

Attached to Hewitt's petition were eight documents:

1. A certificate executed by the assistant comptroller of the University of Washington which disclosed that Rader was on the university payroll in 1938 from January 1 to July 20 and from September 1 to December 31.

2. An affidavit executed by Mrs. Ida Kirby, dated July 24, 1948, notarized by Canwell committee Investigator Aaron R. Coleman and witnessed by Investigator John W. Whipple, which stated that Mrs. Kirby was employed at Canyon Creek Lodge, near Granite Falls, Washington, from 1938 to 1942; that the lodge had

burned "in the early months of 1938" [local newspaper files reveal that it burned February 10, 1938]; that "after the present lodge was built, . . . sometime during the month of August" a man and his wife walked out to the lodge from Granite Falls, introduced themselves as a university professor and his wife, stayed a few days, and departed; that Mrs. Kirby could not remember their names but remembered that the woman was pregnant; that they later came back with "a child or two" and remained at the lodge about a month; that when they departed the second time Mrs. Kirby drove them to an address in Seattle "in the University District and somewhere on 30th Avenue North East"; and that these people had stayed at the lodge during only one summer while Mrs. Kirby was employed there.

3. An affidavit executed by Thomas Grant, dated July 24, 1948, notarized by Investigator Coleman and witnessed by Investigator Evert Pomeroy, which stated that Grant had leased Canyon Creek Lodge from Mrs. Quincy Mueller in 1942 and had been its proprietor since that time; that in "the records left by Mrs. Mueller, a large portion of which I have examined, I fail to find any record indicating the registration of any paid guest during the year 1938"; that Grant did find a file card [which was attached to his affidavit] bearing "a record of one Mrs. Melvin M. Rader, address 6017 30th Avenue, N.E., Seattle, Washington, with the notation penned in ink . . . 'Prof. at U. of Washington, guest for 1 month,' and also the notation in pencil . . . '(L) 8–16–40' " [Mrs. Kirby's affidavit stated that both of these notations appeared to be the writing of Lucille Anderson, niece of Mrs. Mueller]; and that "these records are being turned over to" the Canwell committee "with the understanding that same may be used by them for any purpose . . . [and] that they will be returned to me on completion of their use."

4. An affidavit executed by Mrs. Quincy Mueller, dated July 26, 1948, notarized by Investigator Coleman and witnessed by Investigator Ernest P. Stith, which states that Mrs. Mueller was the proprietor of Canyon Creek Lodge from 1938 to 1942; that the first lodge burned in January, 1938, and a new lodge was completed in May, 1938; that Mr. and Mrs. Rader walked out to the lodge

334

from Granite Falls "in the summer of 1939 or 1940," stayed a few days, departed, and returned later with "a small child"; that Mrs. Mueller could not recall how long they stayed the second time but was sure that the Raders were at the lodge during only one summer between 1930 and 1942; that Mrs. Mueller identified a picture as a picture of Melvin Rader; and that she identified the file card described in Grant's affidavit as one of the records she had turned over to Grant.

5. An affidavit executed by Manning Johnson in New York, which stated that he was a member of the Communist Party from 1930 to 1939; that he "had occasion to appear several times" at the Briehl's farm school in the summer of 1938; and that he recognized an attached photograph of Melvin Rader as a likeness of a person he remembered "as having been present at" the Briehl's farm school in 1938 and a person whom he saw in the executive offices of the Communist Party in New York City "on various occasions in the summer of 1938."

6. An affidavit executed by George Peters in New York, which stated that he was a member of the Communist Party from 1937 to 1939; that "about the summer of 1938" George Hewitt introduced him to "a person called Doctor Rader" at a place "near Second Avenue and 11th Street" in New York City; that about a week later Peters visited the Briehl's farm school and "again met the person known to him as Dr. Rader and had a conversation with him"; and that he recognized an attached photograph of Melvin Rader as the person he met on these two occasions.

7. A copy of the Canwell committee's final report to the legislature.

8. A copy of the transcript of the Canwell committee's second hearing.

When a hearing on Hewitt's petition was scheduled in the New York Supreme Court for Bronx County, Bronx District Attorney Samuel J. Foley advised King County Prosecutor Carroll in Washington of that fact and suggested that he send a representative and witnesses to contest the habeas corpus application. But Carroll announced, "I haven't any of the money of the King County taxpayers to send witnesses and an extradition agent to sit around

New York, and wouldn't spend it that way if I had it." The State of Washington was not represented at the hearing, which was conducted before Justice Aaron J. Levy on May 12, 1948.

Hewitt's petition named the New York City commissioner of police and a city detective as the persons who had Hewitt in custody. These officials were represented at the hearing by Bronx District Attorney Foley and Assistant District Attorney John B. Lee.

The proceedings began with Foley stating to the court that, although he was "well aware that by law and precedent the inquiry is limited to certain points," he felt it "incumbent on me to give you some history" of the case. Foley then described an encounter between Rader and Hewitt in Canwell's office, substantially as set out in the Canwell committee's final report. After Hewitt had completed his testimony before the Canwell committee, Foley said, he remained in Seattle "for two or three days" so that Rader had "every opportunity to bring before the authorities, while this man was in the jurisdiction, whatever of complaint he had." Moreover, the Canwell committee had investigated Rader's story and found that Rader did not tell the truth in his testimony before the committee. The affidavits of the people from Canyon Creek Lodge, Foley said, revealed "that Professor Rader never appeared at the Lodge before the summer of 1940." And the certificate of the assistant comptroller of the university showed that "Rader terminated his paid services on the 20th of June, 1938." Foley concluded with the explanation that he had given the court "what I felt bound to do—the background of this case, with the opportunity to draw whatever inferences concerning motivation might please your Honor—always acknowledging that they are technically irrelevant."

When Foley had finished, counsel for Hewitt called Hewitt, Manning Johnson, and George Peters to testify. Hewitt identified a photograph as a picture of Rader. He did not testify further and was not cross-examined.

Manning Johnson identified the photograph as a picture of a man "I first met . . . at the Communist Party Headquarters with Isadore Begun" in 1938, a man he had seen "a number of times, going in and out of the office" at party headquarters, and a man whom he saw sitting in a class at the Briehl's farm school before which Johnson delivered a lecture in the summer of 1938. Cross-examination by Assistant District Attorney Lee brought out that Johnson was positive in his identification.

George Peters testified that he was a member of the Communist Party from 1933 to 1939; that he recognized the photograph as a picture of a man he first met "around about 11 o'clock" one day in 1938; and that he met the same man again "about the same month in 1938, around about August or September" at Briehl's farm. Cross-examination by Lee brought out that Peters was positive in his identification and that he had seen Rader at Briehl's farm on "about two different occasions."

At the conclusion of this testimony, counsel for Hewitt informed the court that Hewitt was "once one of the most important Communists in the United States"; that he had left the party and had since "helped the Department of Justice, helped the grand jury, helped various legislatures in their investigations of subversive activities"; and that "the Communist Party as a result feels that they must get rid of him." As evidence of the party's attitude, counsel offered issues of the *Daily Worker* which had attacked New York City police for their failure to apprehend Hewitt for extradition, but Justice Levy refused to look at them: "I never saw the *Daily Worker,* and I hope I never will."

Counsel then moved that the writ of habeas corpus be sustained, and Justice Levy, after commending "this heroic District Attorney" for his "proper and human acknowledgment of justice" and his "courage," granted the motion. From what District Attorney Foley had told him and from "what I glean from these [Canwell Committee] reports," Justice Levy said, "I learn that in the State of Washington there is any number of trained and iron-disciplined Communists," many of whom "hold almost impregnable positions of confidence and trust in their communities." In the proceeding before him, Justice Levy added, "there has not been made that showing which in good conscience I consider essential to warrant my sending this man to the State of Washington to eventual slaughter." Rather, "from many things that are in these reports to which the Legislature of the State of Washington certified, I am convinced that this man committed no crime whatever; that

337

if perjury was committed, it was committed by Melvin Rader. . . . And therefore this writ is sustained and the prisoner is discharged."

When news of Justice Levy's decision reached the State of Washington, King County Prosecutor Carroll was reported in the *Seattle Times* as saying that he would "renew his efforts to have Hewitt returned here," and quoted in the *Post-Intelligencer* as saying, "This washes the whole thing up. It's all over now." Justice Levy's decision was not appealed.

While the extradition proceedings against Hewitt were pending, Melvin Rader had been trying to accumulate evidence to prove that he could not have been in New York in the summer of 1938. After checking many records and talking to numerous witnesses, Rader was able to add some details to the account of his whereabouts during that time which he had given in his testimony before the Canwell committee: He taught at the university during the first half of the summer term, which lasted until July 20, 1938. Early in the summer he and his wife took a bus to Granite Falls, Washington, walked from Granite Falls to Canyon Creek Lodge, stayed overnight, and made arrangements to rent accommodations for a month. About August 1, and while Mrs. Rader's sister and her husband were visiting in Seattle and staying at the Rader home, Mrs. Angelo Pellegrini drove the Raders and their eighteen-month-old daughter back to Canyon Creek Lodge. Shortly thereafter the Raders visited a dentist in Granite Falls who extracted a tooth for Mrs. Rader. Midway during their stay at the lodge, Rader broke his glasses. He returned to Seattle, where he visited his doctor and got a prescription for new glasses. While in Seattle he went to his home and saw Mrs. Rader's sister, Louisa Peterson. He also telephoned Mrs. Rader's cousin, Lucille Newman, and told her about his wife's tooth extraction. At the end of the Raders' stay at the lodge, about September 1, Mrs. Ida Kirby drove them back to their home in Seattle. Thereafter, and early in September, Rader and a friend, Malcolm Forbes, took a walking trip to Victoria, British Columbia, where Forbes introduced Rader to an attorney named Theobold Bowen-Calthurst. After this trip Rader stayed in Seattle and resumed his teaching duties when the fall term at the University began on September 26.

This account is corroborated by the following evidence:

Records in the University of Washington comptroller's office show that Rader was on the university payroll in 1938 from January 1 to July 20, and from September 1 to December 31.

Withdrawal cards at the University of Washington library bearing Rader's signature are dated July 29, September 21, and September 28, 1938.

Mrs. Angelo Pellegrini has executed an affidavit stating that she drove Mr. and Mrs. Rader and "a toddler" to Canyon Creek Lodge from their home on 30th Avenue, N.E., in the summer of 1938.

Dr. Raymond O. Loy certifies that he gave dental treatment to Mrs. Rader in his office in Granite Falls "prior to August 7, 1938" and that Mr. Rader was present.

The office records of Dr. Carl D. F. Jensen in Seattle show that Rader had an eye examination on August 15, 1938.

Mrs. Louisa Peterson, Mrs. Rader's sister, has executed an affidavit stating that she and her husband stayed in the Rader home during August, 1938, while the Raders and their only child went to Canyon Creek Lodge, and that she recalls Rader coming to the house on one occasion during that time.

Lucille Newman, Mrs. Rader's cousin, has executed an affidavit stating that she recalls that Rader called her by telephone and told her about Mrs. Rader's tooth extraction shortly before the wedding of her cousin, Jean Simpson, on August 17, 1938, and that Mrs. Rader was pregnant with her second child during the summer of 1938.

Mr. Theobold Bowen-Calthurst, a barrister in Kamloop, British Columbia, has executed an affidavit stating that he met Rader in Victoria early in the month of September, 1938.

The records of M. L. Werner, a tailor in the university district in Seattle, show that he fitted Rader for a suit sometime in September, 1938.

The records of the Seattle city clerk show that Rader voted in the primary election of September 13, 1938, and that it was not an absentee ballot.

Rader's account is also corroborated by Mrs. Mueller and Mrs. Kirby of Canyon Creek Lodge. Mrs. Mueller now recalls pointing out the ruins of the old lodge, which burned on February 10, 1938, to Mrs. Rader while the Raders were at the lodge, and states that these ruins were all cleared away before the summer of 1939. She also recalls that the Raders had one small child with them and Mrs. Rader was pregnant at the time. Birth records in Seattle show that the Raders' first child, a girl, was born in January, 1937, and that their second child, also a girl, was born in February, 1939.

Mrs. Mueller also states that she kept two sets of records at the lodge. One was a loose-leaf register which all guests signed. The other was a card index made up from names in the register. She states further that the handwritten entry, "(L) 8–16–40," on the card which was introduced in the New York habeas corpus proceedings refers not to the time when the Raders stayed at the Lodge but to the date of a letter which Mrs. Mueller wrote to the Raders offering to sell them a part of her property. This statement finds corroboration in the further fact that the address typed on the card, "6017 30th Ave. N.E.," is an address from which the Raders moved in April, 1939, and that in 1940 they lived at 1750 E. 62d Avenue.

Mrs. Kirby, who accompanied the Canwell committee investigators in their search for the Canyon Creek Lodge records, states that on the investigators' first visit, when she made her affidavit for Investigator Coleman [July 24, 1948], they located the card index file but were unable to locate the loose-leaf pages from the lodge register for past years. On a subsequent visit by the investigators when Mrs. Mueller's affidavit was made [July 26, 1948], the old register pages were located, and Mrs. Kirby states that as one of the investigators scanned these pages she heard him say, "There it is, Rader, '38." She also recalls, as stated in the affidavit she gave Investigator Coleman, that when the Raders left the lodge she drove them to an address on 30th Avenue N.E. in Seattle.

Rader's further statements that he spent the summers of 1939 and 1940 in Seattle and vicinity are corroborated by additional documentary evidence which shows that he taught during the university's summer term until July 19, 1939, and was definitely in Seattle on August 1, September 2, 18, and 20, and October 3,

1939, and that he taught during the summer term until July 17, 1940, and was definitely in Seattle on August 5, 12, 19, 26, and 31 and September 3, 10, 12, and 14, 1940.

Obviously, the loose-leaf pages from the Canyon Creek Lodge register were crucial items of evidence in this matter. But those pages were missing. Canwell denied that his investigators had removed any records from the lodge. Thomas Grant, present proprietor of the lodge, stated that all of the records which he received from Mrs. Mueller and which were located by Canwell committee investigators were taken by the investigators, as recited in the affidavit which he gave to Coleman, and had not been returned. And he displayed a printed card which identified Aaron R. Coleman as an investigator for the Washington State committee on un-American activities, on the back of which was written an undated receipt for a card file and "certain register pages," and which recited that they were to be returned to Grant. The receipt was signed "Aaron R. Coleman." Investigator Coleman admitted that he took some records but stated that he brought them to the committee's offices and had no idea what became of them or whether they included register pages. He denied that there was anything in them to indicate that Rader was at the lodge in 1938.

The *Seattle Times* assigned Reporter Ed Guthman, who had covered the Canwell committee hearings for the *Times,* to make an investigation of Rader's case shortly after Justice Levy granted Hewitt's petition for a writ of habeas corpus in New York. Guthman went to see Rader and got an outline of Rader's evidence. He also obtained copies of the affidavits and testimony in the New York habeas corpus proceedings. By August 8, 1949, Guthman had checked all of the documentary evidence in support of Rader's story and had talked to Mrs. Mueller, Mrs. Kirby, and Thomas Grant. He had also talked to Canwell, who refused to give Guthman permission to examine the committee's files and accused the *Times* of giving aid and comfort to the Communists.

The *Times* did not publish the results of Guthman's investigation at this point. According to Guthman, it did not do so for two reasons: (1) *Times* editors were not completely sure that Canwell could not prove that Rader was at the Briehl's farm school, and (2) University President Allen was out of town during the summer of 1949, and *Times* editors planned to take the results of Guthman's investigation to Allen in the hope that there would then be some "official action" which the *Times* could use as a "peg" for its story.

When Allen returned to Seattle in the fall, Rader asked him to consider his evidence and any that Canwell might care to present. Allen arranged for a meeting with Canwell for this purpose, and, after going over Rader's evidence and copies of the testimony and affidavits in the New York habeas corpus proceedings supplied by the *Times,* announced, "The University administration is fully satisfied by the present evidence that Mr. Hewitt's allegations concerning Professor Rader have been disproved."

Canwell also examined Rader's evidence but did not join in Allen's conclusion. He told reporters after the meeting that he intended to check that evidence and "if after I have checked the assertions made in this material, I find them to be correct, then I shall have to say that it is obvious that a conflict exists between this material and the statement made by the Committee's witness." Canwell was also reported as having said, when asked if he would be willing to assist in a search of the committee's files for the missing lodge register, "If you think the register has been suppressed, go find it."

After this meeting the *Seattle Times* went on to press for an investigation to determine whether the Canwell committee had suppressed evidence by concealing or destroying the lodge register pages. Attorney General Smith Troy agreed to make such an investigation.

Before President Allen had issued his statement on Rader's case, Canwell had disclosed that he would seek the Republican nomination to oppose United States Senator Warren Magnuson in the 1950 elections. And after the attorney general's proposed investigation was announced, Canwell branded it a "shyster political trick" inspired by the Democrats to injure his candidacy: "There never has been any suppression of evidence and those who are making the charges know it. It is merely an attempt to reduce the whole thing to politics. . . ."

After four months of investigation, Attorney General Troy

announced that he had learned that Canwell committee investigators took register pages bearing Rader's name from Canyon
Creek Lodge but had not yet been able to locate those pages, and
that he intended to ask the president of the senate and the speaker
of the house for permission to search the committee's locked files.
Canwell immediately declared that the lodge register was not in
the files. "It is not and never has been there. I believe I now know
where it is. I believe it can be made available to the Prosecuting
Attorney of King County, and . . . I will attempt to do so."

Another statement to the press issued by Canwell a few days
later contained his only published evaluation of Rader's evidence:

> The missing register was never of sufficient importance to
> cause us to look for it.
>
> Other evidence presented by Professor Rader made it clear
> that he could not have been in New York City in the summer
> of 1938, as had been charged by a witness against him. And ac-
> tually we had no evidence that Rader had been a Communist
> except the so-far unsupported testimony of that one witness.
>
> .   .   .   .   .
>
> [The search for the missing Lodge register is] just a device for
> getting into the records of our committee to find out our sources
> of information about Communist activities. Those sources were
> responsible for our breaking the Alger Hiss case and the latest
> Harry Bridges trial, so naturally the Communist Party leaders
> would like to identify them.

On April 23, 1950, Canwell delivered a stack of loose-leaf pages
to King County Prosecutor Carroll. The pages contained nothing
but signatures and addresses, some of which were followed by dates
and some of which were undated. There were no pages bearing
dates for the first week in August, 1938. At the bottom of one
page were the undated signatures of Virginia and Melvin Rader
of 6017 30th Avenue, N.E., Seattle. The last dated signature preceding theirs on the page was entered June 12, 1938.

Canwell also wrote Carroll a letter to account for the whereabouts of the register pages during the past twenty-one months:

> Because of the loose-leaf character of the records and the nonde-
> script manner in which they were kept, the Committee's investi-
> gators did not feel that they constituted competent evidence and

343

therefore disregarded them entirely, even though they tended
to refute Rader's alibi. They therefore were set aside to be returned to the Canyon Creek Lodge owners. [They] . . . were
taken by one of the Committee's employees to his home, with the
intention of returning them to the Lodge at his convenience.
He was summoned away on other business . . . and subsequently transferred his residence temporarily to another state.
. . . In the intervening months the records were forgotten and
it was not until the recent highly suspicious clamor was created
over these records that he recalled still having them and so advised me.

Two weeks later, Attorney General Troy released a report of
his investigations: He was satisfied from the discovered evidence
that the Raders were at Canyon Creek Lodge during only one
summer and that they appeared there first in June, 1938, and
made arrangements for a month's vacation which they spent
there between August 1 and September 5 of the same summer.

True, the register pages for the first week in August, 1938, were
still missing, but Troy could only report that they "in all probability will never be found." And the pages which Canwell had
"belatedly delivered" to Prosecutor Carroll "conclusively prove
that at the time the report of the Committee was made, evidence
had been discovered and delivered to the [Committee] headquarters showing that the Raders were at the Lodge in 1938, and
that their first appearance was not in 1940 as stated in the report
to the Legislature."

"The only reasonable conclusion," Troy determined, "is that
George Hewitt did not tell the truth when he testified he had
seen Rader at the school in New York in the fall of 1938."

Troy's report concluded with an observation on the significance
of the committee's performance in the Rader case: "I deeply
regret that it has been necessary to point out the inconsistencies
of the report of the Committee to the 1949 Legislature with the
actual facts as revealed by our investigation as to the Rader phase
of its inquiries. It is sincerely hoped that the errors occurring in
the Rader episode will not becloud the otherwise splendid work
of the Committee in exposing the inroads that the Communists
had made in our community structure."

Following this report, Canwell continued his campaign for the Republican senatorial nomination, and in this campaign "Communist Fighter Al Canwell" reiterated his claims that his committee had "broken" the Hiss and Bridges cases. In the primaries in September, 1950, the Republican nomination went to Walter Williams, former national chairman of the Committee for Economic Development.

Canwell gave Williams his full support in the campaign which followed. They joined in denouncing Senator Warren Magnuson as one who "coddled Communists" and in attacking the national Democratic administration of which he was a part because it had "failed to understand and fight Communists inside and outside the government." In the general election in November, Magnuson defeated Williams by 55,000 of the 744,700 votes cast for the office.

In the same general election, the Democrats retained their majority in the lower house of the state legislature, although it was substantially reduced. They also gained a numerical majority of four in the state senate, but the Republicans retained control there through a working coalition with eight Democratic senators. Former Canwell committee members Kimball and Sisson were re-elected; former committee member Rutter did not seek re-election. An initiative measure to reduce old-age assistance grants and medical care, sponsored by Governor Langlie, was adopted by a vote of 394,000 to 296,000 and the Washington Pension Union's competing initiative measure, which would have further liberalized such aid, was defeated by a vote of 535,000 to 159,000.

When the 1951 legislature convened, Governor Langlie reminded it of the Canwell committee's disclosure of "subversive activity" in the state, advised it that, "in the light of the grave emergency which we now face," he would submit a bill "calculated to give support at the state level to the efforts of our various federal agencies charged with the responsibility of combating . . . forces of tyranny and enslavement." The governor's bill, introduced by Senator Kimball, proved to be a copy of Maryland's Ober Act.[5] After some slight amendments, it was enacted.

The 1951 legislature also expanded the "antisubversive" clause of the Appropriation Act to require recipients of welfare funds,

[5] For a description of the Ober Act, see ch. iii.

345

as well as state employees, to file oaths disclaiming belief in or support of "overthrow of the United States government by force or by any illegal or unconstitutional methods." But Governor Langlie vetoed the entire clause in the 1951 Appropriation Act, stating that he did so because the oath requirement would have imposed the burden of a notary's fee on welfare recipients.

Also before the 1951 legislature was a bill introduced by Representative Sisson and a house colleague to create a new legislative un-American activities committee. Although this bill incorporated some of the safeguards provided in the bill introduced by the Democrats in 1949, it did not include enough of them to satisfy the Democratic majority in the house, and again, as in 1949, the effort to create another committee ended in a stalemate between the two houses.

EVALUATION OF THE COMMITTEE'S WORK

Thus ends the record of the Canwell committee. On that record, there is more than the Rader case to raise doubts about the propriety of the committee's activities and the reliability of the evidence which the committee collected.

The committee concerned itself almost exclusively with the political beliefs and associations of the people it investigated. It collected and published two volumes of testimony naming a great number of persons as members of the Communist Party, members of "Communist front organizations," "fellow travelers," or followers of the "Party line." How is this evidence to be appraised?

In some instances the published testimony has been corroborated by the admissions of the persons concerned. Six of the faculty members named in the committee's hearings admitted past membership in the party. Two others later admitted present membership. But verification of the committee's evidence in eight cases does not demonstrate that it was accurate in all other cases —nor, indeed, that it was accurate in any other case. In fact, Melvin Rader has demonstrated that George Hewitt's testimony about him was completely false. What, then, is the worth of the bulk of the evidence published by the Canwell committee?

346

Much of that evidence is questionable upon its face. The testimony of Witnesses George Hewitt, Howard Smith, and Sarah Eldredge is at points so irrational as to raise serious doubts about their credibility. The testimony of Ellsworth Wills, Ward Warren, Mrs. Costigan, Mrs. Fogg, and Mrs. Winther reveals that frequently when they characterized meetings as "communist," "unit," or "fraction" meetings, or when they named people as members of the Communist Party, they were not testifying from personal knowledge but were merely offering their own opinions or the opinions of someone else, without in either case being called upon to disclose any factual basis for the opinions. The same is true of the testimony of Louis Budenz and Nat Honig when they were asked to testify from "official knowledge." And, although the testimony of other witnesses does not affirmatively disclose this defect, so much of it is clearly a statement of opinion rather than fact that it is impossible to evaluate it.

All of the evidence about "Communist front organizations" is equally dubious on its face. The testimony on this point again consists of the opinions of witnesses, with no disclosure of the facts on which the opinions were based. Although this testimony was liberally supplemented by the introduction of various "lists," the reliability of the lists is similarly open to question.

The three lists issued by the United States attorney general for use in the federal loyalty program, and accepted and used by the Canwell committee as reliable listings of "Communist fronts," were characterized by the attorney general as lists of organizations which are "totalitarian," "fascist," "Communist," or "subversive," or which have adopted a policy of "advocating or approving the commission of acts of force or violence to deny other persons their rights under the Constitution of the United States," or which "seek to alter the form of government of the United States by unconstitutional means." These lists were compiled without notice and hearing to the organizations concerned. To date, the attorney general's office has not revealed either the criteria which were employed in defining these nebulous categories or the evidence upon which it was determined that an organization belonged in one of the categories however defined. But in actions brought by the Joint Anti-Fascist Refugee Committee, the National Council of American-Soviet Friendship, and the International Workers Order—all listed as "Communist" organizations by the attorney general—the Supreme Court has recently held that an organization seeking a court order striking its name from the attorney general's list is entitled to a hearing on the propriety of the listing. Acceptance of these lists as evidence, therefore, is an act of faith. And nothing is added to their persuasiveness by the fact that some of the attorney general's classification were endorsed by witnesses Louis Budenz and J. B. Matthews, who likewise did not disclose the criteria or the facts upon which their conclusions were based.

Similar lists compiled by the United States House Committee on Un-American Activities and by the California un-American activities committee are also based on undefined criteria and on evidence as impossible to evaluate as the testimony taken before the Canwell committee.

There remains the list of "communist front organizations" introduced by J. B. Matthews—compiled by him according to a definition and upon evidence which he did not reveal. This list, like the others, is entitled to whatever weight the judgment of its author is worth, and the general tenor of Matthews' testimony is not such as to inspire great confidence in that judgment.

Even if any or all of these lists could be accepted as persuasive evidence that the organizations listed are "fronts" for the Communist Party, that would demonstrate no more than that members of the party were active in the organizations and sought with varying success to use the organizations' influence in behalf of one or more elements of the party's program—it would not necessarily prove anything about any particular individual member or sponsor or the organization. Even J. B. Matthews admitted in his testimony before the Canwell committee, "There is little or no connection between the sponsor of a Communist front organization and the organization itself subsequent to the time the sponsor agreed to lend his name. . . . [T]he Communist Party . . . probably avoids communicating with its sponsors subsequent to the time they lend their names, lest some of the sponsors should find out what the organization is up to." Yet Matthews' definition of a "fellow traveler" in his testimony before the committee was "any person who has sponsored or been affiliated with twenty or more of these Communist front organizations." And the Canwell committee treated sponsorship of or membership in "Communist fronts" not only as additional evidence against persons on whom it had adduced testimony of Communist Party membership or "following the Party line," but also as evidence worth submitting on persons on whom it had presented no other evidence whatsoever.

The evidence offered to prove that various persons and organizations "followed the Party line" is also, for the most part, nothing but a statement of the witnesses' unsubstantiated opinions. Where specific evidence was adduced in support of the opinion, that evidence suggests that the taking of positions which coincide with positions taken by the Communist Party on three or four issues is enough to demonstrate that the person or organization "follows" the party line. And for this purpose any sort of issue will suffice —whether it be a question of the continuation of an un-American activities committee, urging the San Francisco board of supervisors to take a firm stand on racial discrimination, or entering the United States Army.

Perhaps the committee's evidence is stronger than it appears. Perhaps the opinions of many or most of its witnesses are rational judgments which can be completely substantiated by facts within the personal knowledge of the witnesses. But the committee did not demonstrate that this was so, and the manner in which the witnesses were interrogated does not indicate that the committee was concerned with the basis for the opinions offered.

When a witness testified that some person was a member of the Communist Party or a "fellow traveler," that some organization was a "Communist front" or "Communist-dominated," or that a person or an organization "followed the Party line," he was not asked to explain what he meant or to disclose the basis for his statement. Obviously, that statement was all the committee wanted—interrogation of the witness then went on to other individuals and other organizations.

Indeed, if the witness was slow to offer his opinions, interrogation brought him quickly to the point. Thus, to cite only two of numerous instances: When Louis Budenz was asked about the Seattle Labor School and replied that he was "not very familiar with it," Investigator Houston immediately asked, "You have in your official capacity heard it referred to as a Party organization and Party School?" and was satisfied with the reply, "That's right." When Harriet Riley testified that her husband, as King County secretary of the Workers' Alliance, "worked very closely with the Old Age Pension" in 1938 and 1939, Investigator Whipple asked, "Just for the purpose of clarification of our own record—do you state at this time that the Old Age Pension Union was dominated and controlled during this period by the members of the Communist Party?" Mrs. Riley replied, "Yes, sir," and was not asked to elaborate on her answer.

This sort of interrogation is well designed to produce a collection of rumors, opinions, suspicions, and perhaps hallucinations which will furnish content for newspaper headlines, but it is not likely to get information of much reliability from even the most cautious lay witness. When employed on professional witnesses like Louis Budenz, J. B. Matthews, George Hewitt, and Manning Johnson, and on other witnesses so obviously susceptible to suggestion as James T. Sullivan and Sarah Eldredge, the testimony which it elicits is highly suspect.

Intrinsically, then, the evidence adduced by the Canwell committee appears highly unreliable. There are also extrinsic indications of unreliability.

The evidence accumulated by Melvin Rader to clear himself of the charges of George Hewitt impugns not only the trustworthiness of Hewitt but also that of Manning Johnson, who testified in the New York habeas corpus proceedings in corroboration of Hewitt's story about Rader. And the obstacles encountered by Rader in his attempt to cross-examine Hewitt and in his search for the Canyon Creek Lodge register, as well as the assistance given to Hewitt by the Canwell committee in the New York habeas corpus proceedings, again suggests that the committee's chief concern was not the accuracy of the testimony taken at its hearings.

Moreover, the record of the cross-examination of some of the Canwell committee witnesses at the university tenure hearing raises further doubts about the witnesses' credibility. From that record it is apparent that Joseph Kornfeder was willing to label Consumers Union a "Communist front" although he knew nothing at all about the organization, that the only basis for Mrs.

Fogg's "acceptance" of Ralph Gundlach as a member of the Communist Party was that Gundlach was "acting in the front organizations," that Howard Smith was unable to identify any of the "plenum meetings" where he had seen Gundlach except that possibly some of them were meetings of the Joint Anti-Fascist Refugee Committee, that H. C. Armstrong had taken a false oath in judicial proceedings once while a member of the Communist Party and again after leaving the party, and that Mrs. Costigan's characterization of Gundlach as a "Communist" and her characterization of meetings which Gundlach attended as "Communist meetings" was based on reasoning which proceeded in this fashion: I am a Communist; I am attending this meeting; I know Gundlach is a Communist because he has never made any attempt to convince me that he is not; Gundlach is also attending this meeting; since we two Communists are attending this meeting it must be a Communist meeting; the fact that Gundlach is attending this Communist meeting is further evidence that he is a Communist.

The testimony of Professor Albert Franzke in the tenure hearing also emphasizes the completely haphazard way in which the attorney general's lists of organizations were employed to establish that various individuals belonged to "Communist front organizations." The Seattle Labor School was organized in the fall of 1945. The attorney general first listed the School on December 5, 1947. Assuming with the Canwell committee that this listing demonstrated that the school was a "Communist front" at the time of the listing, it certainly does not demonstrate that it was a "Communist front" at any substantially earlier time. And, according to Franzke—whose testimony on this point is not contradicted by any evidence taken in the tenure hearing or at the Canwell committee hearings—the nature of the school began to change sometime in the fall of 1946. Franzke testified that he resigned his connection with the school in February, 1947, and Gundlach testified that he resigned in March, 1947. Yet the Canwell committee, without taking any evidence on the nature of the school at any time before or after the attorney general's listing, and without disclosing the time during which any individual was connected with the school, cited the connection as an instance of affiliation with a "Communist front" not only in the cases of

Franzke and Gundlach, but also in the case of Mrs. James, Albert Ottenheimer, Professor Phillips, Professor Gundlach, Professor Eby, and several other members of the university faculty.

To the extent that evidence employed by the Canwell committee was used again in the tenure hearing, then, its probative value was seriously impaired by the opportunity afforded in the tenure hearing for cross-examination and for the submission of rebuttal evidence. No such opportunity was allowed in the Canwell committee hearings and the committee explained in its final report that cross-examination was not permitted because "Communist attorneys are notoriously skilled in disruption" and a legislative committee operating without power to punish for contempt could not deal effectively with disruptive tactics. But, whatever the political beliefs of the attorneys appearing before the Canwell committee, and however skilled they may have been as disruptors, Canwell was able to deal with all other "disruptive" moves at the hearings by his command of the attending officers of the State Patrol. And the tenure committee, operating without contempt powers or the assistance of the State Patrol, allowed these same attorneys to cross-examine witnesses and submit rebuttal evidence with no disruption of the proceedings whatever. The result of this testing of evidence which the Canwell committee accepted without test indicates, moreover, that some risk of disruption must be assumed if facts are to be separated from opinions and fantasies.

But it seems obvious from this report that the Canwell committee was not after facts about the persons and organizations it investigated—it was after charges. And it is equally obvious that the charges which it accumulated and published are much too unreliable to form the basis for any proper sort of legislative action. In fact, the evidence collected by the committee was not acted upon by the 1949 legislature. And, while the 1951 legislature did extend the "anti-subversive" oath requirement to recipients of welfare funds, as recommended by the committee, Governor Langlie vetoed the entire oath requirement in order to prevent its application to such recipients. Hence, the committee's evidence has not produced any new legislation, unless it contributed to the 1951 enactment of the Washington version of the Ober Act. In advising the legislature that his administration would submit the bill which became the Washington Act, Governor Langlie adverted to the Canwell committee's "disclosures" of "the degree to which disloyal groups had infiltrated into organizations of our senior citizens, into various economic and educational groups" and declared that "additional action . . . must be taken immediately" "in the light of the grave emergency which we now face." But there is no available evidence of the extent to which the Canwell committee's "disclosures" may have influenced those members of the legislature who voted in favor of the governor's bill.

Apart from its possible influence on the legislature, a number of other consequences are traceable to the publicity given the testimony of committee witnesses. The damage done to Professor Rader and his family by the false testimony of George Hewitt is apparent—they were forced to live and work under the "Communist" label for more than a year before Rader, at considerable personal effort and expense, was able to clear himself of Hewitt's charges. The more lasting damage done to the Seattle Repertory Playhouse by the testimony of Hewitt and others of no more obvious trustworthiness is also apparent. Similar damage to many other persons who were identified as "Communists," "fellow-travelers," or followers of the "Party line," and who have had no opportunity to disprove the charges against them, is incalculable.

On the full record of the Washington investigation another conclusion also seems obvious: Neither in the investigations conducted by the legislative committee on un-American activities nor in any investigation resulting from the committee's work has there been any disclosure of "un-American activities" on the part of the persons or organizations investigated. This conclusion is apparent without any necessity for speculation about the meaning of the term "un-American," in view of the nature of the activities disclosed.

Very little of the evidence accumulated in the Washington investigation discloses activities of any sort—most of it is confined to matters of individual belief and affiliation. True, it is a currently popular theory that affiliation—where it is affiliation with the Communist Party—involves participating in a "conspiracy" to overthrow the government by force and violence, and that

353

every member of the party is therefore vicariously responsible for the activities of all his "coconspirators." And support for this theory is drawn from the Supreme Court's recent affirmance of the conviction of eleven leaders of the Communist Party on such a "conspiracy" theory. This theory is, of course, an application of the doctrine of guilt-by-association which evades the difficult problem of proving individual wrongdoing by assuming it. And, while our legal system does recognize a crime of conspiracy which Justice Jackson has characterized as "so vague that it almost defies definition," and which has now been extended to reach national officers of the Communist Party, it has not yet been extended to reach every member of the party.

Without the aid of the "conspiracy" theory, the evidence produced in the Washington investigation, even when supplemented by events not recorded by the investigators, reveals only the following activities:

1. In 1942 and 1948 the Washington Pension Union resorted successfully to popular initiative, and in other years resorted successfully to pressure on the state legislature, to increase the minimum old age pension from $30 to $60 and to liberalize eligibility requirements and medical benefits. In 1950 Governor Langlie's administration resorted successfully to popular initiative to reduce the old age assistance and medical benefits from the high point reached in 1948.

2. While Thane Summers was a student at the University of Washington from 1933 to 1936 one or more of his instructors introduced him to books which his father concluded, after "more or less superficial examination," were "very radical in their essence and influence."

3. A great many people attended a great many meetings—including the meetings of the "university group" of the Communist Party and the meetings of the "Communist cell" in the Washington State legislature. But the only evidence of what was done in those meetings is the testimony of Professor Winther that the "university group" reviewed books and the recollection of Canwell committee member Thomas Bienz: "Many a time I have heard the strains of the Communist International being sung by

354

the Communist legislators as I passed by their committee room (no. 13) on the second floor in the State capitol building."

More alarming than any of these activities are the activities of the Canwell committee and those who aided it in connection with the Rader case. Clearly, it was not within the proper function of the Canwell committee to confiscate and withhold evidence relevant to the perjury charge against Hewitt. Nor was it proper for the Canwell committee, or officers of the federal Immigration and Naturalization Service, or County Commissioner McLean, to bring pressure on the King County prosecuting attorney to compel him to drop criminal charges which he considered well founded.

Indefensible also is the performance of the Bronx County district attorney's office and of New York Supreme Court Justice Aaron Levy in employing habeas corpus proceedings for a purpose clearly forbidden by the Supreme Court of the United States. On the basis of this obviously deliberate misuse of the proceedings and of District Attorney Foley's distorted version of the facts, and without considering any of the evidence upon which the perjury charge against Hewitt was based, they reached the conclusion that there was no foundation for the charge—a conclusion which on this record is clearly erroneous. Acting on that conclusion, they effectively prevented a determination of the validity of the charge in a proper proceeding and insulated Hewitt from the responsibility which the laws of every state impose upon witnesses who give sworn testimony in official proceedings.

True, King County Prosecutor Charles Carroll might have prevented this action by sending a representative to the proceedings. And, that failing, he could have sought reversal of Justice Levy's decision by appealing from it—even Assistant District Attorney John B. Lee, who prepared the case for Foley's office, admits that the decision was "technically incorrect." But the fact that Carroll demonstrated no more diligence in prosecuting the extradition proceedings than was displayed by New York City police in apprehending Hewitt for extradition merely adds to the instances of inexcusable conduct by government officials. It in no way mitigates the impropriety of what was done in the New York habeas corpus proceedings.

To this record of improper action by government officials must be added the discreditable performance of the Seattle press. The flamboyant manner in which both the *Post-Intelligencer* and the *Times* reported the irresponsible charges of the Canwell Committee seems to be accepted journalistic practice today. But, in the case of the *Times,* this performance affords a strange contrast to its editors' unwillingness to publish Melvin Rader's evidence until University President Allen had accepted it, although Allen's acceptance adds nothing to the overwhelming persuasiveness of that evidence. The best that can be said for the *Seattle Times* is that, while its editors lacked the courage necessary to expose some of the most irregular activities of the Canwell committee, they sought to encourage others to do so.

But if the performance of the *Times* was timorous, that of the *Post-Intelligencer* was reprehensible. The *Post-Intelligencer* joined with the committee in some of the committee's improper activities. True, Managing Editor Edwart T. Stone denies that this is so:

> We had and have no interest in the Canwell Committee except for news coverage. Mr. Niendorff was assigned to the Canwell investigation as a reporter and because of the extraordinary interest in and importance of the investigation devoted considerable time to it as any good reporter should. . . . However, the Canwell Committee was created by legislative enactment without any pressure from this paper . . . and the Committee functioned on its own so far as the Post-Intelligencer is concerned.

Perhaps a "good reporter" for the *Post-Intelligencer* is supposed to write consistently distorted accounts of the testimony of witnesses in a legislative hearing. And perhaps this sort of performance is all that Canwell committee member Sydney Stevens had in mind when he characterized Niendorff as "the Committee's guiding light." But neither this denial nor the one Stone previously published in his paper demonstrates the propriety of the use of Stone's office for, and the participation of Stone and Niendorff in, a conference called to induce the prosecuting attorney to drop the perjury charge against Hewitt.

The activities of the committee and its allies are clearly more subversive of established legal processes than any activities disclosed by the committee's investigation. Indeed, by the standards which the committee professed to follow in its work, the actions of the committee, of officials of the federal Immigration and Naturalization Service, of certain New York officials, and of County Commissioner McLean, were "un-American." The Brookings Institution's *Suggested Standards for Determining Un-American Activities* states:

> It is un-American for any department, agency, or officer of the government to exercise or attempt to exercise any power not conferred by law or to use any power in a way not authorized by law. . . . [T]he objectives of the Committee . . . are not . . . to attempt to try, prosecute, or punish any individual or group for any crime or misdemeanor, or alleged crime or misdemeanor, or to interfere with the prosecution of any individual or group by the duly constituted authorities.

The resolution which created the Canwell committee authorized it to "investigate . . . individuals, groups or organizations whose activities are such as to indicate a purpose to foment internal strife, discord and dissension; infiltrate and undermine the stability of our American institutions; confuse and mislead the people; and impede the normal progress of the state and nation." On this record, the only activities which clearly indicate the proscribed purposes are those of the Canwell committee and some of its supporters.

VII. A GENERAL VIEW

By WALTER GELLHORN   *January 1, 1951*

THE CHAPTERS in this book revolve around a single central
problem. They deal with efforts of the several states to forestall
subversive activities. The differences among the chapters reflect
differences of emphasis among the states themselves—New York
and Maryland in the East, California and Washington in the
West, Illinois and Michigan in the Midwest.

The first and deepest issue these diverse chronicles raise is
whether there has been excessive rather than reasonable preoccupation with "subversion." The American system of government
is based upon freedom and especially upon freedom of ideas. As
the preceding chapters show, that freedom has sometimes been
threatened and, indeed, impaired by efforts to preserve it. Legislative intrusion upon education, upon personal privacy, and even
upon the opportunity to appeal publicly to the electorate has become frequent rather than unusual. Usually this has been justified
as a measure of needed protection against communism. Whether
it is *for* democracy as well as against communism is a question that
sometimes remains unexplored. The unexplored question is a
basic one for our generation. Today as perhaps never before
Americans need an affirmative ideal instead of a merely negative
conviction.

Every democratically minded person properly detests the bru-
talities and excesses of dictatorship, whether "proletarian" or any
other. Every patriot understandably views with acute suspicion
the maneuvers of a giant rival—a rival that preaches the inevita-
bility of world revolution and meanwhile practices the coldly

[Mr. Gellhorn is professor of law in Columbia University.]

358

cynical power politics of old-fashioned nationalism. Every political observer appreciates that the future's grim uncertainties on the international plane inevitably produce domestic insecurities as well.

But when all this has been fully acknowledged, one has still to ask whether the people of the United States have perhaps yielded to an overexcitement that will debilitate them if not soon controlled. Prudence can be overborne by hate and fear as well as by carelessness. Reviewing the record of state action may help us to discover whether emotion is supplanting reason in matters of urgent national concern.

THE LAWS ON THE BOOKS

When the American state legislatures had adjourned their 1950 sessions, they left behind them statute books containing well over 300 enactments aimed at what may be lumped together as subversive activities. One hesitates to define a term that the states themselves use without precision. Subversion, say the legislatures, is to be stifled or investigated; but often they leave it to others to supply a fuller conception of what is meant.

There can no doubt be general agreement that, at the very least, subversive activities include (1) the use of violent or otherwise unconstitutional means to change this country's political or economic institutions; (2) the commission of espionage, sabotage, and other crimes of stealth in behalf of foreign enemies or domestic cliques; (3) the bearing of arms against the United States, or other affirmative behavior in aid of hostile forces; and (4) the entry into a conspiracy to perform these acts or the actual though unsuccessful attempt to do them. Conduct of these types is unquestionably within the reach of criminal laws in every American state. It is well that they should be.

During the present century, however, the catalogue of crimes has expanded. The laws today reach beyond the forbidden activities. They often touch as well those who advocate or teach the propriety of forbidden activities in any circumstances. The advocates are themselves held to be engaged in illegal conduct, even though their advocacy may have created no imminent likelihood of actual misconduct.

359

Even more significant than this development has been an enlarged concern about groups as distinct from individuals. Traditionally the criminal law has dealt with the malefactor, the one who himself committed an offense. Departing from this tradition is the recent tendency to ascribe criminal potentialities to a body of persons (usually, though not invariably, the Communists) and to lay restraints upon any individual who can be linked with the group. This, of course, greatly widens the concept of subversive activities, because it results, in truth, in forgetting about activities altogether. It substitutes associations as the objects of the law's impact. Any attempt to define subversion as used in modern statutes must therefore refer to the mere possibility of activity as well as to present lawlessness.

Since violence has not been the norm of politics within the states of this country, the abundance of penal statutes dealing with forcible assaults upon government may perhaps arouse wonder. Two explanations are immediately apparent.

First, criminal laws are adopted only rarely as a response to an existing crime wave. Rather, they prescribe the consequences of antisocial conduct should it occur, though everyone hopes it will not. Law expresses a community sense about evil. Embodying this sense in a formal utterance may in itself serve to reinforce the group ethic. Whatever discourages misdeeds is all to the good.

Second, the legislatures of many states may face somewhat the same problems and pressures at about the same time. When this happens, some of the legislatures may fail to analyze the issues with calm independence but may instead merely seize upon a conveniently available example. Thirty-two of the states, for instance, have passed laws against the display of red flags, apparently on the theory that abolition of the symbol will prevent the reality of revolution. Twenty-six of these thirty-two laws were enacted in a single year, 1919. The style trend swept the nation with the inexorable force of the onetime craze for Empress Eugénie hats or the autosuggestive theories of Dr. Coué.

Similarly, the criminal syndicalism laws reached the peak of their popularity during the Red Scare days immediately after World War I, when some seventeen states adopted them; more than two decades passed before an eighteenth state was added to the list. Eighteen states placed sedition statutes in effect during the same brief period. Various "oath laws" have had their vogue, too, not because of fully demonstrated efficacy but apparently because their passage gave their backers a sense of purposeful accomplishment.

At the present moment one may anticipate a surge of sentiment for measures that resemble Maryland's antisubversion statute of 1949. This law, discussed at length in an earlier chapter by Professor Prendergast, bars "disloyal" persons from public employment, outlaws the Communists and organizations that are foreign-controlled with subversion as their objective, and establishes machinery to expose the malign political forces that, as the legislature declared, are weakening democracy's foundations. At the very first opportunity the legislature of Mississippi exhibited its zeal to emulate. It solemnly found in 1950 that heroic measures were needed to save Mississippi from being undermined by the plotting minions of a foreign power. And so it copied into its statute books a considerable portion of the Maryland law. J. Edgar Hoover has recently informed a Congressional committee that the Communist Party in Mississippi consists of exactly one man. This lone conspirator must be kept busy indeed as he fulfills the duties of state chairman of his party, its rank-and-file membership, and the foreign-directed forces that menace the state.

To some extent the blossoming of yet further antisubversion laws may simply reflect imperfect analysis of the problems to be faced. Not long ago, for example, Colorado's attorney general was quoted as having declared that according to "unimpeachable" information seventy-five Communists had met in Denver and had individually been assigned "a specific job, such as bombing a radio station, or the telephone company, or the public service company." One might have supposed that at this point the attorney general would have examined the state's sabotage prevention law and the judicial decisions dealing with conspiracies and attempts to commit crimes. Then one might have surmised either that the attorney general would move against those whose criminal plans could be unimpeachably proved, or that he would suggest plugging up whatever gaps he might unexpectedly find in the existing laws. Not so, however, in Colorado. Instead of coming to grips directly with what he regarded as a "master sabotage plan for the state," the attorney general announced his determination to draft a bill that would outlaw communism and subversion.

In all truth, as one reads the many laws that already denounce the dangerous conduct to which Communists are deemed committed, one may wonder at the continuing demand for additional legislation. If the American Communists are as intent upon lawlessness as they are said to be, there appears to be a generally adequate body of statutes to cope with their misdeeds. If, on the other hand, the domestic devotees of Stalin do not violate the existing prohibitions, one wonders whether they are really so menacing that still more laws are needed in order to save the rest of us. Of course, many legislatures are concerned about the possibility of political lawlessness in the future rather than about crimes in the immediate present. For that reason they seek ways to imprison Communists in anticipation of criminality that has not yet occurred and as a means of forestalling it. This is the essential purport of laws that address themselves solely to political identification. Statutes of this type have their appeal because it is often easier to prove that a man is a Communist than it is to prove the commission of some specific offense. There is grave question, however, whether "anticipatory criminality" ought to gain recognition in American law.

Moreover, the influence of American Communists seems on the whole to be at low ebb, rather than ever mounting as the state legislatures formally declare. The Communist movement may possibly have had allure for idealists in the early years after the Russian revolution. Certainly by now that allure has been dimmed if not altogether extinguished by the character of the Soviet regime. Recruitment of Americans by the Communists has been virtually stopped by the steady betterment in this country's economy and social conditions during the past generation. Furthermore, most Americans are utterly repelled by the Communist Party's unbending support of the Soviet Union's policy of the moment. Few persons are likely to embrace a movement that, ascribing all virtuous wisdom to Russia's leadership, propagates the myth that whatever benefits the U.S.S.R. is good for the U.S.A.

One may fully accept the proposition that the Communist Party in this country would, if it could, suppress for others the freedoms it now seeks to claim for itself. One may accept, too, that among the Communists there are individuals who might readily embrace espionage or sabotage as instruments of political action. But when all is said and done, American legislation constantly strays from the point. At times legislative ingenuity seems to be exercised not so much to protect the commonwealth against lawlessness as, in essence, to find new ways of expressing loathing. Pennsylvania, for example, bars subversives from the benefits of its various welfare and public aid programs, except that it does allow a *blind* Communist to receive a grant. Similarly, Ohio requires unemployment insurance recipients to swear that they have no tie with a party that advocates forcible overthrow of the government, which is one of the conventional legislative circumlocutions for "Communist Party." So it goes in state after state.

Almost inescapable is the conclusion that at least some of the antisubversion, or anti-Communist, laws are not intrinsically justifiable as societal safeguards. They have been enacted because thus the legislators can demonstrate hatred of communism.

THE PRESSURES OF POLITICS

In part this satisfies a sincerely felt hunger for expression. In part it may merely satisfy a desire for personal advancement. The instinct for political self-preservation has undoubtedly underlain some of the votes cast in recent years in support of purportedly anti-Communist legislation. Proponents of measures that could well be opposed as needless or otherwise unmeritorious, have discovered an easy way to forestall serious debate. Once the issue can be cast in the black-and-white terms of "voting for the Communist Conspiracy or against it," even an extreme program may pass with flying colors. Only the most courageous legislator runs the political risk of casting a negative vote that can be interpreted as sympathy with communism.

Martin Dies was an early exploiter of this reality of contemporary politics. When his temporary Committee on Un-American Activities came before the House of Representatives for renewed life or for enlarged appropriations, many Congressmen privately denounced but publicly supported Dies's work. To oppose his requests was to invite distortion of the objector's motives. Since for many legislators re-election to office is a more important desideratum than is the proclaiming of an abstract truth, the Dies brand of persuasion was highly effective.

The Dies example has been followed successfully in the states. One of the most complex and far-reaching problems of our times has thus been reduced to a simple formula.

In Maryland, as an illustration, the wide-ranging Ober Law of 1949 scarcely required debate. The choice was appealingly and clearly presented: Americanism against Communism. On that question there could be no substantial division. The senate adopted the proposed legislation unanimously, the house by a vote of 115–1. The lone dissenter was chastened by defeat in the next election.

In Detroit the electorate was called on to approve a charter amendment that would create a full-blown "loyalty program" involving inquiry into municipal employees' associations and beliefs. As the day for voting drew near and as a campaign against the amendment's merits was gaining momentum, the proposal's supporters tended to fall back to safe ground. A vote against the amendment, they said, "will be seized upon and broadcast throughout the world as votes for Communism in Detroit." Few "votes for Communism" were tallied after that warning.

In Massachusetts a legislative committee bottled up from November, 1949, until July, 1950, a resolution calling for a state investigation of subversive and un-American activities. Responsible leaders of the legislature steadily opposed the inquiry as unnecessary. Only a small segment of the press was sympathetic to the idea. The powerful rules committee formally issued an adverse report, declaring that the suggested probe was both needless and unwise. This is serious opposition, indeed. It did not suffice. When the measure was brought before the Massachusetts house on a roll call vote, its sponsors declared ominously that the record would now expose who was for communism and who was against. The tabulated vote showed 190 in favor of the investigation and only 19 opposed; the senate quickly approved on a voice vote. Hailing the outcome, Representative Edmond J. Donlan (Democrat, Boston), the initiator of the project, exclaimed: "Mas-

sachusetts has told the world we are united behind our leaders in
the determination to oppose Communist aggression. . . . Massachusetts boys, fighting and dying in Korea, will know that we at
home stand solidly behind them and will not tolerate attempts at
home to weaken our will to resist the common enemy."

How many patriots, when the issue is put in those terms, could
bring themselves to vote "no"? Obviously, not very many. Unfortunately, demagogy is reinforced by each concession, for conces-
sions fortify the presuppositions on which demagogy builds.

Only occasionally in the recent past has it seemed feasible to
refocus a debate that has been led onto the false ground of "for-or-
against Our Country." The 1949 legislative session in California
offers one of the most dramatic examples.

In that year the investigating committee that had functioned
since 1941 under Senator Tenney's leadership brought forward
for the first time a comprehensive legislative program. Ten bills,
two constitutional amendments, and a concurrent resolution were
offered. They dealt with such varied matters as the legal profession,
the schools, and the labor movement; the teaching of "any other
system or plan of government except the American system or plan"
with intent to create a preference in students' minds for anything
different; and the taking of loyalty oaths by candidates for office
and even by elected legislators. Senator Tenney from the start
sought to create an atmosphere in which cautious evaluation
would be unlikely. Opponents of his proposals, he opined, "are
guilty. People who are not Communists have nothing to fear."

Nevertheless, a first ripple of opposition to some of the proposals came after a while from the non-Communist California
League of Women Voters. The bravery of this disinterested act
was quickly recognized by an unnamed senator who, congratulat-
ing the league, wrote revealingly as follows: "One hesitates to
express his honest convictions in a public forum because of the
danger of being misunderstood and forever labeled as being a
'Fellow-traveler,' leftist, disloyal, or some other derogatory term,
which may prejudice people against him and seriously handicap
his future usefulness."

That the cautious senator's fears were not unfounded was soon
demonstrated. One of Tenney's aides and leading propagandists

quickly proclaimed that all who stood against the bills, "be he Communist, fellow-traveler, or yellow-traveler, is as dangerously un-American as the openly avowed Red traitors. Such individuals should be and must be forced to a showdown to stand up and be counted on this simple challenge: Are you a loyal American, and are you actively opposed to Communism?"

The time for voting within the senate drew near. Each of the Tenney bills underwent heatedly serious discussion, for their implications were indeed broad. But when the votes were taken, the opposition all but vanished. Passage was by margins of 32–1, 33–1, 27–0, 31–0, and 27–4.

Only when the Tenney program reached the assembly did it lose momentum. There, for reasons still unclear, the conservatively disposed speaker and an assemblyman of known anti-Communist views joined in opposing the senate-approved measures, which thereupon were allowed to die in committee. Their acts proved that others than "Red traitors" could doubt the desirability of Tenneyism. In the end the Tenney committee was undone by its own insistence that all opponents were Communist sympathizers. But it took many years and many excesses before the Tenney proposals could be weighed on their own merits instead of on the demerits of communism.

Still, there are unpredictabilities in this field as in others. In 1949 one might have asserted that Oklahoma was on the verge of an educational pogrom. Legislators who were hostile to the University of Oklahoma had created a committee to inquire into the Communist forces that were by hypothesis always at work in the state's educational institutions; and stringent oaths for teachers and students alike, going far beyond the conventional commitments to support the constitution and observe the laws, had been proposed for enactment.

Within the space of a few days rather than a few years, however, the crisis passed. An astute legislator observed that the suggested oath requirements, which bore with special heaviness on out-of-state students, were capable of producing a public catastrophe; if they had been literally applied, he exclaimed, they might conceivably have barred as a student a distinguished football player who had migrated to Oklahoma from a nearby state. Still reeling from this blow, the sponsors of inquiry into communism in higher learning held their first hearing. The chairman's difficulty with rules of elementary grammar gave newspaper writers a chance to wax satirical. And a parade of witnesses—deans and department heads who were of exemplary political purity—made a farce out of the fears that had launched the investigation. Almost before it commenced, it was over. Ordinarily, the fever endures much longer before it has run its course.[1]

ONE POOR ACT BEGETS ANOTHER

The legislative campaign against subversive elements rarely ends with the passage of one law or even a series of laws. First attempts to suppress or correct the detested doctrines and their adherents having failed to produce the desired sense of security, proponents of statutory controls feel that a fresh start must be made.

What high hopes attend the enactment of loyalty oath laws! What comfort there is in believing that at last the ranks of public employees and educators will be purified! Yet, once the laws are changed, the old doubts survive. Communist infiltration is still possible, for the really dangerous "Reds," the unidentified plotters, are unlikely to stickle at taking the oaths required of them. Of course, a few people always balk, but they seem to be the wrong

[1] The above lines were written at the end of 1950. In 1951 there was a recurrence of the 1949 fever. In the spring of 1951 the Oklahoma legislature imposed an oath requirement that includes a disclaimer of affiliation with, and membership during the preceding five years in, any "group" which has been "officially determined by the United States Attorney General or other authorized public agency of the United States to be a communist front or subversive organization." In addition to this vague and retroactive provision, the statute requires a declaration of willingness to "take up arms in the defense of the United States in time of War, or National Emergency, if necessary." Numerous members of the staffs of Oklahoma University and Oklahoma Agricultural and Mechanical College (among them a British exchange professor) were instantly dismissed on May 19, just before the end of the academic session, for failure to execute the oath. The oath requirement has since been declared valid by the Oklahoma courts.

people. After some years of operation, the loyalty oath required of Detroit's municipal employees had claimed a single casualty— a member of the sect of Jehovah's Witnesses. The first effect of the Ober Act in Maryland was to snare three Quakers whose religious rather than political dogmas prevented their conscientious compliance with the statute. In California a number of academics lost their appointments because they were unwilling to assert their innocence of communism, even though nobody so much as hinted that they were in fact guilty. In short, the bag has been a disappointing one.

Identification of the enemy is therefore sometimes sought by another device—the enforced registration of organizations that are under foreign control or that advocate overthrowing the government. In 1940 Congress enacted a statute that organizations of those types must register with the attorney general, under dire penalties for disobedience. But the Communist Party, one of the targets of the Voorhis law, has never registered, nor has it been prosecuted for failing to do so. A similar statute in California, enacted as long ago as 1941, and a Michigan law of 1947 have equally failed to arouse a wave of confession and repentance. Organizations at which they were directed have not caught the hint. Not a one has registered.

Of course, that does not mean that the registration device has been abandoned. Instead, it is given fresh application, as in some of the provisions of the Internal Security Act of 1950. Even though this type of law may not lead organizations to register themselves with the authorities, the statutes may open the way to prosecution for nonregistration. Meanwhile, though, something else must be done to provide the protective coating American society is thought to need.

Sometimes the substitute proposals can bestir a chuckle. In New York, for example, the legislature once considered requiring that all school buses be painted red, white, and blue. Multicolored transportation, it was thought, might rouse in the young riders a patriotic fervor that would offset the doubtful teachings of their instructors. Usually, however, the measures are marked by severity rather than levity.

Texas not long ago decided to require expulsion of "disloyal"

368

students from its institutions of learning. When a distinguished professor and a delegation of students sought to be heard in opposition on traditionally respected civil libertarian grounds, they were roughly received. The professor, shouted one of the legislators, "ought to be run out of the University and State," while the students "ought to be locked up in an insane asylum." His oratorical outburst seemingly reflected the sentiments of many colleagues, for the bill passed the house unanimously and was speedily approved by the senate.

Expressions like these can of course be discounted as hotheaded contributions to debate. At the same time they are not entirely unsymptomatic of an increasing impatience. When "subversion" stubbornly resists being suppressed, it is an easy next step to deportation or detention. Michigan in 1950 went so far as to provide life imprisonment as a penalty for writing or speaking subversive words and created a secret political police force to obtain evidence of transgressions.

One shudders to think of the next step after that. Michigan has abolished the death sentence, so life imprisonment is the supreme punishment there. But capital punishment is still legal in most states.[2]

FAULTY ESTIMATES MAGNIFY THE MENACE

The demand for *action* and *results* is not likely to be fulfilled by the various antisubversion programs. The programs themselves have usually been based on thoroughly inflated estimates of the lawlessness they will curb or expose. They have been unable to perform prodigious feats for the good reason, in most instances, that the feats were not there to be performed. One cannot with assurance say that no dragons remain to be slain anywhere in the world. But if an enthusiast for dragon hunting were to organize a safari for the purpose of slaying whatever ferocious specimens he might find in, say, the Free State of Maryland, he would probably

[2] After this chapter was delivered for publication, Tennessee did in fact take the next step. A 1951 statute of that state makes the death sentence a possibility in cases of unlawful advocacy.

have to content himself with the shooting of somewhat smaller game.

In effect, that is the foreseeable fate of Marylanders who, armed with the Ober Act, seek today to substantiate the legislative finding that the state is imperiled by boring from within. In 1948, before the passage of the Ober Act, a Communist was found in (and promptly ousted from) one of Baltimore's kindergartens, where she was presumably indoctrinating her charges with the spirit of revolt. And in 1950 a suburban high-school teacher of English was discovered to be a possible though not certain member of the world-wide conspiracy. Otherwise the public service of Maryland has not been shown to be infested.

Sometimes a patent mathematical error is the generator of political decisions. Consider the case of Detroit, for example. A responsible official in that city publicly estimated in 1949 that 150 Communist supporters were employed by the city government. Almost immediately, as is shown more fully by Professor Mowitz in Chapter IV, Detroit launched the country's first municipal loyalty program, to weed out these camp followers of the enemy. The only thing wrong with the picture is that the initiating estimate was fallacious. It was based on belief that 0.5 per cent of federal employees were Communist sympathizers and that presumably the same percentage of Detroit's employees would prove to be tainted. In fact, however, the federal loyalty program had proved after three years of operation that the loyalty of federal employees could be reasonably challenged not in one-half of one per cent of the cases but in only one-twentieth of one per cent—not .005, but .0005.

It is too early to say what the Detroit program will ultimately show. Thus far it has produced suspicions, though as yet no proofs, against a single garbage collector. One doubts that it will uncover large numbers of strategically placed partisans, for their supposed presence is merely a reflection of a gross arithmetical blunder. But will the voters now be persuaded that the city government is not after all overrun by the Communists? More likely they will be convinced that the "Reds" have yet again demonstrated their extraordinary wiliness. The stage will then be set for some new, more stringent approach to ridding the municipality of its hypothetical underminers.

Once the thirst for positive action has been aroused, it is not slaked by dry statistics. In New Hampshire in 1949, for example, a clamor was heard about the need of investigating the Communist menace especially, though not exclusively, in the state's educational institutions. Now, the F.B.I. says that there are only forty-three Communists in all of New Hampshire. And the election returns tell us that the Progressive Party—which almost certainly contained every Communist supporter as well as many persons who are not Communist sympathizers at all—was able to poll only .0084 of the presidential vote and .0049 of the gubernatorial vote in New Hampshire's 1948 elections. With these fresh figures at hand, the legislature might fruitfully have focused on other threats to the state's future, such as the inability of the state university to open its library regularly in the evenings because of inadequate funds.

This was not to be. A former national commander of the American Legion spurred legislative concern by speaking of a "communist cell" in Durham, the seat of the university. He reported, too, that "several parents" were worried about conditions; one of them feared that his son was "in the process of losing his religious belief because of what was going on at the University." The legislature concluded that an investigation was needed to "prepare a program designed to protect the democratic principles and ideals of this state, and to expose and expurgate subversive and other illegal activities in this state."

After a year of deliberation the New Hampshire commission declared that it had obtained from law enforcement agencies only "very meager" information as to the existence of subversive activities in the state. In its final report the commission reprinted the names of organizations listed by the attorney general of the United States for use in the federal loyalty program, said that exposure of Communist activities was a job for a national rather than a local police organization, and recommended no additional legislation. Will those who nurtured the inquiry be content with such negative results?

371

There is a widely held opinion that the Communists, somewhat like Satan, are omnipresent and at the same time masters of deceit. Moreover, lack of success in exposing them is not always attributed solely to their own skill. It is sometimes ascribed to the inefficiency or, even, the corruption of the searchers.

So, when Martin Dies turned over a list of more than a thousand "hot suspects" to the F.B.I., and the F.B.I. found that only three persons on the list might properly be regarded as Communist sympathizers, Congressman Dies did not have to confess error. He simply charged that the attorney general was covering up the Communists in order to discredit Dies. And apparently he was widely believed.

A similar reaction could be observed when the federal employee loyalty program, after functioning for a considerable time, had not netted hordes of Communists or other disloyal persons on the public payroll. Senator Ferguson, speaking for an important senate committee, was not moved to congratulate the public upon the demonstrated faithfulness of its servants. Instead he denounced the administration for not locating the undesirable employees that everyone knew must be there.

When Senator McCarthy in 1950 declared that the State Department harbored many Communists, his later inability to prove his charges, and the State Department's insistence that full investigation had shown them to be false did not dissipate the accusations. Even a senate inquiry that energetically characterized McCarthy's assertions as reckless, inexact, and ill founded did not suffice, for the inquiry was itself discounted as a political whitewash. There remains a widespread belief that the State Department has been infiltrated by the enemy.

These examples suggest what may by now be accepted as a normal cycle. First, the legislature responds to popular fears by passing a statute or ordering an investigation against subverters. This action, while initially a reflection of the emotions and alarms that well up within the public, itself stimulates precisely the concern it was intended to allay. The very fact that the legislature acted is interpreted as confirming the existence of a gravely urgent problem.

Next, to everyone's dismay, the threats to national and state security seem to continue despite what has already been done defensively. There are still evil men within the Kremlin, and their lackeys are still within the state. So the legislature must speak again—and again. Each time the effort to produce satisfactory results is somewhat intensified.

When the matter is left to the executive (as, for example, in investigating public employees), the testing process is made more and more rigorous in order to produce at least some of the findings that were expected. If espionage, violence, and other objectively provable crimes are not detected, then it becomes necessary to expand and dilute the definition of what constitutes subversion, disloyalty, or whatever the operative word may be.

In the end, the failure of legislation or investigation to banish the fears that started the whole spiral is rarely taken as showing that the fears were perhaps ill founded. It is taken as showing, rather, that more and more remains to be done.

THE BALLOT BOX AND THE SCHOOLHOUSE

The legislatures, it has already been said, have been especially ingenious in coping with possible preliminaries to conduct as well as with the actualities of conduct. Without now reviewing the whole range, one may isolate two problems that emerge with special clarity.

Barring Access to the Ballot

Some fifteen states today exclude from elections any political group that, in the slightly outmoded phrase, advocates the overthrow of the government by force or violence—or, in the modern variant, is foreign-controlled. On the surface it seems plausible to withhold from the enemies of democracy the use of its machinery. On the other hand, it may well be argued that democratic institutions are not truly preserved by blocking appeals to the electorate. The foundation of our governmental structure is the voters' opportunity to choose freely the candidates, principles, and policies they prefer—to choose wisely or unwisely, but in any event freely. When insurmountable barriers are erected between vote-

373

seekers and vote-givers, credence is lent to those who insist that only revolution can produce change.

This is a position eloquently urged a full generation ago by Charles Evans Hughes. In 1920 five elected Socialists were denied their seats in the New York legislature because their organization was deemed subversive. Neither they nor their party had been charged with any crime, nor was any such charge ever to be made formally against them. The Socialist group at that time, however, were viewed with the fear and distaste that are reserved today for the Communists. Hughes, arguing on behalf of a prominent bar association that the Socialists be permitted to take the places for which they had been chosen, declared:

> I count it a most serious mistake to proceed, not against individuals charged with violation of law, but against masses of our citizens combined for political action, by denying them the only recourse of peaceful government; that is, action by the ballot box and through duly elected representatives in legislative bodies.

The Lusk committee (one of the earliest of the un-American activities committees) prepared, and the legislature overwhelmingly approved, a bill to bar from New York elections any party whose doctrines and policies would *"tend,* if carried into effect, to the destruction, subversion, or *endangering* of the existing governments. . . ." Governor Alfred E. Smith vetoed the measure with a ringing message. Smith, like Hughes, thought that democracy was not likely to be conserved by closing the ballot boxes.

Indiana, Texas, and the other states that exclude antidemocratic parties from their polls apparently disagree. In Indiana the generalized statutory prohibitions do not suffice. Each local election board in that state is under a positive duty to "determine the character and nature of the political doctrines" of all who seek a place on the ballot, in order to assure that the doctrines are consistent with the legislative policy. Texas bars groups "whose principles include any thought or purpose of setting aside representative government."

Limitations like these are understandable in emotional terms. But if we hope to discourage violence, we must assure an ever-present peaceable alternative. Impairing the freedom of elections may be a step in the wrong direction.

Education

Nowhere has concern about subversive activities been more steadily manifest than in the educational process. Although only eighteen states specifically exclude subversive persons (variously defined) from employment in government service, twenty-six states bar them from teaching in public schools and state universities. Almost without exception the publicly supported school is a leading target, if not the primary target, of state legislative investigations into un-American activities.

Interest in educational subversion is by no means confined to personnel problems. Censorship of schoolbooks has frequently occurred. In a western state, for example, a text underwent legislative editing because it contained the un-American acknowledgment that "one-third of our people are poorly housed." The school board of a Texas city found intolerable an author's assertion that even in the United States there were occasional "bits of socialism," such as the postal system. These are not isolated instances. They are matched, on the affirmative side, by efforts to prescribe exactly what is to be taught and how.

To be sure, we Americans have not just recently begun tinkering with schoolteaching. As long ago as 1647 the Puritans of Massachusetts were directing what should and should not be done in the schoolhouse, believing that thus they could "thwart that auld deluder Sathan" and set at naught his "cheife project to keep men from ye knowledge of ye Scriptures." Three hundred years later some among today's state lawmakers with equal confidence perceive how to defeat the machinations of that auld deluder Stalin.

Senator Tenney and his California committee, according to his own statement, "definitely concluded" that a high-school course in marriage and family relations "was a Communist plot to destroy the fibre of youth"; and the Tenney influence overcame the urgings of educators, Y.M.C.A. leaders, and others that California permit its teachers colleges and high schools to establish courses of this type.

The Nebraska legislature in 1949 adopted a more positive approach to the curriculum. It directed each local school board to designate a "committee on Americanism." This committee was then to inspect all the American history and government textbooks and to "assure themselves as to the character of all teachers employed, and their knowledge and acceptance of the American form of government." Finally, to make certain that the sterilized schoolbooks and the pasteurized teachers would be put to good use, the legislature commanded that grammar schools devote specified hours to memorizing "The Star Spangled Banner" and to reciting stories having to do with history "or the deeds and exploits of American heroes." When a child reached high school, he was to be given at least two full-year courses, lasting not less than three hours each week, in which (among other things) attention must be directed specifically to "the benefits and advantages of our form of government and the dangers and fallacies of Nazism, Communism, and similar ideologies." As one Nebraska orator put it at the time, "Borrow a lesson from Hitler and Stalin and teach our children Americanism!"

This is not the place to discuss at length the role of education in American society. Public opinion about the matter has not yet crystallized into a single fixed conviction. Some persons sincerely believe that the schools should propound only views that have already been approved; the demand that they instill a love of country is sometimes merely a subtle way of saying that they should not criticize the status quo. In totalitarian countries—and, as educational studies have shown, this is very markedly true in the Soviet Union—schoolchildren are taught exactly what they are to think but are not encouraged to develop the habit of intellectual independence. Wittingly or not, many earnest proponents of the American way apparently feel that the totalitarians have the correct approach in this respect.

On the other side is the feeling that schools should heighten their students' capacity to analyze problems, to organize and apply the pertinent factual materials, and to maintain a genuine open-mindedness, if not an active skepticism. The New Jersey state board of education, for instance, urged in late 1949 that public-school teachers in that state should freely discuss "controversial questions" in their classrooms, being careful to present both sides of all issues. Of course this prompting may not instantly stir response in every New Jersey teacher. Confidence has been shaken by other school boards' dismissals of instructors for allowing two-sided discussion of race relations, international organization, and "radicalism," or for believing in disarmament, or for doubting the ultimate wisdom of the Daughters of the American Revolution. Being actively orthodox rather than open-mindedly inquiring has been the safer course for public educators. Their enforced timidity must first be overcome if passively uncritical attitudes are to be replaced by fresh thinking and a warm social conscience.

In late years the political identification of teachers, especially those at the college level, has been stressed even more than the character of what they taught. The policy that Communists should not be allowed to remain on faculties has gained wide acceptance despite the pleadings of the American Association of University Professors and a few other traditional upholders of academic freedom. Support for that policy has come from many reputable sources as well as from the professional heresy hunters. Numerous educators, including the University of California faculty, and organizations like the National Education Association endorse it. The University of Washington put it into practice by dismissing two avowed Communists and a professor whose relations with the Communist Party were thought to be ambiguous.

The theory underlying the proscription of Communists as teachers rests on two propositions: first, that their political obligations include surrender of their intellectual freedom; and, second, that they will abuse their academic privileges by seeking to indoctrinate their students. Both of these propositions may be true, in whole or in part, in all cases or in some. But the fact must candidly be reported that their invariable truth has simply been assumed rather than tested in the various state investigations thus far held. By reiteration they have acquired the character of dogmas. This makes it impolitic to inquire into their soundness. Like other dogmas, however, these may be correct or mistaken in particular instances. The states have made no sustained efforts to demonstrate their validity by collecting concrete proofs.

The University of Washington based its action against its er-

377

rant faculty members on the supposition that they had abandoned their brains to some other person's dictation. If this had occurred, the professors were no longer free to seek the truth, to perceive it according to their ability, and to expound ideas with integrity. Thus they were unfitted to remain within a community of scholars. Interestingly enough, however, the evidence that was introduced about the affected trio tended to show that they taught objectively and, in their extracurricular affairs, were personally convinced of the soundness of the opinions they espoused. At the same time, the University of Washington investigation revealed that others of the faculty had been members of the Communist Party at various times but had left it without any difficulty whatsoever upon finding themselves in disagreement. This suggests that at least in the Seattle group of Communists (whatever may be the case elsewhere), individuals were free to accept or reject the partisan dogmas their leaders might proclaim. If they accepted them, presumably they did so because they wished to do so rather than merely because they feared for their well-being should they depart in dissent. The prevalence of repentant or repudiated Communists casts considerable doubt on the notion that the constraints of membership have been uniformly unyielding, though the pressure to conform to group patterns—or, as it is sometimes phrased, "to accept discipline"—appears indeed to be strong within the Communist Party as it probably is within other semiclandestine bodies.

There is, in any event, another aspect of the matter. Communists are generally believed to modify their asserted beliefs in order to meet the tactical needs of the immediate moment. Thus, for example, an historian might be called upon to distort historical facts in order to further some partisan object. Although he might fully realize that his historical observations were spurious, he might nevertheless be willing (if a Communist) to be intellectually dishonest for his party's purposes. It is especially in this sense that acquiescence can be said to be a product of party discipline. It is especially in this sense, too, that the surrender of the mind would render a teacher unworthy of his profession.

Here again, the investigations of the states simply assert the existence rather than demonstrate the specific occurrence of this sort of impropriety. Full reliance has been placed on quotations from Lenin, from party writings of various kinds, and from Communist utterances in other days or contexts; these are used as though they equally reflected the active personal philosophy of every single Communist without the slightest modification or variation. Little effort has been made to show that a particular individual has behaved in an unprincipled manner. Evidence that an instructor is a Communist has not been regarded merely as justifying an inquiry by the appropriate academic authorities into what sort of teacher he is. Instead, it has been taken, standing quite alone, as conclusive proof that he has frittered away his intellectual freedom and is therefore no longer fit to teach. If a teacher is to be ousted on that ground, one may ask whether a more particularized and personalized body of evidence should not be brought forward to establish the facts of the matter. General propositions, to paraphrase Justice Holmes's words, ought not decide concrete cases.

As for the question of indoctrination, here again the state investigations have assumed rather than found that every Communist perverts his academic duties. The Washington proceedings carefully omitted any charge that the affected professors had misused their lecture platforms; such evidence as did come in on this point supported the professors' assertions that they had not been propagandists. In New York an extensive investigation of possible Communists stopped short at any inquiry about their classroom performance; their political impurity in itself was thought to establish their unfitness as instructors. In New Hampshire, where the work of two faculty members was in fact carefully and quietly scrutinized for many months after their political vagaries had stirred suspicion, the university president in the end announced that their behavior was above reproach.

The New York legislature in 1949 enacted a law to facilitate the ouster of Communist teachers. Communists, the legislators declared, ought not be permitted to teach because they disseminate propaganda—a propaganda, they added, that was frequently "sufficiently subtle to escape detection in the classroom." No doubt this insidious subtlety accounts for the fact that rarely is a "disloyal" teacher charged with indoctrinating pupils with his hated ideas. His misconduct is simply assumed even though no proof of its existence can be brought forward.

This element of objection—that is, that a Communist teacher might indoctrinate—has tended to become a formal rather than substantial justification for concern about the matter. Not long ago an Illinois investigation trained its guns on a professor whose work was limited to cancer research on mice rather than pedagogical contact with students. Pretty clearly the real opposition to a Communist as a teacher is that he is a Communist rather than that he is a teacher of communism.

Even if one were unreservedly to accept the articulate suppositions that underlie the policy of getting rid of Communists as teachers, an important question remains. In purely practical terms, is a campaign to identify and eliminate "disloyal" persons from academic posts socially worth while? Is the possibility of having undetected Communists on the campus more dangerous to American education than is the investigation of faculty members' ideas and behavior?

Let there be no mistake about what happens when the search is launched for Communists. Once one agrees that Communist teachers should be ousted because they are Communists rather than because they have demonstrated any personal unfitness, it is only natural to try to discover whether there are any. Communists, if any, are unlikely to offer themselves up for dismissal. Requiring everyone to swear to his purity does not serve to differentiate the good from the bad with complete certainty, because if people are bad enough, they rarely hesitate to add lying to their other vices. So, in order to find out whether a pedagogue is a concealed Communist, there is a strong likelihood that inquiry will be made into his opinions, his private activities, and his nonacademic associations.

Of course, when teachers feel that risk to be imminent, they may seek personal security through academic sterility, with heavy loss to the community. "Any teacher worth his salt or his salary," Irwin Edman once wrote, "believes in working toward a better world. On what else is teaching based but on a faith that through the education of the young the world may indeed be a better one in the next generation . . . ? It would be deplorable if suspicion of propaganda should lead to suspicion of critical intelligence, the very nerve center of a democratic society."

The Communist professor, it is pertinent to recall, is only one among many teachers; only one among all the influences—home, church, community, and all the others—that help shape a student's outlook on life. His Communist ideas, even if fully communicated to his students, comprise only a small part of the great mass of recorded thought, experience, and idealism that are the building materials of organized education. How can it be supposed that the Communist and the philosophy he espouses are so influential and effective that they overshadow all the rest?

Surely there is a measure of unreality in behaving as though the Communists, who have been notably unsuccessful in winning the minds of American youth or of any other numerous group in this country, are so powerfully persuasive that we must push the academic world into turmoil while assuring ourselves that none of the scoundrels survive. In fact, after the turmoil has died down, we usually discover that there were few if any Communists in the teaching ranks in the first place. The oaths and inquisitions and contract clauses with which the Communists were to be confounded, we then learn, have merely disturbed, distracted, and sometimes intimidated a number of people who might better have been left alone to continue their academic labors.

It may be argued that contemporary dangers are so pressing that the democratic community cannot gamble on the wholeheartedness of its teachers and must therefore risk a few collateral casualties in order to extirpate the Reds. But only times of crisis test the American principles of fairness, wisdom, and freedom. If they are not valid then, they have little substance. Moreover, if they are honored only in periods of calm and comfort, they are unlikely to have much of a future. The world, one hopes, will some day return to its usual placidity. The only thing that has been "usual" for a whole generation, however, has been an unusual series of domestic and international tensions. Only a bold man would predict that the tensions will soon relax. If normality must be awaited before teachers are to be assured their traditional freedom—a freedom limited by professional standards rather than by associative political tests—the old tradition is not likely to survive the long delay. A newer tradition, a tradition symbolized by the censorious eye of such bodies as the California committee on un-American activities, may supplant it.

The Educational Policies Commission of the National Education Association concluded in 1949 that Communist Party members should not be employed as teachers. Their "surrender of intellectual integrity" and their adherence to doctrines "completely inconsistent with the principles of freedom on which American education depends" render them unfit as educators. At the same time the commission condemned "the careless, incorrect, and unjust use of such words as 'Red' and 'Communist' to attack teachers and other persons who in point of fact are not Communists, but who merely have views different from those of their accusers. The whole spirit of free American education will be subverted unless teachers are free to think for themselves."

This distinction between the unfit and the fit is clear enough in statement but peculiarly indecisive in action. The appraisal of ambiguous evidence about political adherence results in the very carelessness and injustice the National Education Association deplores. This is the almost inevitable consequence of focusing on the group to which an individual teacher belongs rather than on what that teacher himself actually does. If the reason for ousting a suspected Communist from a teaching post is that he behaves improperly because he is a Communist, the improper behavior ought to be demonstrable rather than merely supposed to exist. When that can be done, the individual should be discharged because he has not fulfilled his obligations rather than because of his known or suspected associations. Perhaps we would be on sounder ground today if we shared the *New Yorker* editorialist's belief that "teachers should be fired not in blocks of three for political wrongness, but in blocks of one for unfitness."

LOCAL EFFORTS TO BANISH COMMUNISM

Municipal endeavors to contain the spread of communism were among the interesting phenomena of 1950. In localities scattered across the land—Birmingham, Alabama; Jersey City, New Jersey; McKeesport, Pennsylvania; Miami, Florida; Los Angeles, California; Cumberland, Maryland; New Rochelle, New York, to name

only a few—ordinances required Communists and others to regis-
ter with the police or, in some instances, to leave town entirely.
Some thirty cities and three counties passed edicts against the
Reds.

After Birmingham had adopted its new laws, Communists were
allowed only forty-eight hours to quit the city. Macon, Georgia,
quickly copied Birmingham's idea, and others began to follow
suit. Jacksonville, Florida, took no chances on letting a Red agent
slip through its *cordon sanitaire;* it created a drastic presumption
that a person is a Communist and must therefore be expelled from
the municipality if he distributes "Communist literature" or even
if he so much as communicates with a present or former Communist.

Detroit has closed up newspaper stands that sold the *Daily
Worker* and similar Communist publications—not, the authorities
cynically emphasized, because the news vendors distributed "subversive literature" but because the stands were a nuisance on the
public thoroughfares. Cumberland, being franker than is sophis-
ticated Detroit, flatly makes it a crime to sell or give away Communist publications on the city streets. Oklahoma City, operating
without benefit of any law, achieves the same result by direct
police action. There, Communists are arrested on the nominal
charge of disorderly conduct. As the police chief remarked after
five persons had been arrested for the disorderly conduct of pos-
sessing "Communistic literature," the disorderly conduct charge
had to be used because "the city has no ordinance" forbidding
Communists to gather together or to read their own effusions.

A number of the local laws have already been declared unconstitutional, and perhaps others will fall by the wayside if they are
subjected to legal analysis. Whether or not they are compatible
with the constitution, their wide enactment is in itself a fact of
sociological significance.

The burning or banishing of heretics blots many of the pages
of man's history. The fervor that produced these contemporary
measures is not wholly unrelated. The local deportation of the
political outcast has something of the same ritualistic quality that
marked the stoning of the religious deviator in days when religion
was a more pressing concern than politics. His very presence in

383

the community is a pollution of its purity. Not a moment is to be lost. Out he must go. He is evil incarnate—which is to say that his mere existence is an offense to good citizens and a lively threat to public order.

Irrationally magnified fear about the Communists—as though they were the dripping carriers of an infection the community could not possibly resist—does not stop at any sharply drawn line. One example can be recorded here as illustrative of, alas, too many.

In the early autumn of 1950 the District of Columbia board of education and its superintendent of schools announced an approved list of persons who could be invited as special lecturers in the local schools. Beforehand the list had been checked with the House Committee on Un-American Activities. If one of the proposed lecturers was mentioned in the House committee's files, he was dropped. The House committee has accumulated thousands upon thousands of names; the reasoning that led to their being listed has not always been tenable; and even the committee admits that its data are not conclusive. Hence it is apparent that the anti-Communist phobia is seriously extended when it results in cutting off everyone on whom a dossier may be kept by a notably unprecise committee. The school superintendent, however, simply thought he was proceeding with proper caution. "I wouldn't run the risk of employing anyone about whom there is any question at all," he told the press with quiet satisfaction.

So he wiped from his list three suspect persons. A later journalistic investigator satisfied himself that one of them was not in the House committee's records at all but had been confused with a similarly named person who was. Another of the banned lecturers was in the House committee's big black book, sure enough—apparently because in 1948 he had opposed the committee-supported Mundt-Nixon Communist control bill as a measure that would "drive Communists underground" and was "against freedom of speech." The third dangerous character had been a member of the National Council of American-Soviet Friendship during World War II and had thus achieved her place in the committee's records; she had long since dropped her membership and, speaking

384

as a Catholic, said that she was "much opposed to the methods and tactics of communism."

In any event, the District of Columbia schools were indeed spared the experience of having contact with "anyone about whom there is any question at all." Severe limitations may be the ultimate reward of continued use of so loose an eligibility test. The school system may find itself unintelligently restricted in its choice of lecturers, for every question that is raised about an individual is, after all, not necessarily an intelligent one. A question is merely something to be answered; it ought not be treated as though it were a tempered conclusion. Secondly, the lecturers and teachers in the system may become improperly constrained, for in order to preserve their status they may have to avoid any area of controversial discussion that might lead to question.[3]

STATE LEGISLATIVE INVESTIGATIONS OF "SUBVERSION"

The tendency to punish or banish the political irregular has been especially marked in some of the state legislative investigating committees. The Tenney committee in California, as Professor Barrett has written, was especially aggressive in seeking to wall off the community from anyone whom it regarded unfavorably.

Efforts were made to prevent association with him, to forbid lawyers defending him in his troubles with the law, to cause his employer to discharge him and his union to expel him. People were warned that they should not rent him a hall for a meeting, or join any organization of which he was a member, or read any book or attend any play or motion picture written by him, or even espouse any cause espoused by him.

Committees of this type need no legislation to enforce their dictates. They have the power to emit odious publicity. Their denunciations can never be fully challenged. Few can withstand

[3] In 1951 the District of Columbia practice was substantially modified so that eligibility is no longer made to turn on mere mention of a name in the files of the House Committee on Un-American Activities.

their coercive pressures. Professor Countryman's discussion of the Canwell committee's work in Washington shows how quickly and deeply those pressures make themselves felt. The fate of the Seattle Repertory Playhouse furnishes an apt example. This was a prospering nonprofit dramatic organization; its series of plays for children and for adults were generously supported, and it afforded interested persons a local opportunity to work in the theater. At no time was criticism directed against the character of plays presented in the past or planned for the future. Nevertheless, when the Canwell committee attacked the politics of some of its officials, it fell almost immediately into financial disaster. In short, contemporary careers shrivel speedily when touched by political scandal.

If scandal were legislatively disseminated in a cautious and orderly way, perhaps it would hurt only those who deserve nothing better. As other chapters in this book amply indicate, however, caution and order are not the main preoccupations of committees in this field.

The prevailing carelessness in so sensitive and complex an area is explicable on several counts. First of all is the fact that some of the committees set up to investigate subversion have been tempted to perpetuate themselves. If they aspire to be continuous and all but permanent, they must produce sensations, especially when they need more funds. Even those that appear to be but episodes in a state's life rather than a part of its continuing structure batten on the exclamatory accusation rather than on quiet exposition of issues. Names make news, and news makes headlines. When chairmen of investigating committees are interested in personal publicity, as many an ambitious legislator is, the temptation to make charges and thus capture the headlines must be strong. That is one reason why an investigation of subversive activities almost inevitably becomes an investigation of persons rather than deeds. Whatever sickness there may be in the body politic is ignored. Instead, attention is fixed upon possible symptoms. That is to say, inquiry into conditions and problems is crowded off the agenda by a sort of unperfected police-work identification of allegedly evil persons.

Legislative investigations are rarely the best means of placing individuals on trial. Their procedure is designed to permit amassing general data from which policy conclusions can be drawn, but not to determine the facts of particular cases. To be sure, legislative committees have sometimes with great ability exposed the failures of law enforcement agencies, as happened, for example, in the Teapot Dome affair in the early twenties. On those occasions a committee has sat almost as might a trial court and has done the needed job with distinction. Again, committees have highlighted a broad problem by showing individual irregularities, as was done in the thirties by the Senate's inquiry into financial practices. So one cannot say abstractly that the committees on subversive activities definitely transgress their legislative function whenever they undertake to judge an individual, nor can one say that it is absolutely impossible for them to do creditably responsible work.

Nevertheless, the substitution of legislative condemnation for the more conventional trial process is, generally speaking, of very dubious utility. Judges and juries need to hear both sides in order to reach sound results; legislative investigating committees cannot arrive at fair decisions after the one-sided presentations that customarily mark their proceedings. The leading of "friendly" witnesses, the harassing of those who are being investigated, and the absence of either cross-examination or opportunity to present an affirmative defense are poor methods of searching for the truth about a challenged individual. This is all the more so when, as is usually the case in connection with "subversive activities," neither the legislature nor its investigating arm has spelled out the offense for which the individual is, in effect, being tried. An objective measurement of guilt might itself be a protection against an abusive procedure. But, as has been seen, no such measurement is ordinarily furnished.

The truth of the matter, revealed by all the studies in this field, is that the state committees' hearings have rarely been held for the purpose of inquiring into facts at all. Rather, they are held to publicize conclusions already reached. Their object is to spread before the public the assertions the committee has previously resolved to make. The Broyles committee in Illinois stated this point with charming candor. Having determined to hire an investigator, the committee wrote in its official minutes: "It was agreed that the primary purpose of the investigator would be to investigate and find proof and basis for the need of the legislation to be recommended. The investigator would substantiate the legislation by his findings." This seems to be essentially the route followed as a matter of course by committees in this area. Make charges or decide on proposed legislation; then "investigate" in order to substantiate the position already adopted; and finally have a "hearing" at a strategically opportune time in order to unveil the "full story."

Another facet of the problem is revealed by study of state committees. The present interest in exposing the "Reds" has given rise to a corps of specialists in the field. The professionals tend to be impatient with the amateurs. The Tenney committee in California, for example, was highly critical of the Los Angeles board of education for undertaking to investigate two allegedly radical high-school teachers. "It should be obvious," said the Tenney report, "that the task of investigation was one for professional investigators trained in piercing smoke-screens. The employment of members of the teaching profession in such an investigation is a waste of energy." It was no surprise to Senator Tenney that an inquiry under nonprofessional direction produced a "palpable whitewash of the affair."

Helping to supply the needed professionalism is a troupe of experts who bob up in one state after another, much like a party of lecturers on the Chautauqua Circuit. J. B. Matthews, who served as Martin Dies's chief aide, and former Communists like Louis Budenz, Benjamin Gitlow, George Hewitt, Joseph Zack Kornfeder, and Howard Rushmore appear as expert witnesses or "research" men again and again. Naturally enough, their analytical techniques and their sources of information do not vary a great deal from one state to the next. Though they may perhaps be sincere men, they clearly have a financial stake in continuing the present standards, methods, and values of investigations into subversion. For better or worse their influence, coupled with the influence of local emulators, has been considerable in setting the tone and shaping the course of a number of the state investigations.

INVESTIGATION WITHOUT
SENSATIONALISM

In a few states—notably Arizona, Florida, and New Hampshire —the legislature has created committees on un-American activities that have thus far remained quiescent.

The Arizona resolution is noteworthy because it called for a committee "on the promotion of American activities" in order "to strengthen . . . American ideals . . . against the encroachment of subversive and un-American propaganda in Arizona." So far as is known, this is the only instance of an affirmative approach in the present context. Unfortunately, the Arizona committee became inactive after several preliminary meetings. Its authority terminated in 1949, and its chairman retired from the legislature without suggesting how to reinforce American principles.

New Jersey has a commission, appointed by the governor rather than by the legislature, "to investigate communistic and un-American teachings and activities in the public schools and universities." The body had an interesting origin. On March 10, 1947, a group describing itself as the "New Jersey Youth Legislature" paid a visit to the legislature. A Republican representative, Assemblyman Griffiths, expansively sponsored a resolution of welcome to the young sightseers. To his deep pain and embarrassment a Democratic colleague took the floor an hour later to charge that he had welcomed a Communist-front organization. Mr. Griffiths was flabbergasted but not undone. On the next day, having rallied, he proposed a resolution instructing the governor to name a commission to report on communism in education. Thus at one stroke he demonstrated his political acumen and rehabilitated his reputation for sound Americanism.

The commission appointed by Governor Driscoll has proceeded quietly for more than three years. Headed by an experienced educational administrator, its members have no apparent political aspirations. Inquiry reveals that it has met in executive session frequently but plans no open hearings until it submits its report. Any evaluation of the commission's deliberations is obviously impossible, since they have been secret. This much can be said.

389

Having avoided the issuance of charges and inflammatory statements, New Jersey's investigators have at least thus far damaged no reputations by design or inadvertence.

Another instance of nonlegislative, nonpolitical inquiry occurred not long ago in the District of Columbia. An investigating committee operated there so quietly that its very existence was almost unknown. Its final report was not published, and copies cannot now be obtained from official sources.

Briefly, the District commissioners appointed a "Loyalty Committee" to consider all phases of a loyalty program for the District. After a long survey of local government jobs, the committee concluded that there were 3,019 positions in the District of Columbia government that might possibly be "sensitive to national security." Then the committee looked at experience in the federal employee loyalty program. It learned that there was not even any debatable cause to investigate more than three out of every thousand employees and that serious questions about loyalty arose in only a very small fraction of this already small fraction. As the committee noted, "If the experience of the Federal loyalty program was applied to the number of employees to be investigated under the District of Columbia program it would mean that only nine persons would have to be subjected to a full field investigation and not one would be charged." Moreover, the loyalty committee was confident that "the personnel of the District Government and its organization are such that the identity of any disloyal person would soon become known; and that adequate legal authority exists for the removal of such persons should any be identified." So the committee unanimously recommended abandonment of the proposed investigation of public employees.

The difference between the District of Columbia committee and the state investigations discussed elsewhere in this volume is very plain. The District body carried on an investigation to find out whether there was anything that needed to be investigated. The others "investigated" in order to support a determination already made. The legislature adopts some member's resolution calling for a committee to root out the subversive activities that (so the resolution "finds") are striking at the commonwealth's vitals. The resolution's sponsor then becomes chairman of the investigating committee he demanded. After that sequence of events the committee is not very likely to acknowledge that the menace was, upon close examination, found to be slightly exaggerated.

CONCLUSION

The struggle to preserve American democratic principles against invasion from any source commands enthusiastic adherence. The struggle, however, needs to be waged with ourselves as well as against our enemies. The record till now suggests that Russian communism and its ineffectual allies are unlikely to succeed in wresting away our freedoms without our co-operation. If our freedoms are lost, it will be because our own timidity, our own lack of confidence in the solidity of American institutions and traditions, led to their repudiation by us rather than to their destruction by others.

Today as always the path of freedom is perilous. Yet, departure from it is an even larger peril. Once lost, freedom is hard to recapture. And the loss, if the first steps are taken heedlessly, may come upon us unsuspectedly. Freedom, as Arthur Koestler well said in *The Yogi and the Commissar,* is a matter of degrees; "the great danger for those who have not been immunized by experience is the smoothness of transition to successive degrees of unfreedom." Catastrophic change comes not in a sudden swoop of completeness, but in an accelerating glide that may extend over a lengthy period. At precisely what point, Edmund Burke asked, does day become night? Though darkness is the opposite of light, does one sense each encroachment of the one on the other?

The statutes and the investigations considered in this volume were intended to strike at enemies of freedom. In many instances, however, they hit others instead—educators, public employees, political minorities, and even religious groups. Unmeasurably but nonetheless surely they created a general uneasiness about dissent, about advocacy, and about ideas unrelated to acts or threatened acts. All of this flows in part from failure to maintain a constant focus on subversive *activities.* What the states need now, generally speaking, is not an ever-growing body of laws to deal with supposedly subversive persons or beliefs. For their legitimate protection they need merely to enforce the already large body of laws that concentrate on actions instead of opinions and associations.

The dreaded subversion of today is not a novelty, as a backward glance readily shows. The alarm bells rang loudly and steadily yesterday as well. For decades the states have been menaced, and with special intensity during the whole generation since World War I. Possibly the present period demands not more and more bulwarks, but a slight enlargement of calm and common sense. If the state legislative declarations of the past had been fully justified, the nation could not have maintained its essential stability while through the long years it steadily underwent subversion. Now it is said that all we hold dear is in grave danger of being subverted anew. Perhaps, in David Cavers' felicitous phrase, it is this very "capacity for perennial subversion which makes a fundamental law or institution fundamental."

APPENDIX A[1]

Description of the Types of State Statutes Relating to Subversive Activities as of January 1, 1951

IN THIS appendix, in addition to the various state statutes that are concerned with subversive activities, the statutes of Alaska and Hawaii are also described.

As an aid to analysis these statutes have been grouped in categories reflecting their main features. Any absolute classification is almost impossible because of the varieties of language and phrasing, but broad identification is necessary if this type of legislation is to be understood. Upon closer investigation it will be found that some statutes do not fit neatly into any of the various types described, and occasionally there is room for difference of opinion as to whether the correct classification has been made.

A mere collection of state statutes, no matter how complete, is only a part of the picture concerning subversive activities. There may be administrative regulations and rules by the state or its counties and municipalities, never put in statutory form, which may be as effective as or more effective than the statutes. With the exception of the administrative regulations concerning teachers' oaths in a few states these are not included in the survey here presented.

In Appendix B, which follows, the precise statutory citations may be found grouped under the names of the respective states.

[1] This appendix was prepared, in the main, by William H. Rockwell of the New York Bar, under the supervision of Walter Gellhorn.

INDEX TO TYPES OF STATE STATUTES

A—Treason
B—Rebellion and Insurrection
C—Sedition
D—Criminal Syndicalism
E—Criminal Anarchy
F—Red Flag Laws
G—Sabotage
H—Masks and Disguises
I—Statutes Excluding Groups from Recognition as Political Parties
J—Statutes Excluding Persons from Elective Office
K—Statutes Excluding Persons from Public Office
L—Statutes Excluding Persons from State Employment
M—Registration Statutes
N—Teacher's Oath Statutes
O—Statutes concerning Teachers' Loyalty Other Than by Oath
P—Miscellaneous School Statutes
Q—Statutes Excluding Persons from Incidental Benefits

TYPES OF STATUTES

Type A—Treason

A-1. Treason. The crime of treason is defined in the United States Constitution (Art. III, sec. 3) as follows: "Treason against the United States, shall consist only in levying war against them, or in adhering to their enemies, giving them aid and comfort. No person shall be convicted of treason unless on the testimony of two witnesses to the same overt act, or on confession in open court."

It will be noted that it is necessary to the commission of treason that war be actually levied against the United States, and a mere conspiracy to wage war against it is not treason.

The definition above is the standard definition given by all the states except New Mexico, which has no provision against treason. The definition is usually set forth in the state constitution and

394

supplemented by appropriate statutes. The fact that it is set forth in the constitution would seem to deprive the legislature of the power either to extend or limit its meaning.

A-2. Misprision of Treason. This crime consists of the concealment of knowledge of the commission of treason or the failure to give information to the appropriate authorities regarding such commission, without otherwise assenting to or participating in the crime.

A typical statute is the California law (Cal. Penal Code sec. 38 [1941]), which reads as follows: "Misprision of treason is the knowledge and concealment of treason, without otherwise assenting to or participating in the crime. . . ."

The following thirty-three states have constitutional provisions or statutes prohibiting misprision of treason: Alabama, Arkansas, Arizona, California, Connecticut, Florida, Georgia, Illinois, Indiana, Iowa, Kansas, Louisiana, Maine, Massachusetts, Michigan, Minnesota, Missouri, Montana, Nevada, New Hampshire, New Jersey, North Dakota, Ohio, Oregon, Pennsylvania, Rhode Island, South Dakota, Tennessee, Texas, Vermont, Virginia, Washington, and West Virginia.

Type B—Rebellion and Insurrection

B-1. Rebellion and Insurrection. The two terms "rebellion" and "insurrection" can be used synonymously in a general sense to mean open and active opposition of a number of persons to the existing government of their country. The term "rebellion" connotes a deliberate, organized resistance, by force and arms, to the laws or operations of the government by one of its subjects (Black's *Law Dictionary,* 3d ed. [1933], p. 1500) where the object is to overthrow and supersede entirely the existing government, while the term "insurrection" connotes something less than rebellion, an active and open resistance to the authority of the government whose object may not be to overthrow the existing government entirely but merely to effect, by force and violence, a lesser change in the form and operation of government. *Prize Cases,* 2 Black (67 U.S.) 635, 666–667 (1862). An insurrection may grow to a rebellion which in turn may grow into a war against the existing

395

government which would make the participants guilty of treason (see above).

Twenty-five jurisdictions have statutes or constitutional provisions making this type of conduct illegal. They are Arkansas, California, Florida, Georgia, Illinois, Indiana, Iowa, Kansas, Maine, Maryland, Minnesota, Missouri, Nebraska, Nevada, New Jersey, New York, North Carolina, Ohio, Oregon, Pennsylvania, Rhode Island, Virginia, Washington, West Virginia, and Wyoming. Even without express statutory power such activities are illegal. As the Supreme Court has said, "the State has inherently the right to use all means necessary to put down the resistance to its authority, and restore peace, order, and obedience to law." *White v. Hart,* 13 Wall. (80 U.S.) 646, 650–651 (1871). A fortiori there would seem to be no question of the constitutionality of such legislation.

It should be noted that both these crimes involve overt acts of resistance by force or violence, an actual arising against the government. In this respect they differ from the crime of sedition (see below).

The statutes of the various states vary a great deal. Here is what one might call a typical provision. Ga. Code Ann. sec. 26–901 (1936).

"Insurrection shall consist in any combined resistance to the lawful authority of the State, with intent to the denial thereof, when the same is manifested or intended to be manifested by acts of violence."

B-2. Statutes Giving Authority to Governor to Call the Militia or Police Forces to Suppress Insurrection. Whether or not a statute so provides in specific terms, the power to suppress insurrection is an implied corollary of its illegality. Fourteen states, however, have statutes which expressly give the governor authority to declare that a state of rebellion or insurrection exists, in the event he is satisfied that such resistance endangers law and order in the state, and to call the militia or the police force, declare martial law, and suspend the writ of habeas corpus.

Statutes of this type are to be found in Arkansas, California, Georgia, Maine, Minnesota, Missouri, Montana, Nevada, New York, Oklahoma, South Carolina, West Virginia, Wisconsin, and Wyoming.

396

In other states the matter is dealt with under the ordinary criminal statutes prohibiting riot and unlawful assembly, for example, Alaska Comp. Laws secs. 65–10–1—65–10–2 (1949).

Type C—Sedition

The crime of sedition consists of advocacy by word of mouth, publication, or otherwise which incites discontent and contempt for the present form of government, causing persons to flout its laws and tending to destroy the government itself. It includes advocacy which incites to overthrowing the existing government, by force and violence, to bring into contempt the form of government, its public officers, its military forces, flags, and other symbols.

No overt act is required for the commission of sedition. Mere advocacy alone which is likely to incite is the essence of the crime.

An example of this type of statute is Conn. Gen. Stat. sec. 8346 (1949), which reads as follows:

> Any person who shall speak, or write, print and publicly exhibit or distribute, or who shall publicly exhibit, post or advertise any disloyal, scurrilous or abusive matter concerning the form of government of the United States, its military forces, flag or uniforms, or any matter which is intended to bring them into contempt or which creates or fosters opposition to organized government, shall be fined. . . .

These thirty-one jurisdictions have sedition statutes: Alabama, Alaska, Arkansas, Colorado, Connecticut, Delaware, Florida, Hawaii, Illinois, Indiana, Iowa, Kansas, Kentucky, Louisiana, Maryland, Michigan, Minnesota, Mississippi, Montana, Nevada, New Hampshire, New Jersey, North Carolina, Pennsylvania, Rhode Island, Tennessee, Texas, Vermont, Virginia, Washington, and West Virginia.

These statutes are by no means uniform in wording or phraseology but vary greatly.

For a collection of state cases discussing the constitutionality of these statutes see 1 A.L.R. 336 (1918), 20 A.L.R. 1539 (1922), and 73 A.L.R. 1495 (1930). For a general recent discussion see Antieau, "The Rule of Clear and Present Danger: The Scope of Its Applicability," 48 Mich. L. Rev. 811 (1950) and Note, "Conduct Proscribed As Promoting Violent Overthrow of the Government," 61 Harv. L. Rev. 1215 (1948).

Type D—Criminal Syndicalism

D-1. Criminal Syndicalism. The doctrine of criminal syndicalism as defined in Cal. Gen. Laws act 8428, sec. 1 (1944) is as follows:

> The term "criminal syndicalism" as used in this act is hereby defined as any doctrine or precept advocating, teaching or aiding and abetting the commission of crime, sabotage (which word is hereby defined as meaning willful and malicious physical damage or injury to physical property), or unlawful acts of force and violence or unlawful methods of terrorism as a means of accomplishing a change in industrial ownership or control, or effecting any political change.

Under these statutes it is made a felony to advocate or teach criminal syndicalism, orally or by printing, or to organize a society which advocates it, or knowingly to become a member of such society.

Twenty jurisdictions have this type of statute. They are Alaska, Arkansas, California, Hawaii, Idaho, Iowa, Kansas, Kentucky, Michigan, Minnesota, Montana, Nebraska, Nevada, Ohio, Oklahoma, Rhode Island, South Dakota, Utah, West Virginia, and Wyoming.

Sabotage is incidentally defined and made a crime by this type of statute. (See Type G-2, below.)

For a collection of cases discussing the validity of these statutes see 20 A.L.R. 1543 (1922) and 73 A.L.R. 1498 (1930).

The Supreme Court of the United States has passed on the validity of these statutes in four cases. In *Burns v. United States,* 274 U.S. 328, 71 L.Ed. 1077, 47 S.Ct. 650 (1927) the California statute was applied to an organizer of the I.W.W. The evidence showed that this organization advocated and taught sabotage and aided in various acts of sabotage as defined in the statute. The court held the statute so applied to be constitutional and not in contravention of the Fourteenth Amendment. In *Whitney v. Cali-*

fornia, 274 U.S. 357, 71 L.Ed. 1095, 47 S.Ct. 641 (1927) the California statute was applied to an organizer of the Communist Labor Party which the jury found on the evidence submitted to be organized for the purposes prohibited in the statute. The court again upheld the statute as applied. It held that it was constitutional to prohibit and punish becoming a member of and organizing such a group as in the Burns case.

In *Fiske v. Kansas,* 274 U.S. 380, 71 L.Ed. 1108, 47 S.Ct. 655 (1927) the section of the Kansas statute which prohibited any person from advocating criminal syndicalism was involved. The court held that the language appearing in the preamble to the constitution of the I.W.W. to the effect that the working class and the employing class have nothing in common, and that as between them there must be a struggle until the workers of the world organize as a class, and other similar statements did not constitute a showing that the organization advocated criminal syndicalism and held that the section as applied to the accused, a person who solicited members in a branch of the I.W.W., was unconstitutional in violation of the due process clause of the Fourteenth Amendment, as no violation of the statute was shown.

In *De Jonge v. Oregon,* 299 U.S. 353, 81 L.Ed. 278, 57 S.Ct. 45 (1937), discussed in Spencer, "Criminal Syndicalism, De Jonge v. Oregon," 16 Ore. L. Rev. 278 (1938), the Oregon statute was applied to a person who aided in the conduct of a meeting organized and sponsored by the Communist Party protesting the activities of the local police in connection with a strike. The Supreme Court of the United States held the statute unconstitutional as applied. There was no evidence of the teaching or advocacy of the prohibited doctrine at the meeting in question. Although it was found by the Oregon Supreme Court that the Communist Party did advocate criminal syndicalism and that the accused was a member, the court felt this was irrelevant and quashed the conviction and held the statute as applied unconstitutional—as a violation of freedom of speech and assembly.

See also Note, "Criminal Syndicalism and Civil Liberties," 36 Ill. L. Rev. 357 (1941).

D-2. Forbidding Assembly and Leasing of Place of Assembly of Criminal Syndicalists. In some statutes there are additional provisions similar to those of the New York Criminal Anarchy Act (N.Y. Penal Law secs. 162, 163), which reads as follows:

Section 162. ASSEMBLAGES OF ANARCHISTS

Whenever two or more persons assemble for the purpose of advocating or teaching the doctrines of criminal anarchy, as defined . . . such an assembly is unlawful, and every person voluntarily participating therein by his presence, aid or instigation, is guilty of a felony. . . .

. . . . .

Section 163. PERMITTING PREMISES TO BE USED FOR ASSEMBLAGES OF ANARCHISTS

The owner, agent, superintendent, janitor, caretaker or occupant of any place, building or room, who wilfully and knowingly permits therein any assemblage of persons prohibited by Sec. 162, or who, after notification that the premises are so used permits such use to be continued, is guilty of a misdemeanor. . . .

Fourteen jurisdictions have these provisions in their criminal syndicalism statutes. They are Alaska, Hawaii, Idaho, Iowa, Kansas, Kentucky, Minnesota, Montana, Nebraska, Nevada, Ohio, Oklahoma, South Dakota, and Utah.

Type E—Criminal Anarchy

E-1. Criminal Anarchy. The crime of criminal anarchy as defined by the New York Criminal Anarchy Act of 1902 (N.Y. Penal Law sec. 160) is as follows: "Criminal anarchy is the doctrine that organized government should be overthrown by force or violence, or by assassination of the executive head or of any of the executive officials of the government, or by any unlawful means. The advocacy of such doctrine by word of mouth or in writing is a felony."

The other state statutes take their origin from the New York statute, and it is followed in many cases verbatim.

Sixteen jurisdictions have criminal anarchy statutes. They are Alabama, Colorado, Connecticut, Delaware, Florida, Hawaii, Iowa, Louisiana, Massachusetts, Nevada, New Jersey, New York, Rhode Island, Vermont, Washington, and Wisconsin.

In *Gitlow v. New York,* 268 U.S. 652, 69 L.Ed. 1138, 45 S.Ct. 625 (1925) a conviction under the New York statute was upheld by the United States Supreme Court, which held that this was a reasonable exercise of the state police power. Justices Holmes and Brandeis dissented; they urged the court to accept the "clear and present danger test," which was later adopted, making this case questionable authority today.

E-2. *Forbidding Assembly and Leasing of Place of Assembly of Criminal Anarchists.* In four jurisdictions there are provisions similar to Type D-2, above. They are Alabama, New York, Washington, and Wisconsin.

Type F—Red Flag Laws

These statutes in general prohibit the display of certain types of flags and other emblems as symbols of the advocacy of or belief in activities antagonistic to the present form of government.

The present California law, Cal. Mil. and Vet. Code sec. 616 (1943), is typical. It reads as follows:

"Any person who displays a red flag, banner, or badge or any flag, badge, banner, or device of any color or form whatever in any public place or in any meeting place or public assembly, or from or on any house, building, or window as a sign, symbol, or emblem of forceful or violent opposition to organized government or as an invitation or stimulus to anarchistic action or as an aid to propaganda that advocates by force or violence the overthrow of government is guilty of a felony."

Thirty-four jurisdictions have this type of statute. They are Alabama, Arkansas, Arizona, California, Colorado, Connecticut, Delaware, Idaho, Illinois, Indiana, Iowa, Kansas, Kentucky, Massachusetts, Michigan, Minnesota, Montana, Nebraska, Nevada, New Jersey, New Mexico, New York, North Dakota, Ohio, Oregon, Pennsylvania, Rhode Island, South Dakota, Texas, Utah, Vermont, Washington, West Virginia, and Wisconsin.

For convenience in classification we have broken down the various types of Red Flag laws as follows:

Type F-1: prohibiting red flags

Type F-2: prohibiting black flags

Type F-3: prohibiting emblems symbolizing opposition to organized government

Type F-4: prohibiting emblems symbolizing disloyalty to the state or the United States

Type F-5: prohibiting emblems which might incite and lead to breach of peace

Type F-6: miscellaneous types

For a collection of cases discussing the validity of these statutes see 20 A.L.R. 1545 (1922).

In *Stromberg v. California,* 283 U.S. 359, 75 L.Ed. 1117, 51 S.Ct. 532, 73 A.L.R. 1484 (1931) the accused was in charge of a children's camp in California where each day she directed a ceremony where the flag of the Communist Party was raised while the children pledged allegiance. The accused was indicted and convicted under the former California statute (Cal. Penal Code sec. 403a [1931]) which prohibited the display of a red flag "as a sign . . . of opposition to organized government." The United States Supreme Court held the clause in question void for vagueness and indefiniteness, stating that its terms might include peaceful and orderly opposition to a government organized and controlled by a political party, as well as a Communist organization. The California statute was then amended (see above).

Type G—Sabotage

The crime of sabotage generally prohibits the wilful destruction, injury, or damage of physical property belonging to another.

When reference to sabotage is merely incidental to the state criminal syndicalism statute (as, for example, in the California statute quoted in Type D-1, above), the focus is on activities engaged in by workers against their employer's property.

The uniform Sabotage Prevention Act, on the other hand, is by its terms applicable only in time of war and is aimed at activities of enemy agents and their sympathizers.

For convenience we have broken down the types of sabotage statutes as follows:

G-1. Uniform Sabotage Prevention Act. See Ark. Stat. Ann. secs. 41-4111—41-4113 (1947). Fourteen jurisdictions have this type.

They are Arkansas, California, Colorado, Florida, Hawaii, Maryland, New Hampshire, New Mexico, Oklahoma, Pennsylvania, Tennessee, Utah, Vermont, and Wisconsin.

G-2. Sabotage Prohibited in the Criminal Syndicalism Statutes. Thirteen jurisdictions have defined and prohibited sabotage in their criminal syndicalism statutes. They are California, Hawaii, Idaho, Iowa, Kansas, Kentucky, Minnesota, Montana, Nevada, Ohio, Oklahoma, South Dakota, and Utah.

G-3. Miscellaneous Type Sabotage Statutes. Six jurisdictions have atypical sabotage statutes. They are Louisiana, Mississippi, Nebraska, New York, South Carolina, and Washington.

There seems to be no question of the right of a state to punish criminally anyone who intentionally destroys or damages the property of others. *Burns v. United States,* 274 U.S. 328, 331, 71 L.Ed. 1077, 47 S.Ct. 650 (1927).

Type H—Masks and Disguises

Many states have enacted laws controlling the wearing of masks and disguises to conceal identity. The laws are of a general nature and apparently not directed at subversive activities.

The California statute (Cal. Gen. Laws act 4707, sec. 1 [1947]) is set forth as an example and reads as follows:

"It shall be unlawful for any person, either alone or in company with others, to appear on any street or highway, or in other public places or any place open to view by the general public, with his face partially or completely concealed by means of a mask or other regalia or paraphernalia, with the intent thereby to conceal the identity of such person; provided, however, that this act shall not be construed to prohibit the wearing of such means of concealment in good faith for the purposes of amusement, entertainment or in compliance with any public health order."

Twelve jurisdictions have this type of statute. They are California, Florida, Louisiana, Maine, Massachusetts, Michigan, New Mexico, New York, North Dakota, Oregon, Texas, and Washington.

Type I—Statutes Excluding Groups from Recognition as Political Parties

This type of statute would exclude from a place on the ballot those groups who advocate what is considered to be subversive or objectionable. This is done either by the simple mechanics of refusing to certify them as a political party if they fall under the statutory proscription or by compelling the officers of the group to sign sworn affidavits to the effect that the group does not advocate the proscribed doctrines or that it is not affiliated in any way with such a group. These statutes are to be found under the state election laws and can be classified as follows:

I-1. Those Excluding Groups Which Advocate Forcible or Unlawful Overthrow of the Government. Fifteen jurisdictions have this type of statute. They are Alabama, Arkansas, California, Delaware, Illinois, Indiana, Kansas, Maryland, Ohio, Oklahoma, Pennsylvania, Tennessee, Texas, Wisconsin, and Wyoming.

I-2. Those Excluding Groups Which Advocate or Carry Out Programs of Force, Violence, Sabotage, Sedition, or Treason. Twelve jurisdictions have this type of statute. They are Arkansas, California, Delaware, Illinois, Indiana, Kansas, Maryland, Ohio, Oklahoma, Tennessee, Wisconsin, and Wyoming.

I-3. Those Excluding Groups Which Use "Communist" in Their Respective Names or Are Directly or Indirectly Connected with the Communist Party of the United States. Eight jurisdictions have this type of statute. They are Arkansas, California, Illinois, Kansas, Maryland, Oklahoma, Wisconsin, and Wyoming.

I-4. Miscellaneous Types. California and Texas have statutory provisions which do not fall into any of the above groupings. North Carolina forbids the existence of any secret political or military organizations, and Oklahoma forbids societies which require their membership to take an oath against the state or federal constitutions.

There have been few cases passing on the constitutionality of these statutes. The California statute was held unconstitutional in *Communist Party v. Peek,* 20 Cal. 2d 536, 127 P.2d 889 (1942). The Arkansas statute was upheld in *Field v. Hall,* 201 Ark. 77, 143 S.W.2d 567 (1940).

404

See also Note, "May the States, by Statute, Bar Subversive Groups from the Ballot?" 25 Notre Dame Lawyer 319 (1950) and "The Communist Party and the Ballot," 1 Bill of Rights Rev. 286 (1941).

In *Washington ex. rel. Huff v. Reeves,* 5 Wash.2d 637, 106 P.2d 729, 130 A.L.R. 1465 (1940) the secretary of state of Washington attempted to bar the Communist Party from the ballot without a statute, and the Supreme Court of Washington refused to allow it.

Type J—Statutes Excluding Persons from Elective Office

This type of statute excludes certain persons from elective office or from candidacy for elective office. These statutes are to be distinguished from those which exclude persons from holding public office (Type K) and those which exclude persons from ordinary state employment (Type L).

We have classified the statutes generally by criteria and method as follows:

J-1. Those Excluding Persons Who Advocate Forcible or Unlawful Overthrow of the Government. Eight jurisdictions have this type of statute. They are Alaska, Florida, Kansas, Maryland, New Jersey, Oklahoma, Oregon, and Texas.

J-2. Those Excluding Persons Who Advocate or Carry Out Programs of Force, Violence, Sabotage, Sedition, or Treason. Two jurisdictions have this type of statute: Maryland and Oklahoma.

It will be noted that Type J-1 would ordinarily include persons guilty of sedition, so that there might be some overlap. However, we have drawn the line closely and limited Type J-2 to those which are worded almost exactly as described.

J-3. Those Excluding Persons Who Are Members of Organizations Which Advocate Either of the Above Doctrines As Set Out in J-1 or J-2. Six jurisdictions have statutes of this type. They are Alaska, Florida, Kansas, Maryland, New Jersey, and Oregon.

J-4. Those Excluding Persons Who Are Directly or Indirectly Affiliated with the Communist Party. Seven jurisdictions have this type of statute. They are Alaska, Arizona, Florida, Georgia, Maryland, New Jersey, and Oklahoma.

J-5. Statutes in Which the Method of Ascertaining the Above Characteristics Is by Sworn Oath or Affidavit. Eight jurisdictions have statutes of this type. They are Alaska, Arizona, Florida, Georgia, Kansas, Maryland, New Jersey, and Oklahoma.

J-6. Statutes Which Authorize Loyalty Investigations of Such Persons. Maryland is the only state with this type of statute.

It will be noted that Types J-1, J-2, J-3, and J-4 are concerned with substantive criteria, while Types J-5 and J-6 are concerned with the procedural method of ascertaining the relevant facts. The most common method is by the so-called loyalty oath or by sworn affidavit by the person concerned. Those jurisdictions using neither of the methods set out simply prohibit such persons from holding office or forbid the elections officials to allow them to run for office.

It will also be noted that this type of statute is another method of accomplishing the same end as is accomplished by the political party statutes (Type I, above).

In *Imbrie v. Marsh*, 5 N.J. Super. 239, 68 A.2d 761 (1949), affirmed 3 N.J. 578, 71 A.2d 352 (1950) the court held the New Jersey oath law unconstitutional as in contravention of the New Jersey constitution in that it prescribed a different oath from that provided by the constitution.

Type K—Statutes Excluding Persons from Public Office

This type of statute excludes certain persons from holding any public office in the state or territory. These statutes are to be distinguished from those which exclude persons from elective office (Type J) and those which exclude persons from state employment (Type L).

These statutes have been classified generally by criteria and method in the same manner as were the Type J statutes, as follows:

K-1. Those Excluding Persons Who Advocate Forcible or Unlawful Overthrow of the Government. Nine jurisdictions have this type of statute. They are Alaska, Florida, Hawaii, Illinois, Kansas, Maryland, New Jersey, New York, and Oklahoma.

K-2. Those Excluding Persons Who Advocate or Carry Out Programs of Force, Violence, Sabotage, Sedition, or Treason. Two jurisdictions have this type of statute. They are Maryland and Oklahoma.

K-3. Those Excluding Persons Who Are Members of Organizations Which Advocate Either of the Above Doctrines As Set Out in K-1 or K-2. Seven jurisdictions have this type of statute. They are Alaska, Florida, Hawaii, Illinois, Kansas, Maryland, and New Jersey.

K-4. Those Excluding Persons Who Are Directly or Indirectly Affiliated with the Communist Party. Seven jurisdictions have this type of statute. They are Alaska, Florida, Georgia, Illinois, Maryland, New Jersey, and Oklahoma.

K-5. Statutes in Which the Method of Ascertaining the Above Criteria Is by Sworn Oath or Affidavit. Eight jurisdictions have this type of statute. They are Alaska, Florida, Georgia, Hawaii, Kansas, Maryland, New Jersey, and Oklahoma.

K-6. Statutes Which Authorize Loyalty Investigations of Said Persons. Maryland is the only state with this type of statute.

It will be noted that Types K-1, K-2, K-3, and K-4 are concerned with substantive criteria, while Types K-5 and K-6 are concerned with the procedural methods of ascertaining the relevant facts. The most common method is by the so-called loyalty oath or by sworn affidavit by the person concerned. Those jurisdictions using neither of these methods simply prohibit such persons from holding office or forbid their appointment.

As to the validity of this type of statute see the comments following Type J and Type L.

Type L—Statutes Excluding Persons from State Employment

This type of statute excludes certain persons from employment by the state or territory. Although most of these statutes are phrased generally so as to include all forms of employment by the state, some apply only to specific types of state employment, as, for example, the state police. Consequently, most of these statutes also apply to teachers in public schools. (See Types N and O.)

These statutes are to be distinguished from those which exclude persons from elective office (Type J) and those which exclude persons from public office (Type K).

These statutes have been classified generally by criteria and method in the same manner as were Type J and Type K, as follows:

L-1. Those Excluding Persons Who Advocate Forcible or Unlawful Overthrow of the Government. Fifteen jurisdictions have this type of statute. They are Alaska, California, Florida, Hawaii, Illinois, Kansas, Maryland, Massachusetts, New Jersey, New York, North Carolina, Oregon, Pennsylvania, Utah, and Washington.

L-2. Those Excluding Persons Who Advocate or Carry Out Programs of Force, Violence, Sabotage, Sedition, or Treason. Three jurisdictions have this type of statute. They are California, Maryland, and New Mexico.

L-3. Those Excluding Persons Who Are Members of Organizations Which Advocate Either of the Above Doctrines As Set Out in L-1 or L-2. Eleven jurisdictions have this type of statute. They are Alaska, Arkansas, California, Florida, Hawaii, Illinois, Kansas, Maryland, New Jersey, New York, and Washington.

L-4. Those Excluding Persons Who Are Directly or Indirectly Affiliated with the Communist Party. Eight jurisdictions have this type of statute. They are Alaska, Arkansas, Florida, Georgia, Illinois, Maryland, New Jersey, and Washington.

L-5. Statutes in Which the Method of Ascertaining the Above Facts Is by Sworn Oath or Affidavit. Eleven jurisdictions have this type of statute. They are Alaska, California, Florida, Georgia, Hawaii, Kansas, Maryland, Massachusetts, New Jersey, Oregon, and Washington.

L-6. Statutes Which Authorize Loyalty Investigations of Said Persons. Only Maryland has this type of statute.

It will be noted that Types L-1, L-2, L-3, and L-4 are concerned with the substantive criteria, while Types L-5 and L-6 are concerned with the procedural methods of ascertaining the relevant facts. The most common method is by the so-called loyalty oath or by sworn affidavit by the person concerned. Those jurisdictions using neither of these methods merely forbid the employment of such persons. Another method, which, as far as can be ascertained, is used by only one state, is to include a proviso in the annual state appropriation statute prohibiting the employment of certain persons. Wash. Laws 1949, c. 242, sec. 2, p. 948.

Type M—Registration Statutes

Statutes requiring the registration of certain organizations have been enacted in five jurisdictions. They are California, Hawaii, Louisiana, Michigan, and New York.

The California statute requires any group which advocates overthrow of the government or which is subject to foreign control to register and to file complete reports with the state, the reports include the names and addresses of all members, the extent of foreign control, their constitutional and charter provisions, the legislative activities, and many other items of information. Periodic statements of changes are required to keep this information up to date. Violations of the act are declared to be a felony and persons attending a meeting of such an organization knowing it has failed to comply with the statute are guilty of a misdemeanor. The 1947 Michigan statute is a similar measure for the regulation and control of foreign agencies operating in that state.

The New York law is not quite so broad in scope as it requires only that all oath-bound societies, with the exception in favor of such groups as college fraternities and other fraternal societies, to register with the state their constitutions, bylaws, membership lists, and other pertinent data.

The Hawaii statute makes it unlawful for a person to organize, form, or maintain any "secret association" for any purpose unless the organization applies for and gets a license from the governor. Such "secret association" is nowhere defined, but presumably the statute could be used against subversive organizations.

The Louisiana statute provides generally that the officers of any fraternal, patriotic, charitable, benevolent, literary, scientific, athletic, military, or social organization shall file with the secretary of state certain information. It is made a misdemeanor if the officer fails to do this, and the holding of any meeting until this is done is prohibited.

This type of statute is an information-inducing type designed to expose all secret or subversive groups to the public authorities. With the exception of the Michigan and California statute such statutes are not aimed at subversive activities primarily but could be so used.

The validity of the New York statute was upheld as applied to the Ku Klux Klan in *Bryant v. Zimmerman*, 278 U.S. 63, 73 L.Ed. 184, 49 S.Ct. 61, 62 A.L.R. 785 (1928).

The California statute was applied in *People v. Noble*, 68 Cal. App.2d 853, 158 P.2d 225 (1945), where the court reversed the judgment against the accused for lack of evidence, and in dictum pointed out that they were in grave doubt as to the constitutionality of the statute.

Type N—Teacher's Oath Statutes

Twenty-seven jurisdictions have prescribed teachers' oaths of various types.

N-1. Those in Which the Oath Is Prescribed by Statute. Twenty-three jurisdictions have this type of statute. They are Alaska, Arizona, California, Colorado, Florida, Georgia, Indiana, Maryland, Massachusetts, Michigan, Mississippi, Montana, Nevada, New Hampshire, New Jersey, New York, North Dakota, Oregon, South Dakota, Texas, Vermont, Washington, and West Virginia.

It is to be noted that statutes of Type L-5, above, would also apply to teachers as state employees. This type is therefore duplicated in those instances where they would presumably apply to teachers.

N-2. Those Which Have a Teacher's Oath Prescribed by the State Department of Education. Four jurisdictions have this type of oath law. They are Rhode Island, South Carolina, Tennessee, and Virginia. In these jurisdictions either by a general or specific enabling statute the state board of education or the local municipal or district board is empowered to prescribe an oath for teachers.

Most states, by their respective education laws, empower the administrative agencies, either state, county, or municipal, to certify and hire new teachers and to discharge persons now teaching. The statutes generally provide certain minimum requirements, and much is left to the discretion of the agency. In those states with no oath laws it would probably not be beyond the authority of these agencies to establish oath requirements or loyalty tests of their own.

It is important in these statutes to distinguish between the various types of oaths according to their content. Ordinarily the older oaths merely stated that the person would "support and defend the constitution." The newer oath laws go much further. An example is the new 1949 Alaska oath law (Alaska Laws 1949, c. 113, p. 290), which reads as follows:

> I . . . do solemnly swear (or affirm) that I am not a member of the Communist Party or any subversive parties or affiliated with such party, that I do not believe in, am not a member of nor do I support any organization that believes in or teaches the overthrow of the United States Government by force or by any illegal or unconstitutional method, that I will defend and support the Constitution of the United States, and perform all the duties of the office or position on which I am about to enter, and therein do equal right and justice to all men, so help me God.

In most states the oath is required only of public schoolteachers in the elementary and secondary schools. In some, however, oaths are required of teachers of all schools, public or private, elementary or higher.

Type O—Statutes concerning Teacher Loyalty Other than Oath Type

Nine jurisdictions have this type of statute. They are Arkansas, California, Illinois, Maryland, Massachusetts, Nebraska, New York, Oklahoma, and Tennessee. Most of these are of the L-1, L-3, or L-4 type, which relate to state employment generally without specific reference to schoolteachers.

The New York *Feinberg Law* (N.Y. Education Law secs. 3021–3022) is exceptional in that it empowers the New York Board of

Regents to make a list of organizations it finds to be "subversive" and provide in its rules that membership in any listed organization shall constitute prima facie evidence of disqualification for any office or position in the public schools of the state.

Type P—Miscellaneous School Statutes

Five jurisdictions have what we have classified as miscellaneous school statutes. They are California, Illinois, Maryland, New York, and Texas.

The California and Illinois statutes prohibit the use of school facilities by subversive organizations. The Maryland statute requires that self-initiated loyalty investigations be undertaken by any private institution of learning before it gets any public funds. The New York statute prohibits the use of textbooks containing seditious or disloyal matter, and the Texas statute requires students who wish to attend any publicly supported institution of higher learning to take loyalty oaths.

Type Q—Statutes Excluding Persons from Incidental Benefits

An indirect sanction against subversives is employed by some states through withholding various legislative benefits.

Thus Pennsylvania renders persons ineligible to receive public assistance if they are active in subversive activities—provided they are not blind. Ohio requires of a person seeking unemployment benefits an affidavit stating whether or not he is a member of a party which advocates overthrow of government by force. Rhode Island, in appropriations bills extending through the fiscal year 1951, prohibits the grant of scholarships until the attorney general and director of education are satisfied that the beneficiary does not employ anyone associated with a group advocating violent overthrow of the government. And South Carolina specifies that no part of its appropriations to state institutions of higher learning shall be used in connection with visits from persons belonging to an un-American organization branded as such by either the United States or state attorney general. Montana, in a unique statute and

412

without providing any sanctions, declares it to be the legislative policy of the state that any position vacancy of any business or industry shall not be filled by any person who is a member of the Communist Party or the German-American Bund.

APPENDIX B[1]

Statutes Listed by State
as of January 1, 1951

ALABAMA

Treason and Misprision of Treason (Types A-1 and A-2)
    Ala. Const. (1901) Art. I, secs. 18, 19.
    Ala. Code Ann. tit. 14 secs. 424, 425 (1940).
Sedition (Type C)
    Ala. Code Ann. tit. 14, sec. 22(1) (Supp. 1947).
    Note: Discussion of this type of statute in *Barton v. City of Bessemer,* 234 Ala. 20, 173 So. 626 (1936).
Criminal Anarchy (Types E-1 and E-2)
    Ala. Code Ann. tit. 14 secs. 19–22 (1940).
Red Flag Law (Types F-4 and F-6)
    Ala. Code Ann. tit. 14, secs. 195–196 (1940).
    Ala. Code Ann. tit. 35, secs. 18(1), 18(2) (1940).
Political Parties (Type I-1)
    Ala. Code Ann. tit. 14, sec. 22(2) (Supp. 1947).

ALASKA

Sedition (Type C-1)
    Alaska Comp. Laws secs. 65-11-1—65-11-2 (1949).
Criminal Syndicalism (Types D-1 and D-2)
    Alaska Comp. Laws secs. 65-11-3—65-11-6 (1949).
Sabotage (Type G-2) included in the criminal syndicalism law.

[1] This appendix was prepared, in the main, by William H. Rockwell of the New York Bar, under the supervision of Walter Gellhorn.

Excluding Persons from Public Office and State Employment (Types J, K, and L-1-3-4-5)
Alaska Laws, 1949, c. 113, p. 290 amending sec. 11-1-8 of Alaska Comp. Laws (1949).
Teacher's Oath (Type N-1), see 1949 statute, *supra*.

ARIZONA

Treason and Misprision of Treason (Types A-1 and A-2)
Ariz. Code Ann. secs. 43-5701—43-5703 (1939).
Red Flag Law (Type F-1-2-3)
Ariz. Code Ann. sec. 43-2402 (1939).
State Legislators Oath Law (Type J-4-5)
Ariz. Laws, 1949, House Res. No. 4, p. 570.
Teacher's Oath (Type N-1)
Ariz. Code Ann. sec. 54-1002 (Supp. 1947).

ARKANSAS

Treason and Misprision of Treason (Types A-1 and A-2)
Ark. Stat. Ann. secs. 41-4101—41-4104 (1947).
Rebellion and Insurrection (Types B-1 and B-2)
Ark. Stat. Ann. secs. 41-4109—41-4110, 42-108 (1947).
Sedition (Type C)
Ark. Stat. Ann. sec. 41-4107 (1947).
Criminal Syndicalism (Type D-1)
Ark. Stat. Ann. secs. 41-4111—41-4113 (1947).
Red Flag Law (Type F-3-4-5)
Ark, Stat. Ann. sec. 41-4108 (1947).
Uniform Sabotage Prevention Act (Type G-1)
Ark. Stat. Ann. secs. 41-4114—41-4124.
Political Parties (Type I-1-2-3)
Ark. Stat. Ann. sec. 3-1604 (1947) held constitutional in *Field v. Hall*, 201 Ark. 77, 143 S.W.2d 567 (1940).
Excluding Persons from State Employment (Type L-3-4)
Ark. Stat. Ann. secs. 3-1404, 41-4113(b) and (c) (1947).
Teacher Loyalty (Type O), see statute cited *supra*, Type L.

CALIFORNIA

Treason and Misprision of Treason (Types A-1 and A-2)
   Cal. Const. (1879) Art. I, sec. 20.
   Cal. Penal Code secs. 37–38 (1941).
Rebellion and Insurrection (Types B-1 and B-2)
   Cal. Mil. & Vet. Code secs. 143, 145 (1943).
Criminal Syndicalism (Type D-1)
   Cal. Gen. Laws act 8428 (1944).
   Note: Upheld *Burns v. U.S.,* 274 U.S. 328, 71 L.Ed. 1077, 47 S.Ct. 650 (1927); *Whitney v. California,* 274 U.S. 357, 71 L.Ed. 1095, 47 S.Ct. 641 (1927); *People v. Steelik,* 187 Cal. 361, 203 P. 78 (1921).
Red Flag Law (Type F-1-3)
   Cal. Mil. & Vet. Code sec. 616 (1943).
   Note: Former sec. 403a of Cal. Penal Code held unconstitutional in *Stromberg v. California,* 283 U.S. 359, 75 L.Ed 1117, 51 S.Ct. 532, 73 A.L.R. 1484 (1931).
Uniform Sabotage Prevention Act (Type G-1)
   Cal. Gen. Laws act 8427 (1943).
Sabotage (Type G-2), see Type D-1.
Masks and Disguises (Type H)
   Cal. Gen. Laws act 4707 (1943).
Political Parties (Type I-1-2-3-4)
   Cal. Elec. Code secs. 2540.3–2540.4.
   Note: Type I-3 held unconstitutional in *Communist Party v. Peek,* 20 Cal.2d 536, 127 P.2d 889 (1942).
Excluding Persons from State Employment (Type L-1-2-3-5)
   Cal. Govt. Code sec. 1028 (Supp. 1947) (Type L-1-3).
   Cal. Govt. Code sec. 18200 (Supp. 1945) (Type L-2).
   Cal. Govt. Code secs. 18150–18158 (Supp. 1945) (Type L-5).
   Also see Cal. Govt. Code sec. 1023 (1944) and Cal. Govt. Code sec. 19573 (Supp. 1945).
   Note: See *Steiner v. Darby,* 88 Cal. App.2d 481, 199 P.2d 429 (1948) upholding the validity of oath imposed by a county board.
Registration Statute (Type M)
   Cal. Corp. Code secs. 35000–35302 (1948).

Note: Discussed in *People v. Noble,* 68 Cal. App.2d 853, 158 P.2d 225 (1945).

Teacher's Oath (Type N-1)
Cal. Educ. Code sec. 12100 (Supp. 1949).

Teacher Loyalty (Type O)
Cal. Educ. Code sec. 13521(b) (1944).

Note: *Board of Education v. Jewett,* 21 Cal. App.2d 64, 68 P.2d 404 (1937).

Prohibiting Use of School Property by Subversive Organizations (Type P)
Cal. Educ. Code sec. 19432 (Supp. 1949).

Note: Held unconstitutional in *Danskin v. School District,* 28 Cal.2d 536, 171 P.2d 885 (1946).

COLORADO

Treason (Type A-1)
Colo. Const. (1876) Art. II, sec. 9.

Sedition (Type C) *and Criminal Anarchy* (Type E-1)
Colo. Stat. Ann. c. 48, secs. 21–29 (1935).

Red Flag Law (Type F-1)
Colo. Stat. Ann. c. 48, secs. 18–20 (1935).

Uniform Sabotage Prevention Act (Type G-1)
Colo. Stat. Ann. c. 48, secs. 425(1)–425(13) (Supp. 1949).

Teacher's Oath (Type N-1)
Colo. Stat. Ann. c. 146, secs. 235–237 (1935).

CONNECTICUT

Treason and Misprision of Treason (Types A-1 and A-2)
Conn. Const. (1818) Art. 9, sec. 4.
Conn. Gen. Stat. secs. 8342, 8344–8345 (1949).

Sedition (Type C)
Conn. Gen. Stat. secs. 8346–8347 (1949).

Note: Upheld in *Connecticut v. Sinchuk,* 96 Conn. 605, 115 A. 33, 20 A.L.R. 1515 (1921).

Criminal Anarchy (Type E-1)
Conn. Gen. Stat. sec. 8382 (1949).

Red Flag Law (Type F-1-5)
Conn. Gen. Stat. sec. 8348 (1949).

DELAWARE

Treason (Type A-1)
Del. Rev. Code sec. 5154 (1935).
Sedition (Type C) *and Criminal Anarchy* (Type E-1)
Del. Rev. Code sec. 5156 (1935).
Red Flag Law (Type F-1-2-3)
Del. Rev. Code sec. 5155 (1935).
Political Parties (Type I-1-2)
Del. Rev. Code sec. 1810 (1935).

FLORIDA

Treason and Misprision of Treason (Types A-1 and A-2)
Fla. Const. (1885), Decl. of Rights sec. 23.
Fla. Stat. Ann. secs. 779.01–779.02, 932.50 (1943).
Rebellion and Insurrection (Type B-1)
Fla. Stat. Ann. secs. 779.03–779.05 (1943).
Sedition (Type C)
Fla. Stat. Ann. secs. 250.73, 779.05 (1943).
Criminal Anarchy (Type E-1)
Fla. Stat. Ann. secs. 876.01–876.04 (1943).
Uniform Sabotage Prevention Act (Type G-1)
Fla. Stat. Ann. secs. 779.06–779.20 (1943).
Masks and Disguises (Type H-3)
Fla. Stat. Ann. sec. 843.03 (1943).
Oath for Elected Officers, Public Officers and State Employees
(Types J, K, L-1-3-4-5)
Fla. Laws 1949, c. 25046, p. 102.
Teacher's Oath (Type N-1)
Fla. Stat. Ann. sec. 231.48 (Supp. 1948).
Note: Teachers also required to take oath for state employees,
supra.

GEORGIA

Treason and Misprision of Treason (Types A-1 and A-2)
Ga. Const. (1945) Art. I, sec. 2, par. 2.
Ga. Code Ann. secs. 2-202, 26-701, 26-801—26-804 (1936).
Rebellion and Insurrection (Types B-1 and B-2)

Ga. Code Ann. secs. 26-901—26-904 (1936).

Ga. Code Ann. sec. 86-207 (Supp. 1949). (Type B-2).

Note: Upholding secs. 26-901—26-902, 26-904, see *Carr v. State,* 176 Ga. 55, 166 S.E. 827 (1932); *Dalton v. State,* 176 Ga. 645, 166 S.E. 198 (1933); also *Carr v. State,* 176 Ga. 474, 169 S.E. 201 (1933) and *Herndon v. Georgia,* 178 Ga. 832, 174 S.E. 597 (1934), rehearing denied 179 Ga. 597, 176 S.E. 620 (1934), appeal dismissed 295 U.S. 441, 79 L.Ed. 1530, 55 S.Ct. 794 (1935), rehearing denied 296 U.S. 661, 80 L.Ed. 471, 56 S.Ct. 82 (1935).

Note also: Sec. 26-902 held unconstitutional as applied in *Herndon v. Lowry,* 301 U.S. 242, 81 L.Ed. 1075, 57 S.Ct. 732 (1937).
Oath for Elected Officers, Public Officers and State Employees (Types J, K, and L-4-5)

Ga. Code Ann. secs. 89-311—89-316 (Supp. 1949), as amended Ga. Laws 1950, vol. 1, p. 282.
Teacher's Oath (Type P-1)

Note: Teachers are required to take oath for state employees, *supra.*

HAWAII

Sedition (Type C) *and Criminal Anarchy* (Type E-1)
Hawaii Rev. Laws secs. 11001, 11190–11191 (1945).
Criminal Syndicalism (Types D-1 and D-2)
Hawaii Rev. Laws secs. 11002–11005 (1945).
Uniform Sabotage Prevention Act (Type G-1)
Hawaii Rev. Laws secs. 11621–11633 (1945).
Sabotage (Type G-2), see Type D-1.
Oath for All Public Officers and Territorial Employees (Types K and L-1-3-5)
Hawaii Rev. Laws secs. 600–616 (1945) as amended by Hawaii Laws, 1945, act 131, p. 22 as amended by Hawaii Laws, 1947, act 117, p. 26.
Registration Statute (Type M)
Hawaii Rev. Laws secs. 11641–11647 (1945).
Note: Applicable to secret associations only.

IDAHO

Treason (Type A-1)
  Idaho Const. (1890) Art. V, sec. 5.
  Idaho Code Ann. sec. 9-501 (1949).
Criminal Syndicalism (Types D-1 and D-2)
  Idaho Code Ann. secs. 18-2001—18-2004.
  Note: Upheld in *State v. Dingman,* 37 Idaho 253, 219 P. 760 (1923); *State v. Doyle,* 37 Idaho 296, 219 P. 775 (1923); and *State v. Moore,* 38 Idaho 506, 224 P. 662 (1924).
Red Flag Law (Type F-1-3-4)
  Idaho Code Ann. sec. 18-3402 (1949).
Sabotage (Type G-2), see Type D-1.

ILLINOIS

Treason and Misprision of Treason (Types A-1 and A-2)
  Ill. Rev. Stat. c. 38, secs. 555–557 (1949).
Rebellion and Insurrection (Type B-1)
  Ill. Rev. Stat. c. 134, secs. 10–11 (1949).
  Note: Applying only to telegraphic communications.
Sedition (Type C)
  Ill. Rev. Stat. c. 38, secs. 558–562, 564 (1949).
  Note: Upholding secs. 558–561, *People v. Lloyd,* 304 Ill. 23, 136 N.E. 505 (1922).
Red Flag Law (Type F-4)
  Ill. Rev. Stat. c. 38, secs. 563–564 (1949).
Political Parties (Type I-1-2-3)
  Ill. Rev. Stat. c. 46, secs. 7-2, 8-2, 10-2 (1949).
  Note: Held unconstitutional *Feinglass v. Reinecke,* 48 F. Supp. 438 (N.D. Ill. 1942).
Excluding Persons from Public Office and State Employment (Types K and L-1-3-4)
  Ill. Rev. Stat. c. 127, sec. 166a (1949).
  Ill. Rev. Stat. c. 24½, sec. 8 (1949).
Teacher Loyalty (Type O), see Type L-1-3-4 *supra.*
Withholding Facilities of University of Illinois from Subversive Organizations (Type P)
  Ill. Rev. Stat. c. 144, sec. 488 (1949).

INDIANA

Treason and Misprision of Treason (Types A-1 and A-2)
Ind. Ann. Stat. secs. 9-1615, 10-4401—10-4402 (Burns 1942).
Rebellion and Insurrection (Type B-1)
Ind. Ann. Stat. secs. 10-4403—10-4405 (Burns 1942).
Sedition (Type C)
Ind. Ann. Stat. secs. 10-1302—10-1303 (Burns 1942).
Note: *McKee v. State,* 219 Ind. 247, 37 N.E.2d 940 (1941).
Red Flag Law (Type F-3)
Ind. Ann. Stat. sec. 10-1301 (Burns 1942).
Political Parties (Type I-1-2)
Ind. Ann. Stat. sec. 29-3812 (Burns 1949).
Teacher's Oath (Type N-1)
Ind. Ann. Stat. secs. 28-5112—28-5114 (Burns 1948).

IOWA

Treason and Misprision of Treason (Types A-1 and A-2)
Iowa Const. (1857) Art. I, sec. 16.
Iowa Code Ann. secs. 689.1–689.3 (1949).
Rebellion and Insurrection (Type B-1)
Iowa Code Ann. sec. 689.4 (1949).
Sedition (Type C) *and Criminal Anarchy* (Type E-1)
Iowa Code Ann. secs. 689.4, 689.7–689.9 (1949).
Note: Upheld in *State v. Gibson,* 189 Iowa 1212, 174 N.W. 34 (1919).
Criminal Syndicalism (Types D-1 and D-2)
Iowa Code Ann. secs. 689.10–689.13 (1949).
Note: *State v. Tonn,* 195 Iowa 94, 191 N.W. 530 (1923) and *State v. Sentner,* 230 Iowa 592, 298 N.W. 813 (1941) for a unique application of the statute.
Red Flag Law (Type F-1-3)
Iowa Code Ann. secs. 689.5–689.7 (1949).
Sabotage (Type G-2), see Type D-1.

KANSAS

Treason and Misprision of Treason (Types A-1 and A-2)
Kan. Gen. Stat. Ann. secs. 21-201—21-202 (1935).

Rebellion and Insurrection (Type B-1)

Kan. Gen. Stat. Ann. secs. 21-203—21-204 (1935).

Note: Prohibiting the joining of revolutionary societies.

Sedition (Type C)

Kan. Laws 1949, c. 246, secs. 2–5, p. 408.

Criminal Syndicalism (Types D-1 and D-2)

Kan. Gen. Stat. Ann. secs. 21-301—21-304 (1935).

Note: Holding this statute unconstitutional as applied in *Fiske v. Kansas,* 274 U.S. 380, 71 L.Ed. 1108, 47 S.Ct. 655 (1927); statute applied to the I.W.W. in *State v. I.W.W.,* 113 Kan. 347, 214 P. 617 (1923).

Red Flag Law (Type F-1-3-6)

Kan. Gen. Stat. Ann. secs. 21-1304—21-1306 (1935).

Sabotage (Type G-2), see Type D-1.

Political Parties (Type I-1-2-3)

Kan. Gen. Stat. Ann. secs. 25-116—25-117 (Supp. 1947).

Oath for Elected Officers, Public Officers, and State Employees (Types J, K, and L-1-3-5)

Kan. Laws 1949, c. 246, sec. 1, p. 407.

Teacher's Oath (Type N-1), see Type L, *supra.*

KENTUCKY

Treason (Type A-1)

Ky. Const. (1891) sec. 229.

Ky. Rev. Stat. sec. 432.010 (1948).

Sedition (Type C)

Ky. Rev. Stat. sec. 432.030 (1948).

Criminal Syndicalism (Types D-1 and D-2)

Ky. Rev. Stat. secs. 432.020, 432.040–432.070 (1948).

Red Flag Law (Type F-1-2-3)

Ky. Rev. Stat. sec. 2.070 (1948).

Uniform Sabotage Prevention Act (Type G-2)

Ky. Rev. Stat. secs. 39.100–39.210 (1948).

LOUISIANA

Treason and Misprision of Treason (Types A-1 and A-2)

La. Const. (1921) Art. 19, sec. 3.

La. Code Crim. Law & Proc. Ann. secs. 740-113—740-114 (1943).

Sedition (Type C)

La. Code Crim. Law & Proc. Ann. secs. 1188–1189, 1192 (1943).

Note: Applicable in time of war only.

Criminal Anarchy (Type E-1)

La. Code Crim. Law & Proc. Ann. sec. 740-115 (1943).

Sabotage (Type G-3)

La. Code Crim. Law & Proc. sec. 1208.1–1208.9 (1943).

Masks and Disguises (Type H)

La. Code Crim. Law & Proc. Ann. sec. 871 (1943).

Note: Applied to the Ku Klux Klan in *State v. Dunn*, 161 La. 532,602, 109 So. 56, 81 (1926).

Registration Statute (Type M)

La. Gen. Stat. Ann. secs. 1285–1294 (1939).

MAINE

Treason and Misprision of Treason (Types A-1 and A-2)

Me. Rev. Stat. c. 130, secs. 1–3 (1944).

Rebellion and Insurrection (Types B-1 and B-2)

Me. Rev. Stat. c. 130, sec. 4 and c. 11, secs. 9–10 (1944).

Masks and Disguises (Type H)

Me. Rev. State. c. 122, sec. 31 (1944).

MARYLAND

Treason (Type A-1)

Md. Ann. Code Gen. Laws Art. 27, secs. 605–613 (1939).

Rebellion and Insurrection (Type B-1)

Md. Ann. Code Gen. Laws Art. 27, secs. 607–608, 610–613 (1939).

Note: See also Md. Ann. Code Gen. Laws Art. 85A, sec. 2(a) (Md. Laws 1949 c. 86, pp. 96–105) commonly known as the Ober Act which was held unconstitutional in *Lancaster v. Hammond*, No. 30021-A, Docket 58A–184 (Cir. Ct. No. 2 of Baltimore City, August 15, 1949) reversed in *Hammond v. Lancaster*, 71 A.2d 474 (Md., 1950).

Sedition (Type C)

Md. Ann. Code Gen. Laws Art. 85A, secs. 2–9.

Uniform Sabotage Prevention Act (Type G-1)

Md. Ann. Code Gen. Laws Art. 27, secs. 576B–576P (Supp. 1947) as amended by Md. Laws 1949, c. 85, p. 95.

Political Parties (Type I-1-2-3)

Md. Ann. Code Gen. Laws Art. 85A, sec. 15.

Excluding Persons from Elective and Public Office (Types J and K-1-2-3-4-5-6)

Md. Const. (1867) Art. XV, sec. 11 (added by recent amendment).

Md. Ann. Code Gen. Laws Art. 85A, secs. 10–14.

Excluding Persons from State Employment (Type L-1-2-3-4-5-6)

Md. Ann. Code Gen. Laws Art. 85A, secs. 10–18.

Teacher's Oath (Type N), see Type L, *supra.*

Note: Oath set forth in sec. 13.

Teacher's Loyalty (Type O)

Md. Ann. Code Gen. Laws Art. 85A, sec. 14.

Miscellaneous School Statutes (Type P)

Md. Ann. Code Gen. Laws Art. 85A, sec. 16.

Note: This requires a self-initiated loyalty investigation be undertaken before any public funds go to any private institution of learning.

MASSACHUSETTS

Treason and Misprision of Treason (Types A-1 and A-2)

Mass. Ann. Laws c. 264, secs. 1–4 (1932).

Criminal Anarchy (Type E-1)

Mass. Ann. Laws c. 264, sec. 11 (Supp. 1949).

Red Flag Law (Type F-6)

Mass. Ann. Laws c. 264, sec. 8 (1932).

Note: Upholding former Mass. Red Flag Law (Mass. Acts 1913 c. 678, sec. 2) *Commonwealth v. Karvonen,* 219 Mass. 30, 106 N.E. 556 (1914).

Masks and Disguises (Type H)

Mass. Ann. Laws c. 264, sec. 34 (1932).

Excluding Persons from State Employment (Type L-1-5)

Mass. Ann. Laws c. 264, secs. 13–15 (Supp. 1949).

Teacher's Oath (Type N-1)

Mass. Ann. Laws c. 71, sec. 30A (Supp. 1949).

Teacher's Loyalty (Type O)
    Mass. Ann. Laws c. 264, sec. 11 (Supp. 1949).

MICHIGAN

Treason and Misprision of Treason (Types A-1 and A-2)
    Mich. Comp. Laws secs. 750.544–750.545 (1948).
Sedition (Type C)
    Mich. Comp. Laws secs. 752.301–752.302 (1948).
Criminal Syndicalism (Type D-1)
    Mich. Comp. Laws secs. 750.46–750.47 (1948).
    Note: Upheld in *People v. Ruthenberg,* 229 Mich. 315, 201
N.W. 358 (1924), writ of error dismissed in 273 U.S. 782, 71 L.Ed.
890, 47 S.Ct. 470 (1927).
Red Flag Law (Type F-1-3)
    Mich. Comp. Laws sec. 750.48 (1948).
    Note: *People v. Immonen,* 271 Mich. 384, 261 N.W. 59 (1935);
also *People v. Burman,* 154 Mich. 150, 117 N.W. 589 (1908).
Masks and Disguises (Type H)
    Mich. Comp. Laws sec. 750.396 (1948).
Registration Statute (Type M)
    Mich. Comp. Laws secs. 14.201–14.207 (1948).
Teacher's Oath (Type N-1)
    Mich. Comp. Laws sec. 377.10 (1948).
    Note: *Wilson v. Council of City of Highland Park,* 284 Mich.
96, 278 N.W. 778, 116 A.L.R. 352 (1938) in which the city council
attempted to remove a person from elective office without the aid
of a statute because of alleged subversive activities.

MINNESOTA

Treason and Misprision of Treason (Types A-1 and A-2)
    Minn. Const. (1857) Art. I, sec. 9 and Art. VII, sec. 2.
    Minn. Stat. Ann. secs. 612.01–612.03 (West 1946).
Rebellion and Insurrection (Types B-1 and B-2)
    Minn. Const. (1857) Art. 5, sec. 4. (Type B-2).
    Minn. Stat. Ann. sec. 612.03 (West 1946).
Sedition (Type C)
    Minn. Stat. Ann. sec. 612.07–612.09 (West 1946).

Note: Upholding prior similar act which was aimed at prohibiting incitement to disloyalty in the armed forces during time of war *Gilbert v. Minnesota,* 254 U.S. 325, 65 L.Ed. 287, 41 S.Ct. 125 (1920); see also *State v. Holm,* 139 Minn. 267, 166 N.W. 181 (1918).

Criminal Syndicalism (Types D-1 and D-2)

Minn. Stat. Ann. sec. 613.68 (West 1946).

Note: Upheld in *State v. Moilen,* 140 Minn. 112, 167 N.W. 345, 1 A.L.R. 331 (1918) and *State v. Workers' Socialist Publishing Co.,* 150 Minn. 406, 185 N.W. 931 (1921).

Red Flag Law (Type F-1-2-3)

Minn. Stat. Ann. sec. 614.34 (West 1946).

Sabotage (Type G-2), see Type D-1.

MISSISSIPPI

Treason (Type A-1)

Miss. Code Ann. secs. 2397–2398 (1942).

Sedition (Type C)

Miss. Code Ann. sec. 2399 (1942).

Sabotage (Type G-3)

Miss. Code Ann. secs. 2400–2401, 2402–2405 (1942).

Note: Upholding sec. 2402 (only applicable in time of war) *Taylor v. State,* 194 Miss. 1, 11 So.2d 663 (1943); *Cummings v. State,* 194 Miss. 59, 11 So.2d 683 (1943); and *Benoit v. State,* 194 Miss. 74, 11 So.2d 689 (1943). Judgments reversed and sec. 2402 held unconstitutional in so far as it forbids teachings tending to create a stubborn refusal to salute the flag in *Taylor v. Mississippi,* 319 U.S. 583, 87 L.Ed. 1600, 63 S.Ct. 1200 (1943).

Teacher's Oath (Type N-1)

Miss. Laws 1950, c. 451.

MISSOURI

Treason and Misprision of Treason (Types A-1 and A-2)

Mo. Const. (1945) Art. I, sec. 30.

Mo. Rev. Stat. Ann. secs. 4073, 4267–4269 (1942).

Rebellion and Insurrection (Types B-1 and B-2)

Mo. Rev. Stat. Ann. secs. 4270–4271, 13138, 15018 (1942).

MONTANA

Treason and Misprision of Treason (Types A-1 and A-2)
Mont. Const. (1889) Art. III, sec. 9.
Mont. Rev. Code secs. 94-4501—94-4502, 94-7210 (1947).
Rebellion and Insurrection (Type B-2)
Mont. Rev. Code secs. 94-3538, 94-5312—94-5313 (1947).
Sedition (Type C)
Mont. Rev. Code secs. 94-4401—94-4403 (1947).
Note: Upheld in *Ex Parte Starr*, 263 F. 145 (1920); *State v. Kahn*, 56 Mont. 108, 182 P. 107 (1919); *State v. Wyman*, 56 Mont. 600, 186 P. 1 (1919); *State v. Smith*, 57 Mont. 563, 190 P. 107 (1920); *State v. Fowler*, 59 Mont. 346, 196 P. 992 (1921). These cases all upheld an earlier statute (Mont. Laws 1918 Extra Sess., c. 11, p. 28) similar to sec. 94-4401 but limited to wartime.
Criminal Syndicalism (Types D-1 and D-2)
Mont. Rev. Code secs. 94-4404—94-4408 (1947).
Red Flag Law (Type F-1-3)
Mont. Rev. Code secs. 94-4409—94-4410 (1947).
Sabotage (Type G-2) see Type D-1.
Teacher's Oath (Type N-1)
Mont. Rev. Code secs. 75-4706—75-4707 (1947).
Incidental Benefits (Type Q)
Mont. Rev. Code sec. 77-606 (1947).
Note: This statute declares it to be the legislative policy of the state that any position vacancy of any business or industry shall not be filled by any person who is a member of the Communist Party or the German-American Bund. It contains no sanctions whatsoever.

NEBRASKA

Treason (Type A-1)
Neb. Const. (1875) Art. I, sec. 14.
Neb. Rev. Stat. secs. 28-101—28-103, 29-2015 (1943).
Rebellion and Insurrection (Type B-1)
Neb. Rev. Stat. secs. 28-103, 55-124 (1943).
Criminal Syndicalism (Types D-1 and D-2)

Neb. Rev. Stat. secs. 28-815—28-817 (1943).
Red Flag Law (Type F-1-2-3)
Neb. Rev. Stat. secs. 28-1103—28-1107 (1943).
Sabotage (Type G-3)
Neb. Rev. Stat. sec. 28-580 (1943).
Statutes concerning Teacher Loyalty Other than Oath Type
Neb. Laws 1949, c. 79, secs. 19–21.

NEVADA

Treason and Misprision of Treason (Types A-1 and A-2)
Nev. Const. (1864) Art. I, sec. 19.
Nev. Comp. Laws Ann. secs. 40, 9992–9994 (1929).
Rebellion and Insurrection (Types B-1 and B-2)
Nev. Comp. Laws Ann. secs. 4842–4843, 9993 (1929).
Sedition (Type C)
Nev. Comp. Laws Ann. secs. 10300–10301 (1929).
Criminal Syndicalism (Types D-1 and D-2)
Nev. Comp. Laws Ann. secs. 10560–10563 (1929).
Note: Upheld in *In Re Moriarity,* 44 Nev. 164, 191 P. 320 (1920).
Criminal Anarchy (Types E-1 and E-2)
Nev. Comp. Laws Ann. secs. 10296–10299 (1929).
Sabotage (Type G-2)
See Type D-1.
Teacher's Oath (Type N-1)
Nev. Comp. Laws Ann. sec. 5686 (1929).

NEW HAMPSHIRE

Treason and Misprision of Treason (Types A-1 and A-2)
N.H. Rev. Laws c. 456, secs. 1–3 (1942).
Sedition (Type C)
N.H. Rev. Laws c. 457, secs. 31–35 (1942).
Note: Upholding secs. 31–32 see *State v. Foster,* 80 N.H. 1, 113 A. 211, 114 A. 277 (1921).
Uniform Sabotage Prevention Act (Type G-1)
N.H. Rev. Laws c. 458, secs. 1–15 (1942).
Teacher's Oath (Type N-1)
N.H. Laws 1949, c. 312, pp. 414–415.

NEW JERSEY

Treason and Misprision of Treason (Types A-1 and A-2)

N.J. Const. (1947) Art. I, par. 17.

N.J. Stat. Ann. secs. 2:173-1—2:173-2, 2:173-5 (1939).

Rebellion and Insurrection (Type B-1)

N.J. Stat. Ann. secs. 2:173-4—2:173-5, 2:173-12 (1939).

Sedition (Type C)

N.J. Stat. Ann. secs. 2:173-3, 2:173-10—2:173-19 (1939).

Note: Upholding sec. 2:173-10 see *State v. Boyd*, 86 N.J.L. 75, 91 A. 586 (1914), affirmed 87 N.J.L. 328, 93 A. 599 (1915), reversed on other grounds 87 N.J.L. 560, 94 A. 807 (1915). Upholding sec. 2:173-13 see *State v. Tachin*, 92 N.J.L. 269, 106 A. 145 (1919), affirmed 93 N.J.L. 485, 108 A. 318 (1919), writ of error dismissed 254 U.S. 662, 65 L.Ed. 463, 41 S.Ct. 61 (1920). Upholding sec. 2:173-14 see *State v. Gabriel*, 95 N.J.L. 337, 112 A. 611 (1921).

Criminal Anarchy (Type E-1)

N.J. Stat. Ann. secs. 2:173-7—2:173-9.

Note: Upheld in *State v. Quinlan*, 86 N.J.L. 120, 91 A. 111 (1914), affirmed 87 N.J.L. 333, 93 A. 1086 (1915).

Red Flag Law (Type F-1-3-5)

N.J. Stat. Ann. secs. 2:173-20—2:173-21 (1939).

Oath for Elected Officers, Public Officers and State Employees (Types J, K, and L-1-3-4-5)

N.J. Stat. Ann. secs. 41:1-1—41:1-3 (Supp. 1949).

Note: Held unconstitutional in *Imbrie v. Marsh*, 5 N.J. Super. 239, 68 A.2d 761 (1949), affirmed 3 N.J. 578, 71 A.2d 352 (1950).

Teacher's Oath (Type N-1)

N.J. Stat. Ann. secs. 18:13-9.1—18:13-9.3 (Supp. 1949).

Note: This statute requires the teachers to take the oath prescribed by Type L, *supra*.

NEW MEXICO

Red Flag Law (Type F-1-2-3)

N.M. Stat. Ann. sec. 41-1903 (1941).

Uniform Sabotage Prevention Act (Type G-1)

N.M. Stat. Ann. secs. 41-4301—41-4313 (1941).

Masks and Disguises (Type H)

N.M. Stat. Ann. sec. 41-2901 (1941).

Note: The New Mexico sedition statute (N.M. Stat. Ann. secs. 35-3101—35-3105 (1929) held unconstitutional in *State v. Diamond,* 27 N.M. 477, 202 P. 988, 20 A.L.R. 1527 (1921).

Exclusion from State Employment (Type L)

N.M. Stat. Ann. sec. 10-112 (Cum. Supp. 1949).

NEW YORK

Treason (Type A-1)

N.Y. Penal Law secs. 2380–2383.

Rebellion and Insurrection (Types B-1 and B-2)

N.Y. Penal Law secs. 1850, 2383 (Type B-1).

N.Y. Military Law sec. 8 (Type B-2).

Criminal Anarchy (Types E-1 and E-2)

N.Y. Penal Law secs. 160–166.

Note: Held constitutional in *Gitlow v. New York,* 268 U.S. 652, 69 L.Ed. 1138, 45 S.Ct. 625 (1925), affirming 234 N.Y. 132, 539, 136 N.E. 317, 138 N.E. 438 (1922). Also see *People v. Most,* 171 N.Y. 423, 64 N.E. 175, 58 L.R.A. 509 (1902).

Red Flag Law (Type F-1)

N.Y. Penal Law sec. 2095a.

Note: Held unconstitutional in *People v. Altman,* 241 App. Div. 858, 280 N.Y.S. 248 (1934).

Sabotage (Type G-3)

N.Y. Penal Law secs. 1435–1437.

Masks and Disguises (Type H)

N.Y. Penal Law sec. 710.

Excluding Persons from Public Office (Type K-1)

N.Y. Pub. Officers Law sec. 35a.

Excluding Persons from State Employment (Type L-1-3)

N.Y. Civil Service Law secs. 12a, 23a.

Registration Statute (Type M)

N.Y. Civil Rights Law secs. 53–57.

Note: This statute which requires the registration of oath-bound societies was upheld in *Bryant v. Zimmerman,* 278 U.S. 63, 73 L.Ed. 184, 49 S.Ct. 61, 62 A.L.R. 785 (1928).

Teacher's Oath (Type N-1)

N.Y. Education Law sec. 3002.

Teachers' Loyalty (Type O)

N.Y. Education Law secs. 3021–3022 (Feinberg Law).

Note: Held unconstitutional in *L'Hommedieu v. Board of Regents,* 196 Misc. 686, 93 N.Y.S.2d 274 (1949), reversed 276 App. Div. 94, 95 N.Y.S.2d 443 (1950). Held unconstitutional in *Lederman v. Board of Education,* 196 Misc. 873, 95 N.Y.S.2d 114 (1949), reversed 276 App. Div. 527, 95 N.Y.S.2d (1950).

Miscellaneous School Statutes (Type P)

N.Y. Education Law sec. 704–705.

Note: This statute prohibits the use of textbooks containing seditious or disloyal matter. On the power of the state in this matter see *People v. American Socialist Society,* 202 App. Div. 640, 195 N.Y.S. 801 (1922).

Note: *Application of Cassidy,* 268 App. Div. 282, 51 N.Y.S.2d 202 (1944), reargument denied 270 App. Div. 1046, 63 N.Y.S.2d 840 (1946), affirmed 296 N.Y. 926, 73 N.E.2d 41 (1947), where applicant was denied admission to the bar due to subversive advocacy. See also Anno. 19 A.L.R. 936 (1921).

NORTH CAROLINA

Treason (Type A-1)

N.C. Const. (1868), Art. IV, sec. 5.

Rebellion and Insurrection (Type B-1)

N.C. Gen. Stat. Ann. secs. 14-8—14-10 (1943).

Sedition (Type C)

N.C. Gen. Stat. Ann. secs. 14-11—14-12, 14.21.1 (Supp. 1949).

Excluding Persons from State Employment (Type L-1)

N.C. Gen. Stat. Ann. sec. 14.21.1 (Supp. 1949).

Political Parties (Type I, Note to)

N.C. Gen. Stat. Ann. sec. 14-10 (1943).

Note: This statute forbids the existence of any secret political or military organizations and was applied recently in *State v. Pelley,* 221 N.C. 487, 20 S.E.2d 850 (1942).

NORTH DAKOTA

Treason and Misprision of Treason (Types A-1 and A-2)

N.D. Rev. Code secs. 12-0701—12-0703 (1943).

Red Flag Law (Type F-1-2-3)

N.D. Rev. Code secs. 12-0707—12-0709 (1943).

Masks and Disguises (Type H)
  N.D. Rev. Code sec. 12-4202 (1943).
Teacher's Oath (Type N-1)
  N.D. Rev. Code secs. 15-3701—15-3704 (1943).

OHIO

Treason and Misprision of Treason (Types A-1 and A-2)
  Ohio Code Ann. secs. 12392-12393, 13444-21 (1948).
Rebellion and Insurrection (Type B-1)
  Ohio Const. (1851) Art. IX, sec. 4.
  Ohio Code Ann. secs. 5202, 12394 (1948).
Criminal Syndicalism (Types D-1 and D-2)
  Ohio Code Ann. secs. 13421-23—13421-26 (1948).
  Note: Upheld in State v. Kassay, 126 Ohio St. 177, 184 N.E. 521 (1933).
Red Flag Law (Type F-1-2-3)
  Ohio Code Ann. secs. 12395, 12398-1 and 12398-2.
Sabotage (Type G-2), see Type D-1.
Political Parties (Type I-1-2)
  Ohio Code Ann. secs. 4785-100a and 4785-100b (1948).
  Note: Upheld in *Johnson v. Sweeney,* 140 Ohio St. 279, 43 N.E.2d 239 (1942) and *State ex. rel. Berry v. Hummel,* 42 Ohio Law Abs. 40, 59 N.E.2d 238 (1944).
Incidental Benefits (Type Q) (denial of unemployment benefits)
  Ohio Code Ann. sec. 1345-6, d (Za) (Cum. Supp. 1950).

OKLAHOMA

Treason (Type A-1)
  Okla. Const. (1907) Art. II, sec. 16.
Rebellion and Insurrection (Type B-2)
  Okla. Const. (1907) Art. VI, sec. 6.
  Okla. Stat. tit. 19, sec. 516 and tit. 22, sec. 107 (1941).
Criminal Syndicalism (Types D-1 and D-2)
  Okla. Stat. tit. 21, secs. 1261–1264 (1941).
  Note: Held valid in *Berg. v. State,* 29 Okla. Crim. Rep. 112, 233 P. 497 (1925). See recent application in *Wood v. State,* 76 Okla. Crim. Rep. 89, 134 P.2d 1021 (1943), 77 Okla. Crim. Rep. 305, 141 P.2d 309 (1943); *Shaw v. State,* 76 Okla. Crim. Rep. 271, 134

P.2d 999, 138 P.2d 136 (1943); *Jaffee v. State,* 76 Okla. Crim. Rep. 195, 134 P.2d 1027 (1943).

Sabotage (Type G-2), see Type D-1

Uniform Sabotage Prevention Act (Type G-1)
Okla. Stat. tit. 21, secs. 1265.1–1265.14 (1941).

Political Parties (Type I-1-2-3)
Okla. Stat. tit. 26, secs. 6.1–6.5 (1941).
Note to Type I: Okla. Stat. tit. 21, sec. 1306.
Note: This statute forbids societies that require membership to take an oath against the state or federal constitution.

Excluding Persons from Elective Office (Type J-1-2-4-5)
Okla. Stat. tit. 26, secs. 161, 162, 1626 (1941).
Okla. Stat. tit. 51, secs. 31–35 (Supp. 1949).

Excluding Persons from Public Office (Type K-1-2-4-5)
Okla. Stat. tit. 51, secs. 31–35 (Supp. 1949).

Teachers' Loyalty (Type O)
Okla. Laws 1949, p. 542.

OREGON

Treason and Misprision of Treason (Types A-1 and A-2)
Ore. Const. (1859) Art. I, sec. 24.
Ore. Comp. Laws Ann. secs. 23-301—23-304, 2-902 (1940).

Rebellion and Insurrection (Type B-1)
Ore. Comp. Laws Ann. sec. 23-303 (1940).

Red Flag Law (Type F-1-3-4)
Ore. Comp. Laws Ann. sec. 23-1071.

Masks and Disguises (Type H)
Ore. Comp. Laws Ann. sec. 23-637 (1940).

Excluding Persons from Elective Office (Type J-1-3)
Ore. Comp. Laws Ann. sec. 81-1309 (Supp. 1943).

Teacher's Oath (Type N-1)
Ore. Comp. Laws Ann. secs. 111-2102—111-2104 (1940).

Excluding Persons from State Employment (Type L)
Ore. Laws 1949, c. 311.
Ore. Laws 1949, c. 434, sec. 14.
Note: See the leading case of *De Jonge v. Oregon,* 299 U.S. 353, 81 L.Ed. 278, 57 S.Ct. 45 (1937) holding unconstitutional as applied the Oregon Criminal Syndicalism Law (Ore. Code Ann.

secs. 14-3110—14-3112 [1930] as amended by Ore. Laws 1933, c. 459). This law was later repealed. (Ore. Laws 1937, c. 362). See Spencer, *Criminal Syndicalism,* 16 Ore. L. Rev. 278 (1937).

PENNSYLVANIA

Treason and Misprision of Treason (Types A-1 and A-2)
 Pa. Stat. Ann. tit. 18, secs. 4201–4202 (1945).
Rebellion and Insurrection (Type B-1)
 Pa. Stat. Ann. tit. 18, sec. 4203 (1945).
Sedition (Type C)
 Pa. Stat. Ann. tit. 18, secs. 4207–4210 (1945).
 Note: Upholding sec. 4207 see *Commonwealth v. Blankenstein,* 81 Pa. Super. 340 (1923); *Commonwealth v. Lazar,* 103 Pa. Super. 417, 157 A. 701 (1931), appeal dismissed in *Lazar v. Pennsylvania,* 286 U.S. 532, 76 L.Ed. 1272, 52 S.Ct. 639 (1932); and *Commonwealth v. Widovich,* 295 Pa. 311, 145 A. 295 (1929), cert. denied, *Muselin v. Pennsylvania,* 280 U.S. 518, 74 L.Ed. 588, 50 S.Ct. 66 (1929).
Red Flag Law (Type F-1-3)
 Pa. Stat. Ann. tit. 18, sec. 4209 (1945).
Uniform Sabotage Prevention Act (Type G-1)
 Pa. Stat. Ann. tit. 35, secs. 2101–2109 (1945).
Political Parties (Type I-1)
 Pa. Stat. Ann. tit. 25, secs. 2831, 2936 (Supp. 1949).
Excluding Persons from State Employment (Type L-1)
 Pa. Stat. Ann. tit. 65, secs. 151–154 and tit. 53, sec. 351.13 (Supp. 1949).
Incidental Benefits (Type Q)
 Pa. Stat. Ann. tit. 62, sec. 2509 (Supp. 1949).
 Note: This statute renders certain persons ineligible to receive public assistance if active in subversive activities.

RHODE ISLAND

Treason and Misprision of Treason (Types A-1 and A-2)
 R.I. Gen. Laws c. 603, secs. 1–3 (1938).
Rebellion and Insurrection (Type B-1)
 R.I. Gen. Laws c. 603, sec. 7 (1938).

Sedition, Criminal Anarchy and Criminal Syndicalism (Types C, D, and E-1)

R.I. Gen. Laws c. 604, secs. 1–4 (1938).

Red Flag Law (Type F-3-4)

R.I. Gen. Laws c. 604, secs. 1, 3, 4 (1938).

Teacher's Oath (Type N-2). See Rules and Regulations adopted January 1, 1938 by the Rhode Island State Board of Education governing the issuance of teachers' certificates pursuant to R.I. Gen. Laws c. 176, secs. 1–2 (1938).

Incidental Benefits (Type Q) (exclusion from scholarship benefits)

R.I. Gen. Laws c. 2352, sec. 7½ (1949); House Bill No. 742 sec. 8 (1950), CCH 1950 New Laws 71, 101.

SOUTH CAROLINA

Treason (Type A-1)

S.C. Const. (1895) Art. I, sec. 22.

Rebellion and Insurrection (Type B-2)

S.C. Code Ann. secs. 1390–1393 (1942).

Sabotage (Type G-3)

S.C. Code Ann. secs. 1100-1—1100-11 (1942)

Teacher's Oath (Type N-2)

S.C. Code sec. 5324(3) (1942).

Note: This statute provides that all persons applying for teachers' certificates "shall also satisfy the examining power of his or her loyalty . . ." to the constitution.

Incidental Benefits (Type Q)

CCH 1950 New Laws 335, 348.

SOUTH DAKOTA

Treason and Misprision of Treason (Types A-1 and A-2)

S.D. Code secs. 13.0701–13.0703 (1939).

Criminal Syndicalism (Types D-1 and D-2)

S.D. Code secs. 13.0801–13.0804 (1939).

Red Flag Law (Type F-1-2-3)

S.D. Code sec. 13.0806 (1939).

Sabotage (Type G-2), see Type D-1.

435

Teacher's Oath (Type N-1)
S.D. Code sec. 15.3702 (1939).

TENNESSEE

Treason and Misprision of Treason (Types A-1 and A-2)
Tenn. Code Ann. secs. 11003–11006 (Williams 1934).
Sedition (Type C)
Tenn. Code Ann. sec. 11026 (Williams 1934).
Uniform Sabotage Prevention Act (Type G-1)
Tenn. Code Ann. secs. 11043.1–11043.15 (Williams Supp. 1948).
Political Parties (Type I-1-2)
Tenn. Code Ann. sec. 2045.1 (Williams 1943).
Teacher's Oath (Type N-2)
Tenn. Code Ann. sec. 2540-3 (Williams 1943).
Note: This statute requires oath but does not set it out verbatim.
Teachers' Loyalty (Type O)
Tenn. Code Ann. sec. 2513 (Williams Supp. 1948).

TEXAS

Treason and Misprision of Treason (Types A-1 and A-2)
Tex. Const. (1876) Art. I, sec. 22.
Tex. Stat., Pen. Code arts. 83–85 (1938).
Sedition (Type C)
Tex. Stat., Pen. Code arts. 153, 155 (1938).
Note: This statute is applicable in time of war only. Art. 155 was held unconstitutional in *Ex Parte Meckel,* 87 Tex. Crim. Rep. 120, 220 S.W. 81 (1919), and *Schellenger v. State,* 87 Tex. Crim. Rep. 411, 222 S.W. 246 (1920).
Red Flag Law (Type F-6)
Tex. Stat., Pen. Code art. 154 (1938).
Masks and Disguises (Type H)
Tex. Stat., Pen. Code art. 454a (1938).
Political Parties (Type I-1-4-5)
Tex. Stat., Rev. Civ. arts. 2978a, 2978b (Supp. 1949).
Teacher's Oath (Type N-1)
Tex. Stat., Rev. Civ. arts. 2908a (1942), 2908b (Supp. 1949).

436

Teachers' Loyalty (Type O)
  Tex. Stat., Rev. Civ. arts. 2908a (1942), 2908b (Supp. 1949).
Miscellaneous School Statute (Type P)
  Tex. Stat., Rev. Civ. art. 2908b (Supp. 1949).
  Note: This statute requires students in public supported institutions of higher learning to take an oath.

UTAH

Treason (Type A-1)
  Utah Const. (1896) Art. I, sec. 19.
  Utah Code Ann. sec. 105-32-10 (1943).
Criminal Syndicalism (Types D-1 and D-2)
  Utah Code Ann. secs. 103-54-1—103-54-5 (1943).
Red Flag Law (Type F-3-4)
  Utah Code Ann. sec. 103-26-84 (1943).
Uniform Sabotage Prevention Act (Type G-1)
  Utah Code Ann. secs. 103-54-6—103-54-21 (1943).
Sabotage (Type G-2), see Type D-1.
Excluding Persons from State Employment (Type L-1)
  Utah Code Ann. sec. 36-9-15 (b) (Supp. 1949).
  Note: This statute sets out grounds for dismissal of members of the state highway patrol.

VERMONT

Treason and Misprision of Treason (Types A-1 and A-2)
  Vt. Stat. Rev. secs. 8227–8229 (1947).
Sedition (Type C)
  Vt. Stat. Rev. secs. 8230–8234, 8236 (1947).
Criminal Anarchy (Type E-1)
  Vt. Stat. Rev. sec. 8236 (1947).
Red Flag Law (Type F-1-2-3)
  Vt. Stat. Rev. sec. 8591 (1947).
Uniform Sabotage Prevention Act (Type G-1)
  Vt. Stat. Rev. secs. 7229–7245 (1947).
Teacher's Oath (Type N-1)
  Vt. Stat. Rev. sec. 4301 (1947).

VIRGINIA

Treason and Misprision of Treason (Types A-1 and A-2)
   Va. Code Ann. secs. 4389–4390 (1942).
Rebellion and Insurrection (Type B-1)
   Va. Code Ann. secs. 4391–4392 (1942).
Sedition (Type C)
   Va. Code Ann. sec. 4391a (Supp. 1948).
Teacher's Oath (Type N-2)
   The Virginia teacher's oath is inserted in the *Virginia Contract with Teachers* prepared by the Virginia State Board of Education pursuant to Va. Code Ann. sec. 664 (Supp. 1948).

WASHINGTON

Treason and Misprision of Treason (Types A-1 and A-2)
   Wash. Const. (1889) Art. I, sec. 27.
   Wash. Rev. Stat. Ann. secs. 2317–2319 (1931).
Rebellion and Insurrection (Type B-1)
   Wash. Rev. Stat. Ann. secs. 2318, 4168 (1931).
Sedition (Type C)
   Wash. Rev. Stat. Ann. sec. 2564 (1931).
   Note: Upheld in *State v. Fox*, 71 Wash. 185, 127 P. 111 (1912), affirmed in *Fox v. Washington*, 236 U.S. 273, 59 L.Ed. 573, 35 S.Ct. 383 (1915).
Criminal Anarchy (Types E-1 and E-2)
   Wash. Rev. Stat. Ann. secs. 2562–2563 (Supp. 1941), and secs. 2565–2568 (Supps. 1940, 1941).
Red Flag Law (Type F-4)
   Wash. Rev. Stat. Ann. secs. 2563-7—2563-11 (1931).
Sabotage (Type G-3)
   Wash. Rev. Stat. Ann. secs. 2563-3—2563-11 (1931).
Masks and Disguises (Type H)
   Wash. Rev. Stat. Ann. secs. 2553–2554 (1931).
Excluding Persons from State Employment (Type L-1-3-4-5)
   Wash. Laws 1949, c. 242, sec. 2, p. 948.
   Note: Included in the 1949 state appropriations law.
Teacher's Oath (Type N-1)
   Wash. Rev. Stat. Ann. secs. 4966-1—4966-5 (1931).

Wash. Rev. Stat. Ann. sec. 4845 (Supp. 1949).

Note: Washington Criminal Syndicalism Law (Wash. Rev. Stat. Ann. secs. 2563-1—2563-2 [1931]) repealed. (Wash. Laws 1937, c. 210, sec. 1.) See also *State v. Reeves*, 5 Wash.2d 637, 106 P.2d 729, 130 A.L.R. 1465 (1940) where the secretary of state attempted to bar the Communist Party without a statute from the ballot and the court refused to allow it.

WEST VIRGINIA

Treason and Misprision of Treason (Types A-1 and A-2)
　W.Va. Const. (1872) Art. I, sec. 6.
　W.Va. Code Ann. secs. 5908–5910 (1949).
Rebellion and Insurrection (Types B-1 and B-2)
　W.Va. Const. (1872) Art. VII, sec. 12.
　W.Va. Code Ann. secs. 1179–1180, 5911 (1949).
Sedition (Type C) *and Criminal Syndicalism* (Type D-1)
　W.Va. Code Ann. secs. 5912, 5914 (1949).
Red Flag Law (Type F-1-2-3)
　W.Va. Code Ann. sec. 5913 (1949).
Teacher's Oath (Type N-1)
　W.Va. Code Ann. sec. 1807 (1949).

WISCONSIN

Treason (Type A-1)
　Wis. Const. (1848) Art. I, sec. 10.
　Wis. Stat. sec. 347.01 (1947).
Rebellion and Insurrection (Type B-2)
　Wis. Stat. secs. 347.02–347.09 (1947).
Criminal Anarchy (Types E-1 and E-2)
　Wis. Stat. secs. 347.14–347.18 (1947).
Red Flag Law (Type F-1-3-4)
　Wis. Stat. sec. 348.485 (1947).
Uniform Sabotage Prevention Act (Type G-1)
　Wis. Stat. sec. 343.74 (1947).
Political Parties (Type I-1-2-3)
　Wis. Stat. sec. 5.225 (1947).

WYOMING

Treason (Type A-1)
    Wyo. Const. (1890) Art. I, sec. 26.
    Wyo. Comp. Stat. Ann. sec. 10-1220 (1945).
Rebellion and Insurrection (Types B-1 and B-2)
    Wyo. Comp. Stat. Ann. sec. 30-137—30-138 (1945).
Criminal Syndicalism (Type D-1)
    Wyo. Comp. Stat. Ann. sec. 9-401 (1945).
Political Parties (Type I-1-2-3)
    Wyo. Comp. Stat. Ann. secs. 31-1404—31-1405 (1945).

INDEX

441

INDEX

INDEX

451

453